P9-CBI-990

AN INTRODUCTION TO
SOCIAL ANTHROPOLOGY

VOLUME ONE

EAGLEHAWK INCREASE CEREMONY, KARADJERI TRIBE

The viscera of a dead wallaby are removed and rubbed on a stone, which is the increase centre for the eaglehawk or wedge-tailed eagle.

FRONTISPIECE, PLATE I

AN INTRODUCTION TO
SOCIAL ANTHROPOLOGY

RALPH PIDDINGTON, M.A., PH.D.

PROFESSOR OF ANTHROPOLOGY
AUCKLAND UNIVERSITY COLLEGE
UNIVERSITY OF NEW ZEALAND

VOLUME ONE

OLIVER AND BOYD
EDINBURGH: TWEEDDALE COURT
LONDON: 98 GREAT RUSSELL STREET, W.C.

FIRST PUBLISHED 1950
SECOND EDITION 1952

PRINTED AND BOUND IN ENGLAND BY
HAZELL WATSON AND VINEY LTD
AYLESBURY AND LONDON

TO THE MEMORY OF

A. B. PIDDINGTON

Broken is the shelter
Of my father
Lost to sight
You were the true *maru*,[1] generous to the
common folk.

From a Tikopia dirge, translated by Raymond Firth

[1] A public official in Tikopia.

PREFACE

1. Problems of Presentation

THE present work is designed to introduce beginners, particularly University undergraduates, to the science of Social Anthropology. Such students experience difficulties—especially in regard to terminology—in their initial studies, and misleading impressions are all too easily created on first acquaintance with the unfamiliar, complex and bewildering facts of primitive life. I have tried to overcome some of the initial difficulties and to avoid the creation of wrong impressions, but in the nature of the case I cannot claim to have been fully successful.

My main problem of presentation has been how far the treatment of primitive cultures should be intensive or extensive. As regards the former, it would only be possible in a work of this size to deal at all adequately with about four or five cultures. As every anthropologist knows, such intensive studies constitute the only means by which a full appreciation of the reality and complexity of individual cultures can be gained. On the other hand my teaching experience has made me keenly aware of the dangers of such an approach in the case of elementary students. They are apt to gain the impression that there are at most about a dozen primitive cultures in the world, bounded on the north by the Tallensi and on the south by Tikopia.

This danger can only be forestalled by an extensive treatment of a comparative kind, but this in its turn has even more grave disadvantages. The cursory treatment of a wide variety of cultures does justice to none, and since the detailed discussion of functional interrelationships is necessarily excluded gives a thoroughly unscientific picture of primitive culture.

I have attempted to compromise by stating general principles —both descriptive and analytical—with, for the most part, cursory illustration only and by indulging from time to time in digressions in which bodies of ethnographic data are treated in greater detail. But it must be emphasized that even the latter discussions are very much attenuated, as the reader may and should gather by reference to the original sources.

One of my greatest difficulties of presentation has been the order in which I should place the material contained in the Cooks' Tour of Primitive Peoples on the one hand, and the material in the chapters on Social Organization on the other. The abstract principles of organization involved in the latter remain nebulous until the student has some superficial knowledge of primitive cultures in concrete terms. On the other hand the latter type of description, if endless circumlocution is to be avoided, implies some knowledge of technical terms used in ethnographic description. The necessary disadvantages of the order of presentation which I have adopted will be to some extent offset if the reader follows the advice contained in Section 3 of this preface.

As regards terminology I have tried to include most of the technical terms necessary to an understanding of this book and also to further reading. Those familiar with the classic controversies about the meaning of such terms as "clan", "bride-price", "law", "function" and so on, will realize that anthropologists are still far from an agreed, consistent and comprehensive system of terminology. No statement on the use of terms, therefore, can command universal agreement. I have tried to present a reasonably consistent system of terminology which comes as close as possible to current usage. Other teachers will indicate to their students the extent to which their use of certain terms differs from mine, and more important still, the theoretical implications of such differences.

2. Note for the Teacher

Any treatment of ethnographic material, unless it is to be a mere inventory of cultural traits, must be founded upon a theoretical system of interpretation. But anthropology, like psychology or any other relatively young science, is characterized by the existence of several schools of thought, and even the individual adherents of these differ from each other on questions of theoretical interpretation. Thus though most British anthropologists might be classed as "functionalists", many of them would disagree, to a greater or lesser extent, with my interpretation of this term. Broadly, as applied to British anthropology, the term "functionalism" refers to two quite distinct trends of thought, with many intermediate theoretical interpretations. The first use of the term refers to a type of interpretation which has its roots in the

sociological system of Durkheim and which was first applied in
ethnographic interpretation by Professor Radcliffe-Brown in his
study of the Andaman Islanders, a point of view which he has
elaborated in subsequent writings mentioned in the bibliography. This school of thought, which regards social structure
rather than culture as the subject-matter of social anthropology,
is being increasingly referred to as "structural" rather than
"functional".

The second use of the term "functionalism" refers primarily to
the theoretical system of the late Bronislaw Malinowski, and it is
in this sense that the word is used in this book. It may be
added that the present writer finds no inconsistency or confusion
in the apparently different senses in which Malinowski uses the
term "function". They are all related to, and comprehensible
in terms of, his theory of needs. This theory again is regarded by
many anthropologists as unnecessary to cultural analysis. At
this point I will merely state my view that the postulate of human
needs, whether overtly stated as such or not, is implicit in all
satisfactory cultural analyses; that it is a theoretical concept
necessary to bring social anthropology into relationship with the
other social sciences, particularly psychology; and finally that it
is absolutely essential to the constructive contributions which the
anthropologist should make to human welfare. If one accepts
Professor Lancelot Hogben's definition of the function of science
as being to provide recipes for human conduct, then some
scientifically elaborated system of values is indispensable, and the
theory of needs provides such a system.

I propose to deal with these theoretical points elsewhere, since
an elementary text-book is not the place for such a discussion. I
prefer to state my point of view, which is based upon an acceptance of Malinowski's theory of needs, quite dogmatically,
referring the reader in my bibliographical commentaries to statements of divergent views and critical analyses.

Though the present volume provides a general introduction to
the subject, in which most aspects of primitive culture are mentioned if not fully discussed, I have found it necessary to defer to
the second volume, to be published at a later date, the detailed
consideration of some of the more general aspects of culture—
geographical environment, material culture and the life cycle and
psychology of the individual, as well as the discussion of culture
contact and the application of anthropological methods to the

study of modern communities. A discussion of these more specialized problems cannot be undertaken without a general knowledge
of primitive culture and a grounding in the principles of cultural
analysis such as I have attempted to provide in the present volume.

3. Note for the Student

How to read this book : As you have gathered from the beginning
of this Preface, I have tried to minimize initial difficulties without
giving an over-simplified or superficial impression of what
primitive cultures are like. If social anthropology is an absolutely
new subject to you, and particularly if you come to it direct from
"school" subjects in which teaching has long since become relatively systematized and standardized, you will probably experience difficulty in acquiring that flair for relevance which is
essential to the really competent anthropologist. You may perhaps
flounder about in the following pages, uncertain as to what you
should memorize, how far you should concentrate on facts about
primitive peoples compared with theoretical principles, and so on.
At the risk of appearing didactic I propose to offer some hints as
to how this book may most profitably be read. If you find them
trite or unhelpful, you can skip over them and plunge immediately into the body of the text.

I think that you will gain most from this book if you do not
attempt to read it straight through as you normally do with a
text-book, but adopt the following plan: First read through
Chapter I so that you have a reasonably clear idea of the scope of
our subject. But you should at this stage skip or read cursorily
Sections 7 and 8 of this chapter, the significance of which you will
not fully appreciate until your reading is more advanced. In this
and subsequent chapters you will find certain terms in **bold type**
—it is important that you should try to master the meaning of
these terms, which are of special significance for your understanding of the subject and in the further reading which you will
do. You need not pay so much attention to technical terms in
ordinary italic type.

After reading Chapter I, you should *skim through* Chapters II
and III, much as you might a newspaper article while waiting
for a bus. You will find many terms which you do not understand
—do not worry about this, and do not try at this stage to memorize
any of the material in these chapters.

Next you should read through Chapters IV and V fairly carefully, memorizing in particular the meaning of the terms in bold type. Then re-read Chapters II and III more carefully, though you should still not attempt to memorize details. After this you might do the Exercise in Appendix B.

If you are satisfied that you have a reasonably good grasp of the subject so far, go on to Chapter VI. You will probably find this difficult at first but you should make sure that you know it thoroughly. But do not worry if you cannot follow in detail Section 8 of this chapter. This is merely a digression in which I have suggested a tentative answer to one of the most difficult problems in theoretical anthropology.

It will help you in reading Chapter VI if you refer back from time to time to the earlier chapters where you will find illustrations (though they are not explicitly stated as such) of the general principles of cultural analysis. For example you should try to discern how far the various features of Eskimo culture—including local organization, material culture, magic and religion—are related to the needs for protection against climate, ventilation and the securing of an adequate food supply under exceptionally rigorous geographical conditions. Again, you should reconsider some of the material on Social Organization in the light of the question how far the widely varying systems of kinship, rank and local organization serve to organize the sexual, reproductive and material needs of various communities as well as to satisfy the wider integrative needs for the regulation of economic rights and responsibilities, for the establishment of authority and for the transmission of knowledge, rank and wealth from one generation to the next. You should also be able to see how human activities are organized into institutions, and the complex functions of these in relation to human needs in the case of, for example, Hehe chieftainship, Karadjeri increase ceremonies and various forms of voluntary association. Of course you will find my descriptions inadequate and incomplete and you should refer as far as possible to good original ethnographic records.

Having mastered Chapter VI you should pass on to the remaining chapters. Here the treatment is necessarily superficial, and at this point in your studies further reading becomes absolutely essential to a thorough grasp of the subject.

Collateral reading: While I hope that this work will provide a general outline of our subject, it would be pretentious to make encyclopædic claims upon it. You should therefore do as much collateral reading as possible as advised in the bibliographical commentaries.[1] These may appear formidable in their extent for elementary reading. It is obvious that no student, unless he or she is reading for an honours degree, or intends to become a professional anthropologist, can read more than a very small proportion of the works cited. Why, then, have I been so lavish in my recommendations? For two reasons: Firstly, the shortage of books and periodicals is such that many of the works cited may not be available to the reader and I have therefore tried to provide as many alternatives as possible; and secondly, I personally prefer to encourage students to follow up their own interests in regard to both areas and subjects, rather than to prescribe a set of intellectual hurdles which they must jump during their elementary course. You should therefore, while reading this book, select certain subjects or peoples which particularly interest you, and read more about them. And I would strongly advise you to make your reading intensive rather than extensive—it is better to know two or three books really well than a dozen superficially.

Photographs, Museums and Films: Your interest in, and therefore your knowledge of, primitive peoples will be increased if you can gain as vivid a mental picture as possible of how they look and dress, how they make and handle their artefacts, and the bodily attitudes which they adopt in day-to-day activities and on ceremonial occasions. The simplest means of achieving this is by looking at good photographs in *modern* descriptions of primitive peoples. Such illustrations are usually either good portraits or action photographs showing mundane activities of day-to-day life as well as formal ceremonies. Photographs in many older field records concentrate very largely on the latter, or on portraits of groups of miserable-looking natives lined up as though awaiting a firing squad.

Good photographs tell you more about the appearance of natives than reams of verbal description or masses of anthropometric data. I have deliberately minimized illustration in this work in order to reduce its cost, but I strongly advise you, at an early stage in your studies, to spend two or three hours in the anthropological section of a good library, browsing through the illustrations in modern ethnographic works, particularly those which deal with peoples discussed in the present book.

[1] On the system of references employed in the bibliographical commentaries and elsewhere in the text, see the note at the beginning of the bibliography.

You should also, if possible, visit the ethnological galleries of a good museum. But in doing this you should beware of taking a merely casual interest in the queer, exotic or even æsthetically pleasing artefacts of primitive man. Any good ethnological collection contains, in addition to specimens, photographs and descriptive labels which will tell you something of the social life of the peoples who made and used the material objects displayed before you. It is upon these that you should concentrate. In this way, in terms of what you will learn in Chapter VI, you will be able to appreciate to some extent the anthropological reality of the purely material objects before you, that is, the institutional setting in which they were manufactured and used.

Finally, you should if possible see one or more good documentary films of life in primitive societies. Unfortunately, there are very few such films and they are not often exhibited in commercial cinemas. Among the best may be mentioned *Nanook of the North* and two excellent colour films of aboriginal life in central Australia, *Tjurunga* and *Walkabout*, produced by Mr. Charles Mountford of the South Australian Museum. The latter are available through Australia House, London, as is *Native Earth*, a striking if somewhat over-dramatized documentary on the effects of the second world war on the natives of New Guinea. The film *Ankole*, in spite of technical defects, gives a good illustration of the economic symbiosis of the Bahima and Bairu, while *The Fight for Life* and *Mamprusi Village* show something of the life of peoples of the Northern Territories of the Gold Coast.

Native Terms: You will find a number of native terms in this book. In general, you should not attempt to memorize them. Some, such as the *Potlatch*, the *Kula* and *lobola* are so extensively referred to here and in other anthropological works that you will automatically come to know their meaning. But most of the native terms are used merely to avoid circumlocution in the description of individual cultures and do not form an essential part of your understanding of the general principles of cultural description and analysis with which we are concerned. I have therefore in general minimized as far as possible the use of native terms.

The one exception to this is the section on the Karadjeri tribe in Chapter III. Here I have presented an abbreviated account of my own field-work on the ceremonial and magico-religious aspects of Karadjeri culture. In this section of the book I have deliberately included a number of native terms and details of ritual and mythology. I have not done this in order to increase your difficulties but to enable you to realize the numerous native categories, and the detailed types and variations of belief and formalized behaviour with which any field-worker must cope. You will merely waste your time if you attempt to memorize these *minutiæ* of Karadjeri culture, but you should, after reading through the book as a whole, be able to see them as illustrating certain general principles. For example, the details of the ritual duties of near and distant kin during initiation ceremonies should not concern you; but you should be able to see them as an illustration of the principle that one of the functions of Australian kinship systems is to provide a definition of rights and responsibilities in ceremonial affairs; and also of how members of the novice's own family play an entirely negative, although important, part in the rites, since it is from them that the boy is in a sense being taken in order to become an adult member of the tribe. Again, the totemic characters in the Karadjeri myths, of which a few only are given, are not individually important. But collectively they illustrate how a detailed knowledge of, and interest in, the natural environment and living things which are essential to survival is symbolically expressed in mythology and ceremonial. Finally, this detailed treatment, even if you only read it cursorily, will make you aware of the enormous detail involved in describing even one or two sets of institutional activities in a given culture. For anything like adequate ethnographic description a similar and actually far more detailed description should be given for cultures which are dismissed in a line or two in the Cooks' Tour and in the Ethnographic Directory.

Spelling and Pronunciation : These are apt to be a source of difficulty for the beginner. Many native languages contain sounds not used in English, and furthermore English spelling is notoriously inconsistent. To overcome these difficulties special orthographic symbols have been devised. These will be mentioned in connection with the study of language in Volume II. For the moment I will mention only two, which are commonly encountered in anthropological writings. Firstly the symbol "ŋ", called an eng or ing, is often used to represent the sound of *ng* as in *hang*. In this book I have employed the simple *ng* for this sound and have rendered the *two* sounds represented by ng in *anger* as *ngg*. Thus I would distinguish between the two English words mentioned by writing them as *hang* and *angger* respectively. Secondly there is the glottal stop, represented by the diacritical sign ' or sometimes '. This replaces a consonant, as in the Tahitian word for "chief" which was *ari'i*, a dialectal variation of the term *ariki* found in some other parts of Polynesia. The glottal stop does not usually occur in English, but may frequently be heard in the speech of a Cockney who goes to a foo'ball match or a Scotsman who mixes his whisky with wa'er.

As regards the pronunciation of ordinary letters, there is much inconsistency in ethnographic writings, but a rule commonly observed is that consonants are pronounced as in English and vowels as in Italian, according to the following table of equivalence:

"a" is pronounced as "a" in father
"e" „ „ „ "a" in baby (usually)
"i" „ „ „ "ee" in eel
"o" „ „ „ "o" in robe, occasionally as in tropic
"u" „ „ „ "oo" in soon

It must be emphasized that this is only a very approximate guide, there being many exceptions to the above rules, and that accurate pronunciation is not essential to your understanding of primitive culture. Vowel sounds in particular shade off into each other, and apart from those which are peculiar to native languages there are others, such as the French "u" and the German "ö" which also occur in primitive languages.

Finally, you should refrain from attempting to make a plural of the names of native peoples by adding an "s"—for example, it is quite wrong to speak of the "Maoris", the "Bantus" or the "Eskimos". Some ethnographers have adopted this practice, as in the case of the Reddis, Chenchus and Todas (singular and adjectival forms: Reddi, Chenchu, Toda), and such usages must be taken as traditionally sanctioned. But you should never add a final "s" unless you have actually seen it in print in a reputable work. Contrariwise, when a native name ends with "s" you should be cautious about attempting to make a singular form by dropping the final consonant. An individual native of Manus is not a Manu. Only familiarity with anthropological writings will make you conversant with the inconsistencies of usage, but you should avoid the common solecisms mentioned at the beginning of this paragraph.

4. Acknowledgments

The fact that this volume has been prepared under the stress of post-war teaching conditions makes me keenly conscious of my indebtedness to those who have assisted in its production or have, in one way or another, facilitated my task. Above all, I would like to express the debt which I owe to my wife for her constant inspiration, her invaluable secretarial assistance and her many helpful criticisms. I should also like to say how much this work owes to the collaboration of my colleague, Mr. James Littlejohn, in the final stages of the preparation of the text and in the correction of proofs. Dr. Audrey Richards and Mr. J. C. Trevor have read the earlier sections of Chapters VII and VI respectively, and I am most grateful for their valuable emendations. Professor Raymond Firth has very kindly revised the diagram shown in Fig. 8, and I am indebted to Mr. David Abercrombie for checking the note on spelling and pronunciation. Professors A. L. Goodhart and A. H. Campbell have been good enough to provide me with much interesting information, a small portion only of which I have been able to use, on American Common Law Marriage and on the corresponding custom in Scotland. I am most grateful to Mr. S. F. Collins for preparing the first three maps and several of the diagrams and for much help in connection with the proofs and the preparation of the Ethnographic Directory and Bibliography. I am much indebted to Mrs. D. MacInnes for assistance of a similar kind, and I would also like to express my warm appreciation of the many hours of painstaking work which Miss M. Le Harivel has devoted to the typing of considerable sections of the manuscript.

Various portions of the text of this volume appeared originally in other publications by myself. It is impossible to specify these exactly, as they have been extensively revised, certain sections have been omitted and new material has been interpolated. But I have been saved a considerable amount of rewriting by the permission which I have been given to reproduce them in a revised form in the present work. In this respect I must thank the Editor of the *Aberdeen University Review* for allowing me to use certain extracts from two articles which I contributed to that Journal in 1939; the Amalgamated Press have kindly allowed me to use material from articles which originally appeared in *The Encyclopaedia of Modern Knowledge*; Professor A. P. Elkin has given

CONTENTS OF VOLUME I

PREFACE

CHAPTER I

THE SCIENCE OF PRIMITIVE CULTURE

CHAPTER II

A COOKS' TOUR OF PRIMITIVE PEOPLES: AFRICA AND AMERICA

CHAPTER III

A COOKS' TOUR OF PRIMITIVE PEOPLES: ASIA AND OCEANIA

CHAPTER IV

SOCIAL ORGANIZATION

CHAPTER V

SOCIAL ORGANIZATION (*continued*)

CHAPTER VI

THE PRINCIPLES OF CULTURAL ANALYSIS

CHAPTER VII

FOOD AND WEALTH

CHAPTER VIII

LAND TENURE

APPENDICES

FIGURES, PLATES AND MAPS

FIGURES

PLATES

MAPS

THE SCIENCE OF PRIMITIVE CULTURE

1. The Anthropological Sciences

BECAUSE man's life is lived in society, his interest is inevitably focused upon the thoughts, feelings and actions of his fellows. From birth to death he is continually dependent upon other people for his nourishment, his training, his security, and for the affection and good-fellowship which make life worth while. These material and spiritual debts find expression in his consciousness of kind and his recognition of his place as an individual in the wider scheme of human life.

The limits of these interests vary. They may be confined to the home, the school, the village or other small community; they may be extended to national and international fields; and they may be so wide as to embrace all mankind, including those peoples whom we call "primitive". The study of these is the special province of the anthropological sciences, which are concerned with the manner in which primitive man adapts himself to his environment, geographical, material and social. The three anthropological sciences are Physical Anthropology, Prehistoric Archæology and Social Anthropology. Their interrelationships and fields of study are summarized in Fig. 1.

Physical Anthropology is concerned with the bodily characteristics of man. One of its tasks is the classification and study of existing races of men, involving the measurement of such physical characteristics as the shape of the skull, height, skin colour and hair texture. The recording and analysis of bodily measurements are referred to as *anthropometry* or *somatology*. The study of race also involves a knowledge of *human genetics*, so far as it is concerned with the ways in which racial characteristics are transmitted from generation to generation. This is a complex and highly specialized field of study, in which few very definite conclusions have emerged. In particular, it is impossible to discern any relationship between racial types on the one hand, and differences in mental characteristics or behaviour on the other. Such differences may exist, but there is no scientifically valid evidence to support the many popular theories concerning alleged racial differences in intelligence, temperament or character. Such theories are usually the result, not of scientific enquiry, but of attempts to give justification to lines of policy based on racial antagonisms and political interests.

From our own point of view the more important task of physical anthropology is the description of the evolutionary processes whereby man acquired the characteristics which differentiate him from the anthropoid apes—his upright posture, his manipulative ability, his power of speech, and above all the large and

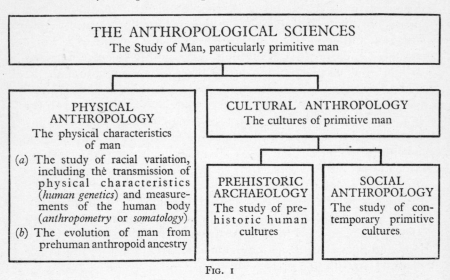

THE ANTHROPOLOGICAL SCIENCES
The Study of Man, particularly primitive man

PHYSICAL ANTHROPOLOGY
The physical characteristics of man
(a) The study of racial variation, including the transmission of physical characteristics (*human genetics*) and measurements of the human body (*anthropometry* or *somatology*)
(b) The evolution of man from prehuman anthropoid ancestry

CULTURAL ANTHROPOLOGY
The cultures of primitive man

PREHISTORIC ARCHAEOLOGY
The study of prehistoric human cultures

SOCIAL ANTHROPOLOGY
The study of contemporary primitive cultures

FIG. 1

complex brain which enabled him to co-ordinate his impressions, to remember, to reflect, to imagine and to anticipate the future.

All these physical developments were related to one another, and enabled man to invent and fashion tools and weapons, to communicate and co-operate with his fellows, and to live in a morally ordered society. These characteristics of human life, which make man's adaptation something quite different from anything found among animals, are summed up in the term *culture*, about which more will be said presently. The other two anthropological sciences are concerned with the study of this specifically human form of adaptation.

Of the earliest cultural achievements of mankind, which are

the province of **Prehistoric Archæology,** we know little, except on the material side. The tools, weapons and implements of pre-historic man are mainly important to us as revealing the significant changes in economic and social life which marked the earliest developments of human culture. Thus the earliest implements of chipped stone, bone and reindeer antler which marked the Palæolithic Age tell us something of the time when man lived exclusively by hunting, fishing and gathering edible fruits, roots or nuts. The wandering existence of the hunter and food-gatherer gave way to the settled life of the cultivator or the more orderly nomadism of the herdsman at the beginning of the Neolithic Age, when spindle whorls, potsherds and stone sickles provide evidence of the invention of weaving, pottery and, most important of all, agriculture.

The adoption of metals as the raw material for tools and weapons saw the development of the specialist craft of the metallurgist, while the transition from copper to bronze necessitated extensive trade to provide the rarer metal tin, to convert copper into the harder alloy bronze. Finally, the use of iron, with the greater control over the environment which its cheapness made possible, brings us to the beginning of historic times, when written records take up the story.

But the conditions of economic, social and political life in pre-historic times can only be discerned in dimmest outline. To study man's family organization, his political institutions, his religion and magic, and his types of economic life under primitive conditions, we must turn to the existing peoples of Africa, Oceania, America and Asia who lack the art of writing and of whom many do not know the use of metals. **Social Anthropology** is concerned with these.[1]

2. *Primitive Culture*

Social anthropologists study the cultures of contemporary primitive communities. The **culture** of a people may be defined as the sum total of the material and intellectual equipment

[1] The term **ethnology** is employed in America, on the continent of Europe, and occasionally in Britain, as a substitute for "social anthropology". But it refers primarily to those schools of anthropology which are largely concerned with historical analyses of the diffusion of culture (see below), sometimes referring also to the data of physical anthropology and prehistoric archæology so far as these contribute to historical reconstruction. For this reason the term is better avoided, but its adjectival form (**ethnological**) is a convenient one. The term **ethnography** refers to the actual collecting and recording of data about primitive culture, as distinct from theoretical interpretation.

whereby they satisfy their biological and social needs and adapt themselves to their environment.[1] The nature of this adaptation varies greatly from one community to another, but is always based on the common biological characteristics of man. Because man is an animal, human beings have the same biological needs the whole world over; and because the conditions of their association in societies are similar everywhere, there are certain general principles of organization common to all human communities, primitive and civilized.

The culture of any people includes two groups of phenomena: firstly, there are the material objects which they manufacture in order to satisfy their wants, such as tools, weapons, utensils, clothing, ornaments, houses and canoes as well as temples, idols, charms, amulets and other objects used for magico-religious purposes. These are called the **material culture** of a people. The smaller objects of material culture are referred to as **artefacts.** (American spelling: *artifacts.*) Logically we should apply this term to all modifications of the natural environment by the hands of man, including houses, temples, canoes, bridges and such alterations to the landscape as fortifications and systems of irrigation. But by convention the use of the term "artefact" is usually restricted to the smaller objects of material culture which may be carried or handled by an individual. The study of the techniques by which objects of material culture are made is known as **technology.**

Secondly, all human communities possess a body of knowledge, belief and values which is just as vital to survival as their artefacts. These intangible phenomena are often referred to as the **spiritual** or **social culture** of a community. The social culture of a people includes their knowledge of natural phenomena and processes, their systems of political and economic organization, their rules of morality, law and good behaviour, and finally their magico-religious beliefs and practices.

It cannot be too strongly emphasized that neither material nor social culture can be scientifically studied in isolation from the other. This is best illustrated by reference to **ecology,** that is,

[1] The reader should be warned against confusing this specialized use of the term "culture" with the more limited meaning attached to it in popular usage, where it refers only to certain specialized types of intellectual activity. From the point of view of anthropology, a steam locomotive, a horse-race, a factory or a popular song are just as much a part of British culture as a symphony, an exhibition of paintings, a university or an edition of the works of Shakespeare.

man's adaptation to his geographical environment. In the getting of food, man employs such artefacts as hunting weapons, snares, fish-hooks and lines, nets and agricultural implements, while he protects himself from the weather by erecting houses, tents or other shelters as well as by the making of clothing. The manufacture and use of these objects cannot be understood without reference to the matrix of social culture in which they occur—systems of land tenure, the economic organization of production, distribution and exchange, the exercise of authority, and finally the beliefs and practices of religion and magic. On the other hand, these elements of social culture are only comprehensible in their material setting of geographical environment and in relation to the objects of material culture by which natural resources are exploited and the material needs of man are satisfied.

We have said that social anthropology is concerned with the culture of **primitive** communities. It must be emphasized that there is no rigid dividing-line between primitive and civilized cultures. A wide range of human adaptations is found in the world today from hunters and food gatherers, such as the Australian aborigines, to the most complicated developments of modern European or American civilizations. There are, however, characteristics of certain cultures which we may conveniently call primitive. These are:

i. Illiteracy; the presence or absence of writing is the most common distinction drawn between civilized and primitive cultures.
ii. The organization of society on the basis of small social groupings, such as the clan, village or tribe, in contradistinction to the state, nation or empire in the case of civilized peoples.
iii. A low level of technical achievement.
iv. Social relations based on kinship and locality are far more important than in civilized societies.
v. In primitive societies generally there is a lack of economic specialization and of the overlapping of social groups which occur in modern civilized communities.

While these criteria will serve as a rough-and-ready delimitation of our subject-matter, it must be emphasized that in the case of each the distinctions are relative. For example, such peoples as the Lepchas of Sikkim or many of the communities of West Africa include some individuals who can read and write. These communities are therefore, strictly speaking, not illiterate, though most of their members are so. Again, many peoples with a low level of technology nevertheless possess an elaborate political organization, a good example being the League of the Iroquois. Thus, while there is a general tendency for the above characteristics to co-exist in certain societies which we call "primitive", the student should not think of "primitive peoples" as a separate breed of men, and caution should be employed in using such terms as "advanced" or "highly developed" cultures.

Since all human cultures are founded on certain common basic principles, it may be asked why social anthropologists should limit themselves to a study of primitive communities.[1] In part this is the result of historical accident, in that most social anthropologists have in fact so limited their studies. But there is a more cogent reason why specialists should concentrate on the study of the primitive: the study of primitive cultures requires a specialized technique which lays emphasis upon the interrelation of all cultural facts. As we shall see, primitive culture is not divided into discrete spheres of human activity such as economic, legal and technological, to the same extent as our own. It follows that such subjects as law, economics and technology cannot be studied in primitive society without reference to their relation to other aspects of culture. We shall therefore take as our field of study any community to which the specific techniques of social anthropology outlined in this book are applicable.

Most of the primitive communities which we shall study were isolated for many centuries from the centres where the major civilizations of the world developed. For example, the Australian aborigines appear to have been completely cut off from the outside world (apart from possible minor contacts in the north with Malays and the natives of New Guinea) since their ancestors first reached the Australian continent. The peoples of Africa, south of the Sahara, were never significantly affected by the civilizations to the north of them—certainly the sociology of a Bantu community is more akin to that of certain Polynesian societies than it is to the historic civilizations of Egypt, Greece, Rome and

---

[1] As a matter of fact, several valuable experiments have been carried out in the application of anthropological techniques to the study of civilized communities. But it remains true that most social anthropologists concentrate on the study of primitive culture.

Islam. Finally, certain Indian tribes which we shall have occasion to mention, though surrounded by highly developed Indian civilizations, nevertheless show characteristics which are essentially primitive.

The historic isolation of primitive peoples has, particularly during the past two centuries, been broken by the widespread diffusion of European and American civilization. Today, "untouched" primitive cultures are rare, surviving only in such places as the less accessible regions of Central Africa, South America, New Guinea and Australia. In most instances primitive communities have been affected to a greater or lesser degree by the impact of civilization, sometimes to such an extent that little or nothing remains of their old culture. This process, which is known as **culture contact,** has raised enormous theoretical and practical problems which are becoming an increasingly important field of study for the social anthropologist.

It should be mentioned that *detribalization*, the breakdown of primitive cultures as a result of culture contact, makes it impossible for the social anthropologist to be both consistent and accurate in his use of tenses in speaking of the cultures of most primitive peoples. In describing a primitive culture on the basis of information collected today (either directly by field-work or indirectly from literary sources), the social anthropologist usually finds that some of his statements about the culture should be cast in the present tense and others in the past. Consistency and precision in the use of terms can be attained only in the case of a few virtually untouched primitive cultures on the one hand and those which have completely disappeared (for example, that of the Tasmanians) on the other. No attempt will therefore be made in this work to achieve consistency in this respect. The reader must, however, be warned that many of the statements made in the present tense regarding the cultures of primitive peoples are no longer true, or although true at the present may not be so in five or ten years' time.

3. The Aims of Social Anthropology

The aim of any science is to study a specified part of the real world and from a study of facts to formulate theories which shall serve as recipes for human conduct, whether that conduct be the carrying out of further research or the taking of practical steps for the promotion of human welfare. This view of the task of science implies a complete rejection of the common antithesis between pure and applied science. The relation of these two aspects of scientific enquiry has been defined by Professor Lancelot Hogben: "It is one thing to say that a discipline can only rank as genuine science when it can also supply us with recipes for the practical conduct of affairs, and it is another to say that scientific research is and must always be confined to topics of immediate social value. If you have to build a railway you need a map. It is obviously superficial to draw a sharp distinction between the work done in mapping the actual track traversed as *useful* work in contradistinction to all the *useless* work of mapping the part of the territory over which no rails are laid down. One reason is that you cannot know what you will have to scrap till your task is finished. Another is that the existence of the railway may make it necessary or desirable to have a water supply, town, or sanatorium in the vicinity. What is easily overlooked is that the part of the map where no rails are laid down, where no town is built, where no wells are tapped, and where no sanatorium is erected would not have been prospected *unless there had first been a definite social reason for constructing the map.*"[1]

In attempts to draw a distinction between pure and applied science, much misunderstanding arises from confusion between the direction and effects of scientific enquiry on the one hand, and the particular motives of individual scientists on the other. Hogben has shown in the work cited how many theoretical advances have been made as a direct result of the realization of new human requirements in a changing culture. On the other hand, it is equally true that useful practical results have emerged from enquiries pursued out of pure scientific interest and with no practical end in view. The most striking example is the statement attributed to the physicist, Hertz, whose researches were fundamental to the development of modern radio, that he did not think that his discoveries could ever have any useful practical application. In social anthropology it is certainly true that researches motivated by purely theoretical interest may have far-reaching practical applications, while those which arise from the pursuit of practical objectives may, provided that they are governed by scientific discipline, lead to the elucidation of abstract theoretical problems. The motives of individual observers are thus seen to be irrelevant to the progress of scientific knowledge.

---

[1] Hogben, *Science for the Citizen*, Epilogue.

Ideally, ethnographic accounts given by a missionary who wishes to convert natives to Christianity, or by an administrator who wishes to govern more effectively, should not differ from those given for the same community by a research worker in social anthropology. But, as we shall see later, the training and background of the different classes of investigators mean in fact that this ideal is not often achieved.

It follows from what has been said that the aims of any science are best defined by reference to the human problems to which it is related. In terms of this criterion, what are the aims of social anthropology?

The physical and biological sciences have enormously increased man's understanding of, and control over, his environment. By comparison the social sciences are "young". Yet an understanding of the laws governing human behaviour and human relations is essential to the proper application of the resources of science to the promotion of human welfare. We who live today are shaping for good or ill the future of our world. It is essential that we should do so intelligently and constructively. Underlying contemporary social and political creeds and policies we can detect certain assumptions which rest upon varying conceptions, or misconceptions, of human nature. We are told that man is naturally communistic, altruistic and peaceful; or alternatively that he is essentially individualistic and aggressive, born eternally to perpetuate the law of the jungle in cut-throat competition and the ruthless extermination of the unfit; that he is instinctively religious, or that religion and ethics are no more than by-products of economic change. These are rich fields for disputation about "human nature" in which primitive people are frequently dragged in by the heels so support the arguments of one faction or the other. Here social anthropology can help by providing a solid basis of empirical evidence.

Though this aspect of anthropological research has not received the attention which it deserves, valuable work has been done by posing concrete problems and considering them in the light of ethnographic evidence. For example: are the emotional crises associated with adolescence in our own society due primarily to biological changes in the growing human organism, or to the culture in which our young are reared? Is the individual family a necessary and universal institution in human society, or could its place be taken by other institutional arrangements? Naturally, social anthropology cannot provide simple and forthright solutions for all current social problems. And at all costs it must not allow scientific knowledge to be distorted to fit in with social and political prejudices. But since most of the suggested solutions for these problems rest upon assumptions concerning human nature, it is useful to know how men live, behave and look upon life in environments vastly different from our own. On the one hand, the complexity of the issues raised by such a study leads us to reject simple formulations; while on the other, the fact that primitive communities are faced with the same sort of problems, which they solve in a variety of ways, that their adjustments are purposive, and in some respects better than our own, leads us to hope that their experience of success and failure may be of help to us in our own work of social reconstruction.

The second aim of social anthropology is related to the study of culture contact, previously mentioned. It is essential to study the effects produced on primitive cultures by the impact of modern civilization. This not only involves problems of considerable theoretical interest, but is also vital to the problems of missionaries, officers in the Colonial Service, and others whose work brings them into direct contact with native peoples. For these, insight into the working of primitive society is of the greatest importance; here, as always, the co-ordination of science and practical affairs is essential to each. Anthropology can derive incalculable benefit from the specialist knowledge of administrators experienced in native government, from missionaries who have gained the trust and affection of the people, and from experts in agriculture, forestry and nutrition, just as these specialists require a knowledge of native political and legal institutions, religious life and systems of land tenure, economics and diet.

4. The Method of Social Anthropology

The method of social anthropology is based upon **field-work**—the direct study of the beliefs and customs of primitive peoples. The field observations upon which theoretical interpretation in social anthropology is founded may be broadly divided into two classes. Firstly, the observations made in the past by observers who were largely untrained, but had the advantage of observing primitive cultures more or less as they existed before the impact of European civilization and, secondly, those made by modern scientific observers trained in methods of field-work. The latter observations usually concern communities whose original culture has been largely broken up or distorted by the process of culture contact.

Field records of primitive peoples began to appear in the late eighteenth and early nineteenth centuries, when such people as travellers and missionaries began to bring home information about the peoples of the remote parts of the world which they visited. But few of these observers had any scientific training, nor had *methods* of studying primitive peoples even been considered. The early observers simply noted what attracted their attention. Consequently their descriptions are faulty by modern standards.

The science of anthropology had its beginnings in the latter part of the nineteenth century, when scholars, under the evolutionary stimulus of Darwin, began to speculate about the meaning and history of social institutions. But these scientists had no actual experience in the field—their theories were based upon the inadequate observations mentioned above. While interpretation was thus separated from observation, no true science of social anthropology could emerge.

During the first three decades of the present century, observations were made by trained scientists, and with this began the building up of a body of scientific information by systematic field-work, which reached a high level of development in the years intervening between the two wars.

This synthesis of theory and practice, of arm-chair interpretation and observation in the field, has produced a body of knowledge which has given to modern social anthropology a truly scientific character. It is now recognized that theoretical interpretation is only valid and valuable when it is founded on a solid basis of observed fact, while the collection of material in the field must be guided and inspired by a systematic body of theory, a clearly formulated set of problems which will enable the observer to collect all relevant facts and at the same time to discriminate between those facts which are relevant and those which are not.

We have said that, ideally, observations carried out by academic anthropologists should be identical with those of the observer with practical interests, provided that both are aware of modern methods of field-work. In fact, however, both are limited. The academic anthropologist sometimes lacks personal interest in the natives he is studying, particularly when he is considering communities which he does not know at first hand. His craving for system and order frequently leads him to reduce the protean stuff of human behaviour to a few simple principles. And when he is addicted to historical reconstruction, this inevitably leads him to ignore or distort the existing reality of the culture he is studying. On the other hand, the missionary or administrator has all too seldom had an opportunity of theoretical training adequate to the demands of the scientific task of studying primitive peoples. In the field he is usually so preoccupied with the responsibilities proper to his practical task that he cannot devote sufficient time and attention to purely scientific studies. And his own social prejudices are apt to distort his judgment to a greater extent than in the case of the scientist. Thus it is true that many valuable records of primitive peoples have been provided by missionaries, but in general they are apt to be biased in their treatment of aspects of primitive social life which conflict with Christian teaching, particularly magico-religious beliefs, polygamy and sexual codes.

Again, when the administrator writes of a primitive people, he is all too apt to concentrate on those features of social life which he encounters in the course of his official duties, particularly those which "give trouble", to the neglect of more recondite problems of native life which demand patient and persevering investigation. His treatment is too often coloured by his profession; for example, in dealing with such subjects as land tenure he often attempts to reduce a complex system of interlocking and counterbalancing obligations to a set of hard-and-fast principles comparable with those found in civilized systems of codified law. The law of land tenure is perhaps easier to handle administratively when regarded in this way, but the treatment, as we shall see, distorts the complex reality of native law and custom.

Both the missionary and administrator are also handicapped by their professional interests and obligations. The administrator finds it difficult to mix on an equal and informal footing with natives, while the missionary must necessarily comment morally on native conduct. Neither can adopt the completely objective and dispassionate mood of enquiry essential to field-work in anthropology as to all scientific research. This mood is particularly difficult to achieve in dealing with primitive culture. The observer is himself the product of a particular (civilized) culture, and when his observations are superficial, they are inevitably coloured by his own cultural background. This leads to a distorted evaluation of features of primitive culture, and of the mentality and temperament of primitive man, in terms of superficial comparisons with certain aspects of our own culture. Distortions so produced are of two kinds, reflecting either a contemptuous dislike of primitive ways of life or an idyllic and romantic interpretation of them.

The reasons for the first of these are fairly easy to understand. The conditions of primitive life are so vastly different from our own that they tend at first to produce amusement, contempt, or indignation rather than an effort at scientific understanding. There seems to be no common element in an exotic carving on a South Sea Island canoe and the achievements of civilized art; the spectacle of a group of Australian aborigines solemnly pouring blood upon a stone to increase their food supply seems at first quite incommensurable with religious life and spiritual aspiration as we understand it; the economic life of primitive man strikes us as thoroughly inefficient, hedged about as it is by magical practices, taboos and superstitious beliefs; and it seems incredible that ceremonies of orgiastic licence, tolerated pre-marital and extra-marital intercourse and other customs which we would regard as immoral, can co-exist with ordered systems of family life, founded upon biological, psychological and sociological bases similar to our own.

This is why so many observers have spoken contemptuously of primitive culture without any genuine attempt to understand its significance for the native. Many years ago an administrator, called upon to report on the manners and customs of the primitive people among whom he was working, sent in the brief report: "Manners none and customs beastly". While most observers today are more sophisticated than this, there still lingers in some quarters the idea of primitive peoples as "barbarians".

The opposite type of distortion is produced by other observers who approach the study of primitive culture obsessed by the defects of our own world, with its increasingly ghastly methods of warfare, its economic depressions, its cut-throat competition, its violent political controversies and its widely publicized cases of violent and sordid crime. Such observers tend to give us a picture corresponding to Rousseau's "noble savage", who is essentially gentle and decent, who lives in a state of "primitive communism", and obeys "automatically" the laws and customs of the community to which he belongs. This idyllic and romantic picture is likewise a distortion of the human reality of primitive life, and is apt to be more pronounced when, as in the case of Elliot Smith, the observer has never carried out systematic field-work in a primitive community. First-hand observation in the field reveals the amount of malicious gossip, backbiting, jealousy and greed which underlie the apparently harmonious day-to-day life of primitive peoples, and the personal antagonisms which from time to time find expression in the performance of evil magic, in murders, or in village brawls. Everybody seems to be hurling abuse at someone else at the tops of their voices, the sentiments expressed are far from "noble", and the behaviour anything but gentle—an amusing example is recorded by Hogbin from a village brawl in Wogeo, in which a man picked up a dog and hurled it at his adversary.

To sum up, it is easy enough, on the basis of superficial and one-sided observation, to caricature primitive man as a fiend or as a saint. It requires the discipline of patient scientific observation to see him as a human being not essentially different from ourselves, capable of brutality and kindness, of greed or altruism, of obedience or defiance towards the social order, according to the culture in which he is born, his individual temperament and the particular circumstances in which he finds himself.

5. The Functional Approach to Primitive Culture

The approach to primitive culture outlined in this book is founded on what is called the **functional method,** based upon the functional theory of human culture. This theory lays down certain principles which are essential to a scientific examination of primitive cultures. It insists that human culture is not a thing of shreds and patches, but an organic unity of which each element is related to every other. And it examines all the phases of human activity—economic institutions, political and social organization, magic and religion—in relation to one another with a view to understanding how they subserve man's biological, psychological and social needs.

This appears at first sight to consist of stressing the obvious. But it is necessary to do so because, both in theoretical interpretation and in actual research, the obvious is frequently ignored. Most of the older anthropological works, and many recent ones, pay no attention to the dynamic factors in social institutions, their complex character and the relationships existing between them.

Systems of family life and kinship have been looked upon as quaint survivals of early adjustments, and their rôle in defining human procreation and in organizing domestic activities has been ignored; volumes have been devoted to technology, without the slightest reference to the use of artefacts in the satisfaction of economic needs, the rules of property defining their ownership, their function as elements of wealth, and the mythological and magico-religious beliefs and practices which centre round them. Finally, religious beliefs and magical practices have been treated as amusing or shocking oddities, as clumsy attempts at scientific thought, or as the obstinate perpetuation of some intellectual blunder, to the complete neglect of their active rôle in organizing collective activity, in providing safeguards against apathy, panic or despair, and in supporting a system of ethical and customary rules upon which a community depends for its very existence.

These criticisms could be duplicated in every branch of anthropological research, and it is necessary on the one hand to formulate a technique for the investigation of living cultures in all their complexity, and at the same time emphatically to reject all lines of enquiry which obscure the genuine scientific issues, which cannot yield verifiable and fruitful results, or which distract attention from the serious study of working human cultures.

As we have indicated, field-work is the key-note of the functional method. This, again, is based upon a general theory of human society which enables us to see beneath the bewildering variety of social customs a certain core of universal human requirements. The older tendency was to lay stress on the differences between human societies, and to ignore their similarities. The modern method is, first, to formulate the fundamental needs of men which all cultures subserve through different institutions, and then to indicate the variety of ways in which these needs are satisfied in different primitive societies.

Man's fundamental needs can be grouped into three classes. In the first place, there are the **primary needs,** given in the biological make-up of the human organism. Hunger and sex are the needs which occur to us at once as the fundamental drives of mankind, but there are also others. Thus, sex does not end at the act of physical intercourse—it leads to pregnancy and childbirth; and the human infant so produced is a helpless creature, who must be fed, cared for and trained during its early life. Some form of shelter against the elements is required, and also means of self-preservation against the attacks of wild animals or hostile communities. These biological requirements are met by culture; thus the family and the working team satisfy man's biological needs of sex and hunger through a system of organization much more elaborate than anything which occurs among animals.

This implies the existence of the second class of requirements— **derived needs.** If the family is to have a home, man must have tools to build it with; to catch fish, he must have nets, traps, or hooks and lines; even in the most primitive pursuit of all, hunting, man does not use his bare hands—he employs spears, snares, bows and arrows, or he trains dogs to hunt for him.

But the fact that man's life is lived in society, that its essence is co-operation and the exchange of services between human beings, gives rise to a system of **integrative needs,** which demand a form of organization that will enable men to live and work together. Thus they must have a religion, using the term in a very wide sense to mean some socially unifying philosophy of life, some source of moral fortitude in the face of illness, disaster or death.

As we have said, not even the primary biological needs are satisfied simply and directly. Men co-operate with men in the production of food and with women in the procreation and training of children; they employ tools, weapons and implements; they communicate to one another, through language, the method of using these material objects; and they live together in defined areas of territory, where they employ the same body of practical knowledge and obey the same moral rules.

It is these systems of human activity, or **institutions,** that are the really significant elements of culture, for they are the means which man employs to satisfy his fundamental needs. Any isolated custom, belief or material object, such as a weapon or implement, cannot be understood except as a part of the institution in which it occurs. We could describe a typical English house, its structure, its measurements, the brick or stone of which it is constructed, without conveying the slightest hint of the meaning of the term "home" for the people who live in it.

Since any human institution can only be understood as a whole, it is important that it should be studied in all its aspects, that nothing which is relevant shall escape observation. The early untrained field-workers failed to do this. As we have seen they went out to live with primitive communities and simply wrote down what interested them or attracted their attention. The result was a one-sided concentration on the strange, the spectacular and the exotic aspects of native life. We were given lurid accounts of sexual customs without a word about family life, or long descriptions of queer ceremonies and weird beliefs without the slightest hint of how the savage obtained his food. Moreover, these investigations were carried out by the "question and answer" method, and without any attempt to see whether the native's behaviour corresponded with his professed beliefs and ideals.

This haphazard procedure gave an artificial and distorted picture of native life. For this reason the modern field-worker insists on going out to his people armed with a theoretical scheme, a programme of investigation which will make sure that he misses nothing that is really relevant. This scheme is based upon a general view of human society which stresses certain aspects of culture that will be found in every community because they are deeply rooted in the biological make-up of the human organism and in the constitution of human society.

6. The Analysis of Culture

Let us imagine ourselves in the position of a field-worker among a primitive community—say, a village on a small island in the Pacific Ocean. At one end of the village some men are preparing for a fishing expedition, mending their tackle, making plans and discussing the prospects of a good catch; in a nearby hut a woman is in labour, and a medicine-man sits outside, intoning a spell for the welfare of mother and child; before the largest hut of all are displayed great heaps of food—fish, pigs cooked whole, yams and coco-nuts—tribute brought to the chief from a neighbouring village; around the spring a group of women are gossiping, and in the distance can be heard the shouts and laughter of small children sailing their toy canoes upon the lagoon.

How, in such a situation, does the modern field-worker approach his problem? How will he bring order and intelligibility into the kaleidoscope of native life which is always presenting to him a new aspect? He must have, first and foremost, a clear idea of what he wants to investigate, and some system of classification which will help him to arrange his facts. This must cover all the aspects of native culture, in order to make sure that there are none of the omissions and gaps in information which characterized the old method of haphazard observation.

First of all, he must have a knowledge of the *geographical environment*, of the climatic setting, of the kinds of food-stuffs and raw materials available, and of the seasonal round which the natives follow, whether they be nomadic hunters, fishermen, pastoralists or agriculturists. Within this setting he will find a complex *economic system*, designed to satisfy the material wants of the people—to organize production, to control distribution, and to determine the rights and claims of ownership within the community.

Probably he will find that this latter system is closely related to the *political organizatian*. The governing authority of primitive peoples, whether it be a headman, a chief, or a council of tribal elders, generally plays an important part in economic life. The chief may direct economic enterprise, may receive vast amounts of wealth as tribute and redistribute it among the commoners. Often he is the titular owner of the land, distributing it among his people and settling the claims of rival parties. This brings us to the *legal aspect* of culture, which is concerned with the maintenance of authority and the enforcement of certain traditional rules.

Every society is constantly renewing itself with fresh human material; as people die off, new individuals are born into the world. But these are at first helpless, being unable to fend for themselves and knowing nothing of the cultural tradition, which must be taught to them. Thus it is that every culture has some system of *education*, using the term in its widest sense—some means by which the traditions of the people, their practical knowledge and techniques, their language and their codes of morals and good behaviour are transmitted from generation to generation.

So far we have been dealing with the practical activities of man, with the matter-of-fact procedure which he adopts to solve his problems. But we have yet to deal with a very vital aspect of his life, his religion and his magic, which together make up the *magico-religious* aspect of culture. Here we are particularly apt to fall into the old attitude of contempt for native custom. There is a tendency to dismiss the whole system of magical and religious beliefs as childish "superstition", but we must delve deeper and seek to find the true meaning which these beliefs and practices possess for the native.

We shall then see his magic, not from our point of view, but from his. We shall find that it plays a part in his life by giving him confidence in the face of difficulty and danger, and also that it serves to organize his practical activities. For example, the magician is often also an expert craftsman or technician. In a fishing expedition the man who carries out magical spells to secure a good catch may also be an expert fisherman; he has a wealth of information concerning seasons and the weather; he is familiar with the habits of fish and sea birds, and with the techniques of craftsmanship required in the making of canoes and fishing tackle. His supposed power as a magician reinforces his authority as a leader, and serves to control and organize the whole enterprise.

Similar considerations apply to the study of religion, of beliefs in immortality, in ancestor spirits, in queer and phantasmic demons and gods. Many of these beliefs appear absurd, but when they are interpreted in terms of human feelings, they appear as man's protest at his own futility before the apparent irrationality of the universe; they carry with them a feeling of human power, of the intelligibility of nature and of the fundamental value of life.

If our study of primitive culture is to be thorough, we must not forget its aspects of *art, recreation* and *ceremonial*. All human communities employ man's sensitivity to patterns of sense impressions, whether it be in music, painting, carving or dancing. Often primitive standards of beauty strike us as perverted, but here, again, we must recognize the fact that they possess a deep significance for the native and serve to enliven, to embellish and to beautify the crude struggle for existence. The same might be said of ceremonial and recreational activity, which provide a relief from the humdrum effort of everyday life, and reflect the social values of the community in which they occur.

Here, then, are aspects of culture which we should find in every society. In addition, we should constantly be brought up against four very general features of human life—material culture, language, social organization and the normative system of sentiments, values and moral judgments which determine human behaviour.

A *material substratum* of weapons, tools, or artefacts of different kinds is to be found underlying every human activity, and the form of institutions is closely related to the material equipment associated with them—family life takes on different forms in a South Sea Island hut and in a modern bungalow or apartment-house, and warfare is largely a different institution according to whether it is carried out with spears and clubs, or with tanks and aeroplanes.

The modern field-worker must also study language, not only because it is an essential instrument in obtaining information, but because language enters into all human institutions, and the manner in which it is employed in effective communication is significantly related to the forms of these institutions. Thus in our own society, speech as used in church, on a parade-ground or in a court of law is different from that employed in a scientific discussion, or, again, in arranging a business transaction; its form is correlated with the differences between the various forms of human activity.

Moreover, in studying language the anthropologist is driven to collect texts, which embody the legends, mythology and historical traditions of the people. These are important, not as an account of what actually happened in the past, but as a body of beliefs which gives a traditional justification for present-day institutions. We are concerned with such historical accounts only in so far as they live in the present, in the form of beliefs, whether true or false, which actually influence the lives of the natives.

Every human community possesses some form of *social organization*, some grouping of the people into social units for purposes of co-operation. The most fundamental unit of social organization is the family, for it is from here that the growing individual starts out to explore the society in which he lives. There are numerous forms of social groupings, the division between the sexes, age-grades, economic classes, small local groups and wider political units such as tribes. The complicated interrelations of these groups, the various functions which they serve, and the manner in which they co-operate—these are some of the most difficult problems which the modern anthropologist has to face.

Finally, every human culture has its *normative aspect*, embodying certain norms or standards which are laid down by tradition. From the simplest practical technique, such as making a fish-hook to the most significant rules of moral behaviour, there is always a "right" and a "wrong" way of doing things, and this is always supported by some form of sanction, whether ridicule, legal punishment or moral condemnation.

But when we have analysed culture into its component parts, we have completed only half our task. We have listed the things which we must study, but we have not fitted them together into an organic whole which reproduces the living reality of human society. This we can do only by recognizing that every aspect of culture is related to every other aspect .We should have to deal in turn with each of the aspects which we have listed and show its relation to every other phase in native life. In dealing with any primitive community, this task of "functional correlation" must be undertaken. To illustrate this, let us take just one of the aspects which we have mentioned—namely the legal aspect—and show that it cannot be considered alone, but must be correlated with every other aspect of culture if it is to be thoroughly understood.

If we are studying primitive legal institutions, we should not deal simply with crime and punishment. We should try to see law in its social context. We should not be content merely to see what happens when the law is broken; we should also ask why it is kept. This would lead us to study law as a part of custom; the economic forces which lead people to obey it; the way in which children are trained to respect the dictates of tradition, and the religious and magical forces of supernatural punishment, which often give to law a binding force.

To show how far-reaching is our functional study of law, we should insist that even art and recreation may have a bearing upon it. Æsthetic factors enter into legal institutions, and give them an added impressiveness, whether it be in the scarlet robes of an English judge or the red feather girdle of a Tahitian high chief. Even recreation may be important in a study of law and morals; the "rules of the game" are often the child's first contact with the social order, and give an early impression of what is "not cricket".

We cannot deal here with the more general aspects of law: with the material substratum of execution, whether spear, axe or policeman's truncheon, together with the emblems and regalia of legal authority; with the linguistic aspect, embodied in legal maxims and verbal tradition; with the ethical significance of law, the manner in which, to be effective, it must be backed by the moral feelings of society; or with the social groups which may administer the law, the people who act for the community in cases of wrong. But we have said enough to indicate that the study of primitive law is not a simple matter, that law is bound up with the whole social system, and that it must be studied in all its aspects if we are to understand how men come to obey laws which very often run counter to the powerful promptings of individual passion and greed.

7. The Classification of Cultures and the Comparative Method

We have so far spoken only of the study of individual cultures. But social anthropology aims essentially at comparison of the different types of human adaptations which make up the wide variety of primitive cultures, and for this purpose some form of classification is essential. In these two tasks—comparison and classification—modern social anthropology has made less headway than in the study of individual cultures, largely because the problems involved are very much more complex and because we must avoid any superficial comparisons which are not based on a full appreciation of the nature of cultural reality in the various cultures studied.

These reservations constitute an objection to the system of cultural classification adopted by many American ethnologists. For them the basic unit of cultural reality is the culture **trait**, that is, a single item of information with regard to either the material or the social culture of any people. Each of the individual standardized types of behaviour which the field-worker observes is a trait of the culture concerned; for example, the use of a particular kind of fish-spear, a prescribed type of marriage between kin, or a method of getting food.

Culture traits usually have a geographical distribution extending beyond the boundaries of any individual tribe. If we review the occurrence of several such traits over a given geographical area, we find that they tend to cluster together into what are called **culture complexes.** Here it is important to emphasize a distinction which is of fundamental importance, but is not always carefully drawn. The aggregation of traits in a complex may be due to functional association or to what is called *adhesion*, that is, the apparently accidental co-existence of culture traits. As an example of the former, Wissler points out that the practice of certain Amerindian tribes in the vicinity of Lake Superior of relying on wild rice for food is a culture trait, but one which is integrally related to certain other traits, such as protecting the growing plants against birds; the gathering, preparation and cooking of the wild rice; the economic principles governing its production and distribution, and the rules of etiquette and magico-religious observances connected with it. Defined in this way, the conception of a culture complex approximates to that of an institution as defined in Chapter VI. But many ethnologists are by no means consistent in their use of this term. Thus Wissler goes on to cite totemism, the couvade, the horse and exogamy as further examples of culture complexes. Here we are dealing with cultural phenomena of widely differing kinds. As we shall see, totemism is not a single cultural reality, but merely a useful label for certain widely differing beliefs and practices which are associated with various types of institution in the different cultures in which it occurs. The horse, again, is a biological and not a cultural reality, since its significance is entirely different if we consider, for example, its place in the cultures of the Bedouin and the Plains Indians respectively.

The significance of this becomes more clear when we come to the next category of classification, namely, the **culture area.** If we study a series of contiguous primitive peoples in any part of the world we find that groups of both culture traits and culture complexes tend to occur together over specific areas, whether as a result of functional relationships between them or because of fortuitous adhesion. Thus the Plains Indian culture area is in general characterized by a large number of traits, among which Wissler mentions dependence upon the bison, the tipi as a movable dwelling, a special bead technique, a strongly geometric type of art, and the simple band as the unit of social organization. In such an agglomeration of culture traits we can discern some which are functionally related to each other. For example, the use of bison hide in the construction of the tipi, coupled with the need for a movable dwelling, can be associated with the dominant food-getting activity—bison hunting—which entails a nomadic existence to which the simple hunting band is probably the most appropriate form of social organization. But such traits as special bead techniques and geometric art do not appear to bear any necessary relation to the major institutional activities of the Plains Indians.

The concept of the culture area, then, is a geographical and not an anthropological one, in the sense in which the functionalist uses the term. It is useful for purposes of superficial surveys and as providing a general impression of some of the dominant characteristics of different groups of cultures. But as an instrument of scientific analysis it is useless, and may even be dangerous, as leading to an entirely wrong conception of culture as a mere agglomeration of traits. Thus we might say that the culture area of Great Britain is characterized by monarchy, the smoking of tobacco, the keeping of dogs as pets, the use of coal and electricity in industry, Christianity, cricket and a high development of the practice of navigation. We could go on *ad nauseam* enumerating such culture traits without even beginning to understand the culture of Great Britain as a mechanism for the satisfaction of human needs, composed of interrelated institutions within the framework of which any isolated culture trait must be considered.

Another type of comparative method seeks to classify cultures on the basis, not of objective culture traits, but upon a subjective assessment of what are called **patterns of culture.** This method, sometimes referred to as the *configurationist* approach, seeks to assess the dominant psychological values in each culture and to compare one culture with another on this basis. It is certainly preferable to the method previously described, in that it treats each culture as an integrated whole and not as a hotchpotch of traits. Unfortunately, however, it has too often led to an over-simplified and superficial impression of the cultures considered. In various attempts to construct neat and consistent "patterns", casual impressions have replaced the orderly scientific examinations of cultural facts; subjective judgments have been used as a substitute for ethnographic documentation; and the postulation of consistent and all-pervasive cultural trends has given an attractive but distorted picture of some at least of the cultures studied in this way, as can be demonstrated by a critical re-examination of the ethnographic evidence.[1]

Actually, no scientific and comprehensive technique of cultural comparison has yet been devised. Such a technique would involve the comparison of functional relationships between cultural phenomena in a series of cultures, since such relationships are the real facts of anthropological science. A few such studies have been made, for example, Professor Radcliffe-Brown's analysis of types of kinship terminology and social organization in Australia in terms of marriage practices and other culturally defined relationships between kin. Again there are such works as Professor Firth's brief comparative survey of certain kinship usages in Polynesia, Professor Schapera's comparative studies of different Bantu legal systems and Dr. Audrey Richards' review of nutritional practices among the southern Bantu. One of the best comparative studies published so far is Dr. S. F. Nadel's survey of the peoples of the Nuba Mountains. Here the author discerns an underlying sub-

---

[1] See, for example, Li An-Che (1).

stratum of something which can be called "Nuba Culture", but also discusses the extensive and detailed tribal variations which occur from one Nuba community to another. This work combines the comparative concept of culture areas with the functionalist's appreciation of the integral individuality of the culture of every human community.

However, the above-mentioned comparative studies, valuable as they are, are limited in their geographical scope. What is needed is some technique of cultural comparison which would enable us, for example, to compare institutions of chieftainship in Africa and in Polynesia in terms of the magico-religious sanctions which support them or in terms of their economic implications. While there are many excellent studies of such functional relationships in individual cultures, no comprehensive technique of comparison exists. In the present state of our knowledge, the most which we can do is to institute *ad hoc* comparisons that illustrate similarities and differences in cultural relationships—for example, to compare the potlatch, the Feasts of Merit of the Nagas and the Chins and the systems of social advancement in Malaita as illustrating a fundamental type of relationship between wealth and prestige, but one which operates in a different way in the various cultures concerned.

Since classification is impossible without a technique of comparison, it follows that there is no really satisfactory way of classifying human cultures. We can, it is true, adopt different criteria such as patriliny or matriliny, segmented or stratified political organization and so on. But this does not help us towards a scientific classification, since we find some segmented societies which are patrilineal and others which are matrilineal, and the same applies to stratified societies. Here again our categories are instituted *ad hoc* according to the purpose of our investigation.

Probably the most useful general type of classification of cultures is according to the dominant type of food-getting activity. We can classify certain primitive peoples either as hunters and food-gatherers, agriculturists or pastoralists, and this is particularly significant in view of Professor Gordon Childe's demonstration of the importance of these types of ecological activity in determining the development of human culture in prehistoric times. But in dealing with contemporary primitive peoples, such criteria can be applied to a limited extent only and must be employed with caution. As we shall see, most primitive peoples have more than one type of food-getting activity. The dividing-line between the different categories is sometimes hard to draw, for example, in the case of certain Amerindian food-gatherers who take some care of the growth of the plants on which they subsist but do not plant seed and cannot therefore be called agriculturists. Again, if we compare the Yukaghir with other peoples of North-eastern Asia, we find that the former are "hunters and food-gatherers" while the latter are "pastoralists". Yet all these communities are largely dependent upon the reindeer for food, and possess very much the same type of culture, the significant difference being that while most of the peoples concerned keep domesticated herds, the Yukaghir do not. Finally, the broad correlations which are evident in prehistory between ecology on the one hand and socio-economic life on the other exist in contemporary primitive societies as general tendencies only. Thus Childe has demonstrated the importance of the availability of an economic surplus in the transition from hunting and food-gathering to agricultural or pastoral stages in prehistoric cultures. Yet we find that the primitive peoples of the north-west coast of America who were hunters and food-gatherers had an economic surplus far more abundant than that of many agricultural and pastoral peoples.

The general conclusion of this section is that though comparisons may be made and classifications instituted *ad hoc*, social anthropology is at present not equipped with any really adequate technique either for comparison or classification. This is greatly to be regretted, and gives some substance to the criticism that functional anthropologists, in their preoccupation with analyses of individual cultures, have not devoted sufficient attention to the wider comparative tasks which our science must ultimately undertake. But things being as they are, it is better to confess ignorance than to institute cultural comparisons which are superficial, misleading or pretentious.

8. Past and Present in the Study of Primitive Culture

The reader may wonder why our definition of the tasks of social anthropology has not included any reference to the study of the history of primitive cultures. Surely, it may be asked, such a study is not only important in itself, but vital to an understanding of the present? Thirty years ago the majority of British anthropologists would have answered in the affirmative, as would most American anthropologists today. But the adoption of the functional method necessarily rules out the majority of problems of origin, not because they are unimportant, but because it is impossible to study them scientifically.

Reconstructions of the history of early forms of culture are very broadly of two kinds, **evolutionary** and **diffusionist**. The former seeks to reconstruct the beginnings of human culture in terms of what has been called "conjectural history", based upon the "known principles of human nature". The difficulty about such reconstruction is that it is possible to adopt an almost infinite variety of conjectures. Thus volumes have been devoted to heated arguments as to whether the family preceded the clan as the basic unit of social organization, whether patriliny preceded matriliny, and whether the worship of ancestors did or did not come before the worship of nature. In dealing with any such two alternative hypotheses, it is possible to adduce evidence of a sort to support either, but the answer really depends upon one's own personal conjectures about the "known principles of human nature", concerning which there is profound disagreement.

To this it must be added that prehistoric archæology, relying as it does upon empirical evidence rather than conjecture, can give us a very general outline of the early forms of socio-economic life. But because of the limitations of the evidence, it cannot throw any light on the more detailed types of historical problems mentioned above.

The evolutionary theories of the nineteenth century regarded the varying types of primitive cultures as "survivals" of stages of social life through which our own ancestors once passed in an evolutionary process, the culminating point of which was European civilization. When similarities between elements of culture were found in different parts of the world, they were explained by the hypothesis of **parallelism** or *parallel development*, based upon the universal similarities of the human mind. The classic example of this is the *couvade*. This is a custom whereby, when a woman is confined, her husband retires to his couch, receives visits from friends, and in general imitates symbolically the confinement of his wife. This custom is found among certain South American Indian tribes, and was also practised by peasants in the Pyrenees until comparatively recently. Obviously, claimed the parallelists, there had been no contact between these peoples, and the similarity in custom must be explained by the operation of similar psychological processes in the two widely separated areas. They applied the hypothesis of parallel development to all aspects of human culture—to artefacts, to religion and to social organization—and some went so far as to affirm that all cultural similarities could be explained in this way.

But this extreme view was challenged by an opposing school, which attributed cultural similarities to **diffusion**, the process whereby forms of technology, beliefs and social customs are learned by one people from another. Here again there are certain clear examples. If we take the islands of the Central Pacific Ocean, we find a number of cultural similarities, for example, in the types of fish-hooks employed, in the names of gods such as Tangaloa, Tane and Maui, and in the prohibitions connected with the word *tápu* or *tábu*, from which our own word "taboo" is derived. Quite clearly these striking similarities in technology, in terminology and in social custom could not have originated independently in all of the many islands of the Pacific, therefore they must have diffused from one area to others.

While there are thus quite clear examples both of parallel development and of diffusion, and the operation of both is now generally recognized, a very large number of similarities are a matter of dispute. Thus the blowgun, a hollow tube through which a poisoned dart is blown, is found in two widely separated parts of the world—in South-east Asia and in South America. Was this weapon invented separately in the two areas, or was it carried by early men to both from a single point of origin or centre of diffusion? As with evolutionary hypotheses, the answer to this question depends upon personal conjecture. One guess is as good as another. And, with the exception of purely local processes of diffusion, this is broadly true of the majority of historical reconstructions in anthropology. Such reconstructions, moreover, necessarily treat human cultures as mere agglomerations of individual traits rather than as integrated systems of human adaptation. They have therefore had a deleterious effect upon research work in the field and upon theoretical interpretation. They are not, in fact, "historical" in the sense in which modern historians understand the term.

Detailed arguments in support of these contentions have been presented in another work [1] to which the sceptical reader is invited to refer. At this stage we shall merely reduce the method-

[1] Piddington (5).

ological assumptions of functionalism, in contradistinction to the diffusionist schools of historical reconstruction, to a series of short statements:

1. Since all elements and aspects of culture are interrelated, no element or aspect can be scientifically understood in isolation, that is, apart from its cultural context.

2. In view of the lack of written records and the inadequacy of archæological data in the case of primitive cultures, historical reconstruction, so far as it is not mere guesswork, must necessarily concentrate on isolated elements or aspects, particularly in the field of material culture.

3. Historical reconstruction cannot therefore be scientific, in the sense in which the functionalist uses the term.

Functionalism, then, is not "opposed to history" as such. Sometimes, but only very rarely, it is possible to study historical problems contextually. The real objection is to the pulverizing technique which concentrates on details of culture torn from their context. This is inevitable in the case of almost all problems of historical reconstruction. Some ethnologists admit the tenets of functionalism and at the same time affirm the value of existing types of historical reconstruction. They resemble the man described by the uneducated woman in one of Galsworthy's plays: "I'm a Catholic, and my husband's a Catholic too, but then, he's an atheist as well."

9. Bibliographical Commentary

There is no better brief introduction to our subject than Firth (1). If possible this should be read by all students before proceeding further in the present work. In addition to discussing the main problems with which social anthropologists are concerned, the first chapter of Firth's book contains a brief review of the concept of race and a criticism of some popular assumptions concerning alleged racial differences in mental capacity and temperament. On this subject see also Huxley and Haddon, *We Europeans* (1935), Ashley Montagu (2) and Morant (1).

Though we have drawn a distinction between the three anthropological sciences, it must be mentioned that this specialization is a recent development in Great Britain. The three disciplines started as a single science, as will be seen by glancing at Marett, *Anthropology* (1912). The activities of the Royal Anthropological Institute of Great Britain and Ireland cover all three sciences, and in America there is still an insistence upon their unity. But the growing tendency in Great Britain is towards a threefold specialization, made essential by the differences in method and scope between the three sciences. No one today can be an anthropologist, in the old sense of the term, unless he is to be jack of all trades and master of none. Though it is true that social anthropology, for example, has many points of contact with physical anthropology and with prehistoric archæology, these are neither more numerous nor more significant than those with such social sciences as psychology, economics and comparative jurisprudence.

On the other hand, it is desirable that students of social anthropology should know something of the other anthropological sciences, and for this purpose reference may be made to Elliot Smith (1), Stibbe (1), Howells (1) and Childe (1–3).

The concept of culture discussed briefly in Section (2) will be elaborated in Chapter VI, where references to further reading are provided. Though the subjects of culture contact and the development of backward peoples are not dealt with in the present volume, the reader is recommended to refer to Malinowski (11), and to Mair (4) for general statements of the scientific and political problems involved and, as a few examples of the many excellent studies of culture change which have been carried out, to Brown and Hutt (1), Fei (1), Hogbin (5), Hunter (2), Keesing (1), Mair (3) and Richards (4). The important subject of methods of field-work, again, is not discussed in the present volume, but reference may be made to the Introduction to Malinowski (1), to Nadel (7) and to Richards (5).

As regards the American concepts of culture trait, culture complex and culture area briefly mentioned in Section 7, see Wissler (1). For the examples of comparative studies carried out in the light of functional principles mentioned in the same section, see Radcliffe-Brown (2), Schapera (1, Chapters VIII and IX), Firth (8, Chapter XVI), Richards (1) and Nadel (5).

CHAPTER II

A COOKS' TOUR OF PRIMITIVE PEOPLES— AFRICA AND AMERICA

1. The Variety of Primitive Cultures

THE teacher of social anthropology is at a disadvantage compared with other scientists in introducing his students to their subject-matter. He has no laboratory, and even ethnological museums, photographs and the exhibition of ethnographic films give but a partial impression of the variety and vitality of primitive cultures. It is impossible to charter an aeroplane and take students to an African kraal, an Australian aborigines' camp or a Melanesian village, where they could observe the day-to-day life and ceremonial activities of primitive peoples. Yet some superficial acquaintance with primitive life is essential before we can undertake our real task—the scientific analysis of the cultural relationships of human beings to each other, to their natural environment and to the supernatural forces in which they believe. We shall therefore embark upon a brief and partial survey of our subject-matter, a Cooks' Tour of Primitive Culture.

This chapter and the next are intended to introduce the reader to the ways of life of primitive peoples. They contain little scientifically organized information, and consist mainly of what might be called "ethnographic gossip". For this reason the reader should not pay too much attention to memorizing material contained in them, though they should be read carefully in order to obtain a conspectus of the types of culture with which social anthropology is primarily concerned. It must be emphasized that the treatment of primitive cultures in these chapters is not only superficial but also very attenuated. The beginner may be struck by the number of peoples mentioned, but these constitute a very minute proportion of the primitive peoples of the world. This will be realized when it is recalled that there are over two hundred native tribes in South Africa and that, so far as the New World is concerned, it has been estimated that there were more than two thousand tribes in North America alone. The Pacific, though its cultures are conveniently divided into Polynesian, Melanesian and Micronesian, likewise contains a bewildering variety of cultures. Even the Australian aborigines, who possess a more or less homogeneous type of culture, present important tribal variations. It will thus be realized that although neighbouring tribes throughout the world are often found to share a similar type of culture, there nevertheless exists an enormous variety of types of cultural adjustment in primitive society. Students should therefore beware of such statements as those beginning: "Among primitive peoples . . ." or even "Among the Australian aborigines . . ." Accurate statements should be couched in such terms as "In the Aranda tribe . . ."; "Among certain African tribes . . ."; "On the North-west coast of America . . ."; or even "Among some primitive peoples. . . ."

A point which must be stressed is the wealth and complexity of each primitive culture. Thus, for Tikopia, a small Pacific island with a population of about 1,300, Professor Firth has written three major works totalling over 1,350 pages, as well as numerous articles. It will therefore be realized that most ethnographic records cover only certain very limited aspects of the cultures concerned. Furthermore, in many field records, particularly the older ones, much of the material recorded is not scientifically relevant, and the functional interrelationships of cultural elements and institutions are largely neglected. As we have already said, the study of these interrelationships constitutes the real task of the science of social anthropology.

Finally, it should be noted that the locations of peoples given in these chapters and in Appendix A are only approximate. No useful purpose would be served by giving a precise definition of tribal boundaries. This would be a lengthy procedure in view of the fact that these boundaries by no means coincide with modern political divisions. The latter provide easily memorized orientations, but it must be emphasized that tribes referred to as inhabiting, for example, an African colony or a state of the U.S.A. did not usually cover the whole of the area mentioned, and on the other hand frequently extended beyond its boundaries into one or more neighbouring divisions. Such extensions are sometimes but not always mentioned. Moreover, the habitat of certain tribes has often changed in comparatively recent times as a result of indigenous wars of conquest or other factors, while many tribes have been wholly or partially exterminated, or have lost practically all of their original culture under the influence of modern civilization. In this connection reference should be made to what was said on p. 7 concerning the use of tenses in anthropological description.

2. *The Cultures of African Peoples*

The classification of African communities is made difficult by the many migrations of peoples which have taken place on the continent over many centuries. These have led to extensive racial, linguistic and cultural admixture. The reconstructions of these migrations of peoples and cultures are often highly speculative, and do not usually contribute much to our understanding of present-day conditions.

Most classifications of African peoples are based upon somewhat confused criteria of language, race and culture. Such terms as "Bantu", "Hamitic", and "Negro" are variously used to denote racial, linguistic and cultural groups. And the boundaries of these different types of groups, even when they can be defined with some degree of accuracy, by no means coincide. Even when each of the three criteria is taken separately, classifications are the subject of considerable controversy, and many "marginal" or "hybrid" communities occur.

As regards language, the following is a simplified version of one classification, but it must be emphasized that the treatment is very sketchy and the delimitation of language groups is only approximate:

1. *Eastern Hamitic.*—This group of languages is spoken over an area of North-east Africa, roughly between the Equator and latitude 25° North. The area is bounded to the west approximately by latitude 30° East.
2. *Western Hamitic.*—The central and north-west Sahara.
3. *Semitic.*—Most of the languages of North Africa from Senegal in the west to Egypt in the east are Semitic, though there exists a considerable amount of Hamitic admixture in this area.
4. *West African Languages.*—These are numerous, and include Sudanic Negro speech, Hausa, Ewe and Yoruba.
5. *Bantu.*—This is the most extensive language group of Africa. Bantu languages are spoken by African peoples south of the Equator except the Bushmen and the Hottentots, who form small but distinct linguistic groups.

The description of African languages is beyond the scope of this work, but reference should be made to a feature of Bantu languages which is apt to lead to misunderstanding. Students reading works on the Bantu-speaking peoples of Africa may easily be confused by the system of *classifiers* typical of Bantu languages. These are prefixes which are functionally not unlike the gender suffixes of Indo-European languages, in that they serve to classify the verbal stems to which they are attached. Gender, however, is not usually a basis of classification. As many as nineteen classifiers exist in individual Bantu languages to indicate such categories as singular, plural, people, language and size. Thus, among the Ganda of Uganda, prefixes placed before the stem "-ganda" indicate classification as follows:

> Ba-: people.
> Mu-: person.
> Bu-: country.
> Lu-: language.

Thus, for example, a person walking through Buganda, the territory of the Baganda, might meet a Muganda, who would speak to him in Luganda. This usage is apt to lead to confusion over tribal names, which are sometimes used with, and sometimes without, their Bantu tribal prefix—for example, Bemba or Babemba, Hehe or Wahehe. In this work the common procedure of dropping the Bantu prefix has been adopted. It will help students in identifying Bantu peoples to recall that the common tribal prefixes are: Ba-, Wa-, A- and Ama-.

The classification of African peoples according to culture is even more difficult than in the case of language. Several classifications have been attempted, but none is entirely satisfactory. The following division, based primarily upon ecology and environment, will serve as a rough guide to some of the main types of African culture:

1. *The Western Forest Region.*—This comprises the coastal region of West Africa and also part of Central Africa, where it overlaps the Bantu area.

2. *Western Park-land and Semi-desert Cultures.*—These occupy the belt of country in West Africa which joins the forest regions in the south with the Sahara Desert in the north. These are primarily pastoral cultures, including some camel-keeping peoples to the north.

3. *The Sahara and marginal regions*, sparsely populated by camel-keeping peoples.

4. *The Anglo-Egyptian Sudan*, comprising pastoral and agricultural peoples.

5. *The Bantu area.*—This comprises the whole of the southern

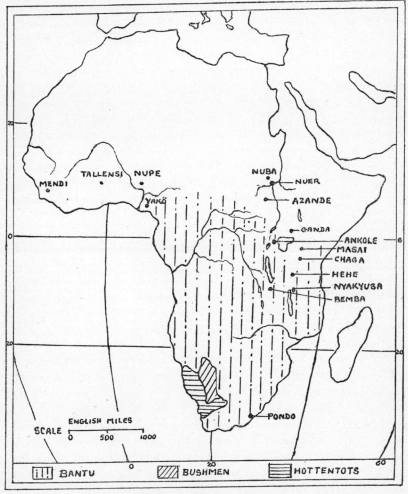

MAP I: Some Cultures of Africa

part of the continent, inhabited by pastoral and/or agricultural Bantu-speaking peoples, except for the Bushmen and Hottentots of South-west Africa, who form two small independent cultural enclaves.

3. *Hunting and Food-gathering Peoples of Africa*

Although the ecology of most African tribes is based upon agricultural or pastoral pursuits, or upon a combination of the two, there exist on the continent a few isolated communities which subsist entirely upon hunting and food gathering. Of these, the best known are the Bushmen of the Kalahari Desert of South Africa and the Pygmies of the Belgian Congo.

The Bushmen lived entirely upon the products of the chase and the gathering of wild vegetable foods. The men hunted larger game, such as the wildebeest, buffalo and zebra, by means of bows and arrows, snares and traps; the women collected roots, berries and other vegetable foods, and also such minor additions to the diet as lizards, termites and locusts. The women were also responsible for the building of shelters, the collection of fire-wood and water, cooking and the tending of children. Owing to the need for mobility, Bushman material culture was necessarily simple. Dwellings took the form of temporary shelters, such as caves or rude huts made of brushwood and bark. Clothing, which was made of skins, was scanty. The Bushmen were dependent upon neighbouring tribes for ironwork, pottery, baskets and certain ornaments. On the other hand, their pictorial art was highly developed and their rock paintings depicting hunting scenes resemble those of Palæolithic Europe.

There is little reliable information about the social organization of the Bushmen. They were apparently organized into small hunting bands which split up from time to time into family groups. The territory of each hunting band was defined by natural features of the landscape, and over this territory the band in question held exclusive hunting rights. Moreover, members of individual families had the right to appropriate such finds as nests of ostrich eggs or beehives. An arrow was stuck into the ground near such finds to indicate family ownership. It is true that another family, if in dire need, might make use of such a source of food, but they were under an obligation to notify the owners afterwards. Large game brought into a camp was generally shared, but the individual hunter kept the valuable hide and sinews for himself and directed the distribution of the meat.

Another group of hunting and food-gathering peoples are the Pygmies of the Belgian Congo. Unlike the Bushmen, they are not all self-supporting. Bands of Pygmy hunters are attached to negro villages under the suzerainty of a negro chief. The Pygmy hunters supply meat to the negro villagers in exchange for agricultural produce. Rights over hunting territories and over the distribution of game appear to be similar to those of the Bushmen. In addition to the Bushmen and the Pygmies, isolated hunting groups occur in part of North-east Africa, notably the Dorobo, who acted as hunters for the Masai.

4. African Pastoralists

The ecology of many African tribes is founded exclusively or primarily on pastoral pursuits. The prevalence of the tsetse-fly, carrier of sleeping sickness, makes cattle-keeping impossible over large areas, notably the west central region, the Coast of West Africa and part of East Africa. The Sahara and neighbouring regions are too arid to support large numbers of cattle. But among most eastern tribes, from the Sudan in the north to the Cape of Good Hope in the south, cattle are kept, and among certain tribes assume a predominant importance. Sometimes both milk and meat are consumed, but many pastoral tribes are reluctant to slaughter their cattle for food. The economic importance of pastoral pursuits among these people is reflected in the social value and ceremonial observances centring around cattle. Among these, one of the most important is the handing over of cattle at marriage by the bridegroom and his relatives to the kin of the bride. This particular form of bride-price is often referred to by the generic term **lobola,** which is one of the Bantu names for the practice.

In other respects also the pastoral peoples of East Africa attach a more than economic importance to their herds. Cattle are often divided into special herds according to their colour and, among certain tribes, beasts have individual names. Numerous magico-religious observances centre around cattle, which are frequently used as sacrifices to ancestors. Thus among the Herero of South-west Africa there exist altars upon which burn sacred fires which may never be extinguished, and around these altars are piled the horns of sacrificed animals. Cattle are also important in the legal and political life of African pastoral peoples, and are the usual form in which tribute is levied by chiefs and fines paid by offenders.

Among certain pastoral peoples, particularly those of the north-east, agriculture is despised or neglected. Thus the Nuer of the southern Sudan, though they practise some cultivation, rely primarily upon the milk from their herds of cattle, to which a very great social importance is attached—as Professor Evans-Pritchard remarks, "most of their social activities concern cattle and *cherchez la vache* is the best advice that can be given to those who desire to understand Nuer behaviour". The Masai, again, live almost exclusively upon the meat, blood and milk of their cattle, and despise agriculture and hunting. It is true that a lion hunter among the Masai is honoured, but hunting for food is regarded as a contemptible pursuit and is relegated to a serf class, the Dorobo. Among the Masai the ceremonial drinking of blood and milk forms a covenant establishing blood brotherhood between men. Similarly, the drinking of ox blood, accompanied by an oath, is a form of ordeal undergone by men accused of crimes.

The Hottentots of South-west Africa likewise relied mainly upon herds of cattle and sheep and, to a lesser extent, on hunting. Unlike the Bantu, the Hottentots assigned dairy work to women, and this again was surrounded by ceremonial observances, for example, a menstruating woman was obliged to abstain from milking until she had been ceremonially purified after her period. The Hottentots seldom slaughtered their cattle or sheep except on ceremonial occasions.

The Fulani of West Africa are another group of pastoral peoples. Here, too, the women do the milking, and the slaughter of animals is confined to ceremonial occasions such as weddings, the naming of children and the observance of Mohammedan festivals. Cattle are inherited in the male line, the inheritance being divided according to the colour of the beasts; thus the eldest son takes all the black cattle, while the white beasts are shared among the younger sons.

In the arid regions in and around the Sahara Desert, camels are of primary importance. One of the camel-keeping peoples of the western Sahara are the Tuareg, or "People of the Veil". The name is derived from the custom whereby men wear a black veil over their face, though the women go unveiled, a reversal of the usual Mohammedan practice. The Tuareg subsist primarily upon milk from camels, sheep and goats, and occasionally meat. Grain is also important in their food supply, though agriculture is despised. According to a Tuareg proverb, "Shame enters a family that tills the soil", and cultivation is normally carried out by negro slaves. The Tuareg carry on extensive trade and purchase cattle from the Fulani. A feature of Tuareg life is the annual trading expedition from Air to Bilma, a distance of about three hundred miles. The object of this is to secure salt, which is extensively traded in the western Sahara. These expeditions over barren country are elaborate enterprises, and usually about five thousand camels are involved.

The Kababish of Kordorfan are a marginal people whose ecology represents a combination of that of the camel-keeping people to the west and the cattle-keeping Hamites to the east. Both types of beast are important, but the emphasis is upon camels, which are of greater significance both economically and ceremonially and are normally used for sacrifice.

5. Agricultural Peoples of Africa and Mixed Ecologies

In certain parts of Africa, notably those affected by the tsetse-fly, the natives rely almost exclusively on agriculture for subsistence. Various grains, yams, and also cassava or manioc (a plant with starchy tuberous roots), form the staple diet for different tribes, supplemented by vegetables, ground-nuts, mushrooms and other relishes. Some African agriculturists practise rotation of crops, but others rely upon shifting cultivation, moving from one area to another as the soil becomes exhausted. A good example of the latter type of agriculture is the *citemene* method of agriculture practised by the Bemba and certain other East African tribes. The method employed is to clear the undergrowth, to pollard the trees, and to burn the brushwood and branches so obtained to make clear patches of ash-fertilized soil. In African agriculture, the hoe is the typical implement employed, though ploughs are found sporadically, particularly in the north-east, and have been introduced elsewhere in historic times by Europeans.

African agriculture is always based upon a traditional division of labour between the sexes, but the nature of this division varies greatly from one tribe to another. Thus in some tribes the men participate in all agricultural operations, while in others their work is confined to heavy labour, such as clearing the bush and hoeing. Agriculture among African peoples is the focus of numerous magico-religious observances, for example, rain-making ceremonies, the ceremonial eating of the first-fruits and the making of sacrifices to secure fertility.

Though three main types of African ecology have been mentioned, it must be emphasized that in the vast majority of cases these are not exclusive. Most African peoples have more than one type of food-getting activity. Even the Pygmy hunters and food gatherers secure agricultural produce by exchange. Both pastoral and agricultural peoples normally supplement their diet by hunting, food gathering and frequently fishing. Usually one or other type of food-getting activity is predominant. Thus the Nuba, though they practise a certain amount of hunting and animal husbandry, are primarily agriculturists. The methods used in stacking and threshing grain by one group of the Nuba are shown in Plate II.

Most Bantu tribes, particularly in the south, have a mixed ecology, in which both cattle-keeping and agriculture are important, though cattle are of primary ceremonial and social significance. Most predominantly pastoral peoples practise a certain amount of agriculture, even though this may be relegated to an inferior class. An interesting example of this type of organization occurs in Ankole, where there exist two distinct strata in the population. The ruling class are the pastoral Bahima, said to be Hamitic migrants from the north, while agriculture is carried out by the Bairu, who constitute an inferior social class of cultivators and craftsmen.

6. The American Indians

The term "Indian" was first used by Columbus in 1493 to designate the aboriginal inhabitants of America, in the belief that his voyage across the Atlantic had taken him to India. The shorter term "Amerind" is occasionally used, but has not been generally accepted. Its adjectival forms, **Amerindian** or Amerindic, however, provide convenient abbreviations.

The wholesale breakdown of primitive culture under the impact of civilization started earlier and proceeded more rapidly in North America than in most other parts of the world. Consequently, the development of modern scientific field-work came too late to provide a really adequate study of any aboriginal North American community. In this field there exists much valuable material on ecology and material culture, but it is difficult to relate this adequately to social institutions. For South America, where "untouched" primitive cultures are still to be found, the amount of really adequate field material so far available is disappointingly small.

In pre-Columbian times a large variety of Amerindian cultures

Threshing

Stacking Grain

existed, from that of the primitive hunters and food-gatherers of
Tierra del Fuego to the Maya, Aztec and Inca civilizations.
Certain characteristics of Amerindian cultures are given in a
valuable series of maps in Wissler (2). These maps show the
distribution of various items of material culture, of patrilineal
and matrilineal clans, of culture areas and of types of food-
getting activity. The latter forms the most convenient starting-
point for a brief survey of Amerindian cultures. It must be emphasized that the food areas overlapped to a considerable extent,
and that the type-food was always supplemented by other items
of diet. Thus, though maize and manioc were the most important
staple foods of different groups of Amerindian agriculturists,
the list of subsidiary cultivated plants includes over twenty-five
varieties, and the native diet was also supplemented by hunting
and food-gathering.

7. Food Areas of the New World

Wissler distinguishes seven food areas in the New World (see
Map II):

i. The *Caribou Area*, covering the continent of North America
roughly north of the Canadian border. This was the habitat of
the caribou (the American variety of reindeer) and other large
ungulates. Ethnologically this region may be subdivided into two
areas: (*a*) the Caribou Area proper, consisting of most of Canada
except the northern littoral, and (*b*) the Eskimo area to the north,
in which the caribou as a source of food was less important
compared with sea mammals.

In the Caribou Area proper these animals, supplemented by
smaller game, and in the vicinity of lakes and rivers by fish and
wild-fowl, formed the staple diet of the Indians. Caribou were
hunted by stampeding the herds into narrow lanes or defiles or
into deep water, where they were despatched by hunters in
canoes. The large herds of caribou moved forward fairly fast,
grazing on the sparse vegetation of the tundra, and the bands of
hunters were forced to keep pace with them. As the rewards of a
successful hunting drive could neither be consumed on the spot
nor conveniently carried, the Indians of this area developed a
specialized type of *cache*. Each successful kill was dressed as quickly
as possible and buried or stowed away in an elevated position,
safe from the inroads of carnivorous beasts. Each group of
hunters thus had a series of hidden stores at various places, upon

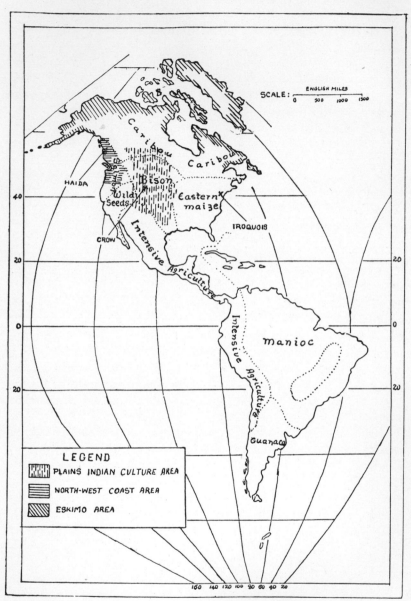

MAP II.—Food Areas of the New World
(*After Wissler and others*)

which they could draw in times of need. The ecology of the
Eskimo was more highly specialized than that of the Caribou
Area proper, and will be described in Section 8.

ii. *The Maize Area.*—The cultivation of maize was carried out
over an extensive area of America, including the eastern and
southern states of the U.S.A. (except Texas), also in Mexico, and
in the north-west and eastern coastal regions of South America.
The eastern maize area of the U.S.A. is the most important
ethnographic division of this area. An interesting feature of
American agriculture was that it was almost entirely women's
work, the men being hunters.

iii. *The Salmon Area of the North-west.*—The north-west coast of
America from San Francisco Bay to Bering Strait was characterized by dependence on fishing. The streams draining into the
Pacific are visited annually by salmon, which penetrate to their
headwaters to spawn. At the periods of these annual "runs", the
natives of the region gathered along the banks of the streams to
catch the fish by means of nets, harpoons and weirs. The major
portion of the large catches of fish so obtained was dried and
smoked to form a reserve of food. The natives of the coast and
adjacent islands also relied on sea fishing throughout the year,
and to a lesser extent on sea mammals. The coastal Indians lived
in permanent or semi-permanent villages, while those of the
hinterland tended to be nomadic, their annual movements being
determined by the salmon "runs", and subsidiary food-gathering.

This region included the famous **North-west coast culture area,**
centring around the Queen Charlotte and Vancouver Islands,
and the adjacent coast of Canada. One of the most distinctive
cultural characteristics of this area was the **potlatch,** an elaborate
system of feasting accompanied by the distribution and sometimes destruction of property, particularly blankets, ornaments
known as "coppers", and whale oil. There were considerable
variations in the form of this institution among different tribes
of the north-west coast. That of the Haida will be briefly described
in Section 10.

iv. *The Area of Wild Seeds.*—To the south of the Salmon area, in
central and southern California, are found a group of predominantly food-gathering peoples, subsisting on wild seeds, roots,
herbs and grasses. This region is sometimes referred to as the
"Acorn Area", because on the uplands and mountains of southern California the staple food consisted of acorns. Flour obtained

from these was treated with hot water to remove the large quantity of tannic acid which it contained, and was made into bread or cakes. Fish, and small quantities of game, were obtained sporadically throughout this area. Lizards and grasshoppers were also eaten.

Representative of this area are the Yokuts and the Paviosto. The latter practised an ingenious method of irrigating patches of ground on which grew grasses and bulbous plants. But they neither planted vegetable foods nor worked the soil, consequently they cannot be called agriculturists.

v. *The Bison Area.*—Between the Salmon and Wild Seed areas to the west and the Maize Area to the east lay a region in which the Indians depended for food mainly on the bison or American buffalo. Large herds of these animals were hunted by methods not unlike those of the Caribou Area. The Bison Area covered an extensive strip of territory, from the Saskatchewan River in the north to Texas in the south. It corresponded very roughly with the **Plains Indian Culture Area,** though marginal Plains tribes to the east practised agriculture (for example, the Hidatsa, Omaha and Pawnee), while those to the west depended less on the bison and more on deer and small game, and also on the gathering of wild vegetable foods. But the central Plains Indians relied almost exclusively on the bison, the flesh of which was dried, pounded with stone hammers, sometimes together with pulverized wild cherries, and stored in sealed bags. This form of preserved meat, known as *pemmican,* would keep for months. It should be mentioned that pemmican, made from the meat of other animals and even from fish, was prepared by several Amerindian tribes outside the Bison Area.

vi. *The Manioc Area.*—Though maize was cultivated on the north-eastern coastal area of South America and on the west coast as far south as Santiago, its place as a staple crop in the central and eastern regions was taken by manioc or cassava. Hunting is also important in many parts of this area.

vii. *The Guanaco Area.*—From the interior of the Argentine southwards to Cape Horn is a hunting area, where the Indians were mainly dependent on the guanaco, a variety of wild llama, which was hunted with bows and arrows and the *bolas,* an entangling device made by joining together stones by means of thongs, which, when thrown, tripped the quarry and brought it to the ground. In the extreme south of this area there was an increasing dependence upon fish and seals. These were practically the only source of food of the natives of Tierra del Fuego, whose ecology thus resembled to some extent that of the Eskimo.

Having surveyed the food areas of the New World, we may now consider certain Amerindian peoples who are of special anthropological interest.

8. The Eskimo

To the north of the Caribou Area proper lies the territory of the Eskimo, which covers the littoral of the northern coast of North America including Labrador, of Greenland and of the neighbouring islands. It extends westwards across the Bering Strait to the easternmost tip of Asia. The Eskimo are of particular interest, because of their highly specialized adjustment to their geographical environment.

An understanding of the seasonal cycle of the Eskimo is essential to an appreciation of their culture. It is divided into four periods:

Winter.—As winter deepens, ice floes begin to form along the coast. In order to breathe, the seals living in the sea below scratch holes in the covering ice. It is upon this habit that the Eskimo relies mainly for his winter food. The best-known method of killing seals is for the hunter to wait beside the hole over which he has placed some form of indicator, such as a feather. When this moves, it shows that the seal has come to breathe, and the hunter then thrusts his harpoon into its muzzle. As each seal has a number of breathing holes, this is a wearisome and relatively unprofitable method of food-getting. The Eskimo food supply in winter is further limited by the very short period of daylight and by the occurrence of fogs or blizzards which may make sealing impossible, and may reduce an Eskimo community to a condition of famine. The following is a description of the conditions which may arise:

"While in times of plenty the home life is quite cheerful, the house presents a sad and gloomy appearance if stormy weather prevents the men from hunting. The stores are quickly consumed, one lamp after another is extinguished, and everybody sits motionless in the dark hut. . . . Their stoicism in enduring the pangs of hunger is really wonderful. At last, when starvation is menacing the sufferers, the most daring of the men resolves to try his luck. Though the storm may rage over the icy plain, he sets out to go sealing. For hours he braves the cold and stands waiting and watching at the breathing hole until he hears the blowing of the seal and succeeds in killing it. . . . If the hunter, however, has tried in vain to procure food, if the storm does not subside, the terrors of famine visit the settlement. The dogs are the first to fall victims to the pressing hunger, and if the worst comes, cannibalism is resorted to. But all these occurrences are spoken of with the utmost horror. In such cases children particularly are killed and eaten. Fortunately, however, such occurrences are very rare." [1]

Seal blubber provides, in the absence of an adequate supply of wood, the best fuel available to the Eskimo, being greatly superior to the fat of the caribou hunted in summer.

Spring.—During the winter the Eskimo live in group settlements, but with the approach of spring, about March, lanes of water form in the ice. The settlements of winter break up into their component families, which hunt seals in the open water or stalk them as they lie basking on the remaining ice. This is the breeding season for seals. With their young, they congregate in large numbers, and hunting them at this time of the year is a more profitable occupation than winter sealing. Large stores of seal blubber are laid by, and the diet of seal meat is supplemented in certain areas by the musk ox—a slow-moving beast which proves an easy prey to the Eskimo and which, with the introduction of firearms, has been largely exterminated.

Summer.—By midsummer the snow has melted on land. Stunted vegetation appears, and the Eskimo turn inland in search of the caribou migrating northwards. The families reunite to form hunting groups, living in summer camps, from which they hunt the herds of caribou by the methods of ambushing or driving into deep water, described above in connection with the southern part of the Caribou area. Smaller animals, wild fowl, fish and very small quantities of roots, berries and other vegetable foods also contribute to the summer diet of the Eskimo.

Autumn.—At the end of summer, the Eskimo hunters return to the shore. Few caribou are left near the coast and it is not yet possible to undertake winter sealing. But if there is an abundance of stored food from the summer hunting, the end of the year is marked by a short period of comparative leisure, festivals and social intercourse between Eskimo communities.

While the above sketch gives a brief outline of the seasonal

[1] Boas (1), p. 574.

cycle of the central Eskimo, it is important to point out that significant variations occurred in the marginal areas. For example, the Polar Eskimo of northern Greenland rely to a much greater extent on sea, as distinct from land, mammals. Though the musk ox and caribou are hunted during the spring and summer, they are relatively less important. It appears that the accumulation of food during the summer is less, and the unproductive autumn period is sometimes one of famine. Rasmussen states that the Polar Eskimo actually welcome the coming of "the great Dark", as autumn gives way to winter.[1] This may be due to the climatic and ecological difference between the central and northern areas just mentioned, but it is possible that he was misled by feigned expressions of pleasure.

Farther to the south, in the sub-arctic areas of Alaska, South Greenland and Labrador, the winter is milder, and the formation of sea ice plays a decreasing part in the ecology of the Eskimo. The same sea mammals provide food, but they are hunted from kayaks (see below) and boats in the open sea. In this area is found the *umiak*, a broad-beamed open boat, which is used in the hunting of larger prey, including whales.

The culture of the Eskimo is admirably adapted to the necessary limitations imposed by the environment. In winter the semi-permanent settlements consist of the well-known snow-houses (*igloo*) or similar structures of stone and slate, heated and lighted by blubber lamps. The two requirements of warmth and ventilation are ingeniously met by the structure of these houses. Cool air enters through an entrance passage, and spreads out over the floor, where the temperature is nearly always below freezing-point. It rises slowly, being heated by the blubber lamps, and finally escapes through a tiny ventilation hole in the roof. The Eskimo household sits and sleeps on platforms at the warmer upper levels where the temperature sometimes becomes so high that they have to divest themselves of most or all of their clothing. For summer dwellings, the Eskimo build tents of skins stretched over wooden poles—formerly narwhal tusks or whale-bones—the skins being held to the ground by heavy stones.

The Eskimo have likewise devised means to protect themselves from the climate when out of doors; for example, their heavy clothing of tailored skins. Snow goggles were made as a protection against snow blindness. These consisted of a mask completely

[1] Rasmussen, *People of the Polar North*, pp. 79–80.

covering the eyes except for two narrow slits through which the wearer could see.

The Eskimo **kayak** is a light canoe which accommodates one person or occasionally two. It is probably, for its size, the most seaworthy vessel ever invented. It consists of a light wooden framework completely covered with skins sewn together in such a way that there is only a small hole just large enough to surround the trunk of the man who navigates it. The air is thus hermetically sealed within the skin covering, so that the kayak can turn upside down without sinking. In fact, a "parlour trick" of the kayak boatman is to tilt his vessel over sideways, submerging himself, and finally coming up on the other side, so that the kayak rotates through 360° on its longitudinal axis. The advantages of a vessel so constructed in a rough and choppy sea are obvious.

Other items of the highly elaborate material culture of the Eskimo, such as their ingenious harpoons, cannot be described here. Those interested should consult the works cited in the bibliographical commentary, and should also, if possible, study the Eskimo specimens displayed in a good ethnological museum.

The social culture of the Eskimo may likewise be correlated with their economic adjustment. It will be clear that the dispersal of their settlements and their seasonal nomadism makes any form of elaborate political organization impossible. Leadership in economic pursuits falls naturally to those possessing the greatest knowledge and skill in the activity concerned. Organized warfare is virtually unknown, and there are hardly any instances of armed conflict between communities. Conflicts over land and movable wealth do not arise. Beliefs in sorcery are virtually absent except in Greenland, illness and other misfortune being attributed to breach of taboo. The cause of illness is diagnosed by a magician, various methods being employed. For example, the magician may subject a sick man to a sort of inquisition, asking such questions as, "Did you work when it was forbidden?" or "Did you eat when you were not allowed to eat?"—questions which the invalid is supposed to answer truthfully. When the cause has been diagnosed by this or other methods the magician prescribes some form of atonement, such as forbidding the villagers to wash for a number of days or imposing restrictions on their diet.

One factor in the peaceful character of Eskimo life is the toler-ant attitude towards extra-marital intercourse. This probably tends to minimize quarrels over women. A man may lend his wife to a visitor as a part of the obligations of hospitality or may assign her to a friend for a season or even longer. Ceremonial wife-exchange is obligatory as part of the autumn festivals. In spite of this, however, it is recorded that quarrels sometimes arise from jealousy over women, though they are far less common than in many other primitive communities.

No detailed account of the causes of quarrels among the Eskimo is available, but it is recorded that they sometimes lead to homicide. This places an obligation to retaliate upon the nearest relative of the victim. The retaliation consists of killing the murderer, or occasionally a member of his family. This second homicide, however, may not be avenged, so that the vendetta is unknown. Murderers and other criminals might sometimes be killed by anyone simply as a matter of justice, but this could not be done without the unanimous consent of the community.

An interesting and unique method of settling disputes among the Eskimo is for one party to challenge the other to a satirical song contest. Each party composes a satirical song about the other, and on an appointed day they meet in public and sing their respective songs. The man who receives the greater acclaim is regarded as the winner and his rival correspondingly loses prestige.

The central theme of Eskimo religion is the myth of Sedna, from which arise many taboos and religious observances. Sedna was a woman who lived alone with her father. Though she had many suitors, she refused to marry until a fulmar (a kind of petrel) came and enticed her away by promising her a life of relative comfort and luxury among his people. She consented and went with him, but when they reached his country she was bitterly disappointed, for her new home was a wretched habitation and she had nothing to eat but poor-quality fish. She regretted her foolish pride in rejecting her other suitors and cried out to her father to come and take her home. When he came to visit her he was outraged at the way his daughter had been treated, killed the fulmar, and took her off in his boat on the homeward journey. When the other fulmars returned to find their companion dead and his wife gone, they set out in pursuit, giving vent to mournful cries which fulmars utter to this day. As they overtook the fugitives in their boat, they stirred up a tremendous storm. The father was terrified and decided to offer Sedna to the birds. He threw her overboard, but she clung to the gunwale of the boat with her hands. The father then took a knife and cut off the first joints of her fingers, which fell into the sea and became whales, the nails forming the whalebone. Sedna still clung to the boat, so her father cut off the second finger joints of her hands and these joints became seals. Then he cut off the stumps of her fingers, which became ground seals. In one version of the myth he gouged out her left eye with his steering paddle, so that Sedna is now envisaged as a sort of female Cyclops. There are different versions of the conclusion of the story, but the upshot of them is that Sedna went down into the lower world, where she lives in a house with her father and receives the souls of the dead. She controls the weather and the sea mammals, the more important of which, it will be remembered, are derived from the joints of her fingers.

Numerous taboos derive from the beliefs concerning Sedna, who is angered by breach of them and may visit disaster upon the offending individual or community. Since sea mammals are derived from her, atonement must be made when one of them is killed—for example, when a seal is brought into a house, all work must cease until it has been cut up. The most interesting set of taboos are derived from a subsidiary legend which accounts for Sedna's traditional hatred of the caribou. A woman, most probably Sedna, created the walrus and the caribou during a famine. She opened her belly, and took from it a small piece of fat which she carried to the hills, where it was transformed into a caribou. When she saw the animal she became afraid and ordered it away, but it turned upon her and would not go. She became angry and knocked out its teeth. It turned around and she gave it a kick which lopped off its tail—this is why the caribou lacks certain teeth and has scarcely any tail. She then took another piece of her fat and threw it into the sea, where it became a walrus. In another legend it is stated that when the walrus and the caribou first appeared, the former had large horns but no tusks and the latter tusks but no horns. This was dangerous to hunters, as the caribou killed its pursuers with its tusks, while the horns of the walrus used to capsize boats. Therefore an old man effected a transfer, as a result of which the caribou today has horns and the walrus has tusks.

The social significance of these legends is that they draw a sharp distinction between the activities of winter on the one hand and summer on the other, a distinction which is reflected in the taboos prohibiting association between the two types of activity. These taboos are explicitly justified by reference to mythology. Thus no work may be done on new caribou skins obtained during the summer until the first ice has formed and the first seal has been harpooned. Then follows a period of intense activity in the preparation of skins, for when the first walrus has been caught, the work must cease again until the following autumn. Thus the hunting of walrus cannot commence until work on caribou skins has been completed. Again, owing to Sedna's hatred of the caribou, the flesh of this animal may not be eaten on the same day as that of the sea mammals associated with her; in fact, the two kinds of meat may not even lie together in the house at the same time. Before changing from one food to the other the Eskimo must wash themselves.

These beliefs and practices reflect vividly and dramatically the Eskimo's emotional attitude to the two phases of their seasonal cycle. Summer is the period of comparative plenty and security, while winter means the constant menace of famine. Thus many magico-religious beliefs and observances are concerned with placating Sedna, who controls the winter environment—there appear to be no corresponding mythical beings or precautionary observances connected with summer activities. Autumn, the period of transition from security to danger, is one of intense magico-religious activity, and great feasts connected with Sedna are celebrated at this time. When the fierce storms begin to rage over land and sea, the Eskimo believe that they can hear in them the voices of malevolent beings threatening sickness, death, bad weather and failure in hunting. The spirits of the dead bring sickness and death to any unfortunate mortal whom they can catch. Sedna herself rises from under the ground at this period.

It is worth noting that among the Polar Eskimo of northern Greenland the psychopathic affliction known as "Arctic hysteria" occurs most commonly in the late autumn. The victim becomes temporarily oblivious of his or her surroundings, the body sways to and fro, and moans, screams and disconnected sentences are uttered. Men sometimes become violent during an attack and have to be restrained by force. It may be suggested that this is an individual manifestation of the current "anxiety state" which finds social expression in the magico-religious beliefs and practices which we are considering.

Next to Sedna, the most important spiritual beings among the

Eskimo are the *tornait*, which have a benevolent influence on the affairs of men. It is from the *tornait* that magicians derive their powers. Autumn is a busy period for the magicians, who are to be found in every house invoking the benevolent spirits for aid against the surrounding spiritual dangers. The hardest task, that of driving away Sedna, is performed by the most powerful magicians. They place a coil of rope upon the floor to represent the breathing hole of a seal. One magician sings a song to attract Sedna, and another stands by the hole and symbolically harpoons her as soon as heavy breathing indicates her presence. She dives downwards, and tears herself away from the harpoon which, stained with her blood, is triumphantly shown by the magicians to the audience. It is obvious that the magicians perform some sleight of hand to stain the harpoon with blood. The expulsion of Sedna and the other evil spirits is celebrated the next day by a great festival, though there are still dangers against which the Eskimo take precautions, such as the wearing of amulets. The festival includes a tug-of-war between two groups, composed of those born in winter on the one hand and those born in summer on the other, called respectively the ptarmigans and the ducks. If the ducks win, it represents the triumph of summer, and fine weather may be expected throughout the winter.

9. *The Iroquois*

One of the most interesting peoples of the eastern maize area were the Iroquois. This name was applied to a group of tribes inhabiting the part of north-eastern America which is now New York State, and extending in parts over its borders. The Iroquois consisted of five tribes, the Cayuga, Mohawk, Oneida, Onondaga and Seneca banded together in a confederacy known as the League, or "Five Nations", of the Iroquois.[1]

The most remarkable features of Iroquois culture are, firstly, its unique development of a federal political authority, and secondly, the unusually prominent part played by women in tribal life.

The social organizations of the Iroquois was marked by the following social groupings:

(*a*) The individual family.

(*b*) The matrilineal and matrilocal extended family, which

---

[1] The original five tribes were joined at the beginning of the eighteenth century by a southern tribe, the Tuscarora. These occupied a subordinate position in the League, which was thereafter known as the Six Nations. It may be mentioned that languages of the Iroquoian linguistic family were spoken by tribes outside the League.

might consist of from fifty to one hundred and fifty members. Their affairs were regulated by the senior female member, from whom all other members (except affinal kin) were descended. This woman might perhaps be described as the "headwoman", since her functions seem to have been analogous to those of headmen of minor groups in other communities. One or more extended families dwelt in a single building of unique structure, the famous "Long House" (see Fig. 2) built of slabs of dried bark placed over a wooden framework. This house was well adapted to the Iroquois type of communal living, since if more space was required, one of the end walls could be pulled down and

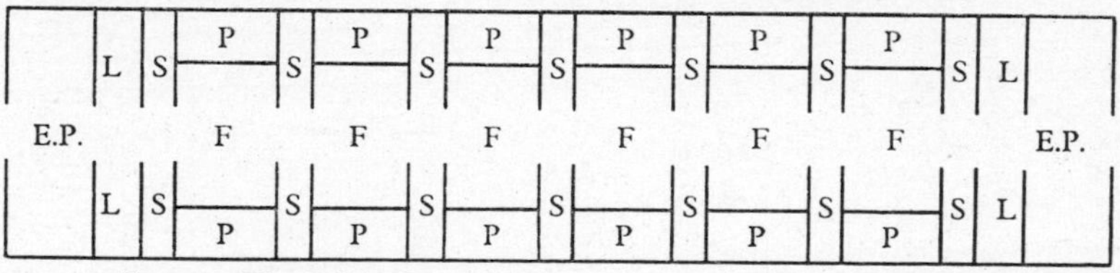

FIG. 2.—Plan of the Long House of the Iroquois (*after Murdock*)
(Not drawn to scale. Usual length, 50–150 feet; usual breadth, 20–30 feet)
P = Raised platforms for sleeping and sitting in cubicles of individual families
F = Fires, each serving two individual families
S = Storage cubicles
E.P.= Exterior porch
L = Lobby for storing firewood

the house extended—in one recorded case a Long House measured 300 feet in length. It should be noted that, in spite of the communal living arrangements of the extended family, the identity of the individual family was preserved.

(c) The matrilineal clan, composed of the related members of a number of extended families. Iroquois clans were totemic, in the sense that they bore the names of animals and birds, but there were no taboos or other ritual observances connected with totemism, and no beliefs concerning descent from the totem. The clans extended beyond the borders of a single tribe, as did the rule of exogamy connected with them—thus, a wolf man of one tribe was prohibited from marrying any wolf woman from another.

(d) The matrilineal moieties, consisting of groups of matrilineal clans. These moieties existed in all the tribes except the Mohawk and Oneida. The functions of the moieties were social and ceremonial rather than political. They opposed each other in various games, but the principal obligation of members of each moiety was to bury and to mourn the dead of the other.

(*e*) The tribe, which was a political unit possessing a common territory and ruled by a council of chiefs representing the component clans of the tribe.

(*f*) The League. Although the Iroquois tribes possessed a considerable amount of autonomy in matters of economics and local administration, they were banded together in the League for matters of common interest, particularly war. The League consisted of a council of fifty chiefs drawn from its component tribes as follows:

Mohawk	.	.	.	.	9
Oneida	.	.	.	.	9
Onandaga	.	.	.	.	14
Cayuga	.	.	.	.	10
Seneca	.	.	.	.	8

50

According to tradition, it was Hiawatha [1] who was largely responsible for the union of the five tribes to form the League for the purposes of arbitrating in cases of disputes between the tribes and of prosecuting wars against neighbouring peoples. In this latter sphere the League was certainly effective. The Iroquois virtually exterminated the neighbouring Huron with the utmost barbarity, and even conducted an expedition nearly a thousand miles to the west to fight against the Pawnee of Nebraska. In their war-making activities the Iroquois suffered considerable casualties, which were to some extent offset by the practice of wholesale adoption, not only of individuals, but also of whole clans and even tribes.[2] Though prisoners of war were habitually tortured and killed, the Iroquois frequently levied tribute in the form of men from conquered and subordinate tribes. In fact, it has been

---

[1] This name is a corruption of Haienhwatha, the title of one of the three chieftainships of the Turtle clan of the Mohawk. The first recorded holder of the title was a great statesman and reformer of the sixteenth century, who took a leading part in the foundation of the League of the Iroquois. His pioneering constitutional work was largely forgotten, and his name became associated with a number of garbled stories of legendary and romantic deeds which form the basis of Longfellow's famous poem.

[2] Where whole groups are thus involved, it is perhaps better to speak of "incorporation" rather than "adoption", which is an individual mechanism serving different functions in the kinship systems of communities which practise it.

estimated that at one time the number of adopted aliens among them exceeded the number of native Iroquois.

The chieftainships within the council of the League were not hereditary, but each of them belonged to a particular extended family, from which the successor to a dead chief was chosen, the nomination being made by the headwoman of the extended family of the dead chief. When a chief died, this woman would call a meeting of members of the extended family and propose a successor. Her candidate was usually a brother or sister's son of the dead chief, so that in fact succession normally followed the ordinary matrilineal principle. Members of other extended families of the same clan were admitted to the meeting called to nominate a new chief, but they had less influence than the members of the extended family in which the chieftainship was vested. The nomination of the headwoman was generally accepted, and the decision of the family council was then communicated by her, first to the chiefs of the "brother clans" (the other clans of the same moiety), and afterwards to the chiefs of the "cousin clans" (those belonging to the opposite moiety). The nomination agreed upon in this way was finally submitted to the chiefs of the League for approval. In the course of this series of councils the original nomination might in theory be vetoed at any stage, but in actual practice it was usually accepted throughout.

A chief thus elected was not free from further supervision. If he proved unsatisfactory he was visited by the headwoman of his extended family, who rebuked him and pointed out his defects. He was expected not to reply to her comments. If, after one or two such warnings, he persisted in his evil ways, she called upon him again and ceremonially deposed him.

The important part played by women was reflected in every phase of life. Economically the Iroquois depended mainly on agriculture. Though a considerable amount of food was gained by hunting, fishing and food-gathering, the cultivation of crops provided the staple diet. This was ritually expressed in festivals in honour of the "three sisters" of Iroquois mythology—Maize, Bean and Squash. Apart from the heavy work of clearing the ground of trees, the work of cultivation was almost exclusively in the hands of the women. They worked in gardening teams under the direction of one of their number, the teams cultivating a series of fields in succession. As we have seen, the affairs of the extended family were directed by the senior female member. The men were strangers to a far greater extent than in other matrilineal societies. As far as political organization was concerned, we have described the pre-eminent rôle played by women in the election of the principal chiefs; and though actual decisions in regard to warfare and other matters of tribal policy rested with the chiefs' council of the League, there is some evidence that women possessed a power of veto in ceremonial matters. Though women might not be members of the League council, they might hold subordinate chieftainships which, though not hereditary, carried with them a considerable amount of prestige. In certain respects the legal code attached more importance to women than to men. Thus atonement was made for murder among the Iroquois by the payment of compensation to the kinsmen of the victim, and the penalty for killing a woman was double that for killing a man. Again, in cases of adultery the woman alone was punished by a public whipping; she was held to have been the only offender, an exception to the more common conception of "seduction" found in the vast majority of communities.

In ceremonial and religious matters, women occupied a position equal, if not superior, to that of men. Each clan elected six officials whose duty it was to organize and supervise ceremonial procedure. Of these six officials, three were women. Again, the Iroquois had a number of secret societies or "medicine lodges", such as the False Face society, who appeased the malevolent Flying Heads which haunted the forests; the Society of the Three Sisters, which carried out the fertility cult of the maize, bean and squash; and several other societies, which were concerned with the promotion of health and the curing of sickness. Membership of these societies was open alike to individuals of both sexes, and in the majority of cases the chief officer was a woman.

10. The Haida Potlatch

The practices connected with the potlatch among the Haida of the Queen Charlotte Islands illustrates very well the way in which this institution conferred prestige on the giver of the potlatch and his kin. The Haida practised several varieties of potlatch, among which may be mentioned the Funeral potlatch, the House-building potlatch, the Face-saving potlatch and the Vengeance potlatch. The Funeral potlatch was carried out by the heir to a chieftainship and was a necessary preliminary to the assumption of the title. The heir invited members of the opposite moiety to assemble in order to erect a mortuary column in honour of his predecessor, and at the conclusion of the work distributed valuable property among them.

The House-building potlatch was an elaborate undertaking. A man and his wife might labour for ten years preparing the necessary food and valuables. Neighbours were then invited to come and work throughout the whole winter obtaining timber, building the house and carving the totem pole. During this period there was much feasting and dancing, the feasts being provisioned by the people whose house was being built. At the conclusion of the building, a potlatch was given, nominally by the wife. Those who had assisted in the house-building assembled and seated themselves according to their rank. The wife distributed furs, blankets, carved dishes and other property among them, finally giving to her husband an old and tattered blanket, symbolizing the exhaustion of the family property. These potlatch goods were distributed according to rank and services performed, and the total value of the property involved amounted in historic times to thousands of pounds.

Social status was acquired by the giving of potlatches. It is important to distinguish between *social status* which was achieved by the giving of potlatches and *political rank* which was hereditary in the female line, subject to the above-mentioned provision that the heir to a chieftainship must give a Funeral potlatch. Status was acquired by potlatching, which, however, affected the social status, not of the man giving the potlatch, but of his children. It was said of a man who had never given a potlatch that "he never did anything for his children".

The differentiation of rank and status meant that a commoner might have a higher status than a chief, this status being marked by the right to wear certain ornaments and to occupy special seats of honour. Individuals whose parents had given a potlatch but who never did so themselves did not thereby lose social status. Their position was not unlike that of the "black sheep" of British aristocratic families.

The Face-saving potlatch was given by a man when he found himself in an embarrassing social position, for example, if he had made an unfortunate slip of the tongue during a speech or suffered some other humiliation. Such a man issued an invitation to all members of the opposite moiety who had witnessed the mishap, and in their presence tore up a number of blankets, the pieces of which he distributed among them. After this ceremony the incident which had led to it was regarded as closed and might not thereafter be mentioned.

The Vengeance potlatch was carried out in order to humiliate a man from whom an individual had suffered an insult. The offended man assembled members of the opposite moiety and also the man who had wronged him, and in their presence destroyed valuable property. For example, he might kill a slave, hack to pieces a treasured canoe or copper, or tear up a number of blankets. His antagonist was obliged immediately to destroy an equal amount of property or to suffer lifelong disgrace.

11. Bibliographical Commentary

Since this and the following chapter are concerned with a general survey of primitive cultures, the reader should if possible refer also to two outstanding works, namely, Murdock (1) and Forde (1), in which concise descriptions of a variety of primitive cultures from many different parts of the world are to be found.

So far as Africa is concerned, a most valuable reference work is Hambly (1), which is well indexed and contains an excellent bibliography which enables the reader to follow up special lines of enquiry connected with African ethnology. On the classification and distribution of African cultures in terms of culture areas, reference may be made to Herskovits (1). Valuable regional surveys are contained in Seligman (1) and Schapera (1). On special problems of African cultures, reference should be made to the journal *Africa*, a few articles from which are cited in the bibliography.

Detailed ethnographic monographs on African peoples are far too numerous to cite individually, but those of Evans-Pritchard, Fortes, Kuper (*nee* Beemer), Mair, Nadel, Peristiany, Richards, Schapera, G. Wilson and M. Wilson (*nee* Hunter) may be specially mentioned. Several of these works are primarily concerned with the problems of culture contact, but provide incidentally an account of the functioning of various aspects of indigenous culture. The same is true of Brown and Hutt (1) which provides an admirably condensed account of a Bantu culture.

A most valuable survey of Amerindian cultures is contained in Wissler (2), which contains a very full bibliography. Hodge (1), though published many years ago, is a valuable work of reference.

Steward (1) and (2) provide useful digests and references bearing on certain South American Indian peoples, and is to be followed by further volumes in the same series. Regional surveys are provided in Kroeber (1) and Swanton (1), while a more popular appreciation of certain Amerindian cultures is contained in Wissler (3).

As regards individual Amerindian cultures, brief summaries of some of them are contained in the works of Forde and of Murdock previously cited, and also in Goldenweiser (1). These works contain references to original field records on the cultures concerned.

CHAPTER III

A COOKS' TOUR OF PRIMITIVE PEOPLES— ASIA AND OCEANIA

1. Primitive Cultures of Asia

ALTHOUGH Asia contains a far greater proportion of the world's population than any other continent, the number of really good anthropological works on Asiatic peoples is far less than that available elsewhere. Ethnographically, it is Asia which is "the Dark Continent".

We are apt to think of Asia in terms of the historic and contemporary civilizations and empires of Japan, China, India and the Middle East. These involve, or have involved, highly developed political institutions, codified laws, philosophically elaborated religions such as Mohammedanism, Buddhism and Taoism, urban civilization, a partially industrialized technology and a complex economic organization. But it must be remembered that the vast majority of people found in the areas covered by the civilizations mentioned live in small and largely isolated communities and are wholly or partially illiterate, while there exist enclaves of primitive cultures which have been but little influenced by the major Asiatic civilizations.

2. Reindeer Peoples of Northern Asia

Reindeer are domesticated throughout northern Asia from Lapland to Kamchatka. Their use, and the degree of importance attached to them, vary from one area to another and even among single peoples. Thus, among the northern Tungus, who are primarily reindeer-herders, the herds belonging to individual households vary from a few dozen to several hundreds. In the case of households with small herds, the men devote most of their time to hunting, and the care of the reindeer largely devolves upon the women. In the hunting of wild reindeer, does from the domesticated herds are used as decoys, especially during the rutting season, and several ingenious methods of hunting are employed. The Tungus also catch squirrels and other fur-bearing animals, the skins of which they barter with Russian traders for guns, knives, utensils and minor luxuries, such as tea and tobacco. The Tungus do not smelt iron from ore, but their smiths manufacture tools and weapons from scrap-iron obtained by barter.

The Tungus rely on the milk provided by their reindeer, and kill them for meat only on ceremonial occasions. Reindeer are used as pack animals, to drag sledges and for riding. Their antlers are often sawn off to prevent them from sweeping a load or a rider from their backs.

The care of reindeer herds is beset with dangers and difficulties. During summer the herds readily stampede under the attacks of mosquitoes, and to prevent this they are moved to higher altitudes during this season. Smoky fires are lit to keep off midges. Does are apt to leave the herds during the mating season. Salt, of which the reindeer are very fond, is provided for them by the Tungus, and helps to keep the herds attached to the human community which owns them. The attacks of wolves are a menace during winter, and from time to time epidemics decimate the herds.

Life among the Tungus follows a well-marked seasonal cycle largely determined by their environment. In winter the poverty of the pasture and the attention devoted to hunting and trapping entail constant movement and long journeys, and during this period the Tungus communities divide into small units composed of one or more family groups. But in summer they tend to settle down in large villages of perhaps a thousand individuals.

The Tungus are divided into patrilineal clans. Two or more of these clans form a tribe, which occupies a specified area of territory and usually speaks a dialect of its own. But the clans alone have names and the tribe is apt to be an unstable unit. The size of the clan varies from a dozen to several hundred households, each household numbering from four to ten people. There are no hereditary clan headmen. War leaders are appointed when necessary, and at the time of summer aggregation the heads of households meet in council to settle disputes and punish offenders. Though herds of reindeer are owned by individual households, the decimation of certain herds by epidemics or the attacks of wolves is followed by a redistribution of stock—ownership is thus not absolute.

The milk of reindeer and the products of the chase are shared by members of the camp group. Nevertheless, individual or family ownership, though limited by traditional usage and mutual agreement, definitely exists. The land rights of tribes are defended if necessary by force, and individual families have customary pastures and hunting grounds scattered over the tribal territory irrespective of clan affiliation. Families likewise build storehouses in which to keep food, clothing and other property. Any Tungus, if in need, may use the contents of these, but a tally must be kept of anything taken permanently, and some recompense at a later date is expected.

Among the Tungus, reindeer are of ceremonial and religious, as well as economic, importance. They are sacrificed at ceremonies connected with marriage and death. Moreover, every clan sets aside a sacred reindeer, which is never milked, saddled or driven. These beasts are believed to carry the souls of men to the land of the dead and to act as intermediaries between human beings and the spirits.

Marriage among the Tungus is almost always monogamous, and polygyny is only approved if the first wife fails to bear children. Frequently, two clans are traditionally associated as intermarrying groups. Cross-cousin marriage (especially matrilateral) is approved, and exchange of sisters is common. Marriages are often arranged while the two individuals concerned are still children. Bride-price, called *turi*, is paid in reindeer by the family of the bridegroom to the parents of the bride, the fellow clansmen of the former often making contributions to it. The size of the *turi* varies with the beauty, skill and social status of the bride, and a large *turi* enhances the prestige of both of the clans concerned. An equivalent of about half the *turi* is returned in the form of a dowry, which also includes the equipment necessary to set up a new household. The exchanges involved are marked by reciprocal feasting. If a family is too poor to provide the necessary beasts, the bridegroom goes for a while to live with his affinal kin, and during this period he hunts for them. No *turi* is paid in the case of sister-exchange.

The dependence of the other peoples of northern Asia upon reindeer is less marked than among the Tungus. The Samoyeds to the north-west, between the Yenesei River and the Ural Mountains, use them for pulling sledges and occasionally make use of their meat and skins. The reindeer of the Samoyeds are neither milked nor ridden, the people depending for food on herds of domesticated deer and on hunting.

The Yakuts, whose territory lies to the north of the Tungus, attempt to raise horses and cattle by gathering scant supplies of hay, constructing winter byres, and even inducing the animals to eat fish and meat. But they are being driven to an increasing dependence upon reindeer as their horses and cattle die out. It appears that they moved to their present habitat from the south-west and, in spite of the unfavourable environment, cling tenaciously to their traditional herds, partly on account of the ceremonial and social values attached to them.

At the north-eastern extremity of Asia the Chuckchi to the north and the Koryak to the south keep reindeer, but also subsist largely by means of fishing and seal-hunting, which resemble the activities of the Eskimo communities inhabiting the extreme north-eastern coast.

An unusual people of this region are the Yukaghir, whose territory lies north of the Verkhoyansk and Stanovoi Mountains. The Yukaghir rely largely on reindeer, which they hunt but do not domesticate. They are (apart from the Eskimo of the extreme north-east coast) the only purely hunting and food-gathering peoples of Arctic Asia. Their indigenous ecology is fast disappearing, and most of them have joined neighbouring communities of reindeer herders.

3. Pastoralists of Central Asia

In west central Asia lies an extensive belt of territory bounded on the west by the Caspian Sea, on the east by the Altai Mountains, and on the south and north roughly by latitudes 40° and 50° North. Though this area is comparatively dry, particularly in summer, there is a good supply of grass. The people of this region depend upon the milk, and to some extent the meat, of their herds of sheep, horses and cattle. Goats, and in certain areas camels, are also kept.

The largest cultural group inhabiting this area are the Kazaks, who occupy most of the western section of it. To the south lies the territory of the Kirghiz and to the east that of the Kalmuck.

The Kazak are divided into patrilineal clans. Groups of twenty or more clans are bound together in loosely knit tribes, and the tribes again have in the past banded together in much larger units known as hordes.[1]

[1] The term "horde" as applied to these large political units, organized for wars of aggression and defence, is used in an entirely different sense from the special connotation given to it in connection with the small local groups of Australian aboriginal society (see section 9 below).

The Kazak hordes and tribes are only important in connection with war. These people have never succeeded in achieving any large-scale political unity. Their basic political and economic units are their clans. Each clan has a headman, who is the senior member of the dominant family of the clan. Each clan has a crest, which is branded on its livestock. The family owners of the herds have traditional pastures, but the poorer members of the community when destitute are fed by more fortunate families. The conditions of pasture and particularly the severe winter are a constant menace to the herds, and families may be reduced by bad luck to complete dependence upon others. Slavery existed among the Kazaks until 1859. The Kazaks are divided into two social classes—the "white bones" and the "black bones". The former, who claim, quite unjustifiably, descent from Jenghiz Khan, form the aristocracy of the Kazaks and refuse to inter-marry with the lower class.

The Kazaks follow a well-marked seasonal cycle. During summer the pastures are poor and will not support herds for any length of time. At this season families and clans do not lay per-manent claim to particular areas, because the richness of any given pasture varies from year to year. The right to use a particular pasture belongs to the first family or clan to occupy it. Families often preserve secrecy as to the pastures they intend to occupy in order to forestall their neighbours.

Life in winter is also precarious, but whereas the Kazaks break up into small nomadic social groups during the summer, the conditions of winter conduce to a concentration of settlement in areas sheltered from the cold. Such areas are permanent terri-torial possessions of the clans.

In addition to herding, the Kazaks practise a small amount of agriculture, which was in the past largely carried out by slaves and is still almost completely limited to Kazak families who have lost all or most of their livestock. Hunting is of little importance, but falconry is practised as a sport by the richer families. The Kazaks are nominally Moslems, believing that the practices of circumcision, head-shaving and alms-giving pave the way to Paradise, but they are not orthodox Mohammedans. They have no priests or mosques and their women are neither secluded nor veiled. They observe the Feast of Ramadan, at which Moslems are enjoined to abstain from food and drink between sunrise and sunset. The Kazaks meet this obligation by feasting all night and sleeping during the day. Moreover, Mohammedanism is supplemented by numerous pagan beliefs and practices.

4. *Some Primitive Tribes of India, Assam and Burma*

Although most of the population of India consists of Hindus, Moslems and representatives of other advanced cultures, there exist numerous more or less isolated areas inhabited by people possessing very much simpler cultures, though these people have adopted cultural elements from their more advanced neighbours. These relatively isolated communities are sometimes referred to as the "aboriginal" tribes of India, but the term "primitive" is preferable. Thus the Lepchas, an agricultural people of Sikkim, are actually of Mongolian race, quite unlike the so-called Dravidians or Proto-Australoids of southern India, though they resemble them in that they form a distinctive cultural enclave isolated from the dominant cultures of India.

Another primitive agricultural people are the Baiga, who inhabit territory in the Central Provinces of India, east and north-west of the Maikal Mountains. They are an agricultural people, cultivating rice and other grain by shifting cultivation on the hills. In spite of rigorous attempts by the Government to induce them to adopt settled plough agriculture in the valleys, they cling tenaciously to their traditional agricultural methods which are socially and mythologically sanctioned. The use of the plough is literally regarded as a sin which may bring misfortune and death to the offender and his fellow-villagers. Elwin (1) deals at length with shifting cultivation and the effects of its prohibition on Baiga life. He includes a comparative section which is of special interest at the present time, when the requirements of soil and forest conservation conflict with native custom in many parts of the world. It may be noted that shifting cultivation has raised similar problems among other primitive Indian tribes, for example, the Reddis of eastern Hyderabad.

Another primitive people of India are the Chenchus of southern Hyderabad. This tribe is divided into three groups. The most important of these, the "jungle Chenchus", inhabit the hills to the north of the Kistna River. They subsist mainly on the gathering of wild forest produce, supplemented by hunting, fishing and the collection of wild honey and Mohua flowers. The latter are used, not only as food, but also for the preparation of liquor. These Chenchus keep a few cattle and sometimes cultivate a little grain, but they are primarily food-gatherers. During a large part of the year they are nomadic, wandering from place to place in search of forest produce.

A group of Chenchus to the north have settled in permanent villages and adopted the agricultural type of life of their Hindu neighbours.

A southern group of the tribe who live on the southern side of the Kistna River in Madras Presidency were originally, like their northern neighbours, semi-nomadic food gatherers. But the Government has taken steps to settle them in permanent villages and to introduce them to agricultural pursuits. It may be noted that, though this policy has certain advantages, it has resulted in an alarming increase in serious crimes among these Chenchus. This is partly due to the breakdown of traditional standards, but even more to the new conditions of life to which the Chenchus are not adapted. Under the nomadic system of the jungle Chenchus, quarrels or strained relations between individuals merely lead one or other party to move off to another area, so that serious consequences rarely ensue. When they are forced to live together in close proximity under conditions of village life, bloodshed is sooner or later the almost inevitable result. This is a good illustration of the dangers of introducing primitive peoples to practices to which their culture is not adapted, even when this is done from entirely disinterested and laudable motives.

An Indian people with an entirely different type of culture are the Todas of the Nilgiri Hills in southern India. The productive labour of these people is almost exclusively devoted to their herds of buffalo, though they exchange their dairy produce with other tribes in return for grain and other goods. Apart from their interesting system of polyandry, the Todas are chiefly remarkable for the elaborate ritual connected with their herds, which are of two kinds. The ordinary herds are tended by men and boys without any special ritual, but the sacred herds are the object of elaborate ceremonial, carried out by a special official dairyman at a sacred dairy.

In the Naga Hills of Assam live a group of primarily agricultural tribes. Most of these cultivate rice by shifting cultivation, but the Angami Nagas have also developed an elaborate system of irrigated terraces, these being flooded when required by water from neighbouring streams and torrents. An interesting feature of this system is the existence of rights of ownership, purchase and inheritance over water. Thus when a man has once dug a channel tapping a new stream, no one is allowed to tap the same stream at a higher level. This rule does not, however, apply to very large streams.

An interesting feature of the cultures of the Naga tribes is the importance attached to feasts, particularly the **Feasts of Merit,** whereby an individual attains social prestige in a manner reminiscent of the potlatch. Social status is achieved by giving a series of feasts, each more costly than the preceding one, and large monoliths are erected in Naga villages to commemorate feasts given by prominent villagers. Similar feasts among the Chins of Burma will be mentioned presently.

Certain Naga tribes are unusual among primitive peoples, in that they believe that an individual's condition in the life after death is determined by his moral conduct during life. The Angami believe that good men go up to the sky, where they lead a pleasant life, while those who have committed breaches of taboo or other offences go to a region below the earth, where their souls pass through seven existences, at the end of which they become extinct. The ideas of the natives on the life after death are vague, and they appear to have little interest in the subject.

Of the many primitive tribes of Burma, such as the Nagas, Lushei-Kukis, Chins, Karens and Shans, few have received detailed anthropological attention. The central Chins occupy a mountainous tract in the Manipur area. Before the advent of British administration, wars and migrations were frequent. The British created new administrative units, which coincided neither with old tribal boundaries nor with traditional political units. Though there are today chiefs of tribes and sub-tribes, the most influential political figure is the hereditary village headman. Villages are situated in easily defended positions on the mountainsides, and consist of anything from ten to three hundred houses, grouped round a *mual*, a place of sacrifice. Houses are well built of planks and thatch, consist of two rooms, and usually have a platform in front extending over a garden. A central aqueduct, sometimes five miles long, of split logs on Y-shaped poles, brings water to the village, and smaller runlets of log or bamboo carry it to each house.

The economy of the Chins centres round agriculture. The mountains of the region rise to 8,000 feet and the cultivable land of a village sometimes extends through 6,000 feet. The land is classified as "hot and cold" and crops are planted to suit each category. The staple crops are rice, three types of millet, sulphur beans and peas. Other crops are runner beans, broad beans and potatoes, while garden produce includes melon, tobacco, cucumber, ginger, chillies, onions and leeks. Each village has a definite territory, the cultivable area of which is divided into fields, about four to each village, which are cultivated or used for grazing in strict rotation. Each field is further subdivided into plots distributed amongst the households of the village. The main crops are also grown in rotation. Formerly agriculture was left to the women while the men mounted guard or raided other territories, but now men work in the fields as much as women. Each household is responsible for the cultivation of its own plot, but labour can be hired, and kinsmen form labour associations to do the heavy work on each other's plots.

Stock-breeding of a variety of cattle known as mithan, and also of pigs, is an important element in Chin economy. A man's wealth is judged by the number of mithan he owns, and meat is the main element in the Feasts of Merit, the giving of which is the road to worldly wealth and glory in the after-life. Jungle and scrub jungle provide game, fruit, honey and other products, altogether forming a substantial contribution to Chin economy. Hunting is both an economic activity and a sport. The most popular form of hunting is the drive, for it allows a large number of men to share the thrills and spoils of the chase. Though each village has its defined territory, a village may hunt in the territory of another village, and hunting parties often travel as much as sixty miles from home. An ingenious trap the Chins have devised consists of a see-saw baited at one end and poised over a steep declivity. Underneath the baited end sharp bamboo stakes are planted in the ground, which transfix the victim as it slips off the see-saw. Even tigers are caught in this way. Chin women are expert hand weavers, potters and basketry makers. There are only two specialists in the Chin village, the priest and the blacksmith. In some villages they are paid by contract, in others they perform all the services required of them in the village and in return have their land cultivated for them by the villagers.

The headman of the village has executive powers to deal with all offences except murder. Assisting him in the guidance of village activities and the maintenance of law and order is a council of village notables. Entry into the council is open to all the males who have given certain of the Feasts of Merit. Labour service and rates in kind are paid to the council by all households (including those of the council members), to meet administrative expenses.

Chin religion is closely bound up with agriculture. For example, before a field is open to cultivation (every three, six or nine years according to the land available) a sacrifice to ensure the goodwill of its guardian spirit must be performed by the village priest, otherwise evil would befall any man who used the field. Thus religious beliefs ensure that the system of field rotation will be strictly adhered to, while the priest is a major figure in organizing the system. To the Chin, heaven and earth are stratified, and the soul of a man at death goes to the stratum which corresponds with what his status has been on earth. A man advances in status by giving Feasts of Merit of increasing lavishness. Religious beliefs here stimulate economic production and distribution.

Succession, inheritance and descent are patrilineal and marriage is patrilocal. Marriage with close patrilineal relations is forbidden. Polygyny exists, but is disapproved and is rare. A bride-price and a dowry of almost equal value are exchanged between the kin of the bride and the kin of the groom at marriage. The value of the bride-price varies according to the status of the girl and her physical condition. Her status depends upon that of her father, and hence upon the number of Feasts of Merit he has given. Her physical condition refers, not to her beauty, but to whether or not she has already borne children. Virginity is not valued, but the Chin youth prefers to marry a woman who has not yet given birth. On account of reciprocal obligations between a husband and his patrilineal kinsmen and between him and his relatives-in-law, most men live within their fathers' villages. The village is thus usually composed of groups of patrilineal kinsmen (and their wives) each related by marriage to other groups in the village.

5. Malaysia

This area includes the Malay Peninsula, Sumatra and the islands and island groups extending eastwards to the western end of New Guinea and northwards to the Philippine Islands. The primitive cultures of Malaysia are extremely heterogeneous, and have for many centuries been affected by religious, political and economic influences from the cultures of India and China, and in recent centuries by European colonization. Thus we find cultures ranging from nomadic bands of hunters and food-gatherers to highly developed native states ruled by rajahs and sultans.

The simplest cultures of this area are found in the interior of the south-eastern extremity of the Malay Peninsula. This region is inhabited by communities of hunters and food-gatherers, the Sakai to the south, and the Semang to the north.

The Semang live in small nomadic groups numbering up to twenty or thirty individuals. Each group has its own traditional territory, but rights to the products of such territory vary according to the value of the food concerned. Thus a man may wander over the territory of a neighbouring group in search of roots or game, but must not take the fruits of valuable trees. The Semang have no crops or domestic animals except half-wild dogs and a few tame monkeys. They subsist primarily by food-gathering, supplemented by the hunting of small game and by fishing. Their principal hunting weapons are the bow and arrow, and the blow-gun and poisoned darts.

Semang habitations consist of rude shelters of palm leaves, and these are usually only temporary structures. The material culture of the Semang is extremely simple, and they make no weapons or tools of metal or even of stone.

The leadership of a band of Semang is usually vested in a man respected for his age, personal qualities or supernatural powers. Certain groups of bands have a feeling of community and share a common dialect, but these larger groups have no political unity.

A man normally marries a woman belonging to a band other than his own. Marriage is by individual choice, and when the two parties have reached an understanding, the man gives presents to his prospective wife's father. After marriage he goes to live with and work for his wife's people for a period of a year or two, and then returns with his wife to his own band.

The Semang carry out some trade with the neighbouring Malays, exchanging wax, resin and other forest produce for salt, beads, cloth and metal articles. This trade is carried out by what is called "dumb barter". The Semang leave their forest produce in a specified place and retire. The Malays come and collect it, leaving in its stead the articles which they have to provide in exchange, and these are subsequently collected by the shy and suspicious Semang. In these transactions the Semang are usually cheated by their more sophisticated neighbours.

Semang bands live at peace with one another. They do not carry on any armed conflict even with the Sakai and Malays, by whom they are sometimes harassed. The Semangs' reaction to attack is to retire from the conflict.

The inhabitants of the Andaman Islands of the Bay of Bengal are also hunters and food-gatherers, but possess in many respects a more advanced type of culture than the Semang. The settlements of the Andamanese are more permanent, and there is a certain amount of economic specialization and trade, which takes the form of gift exchange, between inland and coastal peoples.

Most of the primitive peoples of Malaysia, however, are agriculturists, rice being the most common crop. But this is usually supplemented by other items of diet, as among the Igorot peoples of north-western Luzon, who also cultivate sweet potatoes and indulge in fishing and hunting. Rice is also the staple food among the primitive non-Mohammedan peoples of Borneo, often loosely referred to as Dyaks. Among these may be mentioned the Kayan, who live along the banks of large rivers and who are remarkable for their local organization. They live in "long houses" reminiscent of those of the Iroquois. One or two of these houses make up an independent village unit. The headmen of such villages are the only political authorities.

6. Primitive Cultures of the Pacific

The aboriginal cultures of the Pacific islands are traditionally divided into three groups—those of Melanesia, Micronesia and Polynesia.

Melanesia includes New Guinea and the arc of islands to the north-east of Australia extending southwards as far as New Caledonia and eastwards to Fiji.

Micronesia covers the small islands lying to the north of Melanesia. Very little ethnographic information is available for this area.

The *Polynesian* islands are those of the Pacific roughly east of longitude 180° and also including New Zealand. Polynesia is bounded on the north by Hawaii and on the east by Easter Island. Lines joining these three points cover approximately the so-called "Polynesian triangle". But it should be noted that there are certain western Polynesian "outliers" in the area covered by Melanesia, notably the islands of Tikopia and Ontong Java.

s.a. i—7

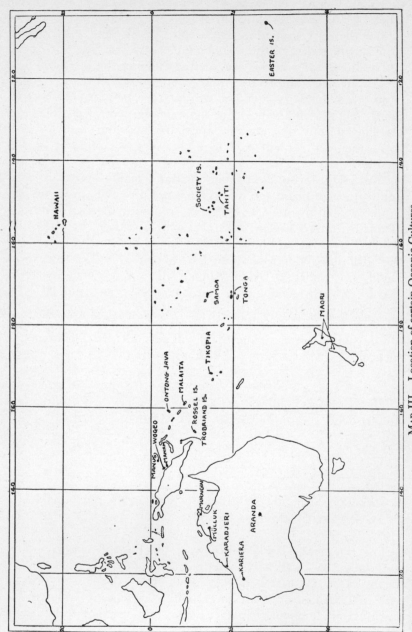

Map III.—Location of certain Oceanic Cultures

The native ecologies of the Pacific are based on cultivation, but no grain crops are indigenous to the Pacific. The natives rely mainly on root vegetables such as taro and yams, and on sago, breadfruit, bananas and, in particular, the coco-nut. The last of these provides, not only food and drink, but also fibre for making string and rope, and also material for bowls, cups and spoons. Nowadays the dried "meat" of the coco-nut (copra) is one of the most important commercial exports of the Pacific. Fishing is an important activity on the smaller islands and in coastal regions of the larger ones, where fish are frequently exchanged with inland people for vegetable produce. Pigs are kept, and are of particular social and ceremonial importance in Melanesia.

7. Polynesia

In spite of widespread similarities of culture and language, a great variety of cultures is to be found in Polynesia. Students should therefore beware of regarding the cultures of Tikopia or of Ontong Java as equivalent to "Polynesian Culture". Much attention is paid to the two islands mentioned because of the quality of the ethnographic records from them, in contradistinction to the larger island groups where detribalization preceded the development of modern methods of field-work. In these large groups the greater population, and later the introduction of firearms by Europeans, made possible the growth of elaborate systems of chieftainship, for example, the dynasty of Kamehameha I, the "Napoleon of Hawaii". Warfare in the large island groups of Polynesia was highly developed.

Throughout Polynesia there were many variations in religion and special developments in material culture. The latter were particularly marked in New Zealand, where the migration of the original Maori during the fourteenth century from the Society Islands to a land with a very much colder climate and with different natural resources produced considerable changes in technology, particularly in the making of clothing.

8. Melanesia

Melanesia also presents a wide variety of cultures, and the danger of generalizing from one or two communities must again be emphasized. Thus, much attention will be paid to the Trobriand Islands because of Malinowski's pioneering field research

in this area (1914–18). But the matrilineal system of the Trobrianders is by no means universal in Melanesia, where both
patrilineal and matrilineal systems occur. Sometimes both forms
of organization co-exist, as in Wogeo, though the people of this
island are predominantly patrilineal.

Again the Trobriand Kula (Chapter VII, section 6), though it
reflects the emphasis upon wealth which is common in Melanesia
generally (in contradistinction to the importance attached to
hereditary rank in Polynesia), is a highly specialized institution.
Finally, the Trobriand system of chieftainship is not typical of
Melanesia, where the political unit tends to be a small clan,
village or group of homesteads. In this respect Malaita and Wogeo
are more representative of Melanesian political organization than
the Trobriands.

In Malaita the basic social unit is the district, composed of a
number of isolated homesteads. Men of importance (*ngwane-inoto*)
acquire authority over one or more districts by lavish distribution
of wealth, but none of them ever has more than about two hundred
followers. The office is not hereditary, though the son of a *ngwane-
inoto* has an initial economic advantage over his rivals. The island
of Wogeo, again, is divided into five districts, but there are no
chiefs ruling over these. Each district contains a number of
villages. The population is divided into patrilineal clans, and
usually two clans occupy each village. Each clan has a headman
and deputy-headman. Cutting across the predominantly patrilineal system there are two matrilineal moieties. These are mainly
ceremonial in their function, and friendship is enjoined between
fellow-members of the same moiety. Culturally, the patrilineal
clans are of far greater importance.

A characteristic feature of Melanesian cultures is the development of magical beliefs and practices and particularly of sorcery.
Though frowned upon by the administration, such beliefs play, as
in other parts of the world, an important part in maintaining
native standards of law and morality.

9. The Australian Aborigines

The Australian aborigines are a hunting and food-gathering
people. They have no cultivated crops or domestic animals except
the dingo (the native Australian dog) which they train to hunt
for them. They are divided into *hordes* of perhaps fifty to one
hundred and fifty individuals. The horde normally consists of the

men and immature females of a patrilineal clan and the wives of its male members. This group occupies a specified area, and its members do not normally trespass on the territory of other hordes. The horde is the basic political unit of native society, the tribe being a linguistic and not a political entity. Great respect is paid to age, and the affairs of the horde are regulated by an informal council of old men, a system which has been termed *gerontocracy*. The old men are important because of their detailed knowledge of local geography and bush lore, and this is reflected in their direction of ceremonies, particularly the elaborate ritual connected with initiation.

Australian culture is remarkable for the elaborateness and complexity of its kinship systems, which regulate all phases of social life, particularly marriage. The prescribed marriages with kin, real or classificatory, fall into the following groups:

1. Marriage with either cross-cousin, as found among the Kariera and other tribes in the vicinity of the De Grey River, Western Australia.
2. Marriage with mother's brother's daughter but not father's sister's daughter, as among the Murngin of north-east Arnhem land.
3. Marriage between cross-cousins prohibited, the preferred marriage being with mother's mother's brother's daughter's daughter, as among the Aranda.
4. Various atypical and intermediate forms of marriage.

Various forms of totemism exist. A common feature of Australian totemism is a series of rites, known as **increase ceremonies.** The object of these is to increase the supply of animals, plants and other natural species upon which the aborigines depend for their existence.

In spite of the general homogeneity of culture in Australia, various Australian tribes present important cultural variations. The danger of generalizing from a single instance must again be stressed. Thus one of the best-known tribes are the Aranda or Arunta of Central Australia, and their somewhat specialized culture, particularly in regard to social organization and magico-religious beliefs, has frequently been treated as synonymous with Australian aboriginal culture. It has moreover frequently formed the basis of theoretical interpretations which are not applicable to other Australian tribes.

10. The Karadjeri Tribe

As an example of Australian aboriginal culture, we may consider that of the Karadjeri, bearing in mind what was said in the preceding section about the danger of generalizing from a particular tribe. Thus the food supply of the Karadjeri is much more abundant than that of the natives of the interior, their initiation ceremonies are more elaborate than in some other Australian tribes, and their kinship system is less systematic and stable than corresponding organizations elsewhere in Australia. Nevertheless, the Karadjeri are a reasonably representative Australian tribe.[1]

Environment and Food Supply

The Karadjeri tribe occupies a strip of coastal territory situated around Lagrange Bay, in north-western Australia, and extending several miles inland. In culture the coastal Karadjeri differ slightly from the inland Karadjeri, especially in regard to kinship usages. The coastal territory consists of belts of bush country, known as "pindan", alternating with tidal marshes; the latter are covered by the sea at the time of the equinoctial tides. There are no streams of fresh water, but the marshes are at intervals invaded by salt-water creeks in which fish are plentiful. In these the white "mangrove mud", extensively used for decoration, is obtained.

Near the coast native wells are plentiful and food abundant, but as one proceeds inland, water becomes more scarce and food correspondingly more difficult to obtain. The climate is not fully tropical. The native year is divided into periods of varying length, as follows:

1. *Manggala* is the wet season, lasting from about the beginning of January till the end of the heavy rains, about the middle of March.
2. *Marul* is a short season between the end of the rains and the beginning of the cold weather, about May.
3. *Pargana* is the cold season, lasting till some time in August.
4. *Wilburu* is another short transitional season; at this time the weather becomes hotter.

[1] The field-work on which this account is founded was carried out by the writer under the auspices of the Australian National Research Council during 1930 and 1931. Many of the cultural features described were even then in a condition of disintegration and no doubt others have since disappeared. (Cf. p. 7.)

5. *Ladja* comprises the later months of the year, when the weather becomes intensely hot; the end of this season, just before *Manggala*, is termed *ladjaladja*.

The Karadjeri draw a distinction between flesh foods (*kwi*) and vegetable foods (*mai*). As mentioned above, there is no lack of food along the strip of coast occupied by the Nadja (coastal) Karadjeri. Fish, turtle, crabs, oysters and other bivalves are available in unfailing supply, and occasionally a porpoise or dugong is washed ashore and eaten by the natives. The Karadjeri have no form of canoe. Crabs, cockles and oysters are collected by the women, but the larger fish are caught by men. Turtle are speared in rock pools at low tide. Fish are caught by several methods, the most important of which are *margu* and *panaing*. In the former a barricade of bushes is built across one of the ramifications of a tidal salt-water creek at high tide, and as the tide recedes, the fish and stingarees are caught.

The *panaing* (or "dry fishing") method consists of wading out over the reef and among rock pools at low tide; the fish are either speared or killed by means of a flat piece of wood resembling in shape a large squash racket.

Second to fish foods, the most common form of *kwi* consists of wallaby flesh, these animals being extremely plentiful in the belts of cadjibut trees which border the patches of pindan country. The most usual means of obtaining wallabies is by the use of dogs, while during the *ladja* season wallabies are sometimes tracked and speared while asleep during the heat of the day. Occasionally a drive is held in which an extended line of natives drives the wallabies out of a patch of country while others wait for the frightened animals, which they kill with hitting sticks. Wallaby is preferred to fish foods, the fat and blood of the animals being regarded as a great delicacy. It appears that bandicoots once formed a regular article of diet, but they are now extremely uncommon.

The two most important birds, from the point of view of food, are the brolga or native companion, and the Australian bustard or wild turkey. These birds are extremely difficult to approach, and are caught by an ingenious method. A yard of bushes is built round a small waterhole, a narrow entrance being left; a native conceals himself near this and, when the bird comes to drink, throws bushes across the opening, thus imprisoning the bird. Smaller birds are killed by means of the boomerang.

Goannas (which are very plentiful) and snakes are a regular article of diet, while witchety grubs, locusts and other insects are also eaten.

Turning to *mai* (vegetable food), we find a variety of bush fruit, including the native plum, as well as nuts and wattle seed which become plentiful during the *wilburu* and *ladja* seasons; but the most common form of *mai* (among the coastal people) is the "nalgoo", a minute ground fruit resembling in shape a small clove of garlic. These are dug up by women at several sandy patches along the coast.

The native knowledge of all matters connected with bush life is very wide; it covers, not only those animals and plants which are used as food, but also the less important aspects of bush lore. This is exemplified in the vocabulary in which every animal, bird, insect or plant has a name, and in the case of the more important species, two or three names.

The coastal Karadjeri have been, since the latter decades of the last century, in contact with white men as well as with the coloured crews of pearling luggers which frequently put into the creeks for supplies of water. However, the settlement of the country by white people has at no time been dense, and the inland members of the tribe have had very little contact with whites or Asiatics.

The effect of white influence upon the culture has been a general weakening of tribal tradition. The aspect of the culture which has suffered most is the local organization; many of the natives are content to live away from their own country for considerable periods of time, but there still exists a very powerful bond between a man and the district to which he belongs. The kinship organization has also suffered disintegration, though the more binding usages and prohibitions associated with it are still maintained. Fights between hordes are becoming less common (though camp brawls are still fairly frequent) and killing is quite rare. It seems probable that even before the advent of the white man the Karadjeri were an exceptionally peaceful tribe.

Kinship

As with all Australian tribes, kinship is a most important and complex feature of Karadjeri culture, particularly in the regulation of marriage. The general marriage rule of the inland Karadjeri is that a man marries his mother's brother's daughter, real or classificatory. But there are certain restrictions on this kind of marriage, and marriages with other types of kin also occur, for example, with sister's son's daughter and with sister's daughter's husband's sister's daughter. The terminology of Karadjeri kinship will be discussed in the next chapter. At this point we may note that, in common with many other Australian tribes, the Karadjeri classify kin into four sections.[1] These sections may be diagrammatically represented as follows:

$$\begin{array}{l} \text{Panaka} = \text{Burung} \\ \text{Karimba} = \text{Paldjeri} \end{array}$$

In this diagram, parallel lines indicate marriage and arrows the allocation of children to sections *according to that of their mother*.[2] Thus a Panaka man marries a Burung woman and the children belong to the Paldjeri section; a Paldjeri man marries a Karimba woman and the children belong to the Panaka section; a Burung man marries a Panaka woman and the children belong to the Karimba section, and a Karimba man marries a Paldjeri woman and the children belong to the Burung section. For ceremonial and descriptive purposes the sections are grouped in different ways. Thus it will be seen that Panaka and Paldjeri together constitute a patrilineal moiety, and the same is true of Burung and Karimba. These patrilineal moieties have no names, but each man calls his own moiety *nganirangu* and the other *kalyera*. Each of the two intermarrying pairs of sections is called *m'reram'rera* and the matrilineal moieties (Panaka-Karimba and Burung-Paldjeri) are called *kagaramada*.

The section organization provides a convenient means of classifying kin, especially for ceremonial purposes, and the same may be said of the various groupings of the sections. Thus, at initiation the ceremonial obligations of various individuals depend upon their *m'reram'rera*, while in the case of totemic increase ceremonies it is the patrilineal moieties which are prominent.

Local Organization

An important feature of Karadjeri culture is the local organization, though it is impossible to give an adequate account of it.

---

[1] In older works on Australian sociology, such groupings are often called *marriage classes*. But this term is misleading, since the sections are primarily ceremonial in function, marriage being regulated by the underlying individual relationships of kinship. It may be mentioned that many Australian tribes, such as the Aranda, have an even more complex way of classifying kin into eight *subsections*, and this again is correlated with their specific types of kinship organization.

[2] This does not mean that the system is matrilineal. Neither is it patrilineal. The diagrammatic representation is one of convenience only. A child belongs neither to the section of its father nor to that of its mother. It belongs to another section altogether, the identity of which is determined by the section membership of both parents.

As elsewhere in Australia, it was the first element of culture to be destroyed by contact with the white man. This difficulty is intensified by the fact that the original local organization varied somewhat from the usual Australian form and that white influence has apparently intensified this deviation. In particular the Karadjeri horde is limited in the proprietary rights which it exercises over its own territory, particularly in the case of the Nadja subtribe. The general Australian practice is that each horde owns a specified territory over which its members may hunt, but on which no members of other hordes may hunt or camp except with the permission or at the invitation of the owners. Throughout the entire Nadja territory, this rule does not exist. Certain small exogamous groups exist, but they lack the solidarity which characterizes the normal Australian horde; small parties composed of less than a dozen individuals from any horde may go on hunting expeditions lasting several months, over the territory of any other horde, without asking the permission of the owners, who would not object.

In spite of the freedom of movement which is possible between them, the Nadja hordes are similar in other respects to the normal Australian local group. Thus in the first place the horde is exogamous, this fact being expressed by the Nadja Karadjeri in the statement that a man may not marry a woman from his own *ngura* (district). There is also a prohibition against marriage between persons whose *ngura* are close together, in fact, there is a very strong feeling that where possible a wife should come from as far away as possible.

One common feature of the Australian horde is that it has a patrilineal clan associated with it; such a state of affairs must necessarily be based upon patrilocal marriage, so that all the men and the unmarried girls of the horde belong to one patrilineal moiety, while all the married women come from other hordes and belong to the other moiety. But it seems probable that the Karadjeri never possessed a rigid clan associated with their local groups, but that there was a general tendency for the majority of men of one locality to belong to one or other of the two moieties, a state of affairs which was probably preserved by the predominance of patrilocal marriages.

As in other Australian tribes, Karadjeri government is carried out by an informal council of elders. In every horde there are several old men who have been initiated into the *midedi* feast, which will be described later. When decisions have to be taken, they meet together and confer, the opinions of the more forceful and intelligent individuals carrying more weight in the discussion than those of others. The leadership of the old men is most prominent in ceremonial activities, in which they decide upon such matters as times of performance, make all preliminary arrangements and actively direct the ceremonies themselves.

Religion and Magic

Karadjeri religion centres around a complex of beliefs and practices connected with initiation and totemic increase ceremonies, which will be described presently. In addition to these collective rites, there is a certain amount of magic of a more individual kind, but at present this plays a comparatively small part in the social life of the Karadjeri. Like other Australian tribes, they have a belief in the powers of certain persons, and the efficacy of certain magical ritual, but this belief does not play an important part in social life. This is probably correlated with a low degree of development in the institution of warfare, since in Australian society affrays which lead to killing, as opposed to minor brawls involving slight wounds and a considerable amount of bad language, are very frequently due to a belief in murder by magic.

The medicine men appear to serve a function conforming to the general Australian type, though neither their powers nor their influence appear to be as great as, for example, among the Aranda. In addition to rain-making and the detection of murderers, their chief powers are killing at a distance (*udja*) and curing sickness. As elsewhere, they receive their status and powers from a mythical water-serpent (*bulaing*), who blows water upon them in a dream. The *udja* method of killing produces a number of deaths in the horde against which it is directed. A heap of mud is made with a hole in it; in the hole is placed spinifex grass which is set on fire, and a *pirmal* [1] is placed upright in the mound. A circumcision knife is rested on the top of the *pirmal*, and fragments chipped from it in the direction in which the deaths are desired.

Sickness is said to be caused by a bad spirit inside the body of the patient; this can be heard by a medicine man making, he

---

[1] *Pirmal* are sacred objects consisting of wooden boards carved on one side with traditional markings. These markings are not totemic, but are connected with the mythology of initiation described below.

says, a sound like a bull-roarer. When the medicine man comes to
the patient, it is believed that he has a spirit *pirmal* inside him.
He lies on top of the patient, who immediately feels cool, and
should soon recover. Sometimes the medicine man bites the
affected part and produces a piece of human-hair string from it.
The belief that such foreign bodies, which may be abstracted by a
medicine man, are the cause of illness is a common feature of
Australian curative magic.

A rain-making ceremony is sometimes carried out during the
ladjaladja season, that is, before the rain sets in. A medicine man
digs a hole near a native well; from this hole he takes quartz
crystals which he throws in the air and then picks up again; the
medicine man then "drinks" the crystals, that is, he places them
in his mouth, where they disappear.

Totemism

The totemic system of the Karadjeri is of fundamental importance in the social life of the natives, since it is functionally related
to every other element in their culture and determines to a very
great extent the attitude towards life of the individual living in
Karadjeri society.

The Karadjeri language has two words for totem, namely
bugari and *kumbali*, but the two words have somewhat different
associations, the former referring primarily to the religious and
the latter to the social aspect of totemism. *Kumbali* also means
"namesake". The term *bugari*, like the word *alchera* among the
Aranda, possesses several meanings. In the first place it connotes
that which has a binding force upon the society; to describe an
institution or custom as *bugari* means that it has a special sanction
which renders it inviolable. This is derived from the fact that all
things which are *bugari* were instituted by mythical beings in
bugari times, that is, in the distant past when the world was
created. Thus the most general meaning of the term when
applied to a social institution or custom is that it has a sort of
categorical imperative associated with it.

Apart from its reference to the period of the world's inception
and the sanction for present institutions derived therefrom, the
word *bugari* is also used to denote the totem of an individual. The
connection is fairly clear when we consider that each totemic
group is derived from an ancestor or ancestors who in *bugari* times
instituted it, and thus in Karadjeri totemism the individual is

linked, through his membership of the totemic group, not only with the other members of the group and the associated natural species, but also with *bugari* times.

Associated with the last meaning is another use of the word to denote dreams; this again is quite clear in view of the fact that the most important aspect of dreams, in the native mind, is that through a dream a father establishes the patrilineal inheritance of the totem by his children.

Every Karadjeri man or woman possesses one or more totems. There is a prohibition against killing or eating the totemic species. Totems are acquired by individuals as follows. Before a child is born its father dreams that he sees his own *bugari* together with a *yardanggal* (spirit child). The scene of the dream is always located in the father's own horde territory, though he may be absent from it at the time; the *yardanggal* subsequently enters the man's wife, who becomes pregnant. Now a man must dream of his own *bugari* in this way, so that totemism may be said to be patrilineal; but he may also dream of other *bugari* of his own moiety. It thus happens that many individuals have three or four totems, and that totems do not belong exclusively to specific hordes, though the increase centres associated with them do, and the increase ceremonies must be directed by a man of the local group in whose territory the centre is situated.

Though the director or leader of the increase ceremonies has full control over the performance of the ritual, he may be assisted by other men and under certain circumstances by women. In cases where the last man of the appropriate totem dies, he bequeaths his title to another man of the same *ngura* (district) and not to a member of the same totem belonging to a different *ngura*. It thus appears that increase ceremonies are associated primarily with the districts in which the increase centres are located rather than with the individual members of the totems.

Though the Karadjeri have localized rites for the increase of natural species, by no means all species have increase centres located in Karadjeri territory. It is, however, essential to note that theoretically (in the minds of the natives) all important natural species have increase centres somewhere, and a number of these in the territories of surrounding tribes can be named as the place where certain increase ceremonies are carried out. People of one or other of the two patrilineal moieties are always conceived as directing the ceremony, though they are assisted by members of the other moiety.

Increase centres are generally located at places where the natural species in question is plentiful. Thus, for example, Birdinapa Point is the best place on the coast for any kind of fishing, and here are located a number of fish increase centres.

Increase ceremonies are usually performed once a year, and when a natural species appears at one season only, the ceremony associated with that species is performed just before it becomes plentiful. On the other hand, the increase ceremonies associated with those foods which are perennial may be carried out at any time.

An invariable accompaniment to Karadjeri increase ceremonies is a series of instructions uttered by the performers as they carry out the ritual; these are of one general pattern, and consist of instructions to the species to become plentiful. They are continued throughout the ceremonies, various *ngura* (districts) being named in succession as places where the totem in question should become abundant. In reciting these lists of *ngura* the natives name only those places in which the species is actually to be found. The instructions are associated with the belief that all increase centres were instituted in *bugari* times, when a number of spirit members of the species were left at the centres; these come out under the influence of the ritual and so ensure the increase of the natural species. Sometimes a song associated with the mythological origin of the ceremony is sung.

At many of the increase ceremonies decorations are worn, but these, probably owing to European influence, are sometimes omitted. The decorations most commonly used are powdered charcoal, red ochre, white mangrove mud, white down from such birds as the native companion, and human blood obtained by boring a hole in the forearm of one of the performers with a pointed wallaby bone. The latter rite may not be witnessed by women or uninitiated males.

The following descriptions of a few typical increase ceremonies will provide some idea of the character of the ritual.

Increase of parrot fish.—The increase centre for parrot fish is situated at Cape Bossut. It consists of an ovoid stone, about eighteen inches in length, partially buried in the ground. This represents a parrot fish. The director of the ceremony digs away the earth from around the stone, at the same time saying that parrot fish are to increase and asking for a plentiful supply. As the earth is dug out it is scattered north and south, various coastal *ngura* being named and the fish being told to be plentiful in these places. When a quantity of earth has been removed the stone is taken out and laid on its side near the hole from which it has been taken. It is then addressed as follows: "At low tide you will lie like this!" After this the stone is painted with charcoal and also red and yellow ochre mixed with grease, replaced in its hole, and packed around with earth. Branches of trees are then held resting on the stone for a moment and then swept down a pathway towards the ocean. This ensures that fish will leave the rock and go down the path to the sea.

The ritual as described above may be witnessed by women, but sometimes human blood is poured upon the stone in the belief that it will make the fish fat, and in this case women are, of course, excluded. The ceremony is performed during the *wilburu* or *ladja* season, and at this time the fish are caught upon the reef at low tide. The ritual belongs to the Burung-Karimba moiety.

Increase of cockles.—On either side of a small mangrove creek at Lagrange Bay are several heaps of cockle-shells. Each of these heaps (on the northern bank of the creek) represents a shell, and a solitary one on the southern bank represents the fish inside. The latter is the cockle increase centre, where a ceremony for the increase of cockles may be performed at any time of the year, since this kind of food is a perennial article of diet. At the ceremony, which belongs to the Burung-Karimba moiety, no decorations are worn, and women may assist. The ceremony is a very simple one, and consists of cleaning out a hole at the top of the mound.

The ceremony was instituted in *bugari* times by Djui (bower-bird) who, together with his wife (who was also a bower-bird), came from a district to the north. Djui made a nest in a tree and a playground; his diet consisted solely of fish and shell-fish. He made a small fish trap consisting of a yard of stones, and one day, on looking into it, saw a number of fish. He then travelled down the coast making the present native fish traps, semicircular rows of stones in which fish are caught as the tide recedes. He killed a mullet, the body of which became a stone, which is now the mullet increase centre, and he also instituted the cockle increase centre.

After a while the exclusive diet of fish began to disagree with

Djui and his wife. They became very sick and finally died, leaving the fish traps, and instructing people not to live on fish alone but to eat meat and vegetable foods as well. They also gave the tradition that men obtain fish, because Djui did so, while women collect and cook cockles because his wife performed these duties.

Increase of crow and pink cockatoo.—This is a type of increase ritual, of which there are other examples, in which the increase centres of two natural species are located close to each other. Between Lagrange Bay and Injidan Plain is a large dark-coloured stone projecting from the ground. This is an increase centre for *djowari* (crow); about twenty yards distant is a centre for the increase of *ngagalil* (pink cockatoo). The two ceremonies are performed together, during the *pargana* season, that of *djowari* first. This ceremony belongs to the Panaka-Paldjeri moiety, and the *ngagalil* ceremony to the Burung-Karimba moiety.

The performers clean away any leaves, sticks or other litter from around the *djowari* stone. They then lay their hands upon the stone, stroking it and asking crows to become plentiful. When this is concluded, they move on to the *ngagalil* increase centre, which consists of several light-red coloured stones just projecting above the ground. These they clean and rub in a similar manner, sitting around them on the ground.

The mythological origin of this ceremony is associated with the legend of a crow man (Djowari) who had two wives, one of whom was also a Djowari and the other a Ngagalil. Of these two women the former was less attractive physically than the latter. For this reason their husband preferred Ngagalil, which made the other wife jealous. Each day the two women used to go collecting ants' eggs. They used to work some little distance from each other, and the Djowari woman used to insult Ngagalil by obscene remarks regarding her sexual attractiveness.

One day the Djowari woman had a large piece of wax in her hand. She threw this at Ngagalil, breaking her leg and killing her. She then returned to their camp, and when her husband asked her where his other wife was, she replied that she had remained in the bush. After waiting several days the man became suspicious, and on searching he found the dead body, which he buried. Returning to the camp, he said nothing to the Djowari woman, but built a large fire into which he threw her. She cried out "*wah*", and so perished. This is why crows are black, and give out mournful cries to this day.

The tracks of Ngagalil are represented in the sky by the four bright stars of Corvus. The tracks of Djowari may be seen as the four brightest stars in Delphinus.

Increase of eaglehawk.—About twenty miles east of Lagrange is a depression in the ground surrounding a native well. Around this are several stones which represent a number of *bugari* birds. The largest of these is an increase centre for *wolaguru* (wedge-tailed eagle or eaglehawk), and here an increase ceremony is performed at the end of the *pargana* or beginning of the *wilburu* season. The ceremony is performed by men, though women of the *wolaguru* totem may help. The ritual belongs to the Panaka-Paldjeri moiety.

A wallaby is killed for the ceremony, and after the performers have cleaned the ground around the stone the animal is eviscerated and the viscera rubbed upon the stone in order to tempt the spirit *wolaguru* within (Plate I, frontispiece). The remainder of the wallaby is subsequently eaten by the natives in the ordinary way.

The mythology associated with this ceremony is described as follows: Wolaguru was camped near the present increase centre. Bilari (pelican) and a number of other "coastal" birds came up, and started to abuse Wolaguru, who in turn insulted them. Bilari and Wolaguru fought, and the former struck the latter on the back with a club. Thus was established the Wolaguru increase centre.

Increase of nalgoo.—There is a centre for the increase of nalgoo near Cape Bossut. The ceremony is of an unusual type, being entirely carried out by women, under the direction of men. At the increase centre are a number of pebbles which are said to represent nalgoo. The women place the pebbles in their wooden dishes, and, holding the latter high in the air, allow the pebbles to fall into heaps on the ground, the dust being blown away from them by the wind as they fall, as does chaff in winnowing. A number of heaps are made in this way. It should be noted that this ceremony must be performed at a time when a westerly wind is blowing, so that the spirit nalgoo may be disseminated over the land. If the ceremony were performed in a south-east wind, they would be blown out to sea and the performance of the ceremony rendered futile.

We have referred to myths connected with increase ceremonies. But it must be emphasized that these form but a part of a much wider system of mythology. Of the many Karadjeri myths of *bugari* times, the majority are totemic, that is to say, they describe the activities of beings who were neither men nor animals,[1] but exhibited alternately the characters of both of these types of creature. This is a common feature of Australian mythology, and of primitive mythology generally. Some of the myths, however, concern mythical beings who are not identified with any natural species, and hence cannot be described as totemic. But one must remember that in the minds of the natives the two types of myth form part of an integrated whole—the legendary history of the aborigines. The sacred myths, which may not be told to women, are concerned mainly with cosmogony, and especially with the institution of the initiation ceremonies to be described presently.

Karadjeri myths have certain structural or stylistic characteristics, and very frequently, in concluding the recounting of a myth, informants offer a moralistic interpretation of the story. The most general form of the myths is as follows. The story opens with a certain state of affairs existing; this is indicated by the natives by describing one day's events and then repeating them for successive days, the series of activities being repeated in exactly the same form over and over again. For the sake of brevity this has been abbreviated by describing the events as occurring every day or on a number of occasions. Given, then, this existing state of affairs, a *dénouement* occurs, generally resulting in the death of one of the characters. By this means some element of either the natural or the moral order is established. This is the most general form of the myths, though variations sometimes occur. A common feature of Karadjeri myths is their association with specific landmarks, such as stones, hills, creeks, or even trees, the traditional institution of increase centres being a particular example of this principle.

Among the Karadjeri the mythology of the heavens plays an important part in the beliefs connected with immortality. It is generally believed that the sky consists of a dome of a very hard substance (rock or shell), the stars representing the spirits of dead men and women, including mythological characters. As to the stars themselves, there is considerable difference of opinion; some say that they are just globes of light, but others believe that they are individual nautilus shells with the fish alive inside them.

[1] The word "animal", as used here, includes birds, insects, reptiles and other natural species.

On the latter view shooting stars are caused by the death of the fish and the dropping of its shell.[1]

The natives think of the various stars in terms of the time of year at which they are clearly visible (that is, when they appear well above the horizon) during the early part of the night. They realize, however, that they are, generally speaking, actually visible for a total period of several months, and can generally give with a fair degree of accuracy the time of the heliacal rising of any large star.

From the extraordinarily rich totemic mythology of the Karadjeri a few traditions may be selected as examples.

Myth of Pardjida and Langgur.—Pardjida (native cat) cut off the hair of Langgur (opossum) with a sharp tomahawk. Langgur made a stick for winding hair, and using it proceeded to make opossum wool thread from his own hair. All night he twirled the stick, the noise of which prevented Pardjida from sleeping. One day Pardjida became so annoyed that he struck Langgur on the chest with a fire-stick made of wood of a yellowish-brown colour. Langgur then took a burning stick of another kind of wood and struck Pardjida with it, the ash marking his body with white spots. The ash of this wood is said to be highly corrosive. So to this day male opossums have a brown mark on their chests and native cats are covered with white spots. The spirit of Pardjida may be seen in the sky as the star Alpha of the constellation Cygnus and that of Langgur as Capella in Auriga. The tracks of Langgur may be seen as several pairs of faint stars between Auriga and Taurus.

Myth of Yalwa and Nalgumidi.—Yalwa (rat kangaroo) and Nalgumidi (bandicoot) decided to go out collecting vegetable food. They went in different directions, and Nalgumidi collected a quantity of *runggur* (a root) while Yalwa obtained *baru* (another root). Each cooked what he had collected separately, and when the food was ready to eat, they both came together in the one camp. Yalwa gave Nalgumidi some *baru*, but Nalgumidi did not give Yalwa any *runggur*, returning instead the *baru* which he had

---

[1] There are, however, two other theories as to shooting stars. According to one of these, a shooting star indicates that an important man has died, the direction of the meteorite indicating where the death has occurred. The other version is that shooting stars represent fragments of the dead body of Marela (a *bugari* culture hero) falling from the tree in which he was buried. Every star in the heavens represents the spirit of some deceased man or woman, while the more important stars and even constellations represent certain objects and persons mentioned in the myths. Theoretically, of course, all such individuals have a place in the sky, but the stars to which they correspond are known in a limited number of cases only.

received from him. Yalwa did not see the way in which he had
been deceived. The same thing occurred every day, Nalgumidi
always keeping the *runggur* to himself and returning Yalwa's *baru*.

One night Nalgumidi accidentally allowed some of his *runggur*
to become mixed with the *baru* which he returned to Yalwa.
When he tasted it, the latter knew that he had been deceived,
and, seizing a stick, he chased Nalgumidi off to the south, where
they both died.

Kunbalubalu myth. — A man had a dingo called Kunbalubalu,
which he used to send to chase kangaroos. Each day the dingo
caught a kangaroo, and the man used to send the dingo out again,
but he never caught more than one each day. This used to annoy
the man, who refused to give him water or the viscera of the
kangaroos which he caught. When a camp was made at night he
used to cover up the well with logs so that the dingo could not
obtain any water to drink. In the morning, however, he used to
give him a small drink of water and send him out again. One
night, the well having been covered up as usual, Kunbalubalu
feeling very hot and thirsty went prowling in search of water.
Some distance from the camp he smelt water and, having located
it, slaked his thirst.

In the morning his master awoke and missed him. Finding
tracks he followed and finally found him. Kunbalubalu attacked
his master, knocking him down and finally killing him. Kunbalubalu thus gave the tradition that men must be kind to their
dogs, must always feed them and give them water to drink.

Djarabalbal myth.—Djarabalbal (top-knot pigeon) was a woman
who used to go out collecting food, but she used to spend a great
amount of time tying her hair up into a pointed knot. As a result
she never collected much food, and this occasioned a considerable
amount of comment among the men at the camp. One day they
followed her and saw the way in which she wasted her time. They
frightened her, and she flew up into the sky, thus giving the tradition that women must not waste time when collecting food, and
also that they must not arrange their hair as men sometimes do,
that is, by tying it up into a pointed structure which is not unlike
the crest of the top-knot pigeon. The spirit of Djarabalbal is
represented by one of the smaller stars in the constellation Auriga.

Kargidja myth. — A man Kargidja (a kind of hawk) used to
approach the camp of a number of people, and, seeing smoke a
little way off, would ask who was camped there. When told that it

was the camp of a menstruating woman, he would approach and have sexual intercourse with her. One day the woman saw him coming near and cried out. This frightened Kargidja, who flew away and died at Birdinapa Point, where he became a stone. Thus arose the tradition that men must not have intercourse with a menstruating woman.

Bardarangalu myth. — A mother Bardarangalu (snake) was always sick, every day and every night. Every night she died and her two sons buried her. The boys used to go away and leave her in the ground, and she would shed her skin and follow them to their camp. The old woman's grave was near the water, and one day a frog came out of the water and saw the dead woman in the ground. He sat on the grave and croaked several times, at the same time wriggling about on his buttocks, and after this the old woman did not rise again. This was the origin of death.

Yindjiyindji myth. — Yindjiyindji (mantis) used to talk all the time, thus producing the south-east wind. The result was that this wind used to blow throughout the year. A number of people wanted to kill him on this account. They used to cut him up into a number of small pieces and leave him to die. But he always recovered and continued to make the south-east wind.

One day a man threw a spear at Yindjiyindji's scrotum. The spear struck its mark and killed him. As a result of this the south-east wind now blows during the cold season only, and not all the year round, as before.

Initiation

Like most Australian tribes, the Karadjeri preserve a strict differentiation between women and children on the one hand and fully initiated men on the other. From the time when he is about twelve years of age until two or three years after marriage every male [1] native is called upon to take part in a series of ceremonies by which his status in the tribe is progressively altered from that of a child to that of a fully initiated man. Even after the last initiation ceremony, the introduction to the *midedi* feast, the respect accorded to a man continues to increase until he becomes a *worara*, a term used to describe the elders of the tribe and also its mythical ancestors of the *bugari* "dream times" when the world was created.

[1] In the case of females there is but little ceremonial, though here also status is determined to a large extent by age. The bearing of children also adds to a woman's prestige, and releases her from certain food restrictions.

Throughout his initiation a youth is constantly instructed in various traditions of the tribe. These consist primarily of certain sacred myths, which he must never relate to women or younger men, and of injunctions to avoid irregular sexual unions.

The most important ceremony connected with initiation is the rite of circumcision, which may be carried out in either of two different ways, each having a somewhat different mythology and ritual associated with it. The other ceremonies have to a large extent fallen into disuse owing to European influence, but it rarely happens that a boy is not circumcised.

The two methods of circumcision may be referred to as the southern tradition and northern tradition respectively, but we shall consider only the first of these.[1] The institution of initiation ceremonies is intimately associated with the cosmogony, and we shall therefore consider initiation mythology in connection with the wider subject of the legendary institution of the world in general. Throughout the cosmogony incidents occur which offer a parallel to details of the initiation ritual as carried out at the present time, though every rite does not possess a parallel mythological incident. If questioned on these aspects of the ceremonies, the natives say that the ritual was carried out in such and such a way in *bugari* times, and must therefore be repeated in an identical manner, though they cannot always give details. Thus the entire ritual of initiation may be said to have been instituted in *bugari* times, many of the rites being accounted for in detail.

The cosmogony consists of a series of incidents which are related in no very definite order. A song is associated with each of these incidents, but the order of the singing of these songs is not fixed. Nevertheless, it is possible to distinguish a general outline in the myths, which is as follows: before the time of two brothers called the Bagadjimbiri there was nothing at all—no trees, no water, no people, no animals, and so on. They made these things, and instituted the world as it is at present. The two brothers arose in territory belonging to the Nyangamada tribe, to the south of the Karadjeri, and travelled north-east, following a route parallel to the coast, several miles inland; in the vicinity of Broome they turned back and came down the coast, making frequent trips inland, thus preserving a zigzag course as far as Nyangamada territory, where they died.

The following is a very abbreviated account of some of the

[1] For a comparison of the two traditions, see Piddington (2).

incidents in the Bagadjimbiri myth: When they first arose from the ground, the Bagadjimbiri were two dingos [1]; they later became gigantic men, reaching up to the sky, and when they died their bodies became water-snakes, while their spirits became the Magellan Clouds.

When the Bagadjimbiri arose, it was just before the twilight of the first day; they heard the note of a small bird, which regularly sings at this time, and saw that it was twilight. Before this they knew nothing. They subsequently saw all animals and plants, to which they gave the appropriate names.

One of the Bagadjimbiri micturated, a function which, of course, had never been performed before. When his brother observed him, he became curious and imitated him. Now black fellows can relieve themselves in this way. They saw a star and the moon, both of which they named.

The Bagadjimbiri then travelled north-east parallel to the coast, instituting various geographical features in the territory of the Mangala, Djualing, Nyigini and Yauor tribes. The Bagadjimbiri saw a number of men and women who were organized in the correct way; the Bagadjimbiri gave them their relationship terms.

Over the whole area covered by them the Bagadjimbiri instituted the water supply in the following manner. Whenever they were thirsty they would look for water and, finding none, since none existed before their time, they would hold their *pirmal* in a perpendicular position and drive them down into the ground. As a result of this a spring or well of fresh water would appear.

Before the time of the Bagadjimbiri men and women had no genital organs. The Bagadjimbiri found a white *pordi* (an elongated toadstool) and a *panora* (bulb-shaped fungus). They saw a number of men and women who, like themselves, had no genital organs. They picked a gum-tree leaf, put it to their mouths and breathed upon it; they then cut the *panora* with the sharp edge of the leaf in the shape of a vulva, and at once all the women were provided with genital organs. Next they cut the *pordi* in the shape of a penis, and at once all the men acquired genital organs. At another time they saw sponges resembling a woman's breast and called them by the same name (*ngama*).

---

[1] Though the legend later tells of their mother, the native insist that the Bagadjimbiri were not born in the usual way, but simply arose out of the ground.

The Bagadjimbiri collected some wattle seed and ate it raw.
They knew that this was wrong and laughed. Then one of the
brothers tried cooking the seed, so that now men may cook their
food. From the top of a hill near the sea they saw a large stingaree,
and threw a *pirmal* at it. The *pirmal* went right through its
body and emerged at the other end, this being the origin
of the sting in its tail. In the territory of the Muli horde
the Bagadjimbiri left a hitting stick. Blackfellows subsequently
found the hitting stick and were thereafter able to make
this type of implement. The hitting stick lost by the Bagadjimbiri is represented in the sky by the pointers of the Southern
Cross.

The Bagadjimbiri instituted the initiation ceremonial associated
with the southern tradition, and used for the first time the sacred
objects employed in the ritual, the stone circumcision knife, bull-
roarer and the large *pirmal*; using the circumcision knife they
carved the characteristic markings on the bull-roarer and *pirmal*.
The Bagadjimbiri differentiated the Nadja and Nangu dialects
of the Karadjeri language.

The Bagadjimbiri saw Tabaring (a snake man) and sang a song
to produce snakes. This song may be sung once only.[1] If sung
more often it might cause someone to be bitten by a snake. In a
similar way the song by which the Bagadjimbiri instituted the
hurricane or "willy-willy" may be sung only once, and that only
when there is good reason, for example, when it is being told to a
young man at initiation.

The Bagadjimbiri had very long hair. They shook their heads
and pulled out a number of their hairs, one of which they gave
to each local group. They saw a native cat man called Ngariman,
and gave him a number of hairs from their heads, which may be
seen at the present time as the black fur on the tails of native cats.
When they saw Ngariman's buttocks they laughed; this annoyed
Ngariman, who, together with some others, killed the Bagadjimbiri with spears. This happened in Nyangamada territory and
Dilga, the mother of the Bagadjimbiri, who was camped near
Lagrange, smelt the south-east wind and detected the odour of
decomposing flesh. Milk came out of her breasts and flowed
underground to the place where the Bagadjimbiri had died.
There it emerged, drowning the murderers and bringing the two
heroes back to life again. Their spirits subsequently went up

---

[1] In contradistinction to other songs which may be repeated *ad nauseam*.

into the sky to form the Magellan Clouds, while their bodies became water-snakes.[1]

Having presented the mythological background of initiation ritual, we may now turn to an examination of the ceremonies themselves. These consist of a series of rites which correspond to stages through which a male individual must pass before he becomes a fully adult member of the tribe. Most of the ceremonies are considered by the natives to be of minor importance, and all except circumcision and the introduction of the *mididi* feast have, generally speaking, fallen into disuse.

Milya rite.—At about the age of twelve a boy is taken into the bush and decorated from head to foot with human blood. About two weeks later a hole is bored through his nasal septum, and the quill of some large bird (wedge-tailed eagle, bustard or pelican) is inserted in the hole. This is worn by the boy for a few weeks and then removed, though a quill is occasionally worn in later life as a decoration. After the milya rite a boy is called *nimamu*, until he goes on his "walk-about" before circumcision, which takes place a year or two later.

Circumcision.—When the time has come for a boy to be circumcised, a man who stands in the relation of elder brother to him (preferably his own elder brother) asks the novice's father's consent to the operation. Though the boy's father is expected to give his permission, it would be impossible to circumcise the boy should he refuse to do so. After the usual discussions the old men agree that the ceremony must take place, and the women are told that the boy is to be made a man, though they do not, of course, know what is to happen.

When it is thus agreed that a boy should be circumcised, a number of members of neighbouring hordes assemble at the boy's camp. The novice is told to sit down by a fire alone. A man who may stand in any relation (except that of father) to him, but who must not be a "near" [2] relative, comes up behind him as he sits

---

[1] There are several versions of the death of the Bagadjimbiri. In most of these their revivification is not mentioned. In the simplest version they simply died of weariness and old age, while other forms of the legend relate how Dilga drowned the murderers either with water, using her digging stick in the same way as the Bagadjimbiri used their *pirmal*, or with her own menstrual blood.

[2] The distinction between near (*lani*) and distant (*kadjeri*) relatives plays an important part in initiation ritual, though it is difficult to fix the precise meaning of the terms. Part of the initiation ritual devolves upon relatives who must be closely related to the novice and part upon persons who must not be in any way closely related. Here, as elsewhere in Australia, the terms "near" and "distant" possess at once a genealogical and a geographical significance.

beside the fire and, throwing his arms around the novice, drags him away, telling him that he is now a *malulu*. This rite, which is termed *badurmana*, may be performed by a JAMBARDU [1] who comes from a nearby horde, such a person being regarded as the most suitable relative to perform the function in question—any other relative performing the rite must come from a distant horde.

The *malulu* is then led by his *badurmana* relative to an old man who weeps with him while everybody assembles. He is then taken to a cleared place where everybody is assembled, sitting closely packed together on the ground, all facing in one direction. The men sit in front and the women behind, certain types of relative being assigned special positions. Thus all those related to the *malulu* as BABALA or KALUJI sit in front of the group; next come his YAGU, TABULU (including his own father, who must be present) and KAGA. A similar arrangement exists among the women; nearest to the men (that is, in the front of the women's group) sit the boy's *kami* and *kabuju*, and behind them his *kurdaing*, *tabulu* and *dalu*.

The novice is taken to his nearest relatives in turn, and they weep over him, a special procedure being adopted. The boy sits on the ground with his back to the relative in question, while the latter places his or her arms around the novice's waist at the same time weeping copiously. Sometimes the person who is weeping will reach for a boomerang or other implement which happens to be lying handy and will strike his head with it, wailing at the top of his voice until someone comes up and, seizing the boomerang, prevents him from inflicting further pain upon himself. The women are particularly vigorous in this self-mutilation.

Each of the individuals to whom the *malulu* is taken must weep, though the emotion exhibited tends to be more formal and of briefer duration in the case of more distant relatives.

Immediately after this weeping ceremony there is a ritual exchange of vegetable food between the members of the boy's local group and the visitors who are present—meat or fish, however, is not exchanged, each party keeping their own supply to themselves. The *malulu* himself is led aside and eats food with one or two younger boys. He must not sit directly upon the ground, but upon leaves laid down for the purpose. Similarly, when he sleeps at night, he must have a couch of leaves and must rest his

---

[1] The meaning of this and other classificatory kinship terms employed here may be ascertained by reference to Fig. 7, p. 123.

head upon a pile of weapons, boomerangs, shields and hitting sticks.

The above ceremonies take place late in the afternoon, and, when night falls, the *malulu* is led away into the bush, where he hears a number of sacred songs for the first time. This ceremony (called *yuna*) acts as a preliminary to the all-night singing which immediately precedes circumcision.

The next morning the *malulu* is again taken to the bush, where a number of men sit around a cleared place, the boy being led aside while preparations are being made. Several men tie ligatures around their arms and pierce a vein in their forearms with a pointed wallaby bone, the blood so produced being allowed to flow into a bark dish. The *malulu*, who is completely naked, is brought up and told to stand over a small fire upon which green leaves have been placed, the smoke enveloping the boy. He then sits down on the ground, his eyes being covered by a man's hand and bark or leaves being placed in his ears. He is forced to drink blood from the bark dish, while a medicine man rubs his abdomen to prevent him from vomiting. While he is drinking the blood he is exhorted not to vomit lest he should offend a spirit (*miruru*), who would kill his father, mother and sisters. After the boy has consumed a quantity of blood, his TABULU, KAGA, BABALA and YAGU also drink some. It is said that the boy believes that the blood will kill him until he sees the older men drinking it. During the whole rite there is much teasing of the boy, who is asked whether he knows the name of the blood, and is held up to derision because he does not reply.

After the drinking of the blood several men loosen the ligatures around their arms and allow the blood to squirt out, directing the streams on to the head of the boy, who sits with a shield resting upon his legs. When a considerable amount of blood has thus been allowed to flow over the novice's body, the latter is sprinkled with powdered charcoal and the blood on it allowed to dry.

The *malulu* then receives a number of human-hair girdles lent to him by various relatives, but these must be placed around his waist by a KADJERI JAMBARDU. The party then move off to the place where the women are waiting and the close relatives of the *malulu* weep over him as before. Again he sits apart for a while with some younger boys, after which he returns to the main group of his relatives, with whom he eats vegetable food— he may not eat meat or fish.

When this ritual meal is concluded, a number of women gather round the *malulu*. One of these who is a *lani kabali, jambardu* or *kami* (the first of these is the most appropriate relative) to the boy gives him a lighted fire-stick, telling him that he must go away as a *malulu* should, observing all the obligations imposed upon him. The boy is told that the purpose of the fire-stick is to light a fire in which his penis is to be burned, and the women are told the same thing.

The novice then sets out upon a journey, or "walk-about". He is accompanied by a party of men who may stand in any relation to him, but who must not be *lani* relatives. The man who specially cares for the boy, instructs him, leads him about and so on is a KADJERI JAMBARDU.

The party visits a number of camps, and at each there is a considerable amount of ceremonial in which the organization of the sections into inter-marrying pairs (*m'reram'rera*) plays an important part. On meeting the members of distant hordes, the novice is required to go through a rite called *ngambal*, that is, a ceremonial embrace in which the abdomens of the two parties are pressed together.[1]

The *malulu* is absent from his own camp for about twenty-four days, during which time he travels about one hundred miles up or down the coast. During this trip the *malulu* is not allowed to speak. If he wants anything he must make a mumbling sound to attract attention, and then indicate by gestures what he wants. Indeed, throughout the whole series of ceremonies, from the *badurmana* rite until after he returns from his seclusion in the bush after circumcision, his attitude is one of complete passivity. While he is a *malulu* he never moves without being led by the hand and moves about with bowed head, his face being completely devoid of expression. If it were not for the readiness with which he responds to instructions, the impression created would be that of a mental defective.

On the return journey the novice is joined by people from those hordes which he passes on the way, to whom we shall refer, for the sake of brevity, as the visitors. The men of this group perform dances around the novice at intervals along the route, and when any camp is approached it is by a series of these dances.

When the *malulu* and the visitors approach the former's horde,

---

[1] This rite may also be carried out with material objects (such as bull-roarers), which are pressed against the abdomen of the individual who is required to *ngambal* them.

the boy is once more decorated with blood, and also with red and yellow ochre. When the members of the novice's local group, whom we may term the hosts, observe the approach of the visitors, they gather on the ceremonial ground, closely packed together and facing in the direction from which the visitors are to approach. The arrangement of relatives has already been described. As the *malulu* approaches, a small group of his more distant female relatives belonging to his own *m'reram'rera* form two lines on either side of and to the rear of the group on the ground. These women sing and dance, their performance being said to be, and bearing every resemblance to, play—certainly it is not taken very seriously. The individuals sitting on the ground, however, preserve a serious mien and appear completely to ignore the laughter and horseplay which are going on behind them. As the visitors approach, several women of the party of the hosts rush out with bushes in their hands—these they wave in the faces of the visitors in an attempt to prevent them from coming close. There are many expressions of hostility between the two groups, culminating in a sort of mock fight between the women of the boy's group and the visitors. The former throw handfuls of vegetable food in the direction of the visitors, while the latter retaliate by throwing boomerangs in the direction of the hosts seated upon the ground. These boomerangs generally fly off to the side, but occasionally someone is struck, in which case a genuine fight, though never a very serious one, ensues.

As the boy is led up, the playing of the women gives way to weeping and vigorous self-mutilation. The *malulu* is led to the group of his BABALA on the ground, where he sits in front of his own TABULU, who weeps with him.

After this the visitors again approach and throw down presents of boomerangs before the hosts, who reciprocate by giving them vegetable food, at the same time saying that the supply is quite inadequate and apologizing for the deficiency. But the visitors must protest that they have been offered more than they need. This discussion, which is purely ceremonial, takes place quite independently of the quantity of food actually provided.

After some further ceremonial, all the visitors (including women) seize the boy and move towards the *yuna* ground where the circumcision is to take place, but the women go a short distance only, after which they return to the camp, where they join the other women in a series of dances which lasts for several hours. All the initiated male relatives of the *malulu* go with him to the *yuna* ground, where most of them remain all night.

The night at the *yuna* is spent in singing and dancing, in which neither the boy nor his father takes part. The dances are of the spectacular type, several men at a time giving pantomimic representations of various mythological events. During the night one or two new bull-roarers, which have been specially prepared for the novice, are passed round, and *ngambal*, the *malulu* being covered over while this is done.

Just before dawn the boy is led away into the bush while preparations are made for the operation. In these the novice's father takes no part. A group of men standing to the boy in the relation of BABALA (*lani* or *kadjeri*) choose from three to five operators, who must not be closely related to the novice nor belong to his horde, and cannot under any circumstances be his KAGA.

The stone circumcision knife is passed round, and *ngambal* by everyone, after which it is fixed to a spear-thrower and is sharpened.

The operators retire some distance from the main group, while the close relatives of the boy lie down in a prone position and hide their faces. Two men standing to the novice in the relation of YAGU lean over, resting upon their shields, which are held perpendicularly to the ground. Under the arch so formed two or three other men kneel, thus forming a human table upon which the novice is placed in a supine position with his legs pointing away from the shields of his YAGU. His human-hair girdles are removed, while one man places a hand over his mouth. His eyes are also covered. The operators, acting in turn, then make an incision around the base of the penis, and keep on cutting until all the skin has been removed from the organ. There is much weeping on the part of the boy's close relatives.

After the operation the novice sits with his YAGU and BABALA and is shown his circumcised penis. The blood, of which there is little, drips on to a shield which is placed on the ground. The initiate sits with bowed head and closed eyes while the operators file past him weeping. They drop boomerangs as presents before him and then leave the *yuna* ground, and the initiate is told their names (which he did not know before). Thereafter he must for a certain period observe a special relationship towards all the men who have operated on him, and must not under any circumstances mention their names.

After the departure of the operators several young men bring up and swing the bull-roarers, which are then shown to the novice for the first time. The swinging of the bull-roarer is for the natives an extremely sacred proceeding; it is always carried out by young men, following the tradition established by the Bagadjimbiri. Starting slowly, it is swung more and more rapidly, the performer himself turning round and round in order to secure a better effect.

At the conclusion of the swinging the bull-roarer is not allowed to fall on the ground, but the string is shortened while it is still swinging and it is held for a moment vertically by the string, still spinning before the performer's abdomen. While still spinning rapidly it is *ngambal,* and if the carved side comes into contact with the abdomen the swinging is concluded. If, however, the back of the bull-roarer happens to come to rest against the skin, the swinging must be repeated until a correct *ngambal* is obtained.

When the blood upon his penis is dry, the novice is shown the circumcision knife. At first he is teased about it, being told that it is goanna fat, but finally he is told its correct name. This concludes the ritual associated with circumcision, and the visitors return to their respective districts. The initiate remains in the bush for several weeks, being forbidden to go near any women, though he may go hunting with the men. During this period the novice is for the first time shown the method of producing human blood. A pointed wallaby bone is stuck in the ground before the novice, surrounded by human-hair string used in swinging the bull-roarer. The initiate's eyes are covered for a moment and then uncovered and he is told to watch. A man sits down facing him and very slowly ties the ligature on his arm. There is much teasing, the novice being told that the man has a maggot in his arm which must be extracted, and the whole proceeding gives the impression of being prolonged as much as possible. Finally the vein is pierced and everybody, including the novice, drinks the blood.

On the day of the novice's return from the bush he sits on bushes and is decorated with blood in preparation for his ceremonial return to the main camp. He then stands holding a spear upright while a JAMBARDU dresses him in a belt and hair-string pubic tassel. He is told not to allow the women to see his circumcised penis or to associate with women or children too much for two or three days after his return.

Meanwhile, at the camp the women and children are covered over with bushes, being forbidden to look up. The initiate is brought up to the accompaniment of the swinging of bull-roarers, and is told to sit down holding a hitting stick behind his neck at right angles to the direction in which he is facing. He sits in this way for some time while the branches under which the women and children are lying are beaten with sticks by several men. After the bull-roarers have been taken away, the women are told to look up and see the newly initiated youth, after which they weep over him and give him food.

Subincision.—After his return from seclusion in the bush, a youth is termed *miangu* for a period of one or two years, after which he may be subincised. This rite is regarded as a minor ceremony, occupying one day only, and very few neighbours are summoned. In the morning songs are sung and at about noon the novice is taken into the bush. Two men lie prone on some bushes and the boy is placed upon them. The operator, whose relationship to the boy is limited in the same way as in circumcision, makes a small slit in the urethra. The blood from the wound is mixed with red ochre or charcoal, and with this mixture sacred markings are made on the youth's back. He is then decorated with human-hair-string belts, which he wears crossed over his shoulders, and a *lara* (an ornament resembling a bull-roarer in shape, but devoid of any hole) is thrust through his headband in a horizontal position at the back of his head. The initiate, who is now called *djamununggur*, is then taken back to the camp. Bull-roarers are not used, nor do the women weep.

Transition to the Bungana stage.—A short time after subincision a young man ties around the upper arm of the *djamununggur* a ligature of opossum wool, which is worn very tightly for about a day. While he is wearing this ligature thus tightly tied, the youth is called *kambil*. When the arm-band is loosened, the youth wears a pearl-shell pubic pendant, for the first time, and thus becomes a *bungana*, a stage at which he remains for several years.

Laribuga ceremony.—About half-way through the *bungana* stage the youth is introduced for the first time to the *laribuga* ceremony held during the *pargana* season and said to have been instituted by Djui. The *bungana* is taken into the bush by the men, and together with other young men he climbs a blood gum tree while the old men stand around the bole and sing a sacred song, the meaning of which is not known, about the tree. The song concludes with an exhalation, and when the singing is concluded the young men come down from the tree and a series of dances are held nearby.

Biliangu feast.—The next ceremony to be shown to the *bungana* is the *biliangu* feast, a ceremony instituted by two culture heroes of the sea. The *biliangu* feast consists primarily of fish, though this may be supplemented by other forms of food. A large quantity of fish is caught in a barricade built across one of the ramifications of a salt-water creek. The fish is taken away into the bush, where it is eaten at a ceremonial feast, the women being forbidden to attend.

Kurangada ceremony.—The ritual associated with the *kurangada* ceremony may be shown to a young man who has reached the status of *bungana*, but it may be shown in the same way to a married man who has not witnessed it before. The ceremony is performed at a place where large bull-roarers are kept, being under the care of two or three old men. The novice is led up with his eyes covered, and sits with one of these old men, while the men standing around bend over him and stroke his shoulders with bull-roarers. The various sacred objects are then arranged in bundles and *ngambal* by the novice, after which they are laid before him, and food which has been provided by the novice is placed with them. The food is *ngambal* by the old man, who then takes a small pellet of it, which he rubs upon the bull-roarers and then places in the mouth of the novice. The old man and the novice eat the food together, and after this the novice is shown certain other sacred objects and is told of their magical properties.

Marriage.—After he has been a *bungana* for several years the young man asks permission to marry. Neighbouring hordes are not summoned, but all members of the young man's own horde are gathered together. The youth puts on all the ornaments which he has received during his initiation, and is painted with a mixture of grease and red ochre. He is told that this is *bala* and is the same as menstrual blood, which is called by this name. A few weeks later the *kulakula*, as the man is now called, may, if a woman has previously been promised to him, go to her horde and claim her.

Mididi feast.—After he has been married for one or two years, a man is introduced for the first time to the *mididi* feast, when he is shown for the first time a series of places where the older men keep the sacred objects known as *pirmal*. These are preserved in a small bough shelter raised from the ground, where they are kept with the carved side downwards. Great care is taken lest the white ants should get to them. They are covered with a mixture of grease and red ochre, which is renewed from time to time, special care being taken of the carved side.

When a novice is being shown the *pirmal* for the first time he is left with the main party some distance from the sacred place where the *pirmal* are kept, while a few men go ahead to prepare them. All the men with the exception of the novice then decorate themselves with powdered charcoal and place leaves in their head and arm-bands. When it is announced that all is ready, the novice is led along a bush track towards the place where the *pirmal* are kept. The novice walks with bowed head and must keep his eyes closed except when he is told to look up. One man walks in front leading him by the hand, and another walks behind the novice with his hand on the latter's shoulder. The remaining members of the party walk, or rather trot, for the journey is made at a slow run, beside and behind the novice, at the same time giving vent to staccato sounds resembling a dog's bark.

Along the path traversed by the party are stationed men holding *pirmal* in various statuesque attitudes. (For example, as illustrated in Plate III.) When one of these is reached, the novice is told to look up and is asked what it is. He says nothing, and, having been told to close his eyes again, is led on to the next figure.

When the party arrives at the bough shelter, they find the *pirmal* laid on a couch of bushes with the carved sides towards the ground. The men sit around these and turn them over one by one, the novice sitting with bowed head while a man immediately behind him holds his arms around his waist. There is a great amount of singing and talking, during which the novice is told of the institution of the *pirmal* by the Bagadjimbiri.

After some time the food which has been prepared is ceremonially placed upon the heap of *pirmal*. At this point in the ceremony there is a remarkable change in the attitude of the participants. They still appear excited, but the hitherto predominant tension gives way to relaxation. There is much laughter as the *midedi* feast is eaten. The party, previously grouped in a solemn circle around the *pirmal*, breaks up into small groups of men eating, talking and laughing together, while some renew their decorations, the novice being decorated with powdered charcoal for the first time in the ceremony.

When the *midedi* is finished the *pirmal* are replaced in their bough shelter, and the men then return to the place where some old women have been preparing more food, and another feast is held there. When the men appear, the women who are sitting

PLATE III

DISPLAY OF PIRMAL, KARADJERI TRIBE

around the food which they have prepared retire to another clearing about twenty yards distant and eat some food, while the men have another feast together.

After being shown the sacred objects at one place, the novice is subsequently taken to all the other centres of the *pirmal* cult in the vicinity of his own horde territory. At each centre the *midedi* feast is repeated, though much of the ritual described above is omitted, and the emotional atmosphere is not nearly so tense as when a man is being shown the *pirmal* for the first time.

11. *Bibliographical Commentary*

In addition to the specifically primitive peoples of Asia, certain rural communities have been studied by social anthropologists, for example Fei (1) and Embree (1). The reindeer peoples of north-eastern Asia are discussed in Forde (1) and the Kazaks in the same work and also in Murdock (1). As examples of ethnographic records of the primitive tribes of India and Burma may be cited Gorer (1), Elwin (1), Fürer-Haimendorf (1 and 2), and Stevenson (1). The latter work is an excellent account of the economics and social life of the Chins. The Todas are described at length in Rivers (1), but the shorter account of them in Murdock (1) should prove adequate for most students.

An extensive survey of the cultures of Malaysia is contained in Cole (1). Both Forde (1) and Murdock (1) provide descriptions of the Semang. Radcliffe-Brown (1) gives an ethnographic account of the Andaman Islanders and an interpretation of their beliefs and ceremonial customs which has become a landmark in the history of anthropological theory. Firth (13) gives an account of the fishing industry of Malaysia as it affects a coastal community of the Malay peninsula.

General surveys of Pacific peoples are contained in Keesing (2 and 3). Among the many accounts of Polynesian peoples may be cited Firth (5, 8 and 10), Hogbin (2) and Mead (1). A general survey of the place of religion in social life in Central Polynesia is given in Piddington (4). Many valuable studies, notably those by Sir Peter Buck, of Polynesian cultures are contained in the publications of the Bishop Museum, some of which are cited, together with the records of earlier observers, in the bibliographies of Williamson (1 and 2).

As far as Melanesia is concerned, reference should be made to the accounts of various aspects of Trobriand Island culture con-

tained in Malinowski (1–5), to the account of Malaita in Hogbin
(5), of Malekula in Deacon (1), of Manam in Wedgwood (2–4)
and of Wogeo in Hogbin (7–10). An excellent account of the
place of sorcery in a Melanesian community is contained in
Fortune (2).

The best general introduction to the study of the Australian
aborigines is Elkin (3). The standard work on Australian kinship, an appreciation of which is essential to the full understanding of Australian communities, is Radcliffe-Brown (2). A valuable
ethnographic record and sociological analysis of the Murngin
tribe is contained in Warner (1). Kaberry (1) discusses the place
of women in Australian culture, and gives incidentally an
excellent impression of life among certain Kimberley tribes.
Spencer and Gillen (1) is a classic description of the Aranda, the
best known of Australian tribes, but the shorter account in
Murdock (1) should prove adequate. A valuable description of
the place of mythology in Aranda culture is given in Strehlow (1).
Specialist articles on various phases of Australian culture, too
numerous for citation, are to be found in the journal *Oceania*,
which also deals with Melanesian and Polynesian communities.
The preceding material on the Karadjeri tribe is taken from
articles in this journal by the writer, especially Piddington
(1 and 2).

CHAPTER IV

SOCIAL ORGANIZATION

1. Social Structure in Primitive Society

By **social organization** (or **social structure**) is meant the division of society into social groups, based upon conventionally standardized social relations between the individuals concerned. In civilized society, families, clubs, trade unions, religious sects, political parties and nations are examples of different kinds of social groups. It will be noticed that these differ according to whether, or to what extent, membership is *obligatory* or *voluntary*. A man cannot change his membership of the family into which he is born or adopted. There are numerous restrictions on changes of nationality. And in totalitarian countries there is no choice in regard to membership of political parties. On the other hand, a man is free to belong to any club, sporting association or recreational group, or alternatively not to belong to any. In modern democratic countries most social groups are of the voluntary type, and here we find the most striking contrast with primitive cultures in which the individual's place in the social structure is determined, in general, by such factors as kinship, locality and hereditary social class which cannot be changed except by certain special social mechanisms which occasionally occur.

Certain types of social grouping are widespread in primitive society, though they do not all occur everywhere, for the social structure of primitive society not only differs considerably from our own, but also varies from one primitive community to another. The most important types of social groups are those founded on:

1. Sex.
2. Age.
3. Kinship.
4. Locality.
5. Social status.
6. Political power.
7. Occupation.

8. Magico-religious functions.
9. Totemism.
10. Voluntary association.

Of these types of social grouping, those founded on *kinship* and *locality* are not only much more important in primitive society than among ourselves, but are more difficult for the European to understand, because they are based on different rules and customs in regard to, for example, marriage and descent. A number of technical terms are employed in social anthropology to define various primitive types of social grouping and the various prescribed or customary relationships between groups

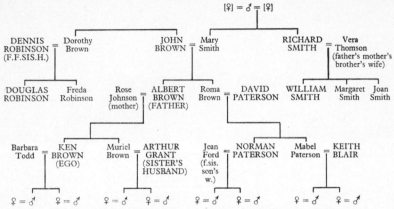

FIG. 3.—Hypothetical English Genealogy (Patrilineal Descent)

and individuals, while certain ordinary English words are given a specialized meaning. In addition, certain conventional forms, which might be described as the *orthography of kinship*, are employed (though by no means consistently) in representing genealogies [1] and describing kinship systems.

These may be illustrated by reference to the hypothetical English genealogy [2] given in Fig. 3. The following points should be noted:

[1] The collection of genealogies is now the recognized basis of the study of primitive systems of kinship terminology. Some early ethnographers followed the procedure of asking an informant in some form of *lingua franca*, or through an interpreter, such questions as: "What do you call your mother's brother?" Because of the complexities of the classificatory system which will be described in Section (4), this led to endless confusion and misunderstanding. The modern method is to write down the *names* of relatives first, and then ask what kinship terms are applied to them. This procedure, known as the *genealogical method*, was first introduced by Rivers in his study of the Todas.

[2] The names in this genealogy and in Fig. 5 are entirely fictitious, having been decided by juxtaposing Christian names and surnames selected at random from two separate lists.

(a) Conventional symbols for males and females ($\male$ = male, $\female$ = female, or $\triangle$ = male, $\bigcirc$ = female), for marriage (=) and for descent ($|$ or ⌐⌐).

(b) In writing either personal names or kinship terms, words representing *MALES* should be written in *CAPITALS*, and those representing *females* in *small letters*, an initial capital being optional in the case of females. This seems unnecessary in a European genealogy where Christian names almost always define the sex of the individual, but the situation is quite different when we come to primitive languages. In a Karadjeri genealogy, for example, the names Yuari and Yeni do not convey the necessary information unless we write them YUARI and Yeni (or yeni). Similarly, it seems pedantic in English to write FATHER and mother, but this usage immediately clarifies the meaning of the corresponding Karadjeri terms, TABULU and *kurdaing*.

(c) In genealogies it is useful to take one individual (called EGO or ego) as a point of reference (KEN BROWN in our genealogy) for the definition of kinship terms, which have been given in a few cases—a larger number would be superfluous in an English genealogy. Other particulars, such as rank, place of residence, membership of a clan or other social group, may be entered below the name of each individual, according to the purpose for which the genealogy is being compiled.

(d) In describing relationships or translating native kinship terms, we should always define the relationship exactly. Thus we should not use the term "brother-in-law" which is equivocal, but either "wife's brother" or "sister's husband", as the case may be. This defines the relationship precisely, as in the case of ARTHUR GRANT. The only terms which should be employed are: FATHER, mother, BROTHER, sister, SON, daughter, HUSBAND and wife. To write out relationships in full in these terms is often cumbrous (e.g. in the relationship of Vera Thomson), so they are often abbreviated. They can all be represented by their initial letter without confusion, except SON and sister. These may be represented as "SON" and "sis", as in the cases of DENNIS ROBINSON and Jean Ford.

(e) Symbols may be entered in genealogies when names are not known, as in the case of EGO'S SON and daughter.

(f) The names of, or symbols for, deceased persons are indicated in different ways by various writers, e.g. by writing names in italics, by attaching an asterisk, or putting them in square brackets. Probably the last of these is the most satisfactory. For example we could tell from our genealogy that EGO's f.m.m. is deceased.

(g) Order of birth of brothers and sisters, and order of marriage of spouses may be indicated by the order in which they appear in a genealogy, reading from left to right. Thus we know that Margaret Smith is older than Joan Smith and that EGO's F.M.F. was married to another woman (deceased) before he married EGO's f.m.m. Where this is not practicable, order of birth or marriage may be indicated by numerals in brackets under or after the names of the individuals concerned.

(h) Generations in lines of descent are described with reference to EGO by the following terms:

Second ascending	e.g. F.F.
First ascending	e.g. F.
Contemporary or Ego's . . .	e.g. B.
First descending	e.g. SON.
Second descending	e.g. SON's SON.

(i) Difficulties of space are frequently encountered in compiling genealogies. These are usually greater laterally than vertically. It sometimes becomes necessary to compile subsidiary genealogies, for example, in the case of several brothers and sisters or when a man is or has been married more than twice.

2. *The Family, Marriage and Kinship*

The basic and universal kinship grouping is the **family** (sometimes called the "individual" family to distinguish it from the "extended" family to be described later). In ordinary usage we are apt to employ the term "family" rather loosely, and with different meanings, as when we speak of a family tree, the Royal Family, or a family gathering. But in anthropology it refers to one type of grouping only—a man, his wife and the children resulting from the union or adopted into the family.[1] In the course of a normal lifetime a person belongs to two individual families—that in which he or she is a child (*family of orientation*) and that in which he or she is a parent (*family of procreation*).

All kinship derives from the existence of one or more families. People are said to be **kin** to each other when their relationship can be demonstrated genealogically. **Consanguineous** kin are those whose relationship, real or by adoption, can be demonstrated genealogically by descent. This is what is commonly called "blood relationship", but this term is unsatisfactory, because many primitive peoples do not think of kinship relationships in biological terms and because it rules out adoption, which is very common in some primitive societies. It is therefore better to employ the more specialized term "consanguineous". ALBERT BROWN, NORMAN PATERSON and Freda Robinson are consanguineous kinsfolk of EGO. **Affinal** kin are those whose relationship, real or by adoption, can be demonstrated genealogically by *marriage*, or by marriage *and* descent, e.g. Barbara Todd, DAVID PATERSON and ARTHUR GRANT.

The family exists in both monogamous and polygamous societies. **Monogamy** is a form of marriage in which no man may be married to more than one woman, and no woman to more than one man, at any one time. **Polygamy** is of two kinds, polygyny and polyandry. **Polygyny** is the system whereby a man may have more than one wife at one time. Because of the approximate equality in numbers between the sexes,[2] it is clear that polygyny can never be universal in any society. To take a hypothetical and unreal example, if the sexes are equal in number and half the men have two wives each, it is clear that the other half must remain unmarried. For this reason polygyny is always limited, either by legal, religious and customary rules or by practical difficulties. Thus, there may be restrictions as to the number of wives a man may have and the classes of men who may be polygynists. The Mohammedan faith limits the number of wives a man may have to four. In the Trobriand Islands only chiefs may be polygynous, and because of the customary giving of *urigubu* gifts by a man to his sister's husband, this ensures ample tribute, in the form of gifts based on kinship, for the chief. In

---

[1] Certain atypical or aberrant forms of the family will be considered later.
[2] Modified by differential birth and mortality rates and, in a few societies, by infanticide.

other societies (for example among the Australian aborigines and to a lesser extent among the Mende) polygyny is regulated by the practice of men marrying at a very much later age than women. This means that the older men are in general polygynous, while young men remain unmarried for a considerable time. The sexual restriction imposed by the latter custom is frequently to some extent offset by tolerated extra-marital licence, whereby youths are allowed from time to time to co-habit with the wives of older men.

Even when polygyny is not restricted by custom, it is often so *de facto* through the need for providing bride-price. This means that only men who can command a certain amount of wealth can be polygynous. The following figures given by Brown and Hutt (1, p. 107) for 4,054 members of the Hehe tribe indicate the incidence of polygyny in a society where the custom is widespread and is not legally restricted to men of rank or wealth:

Unmarried men	1,026, or 25·3 per cent.
Men with 1 wife	1,881, or 46·4 per cent.
Men with 2 wives	838, or 20·7 per cent.
Men with 3 wives	211, or 5·2 per cent.
Men with 4 wives	62, or 1·5 per cent.
Men with 5 wives	24 ⎫
Men with 6 wives	6 ⎬ together, 0·9
Men with 7 wives	4 ⎪ per cent.
Men with 9 wives	2 ⎭

Polyandry is the form of marriage in which a woman may have more than one husband at any one time.[1] True polyandry is extremely rare, and very little is known concerning polyandrous societies. The best-known example of polyandry is found among the Todas. Here a woman may be married to more than one man at one time. If the husbands live together, she resides with them and they share her sexual favours. If they live in different villages, the wife usually lives with each for a month at time, though there is considerable elasticity in the details of the arrangements.

We have said that the individual family exists in both monogamous and polygamous societies. Under polygyny, two or more families are linked by the fact that the same man is the father in

---

[1] Two varieties of polyandry have been distinguished: the *Tibetan, fraternal* or *adelphic* type, in which the husbands of the woman must be brothers, and the *Nayar* (or Nair) type, in which there need not be any relationship between them. But in view of the inadequacy of the ethnographic material, too much attention should not be paid to this distinction. It is probable that many, if not all, alleged examples of fraternal polyandry are in fact forms of cicisbeism (see below).

each, a situation diagrammatically represented in Fig. 4 (*b*). In polyandrous societies, we similarly find a number of individual families linked by the fact that the same woman is the mother in each.

A problem will at once occur to the reader: in polygynous societies the individual link between different mothers and their respective children is obvious from the fact of parturition, but in polyandrous communities, where the physiological father may be unknown, how is paternity established? The answer is that paternity is a social rather than a physiological fact.[1] It is socially established by legal or ceremonial observances. Thus, among the Todas paternity is determined by performance of the "bow

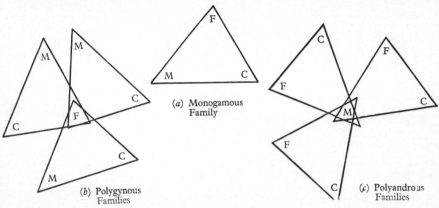

FIG. 4.—The Family in Monogamous and Polygamous Societies

F = Father, M = Mother, C = Children.   In all these cases each triangle represents a distinct individual family group, clearly recognized as such in the culture concerned.

and arrow" ceremony. When a polyandrous woman has been pregnant for about seven months, she goes into the woods accompanied by the man who is to be regarded as the father of her child. He cuts a niche in a tree and places in it a lighted lamp. The relatives of husband and wife assemble and participate in various rites, which link the coming child, not only to its father and mother, but also to their kinsfolk. The wife sits before the tree and the husband gives her a specially prepared bow and arrow, at the same time saying a special word, which is different for each clan. The child is thus affiliated to the clan of its father. The woman raises the bow and arrow to her forehead and gazes

[1] The same is actually true of maternity (e.g. in cases of adoption), but this need not detain us here.

at the lamp for some time. The relatives then return to the village for food, leaving the husband and wife to cook and share a meal in the woods. While some of the symbolism of this ceremony is not clear, we can discern how it singles out one husband (who is not necessarily the physiological father) who will assume the relationship of paternity to the child. Moreover, all subsequent children are regarded as those of this man until another husband performs the bow and arrow ceremony. This establishes the second husband's paternity for subsequent children until the ceremony is again performed by another man, and so on. Thus the mother becomes the centre of two or more individual families, each having its own distinct father whose paternity has been established by the bow and arrow ceremony (Fig. 4 c).

It should be noted that since polygyny is infinitely the more common form of polygamy, the terms "polygamous" and "polygamy" are commonly used to mean "polygynous" and "polygyny".

There is no evidence for the existence of what has been called "group marriage", under which a group of men are said to be married to a group of women. The suggestion that such a type of marriage exists, or ever existed, probably arises from a confusion between marriage on the one hand and forms of tolerated extra-marital sexual relations, which occur in many primitive societies, on the other. Such relations may be casual and temporary or may be more or less institutionalized and permanent. In this case they are termed *concubinage* and *cicisbeism*, the latter term denoting toleration of an extra-marital liaison of a married woman.[1] Concubinage, as it is known in civilized societies, is rarely found among primitive peoples, where women are usually married at a fairly early age. Its place is taken by polygyny, which differs from it in the greater permanence of the union, the continuous living together of the man and the woman concerned and the greater social status of the respective women and their children. But the difference is a relative one. In polygynous societies there are often marked differences between the status and privileges of co-wives and their children, and there are borderline cases which might be regarded either as polygyny or concubinage.

Cicisbeism is fairly common, and often forms part of the obligations of kinship, hospitality or bond-friendship. We have already noted its occurrence among the Eskimo. Similarly in Australia, men frequently lend their wives to kinsmen (married or un-

---

[1] From the Italian word *cicisbeo*, the recognized lover of a married woman.

married) either casually or at special tribal gatherings, such as the famous *pirrauru* ceremony of the Dieri tribe.[1] Such wife-lending among the aborigines is often not only permissive but obligatory—thus a man may force his wife, even against her will, to discharge her extra-marital obligations.

Cicisbeism was associated with bond friendship in Tahiti. Two men entered into a special relationship of pledged friendship, known as *tayo*, one of the obligations of which was that a man's wife was at the disposal of his *tayo*. Similar privileges were also extended to visitors, and one early European traveller who had been adopted as *tayo* by a high chief found himself in a difficult situation because he did not avail himself of the sexual privileges involved. This illustrates clearly the socially recognized and obligatory character of the relationship. Apart from the relationship of *tayo* and the obligations of hospitality, the Tahitians expected their wives to remain faithful.

While the motives dominant in the above examples are social or ceremonial, cicisbeism is often allowed for various practical reasons. Thus, among the Mende, where men tend to be much older than their wives, women often find it impossible to have children by their own husbands. In polygynous Mende households the latter sometimes allow their sons to have access to their wives, though no son would be allowed to do this with his own mother. Again, in the Marquesas, a chief might have in his retinue an official known as his "fire-maker", who, in addition to performing services for the chief, was, in the latter's absence, the official guardian of his wife's virtue. As a reward he was allowed the enjoyment of that which he had to protect, thus preventing promiscuous infidelity.

Several examples of cicisbeism have been given, not because it is particularly important sociologically, but because it is so often confused with polyandry, which can only be said to exist when a woman is bound by the bond of marriage to more than one man, paternity of her respective children being divided between them.

3. Descent, Succession, Inheritance and Residence

Three important features of primitive kinship systems are the rules governing descent, succession and inheritance.

---

[1] This rite was previously regarded as a survival of "group marriage", but the term "marriage" is quite inapplicable to such a relationship, which is essentially temporary in character.

The rules of **descent** are those which regulate the birthright membership of a social group, though such membership may also be acquired, in special cases, by adoption. Descent may be traced through either the father or the mother. In the former case descent is said to be **patrilineal.** This is easy to understand, because our own society is predominantly patrilineal. A child takes its surname (and in Scotland its membership of a clan) from its father, and members of the aristocracy take their titles, not from their mothers, but from their fathers. But this emphasis is quite

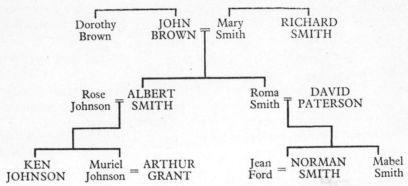

FIG. 5.—Hypothetical Genealogy illustrating Matrilineal Descent of Surname

arbitrary. Every child has two parents. It would be quite as feasible to regard the *mother* as the relevant parent for purposes of descent, and many primitive peoples in fact do so. In these societies descent is said to be **matrilineal,** since it is traced through the mother and not through the father.

In view of the difficulty which is experienced by students reared in a patrilineal society in understanding the principles of matriliny, let us refer to another entirely hypothetical genealogy (Fig. 5) which we may contrast with the patrilineal one previously discussed. We assume that our own society might be matrilineal, and that descent of the surname would follow the same principles as does that of membership of a social group, such as a clan, in a matrilineal primitive society.[1] In this case, when JOHN BROWN

[1] The assumed analogy between surname in our own community and clan membership in primitive society breaks down on one point which is worth mentioning. In our society a woman assumes her husband's name at marriage, and does not normally relinquish it even after widowhood or divorce. In primitive society a woman never, or only very rarely, becomes a member of her husband's clan or he of hers, whether descent be patrilineal or matrilineal.

marries Mary Smith, their children take their name from their mother, and this name is transmitted through the female offspring only.

The vast majority of primitive kinship systems are either patrilineal or matrilineal. In both cases descent is said to be **unilateral,** since only one parent is regarded as relevant for purposes of descent. But in certain kinship groups descent is traced through *both* parents. Such groups are said to be **bilateral.** The most obvious example of this is the family, the child's membership of which depends upon its relationship to both its parents and upon the bond of marriage existing between them— thus, an illegitimate child is not a member of a family in the anthropological sense. But in addition to the family, a few primitive communities have wider bilateral groups, such as the *kindred.*

In addition, there are atypical forms of descent, such as the *ambilateral* Maori *hapu,* in which descent may be traced *either* through the father or through the mother (but not both), and *double unilateral* descent, in which two sets of groups, one patrilineal and the other matrilineal, co-exist in the same society. These methods of reckoning descent will be discussed later.

In older anthropological works the terms "patriarchal", and "matriarchal", or "father-right" and "mother-right", are sometimes used to correspond with "patrilineal" and "matrilineal". But these terms are best avoided, since they may convey misleading implications about the power and status of women in matrilineal communities.

This brings us to the rules of **succession,** which are those regulating the transmission of office or rank. Succession may be patrilineal or matrilineal. In the latter case succession to a male title passes from a man to some other matrilineal kinsman, usually his sister's son. It is important to stress this because of the misleading implications of the term "matriarchal" mentioned above. In primitive society generally women play a negligible part in political affairs, and even when they do exert a significant influence, the actual administration of tribal affairs is mainly carried out by men, as we have seen among the Iroquois, who were once regarded as the classic example of the matriarchate. Matrilineal succession, in fact, means that title or office is transmitted *from* males *to* males *through* females. In both patrilineal and matrilineal systems, succession to rank or office may pass first to a man's younger brothers, reverting later to a younger man in the senior line of descent.[1]

The real difference between patrilineal and matrilineal succession is that in the former a patrilineal kinsman must succeed and in the latter a matrilineal one. In both cases there is usually a certain amount of flexibility in regard to the individual kinsman who actually succeeds. An incompetent, immature or unpopular heir may be passed over in favour of one who is regarded as more suitable—the rules of succession are thus not rigid. Sometimes the chief may himself play a part, before his death, in nominating his heir, and occasionally there are elective mechanisms whereby a suitable successor is chosen from among several alternative aristocratic houses.

It should be noted that in some communities rank is not subject to any rules of succession, but is due, for instance, to wealth. This may result in the *appearance* of patrilineal or matrilineal succession owing to the transmission of property by patrilineal or matrilineal inheritance.

The rules of **inheritance** are those which regulate the transmission of property from one generation to the next. As with succession, it may be patrilineal or matrilineal, but these principles are sometimes modified by the wishes of the original owner, who may have powers of testamentary disposition.

The rules governing distribution between brothers on the death of their father or mother's brother are variable. In some communities a more or less equal division is made, but in others the rule of *primogeniture* prevails. In a few communities, for example among the Kazaks, the rule of *ultimogeniture* gives preference to *younger* sons, but this usually happens when provision has been made for their older brothers during the lifetime of the original owner. For it is important to stress the fact that inheritance, as defined above, is something much wider than the legal rules governing the disposal of property at death. It is the whole mechanism whereby the material wealth of the community is passed on from one generation to the next. For example, a man may hand over some of his property to his heir during his life-

---

[1] In considering matters of kinship and particularly of succession, it is important to distinguish between *age* and *seniority*. We should never confuse the term "senior" with "elder" or "junior" with "younger". "Elder" and "younger" refer to relative age. "Senior" and "junior" refer to lines of descent, irrespective of the relative ages of the persons concerned. Thus, in a patrilineal society if a man is a chief, his son is junior to his younger brother's son, even though the latter may be older in years.

time, or may even dispose of it in a manner contrary to the prevailing rules of inheritance. Thus, in the matrilineal Trobriand Islands a man may hand over certain wealth and magical spells (which may be regarded as a form of wealth in this society) to his son, instead of leaving them to be inherited by his sister's son after his death.

Since primitive communities lack, for the most part, any generalized form of wealth such as money, material possessions usually appertain to one sex or to the other, for example, clothing and certain forms of ornament. Again, because of the division of labour between the sexes, the same is generally true of objects of utility, for example, household utensils, tools, weapons, canoes and so on. The usual custom is for men's property to be handed on in the patrilineal or matrilineal line as the case may be, while that of a woman normally passes to her daughter or sometimes her sister. But there are specific exceptions to this—for example, among the Aranda a woman's *tjurunga* (a kind of sacred object) is inherited by her younger brother, never by her daughter. In regard to certain personal possessions in some primitive communities, the problem of inheritance does not arise, property being either destroyed at death or buried with the dead owner.

The rules of inheritance in regard to *land* are extremely variable and complex. Some examples will be given in Chapter VIII, since they cannot be understood apart from the whole system of land tenure existing in the community concerned.

As with succession, the student must guard against a too rigid impression of the rules of inheritance, which is only too easily gained from some of the earlier field records which usually sought to give cut-and-dried formulations of these rules. There is usually a tendency for either patriliny or matriliny to be emphasized, and for customary rules to determine distribution of property between males and females, elder and younger, and so on. But such rules are constantly modified by particular considerations, such as the wishes of the owner or of the community and the availability of an heir of the appropriate age, sex and character. Thus, sometimes a woman may inherit if there is no male heir, or someone, male or female, not in the direct line of descent may temporarily hold property in trust until an immature heir comes of age. The personal situation of possible heirs may also be taken into consideration so that hardship is normally avoided.

Among the rules connected with kinship in primitive society

are those governing **residence,** particularly residence after marriage, for it is rare in primitive society to find a young married couple "setting up house" for themselves far from the homes of either of them. Usually one spouse moves to the village (or other local group) of the other, often into his or her household. When it is customary for the wife to move and join her husband's group, marriage is said to be **patrilocal.** When the husband moves to join his wife's group, marriage is said to be **matrilocal.**[1] Occasionally matrilocal marriage is a temporary arrangement. Among the Bemba a man goes to live with his wife's family for a period after marriage, returning subsequently with his wife to his own village. During the period of matrilocal marriage he works for the family of his wife, this service taking the place of the *lobola* payment made in other Bantu tribes.

Patrilocal marriage is usually correlated with patrilineal descent and matrilocal marriage with matrilineal descent, but there are a few exceptions to this. In the matrilineal Trobriand Islands marriage is patrilocal. A woman goes at marriage to live permanently in the village of her husband, but her sons are expected to return at maturity to the village from which she originally came, that is, to the village of their mother's brother.

As regards the residence of children, these usually live, as we would expect, with their parents until male or female children move off at marriage under the principles of matrilocal or patrilocal residence respectively. But there are exceptions to the general practice of family residence for children. Among some primitive peoples, a woman returns to her own family for her confinement, and in others it is customary for children to be sent to live with their grandparents for various periods. Again, in Tikopia a child may sometimes be sent away from its parents to live more or less permanently in the household of a member of its *kano a paito* (p. 150). This is not true adoption, since the child retains its own family titles and rights to inheritance. In general, the function of such practices is to emphasize the wider kinship bonds of the child in contradistinction to those of the individual family. We shall see later how important are these wider bonds in primitive society, a feature which contrasts most sharply with our own emphasis on the more limited bonds of the individual family. This is reflected in the linguistic usages connected with kinship

---

[1] The terms *virilocal* and *uxorilocal* are sometimes used as equivalent to patrilocal and matrilocal respectively.

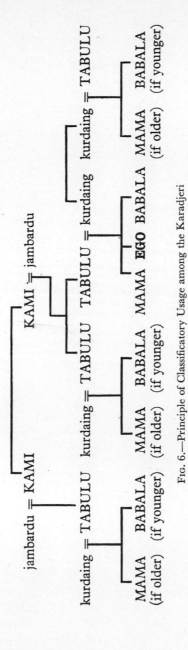

Fig. 6.—Principle of Classificatory Usage among the Karadjeri

terminology, which are extraordinarily elaborate in many primitive societies.

4. Classificatory Terminology and the Language of Kinship

The terms used by primitive peoples to denote kinship relationships differ from our own in the predominance of classificatory terms as opposed to descriptive terms. **Classificatory** terms are those which refer to more than one type of relationship, for example, "aunt", "uncle", "grandfather", "cousin" in our own system. **Descriptive** terms are those which refer to one type of relationship only, for example, "father", "mother", "brother". In the classificatory system of kinship terminology, such terms as those just mentioned are also applied to a number of different kinds of relationship, for example, a man may use the term "father" to denote not only his own father but also his father's brothers, his father's father's sons and so on—the actual grouping varies from one community to another. The most general (though by no means the only) principle underlying most classificatory systems is the equivalence of brothers and of sisters for purposes of terminology. This means that, for example, if a man uses a certain term towards a particular individual, he employs the same term for the brothers of that individual. Thus, a man may have many relatives whom he calls "father", the number depending on the consistency with which the classificatory principle is applied in the community concerned.

In order to give the reader some idea of the appearance of a classificatory system of kinship terminology, a few of the kinship terms of the Karadjeri are shown in Fig. 6. Here it will be seen that a man uses the term TABULU to refer, not only to his FATHER, but also to his FATHER'S BROTHER. The same principle applies to the term KAMI in the second ascending generation. FATHER'S FATHER'S BROTHER'S SON is therefore another TABULU, and his sons are addressed by the term for BROTHER. In the Karadjeri kinship system this logical process ramifies out through the whole genealogy of an individual. This means that two individuals can define their classificatory relationship to each other, even if no genealogical relationship between them can be traced, provided that the relationship of both of them to a third party is known. Thus if A addresses B as KAMI and B addresses C as MAMA, then A knows that he must address C as KAMI also. In this respect Karadjeri kinship is, like

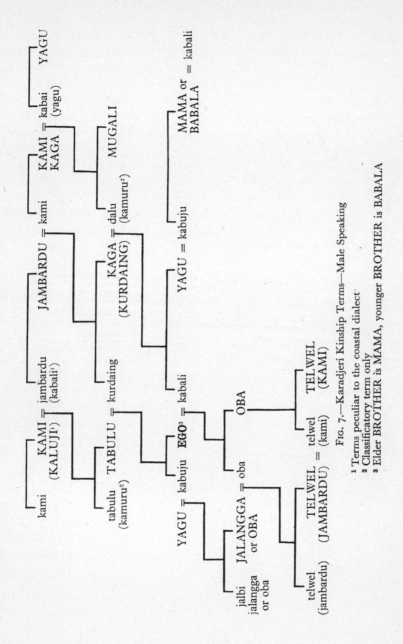

Fig. 7.—Karadjeri Kinship Terms—Male Speaking

[1] Terms peculiar to the coastal dialect
[2] Classificatory term only
[3] Elder BROTHER is MAMA, younger BROTHER is BABALA

all Australian systems, extraordinarily logical and consistent. This usage means that theoretically every Australian aborigine is related to every other, though of course relationships are normally traced only with members of an individual's own local group and neighbouring ones, or groups with which he has special relationships, for example, by marriage.

The tracing of such relationships in Australian society is of vital importance in actual life, since classificatory kinship imposes certain patterns of behaviour between individuals. For example, a Karadjeri man must adopt the avoidance relationship (p. 136) towards his wife's mother; similarly, any man who is called KAGA and is married to a *dalu* is one from whom EGO may obtain a wife. Thus, when a stranger arrives in a camp, the first thing which must be done is to work out his classificatory relationships to its members, so that he knows how to behave towards them and they towards him.

A fuller presentation of Karadjeri kinship terms is given in Fig. 7, to which reference will be made later.[1] It must be emphasized that this is only one of the many classificatory systems which exist throughout the world. As has been mentioned, Australian kinship systems are extraordinarily elaborate, logical and far-reaching in their definition of classificatory relationships. They exemplify in a striking way certain principles which are operative, though usually to a lesser extent, in classificatory systems generally. But the reader must not infer that the diagram presented is by any means typical of classificatory systems. To guard against this impression, some of the kinship terms used in Tikopia [2] are given in Fig. 8.

The use of classificatory terminology does *not* mean that natives cannot distinguish between different kin who are called by the same term, or that all are treated alike. As regards the distinction between different relatives to whom the same classificatory term is applied, the context in which a term is used generally makes its individual reference clear. Where this is not the case, all classificatory systems have certain **indices of identification,**

---

[1] Specialists in Australian kinship will at once see that this figure is over-simplified and artificial. It postulates a series of marriages between men and their matrilateral cross-cousins. In actual fact, this form of marriage is not universal even among the Inland Karadjeri, while the coastal section of the tribe actually prohibit marriage with a man's own mother's brother's daughter.

[2] This again is an over-simplified presentation of the facts. For a more detailed treatment of the terms, and their implications in native life, the reader should refer to the original field-record (Firth, 8, chapter VII).

$\male$ = $\female$
NA
[A

$\female$
taina

$\female$ =
mutu

mak
3.—Sor

man o
D) are

though the incidence of these varies from one community to another, while within the same community different indices are employed at different times. Classificatory kinsfolk may be distinguished from each other by the following indices:

(a) The index of circumlocution or of specification, that is, by describing the individual concerned by characteristics other than his kinship relationship to the speaker, for example, by mentioning the clan or local group to which he belongs. Moreover, most classificatory systems have supplementary terms corresponding to "near", "distant" and "own", by which the meaning of classificatory terms can be clarified.

(b) The nominal index, which consists of adding the personal name to the kinship term, just as we distinguish between classificatory relatives in the case of uncles and aunts. Though this is probably the most obvious index to employ, it is rare in some communities owing to certain taboos on the use of personal names.

(c) The ocular index, that is, when various classificatory relatives of the same relationship are present, by looking at the individual concerned.

(d) The manual index—pointing at the relative indicated, particularly common among young children.

(e) The tonal index. Malinowski records differences in emotional tone in the utterance of classificatory kinship terms, according to whether the relationship is close or distant, but other observers have failed to detect such differences. Their occurrence probably depends, not so much on the need for precision as on the kind of situation in which a kinship term is uttered, for example, whether it is one of day-to-day practical life or one of emotional tension.

Natives, then, are perfectly capable of distinguishing between different individuals described by the same classificatory term. Such distinctions, moreover, apply to conduct as well as terminology. Behaviour towards more distant classificatory kin is apt to be a pale reflection of that towards those who are more closely related. Common residence has an important effect upon the way in which patterns of kinship behaviour are observed. Thus, when classificatory kinsmen live close to each other, they normally meet more frequently than those who are not neighbours. Consequently, they have more opportunities of observing their mutual obligations, such as the giving of presents, and are usually more inclined to do so than when the obligatory kinship bonds are not reinforced by frequent personal contacts.

Classificatory usage may even be extended beyond the point to which genealogical relationships can be traced, as we have seen to be the case in Australia. It should be noted that such usages do not correspond strictly with the definition of kinship given in Section 2. This is even more marked when the use of classificatory terms depends upon membership of a group irrespective of genealogical connection. Thus, in some primitive societies a man may call other men of his clan "brother", though he cannot trace relationship to them. Again, in Wogeo a man uses the term corresponding to "mother" to apply to the wives of all his fellow-clansmen. Such usages are best described as *fictional kinship*.

We have described the general features of the classificatory system,[1] not only because of its prevalence in primitive society, but because it has in the past led to more misunderstandings and misinterpretations in anthropological theory than any other feature of primitive culture.

Some primitive kinship systems have two terms for a single type of relationship—a term of reference and a term of address. A **term of reference** is used when speaking *of* a relative, and a **term of address** when speaking *to* them. Some of our terms, for example, "mother", are used in both ways; but such terms as "mother-in-law", "son", "daughter" are not used as terms of address. In some primitive societies there are two different sets of terms, one of address and the other of reference. Thus in Tikopia, for which we have given the terms of reference, a man refers to his father as TAMANA when speaking to a third person, but addresses him as PA. A similar distinction is observed in the case of certain other relatives, though for some (for example, TUATINA = MOTHER'S BROTHER) the same term is used in both ways. In other kinship systems there is no distinction between the two types of term. For example, a Karadjeri man speaks of his father as "*nyundu* TABULU", "my father", and also uses the term TABULU in addressing him.

[1] In view of the definitions of classificatory and descriptive terms given above, it must be recognized that the use of the term, "classificatory *system*", is generally a loose one indicating a general tendency rather than absolute consistency. Thus, though the Karadjeri system is entirely classificatory, the terms of reference in Tikopia include two descriptive ones. Again, our own system is generally called descriptive because of the relatively large number of descriptive terms in it. But, as we have seen, it also includes classificatory terms.

When the same kinship term is used by two relatives in speaking of or to each other, the term is said to be *reciprocal*; for example, when there is a single term for FATHER'S FATHER and SON'S SON. Our own term "brother" is a reciprocal one, but "uncle" is not.

Many systems of kinship terminology have separate terms for a single relationship according to whether the relation is older or younger than the speaker; for example, there may be one term for "elder brother" and another for "younger brother", as among the Karadjeri.

In some primitive kinship systems there is a practice whereby, when a man becomes a father, he is habitually referred to and addressed as "Father of X", "X" being the name of the infant. Similarly, the mother may be called "Mother of X". This custom is known as **teknonymy.**

Certain technical terms are useful in referring to groups of relationships which are not easily described in English kinship terminology. The term **sibling** refers to children of the same mother and father irrespective of sex, that is, it covers both brothers and sisters. One application of this term is found in Tikopia and other Oceanic societies, where, instead of words corresponding to "brother" and "sister", there are terms which can only be rendered "sibling of the same sex" and "sibling of the opposite sex". Thus, in Tikopia terms for siblings can be translated into English only by reference to the sex of the speaker, as follows:

> Brother (man speaking):   TAINA
> Brother (woman speaking):   KAVE
> Sister (man speaking):   Kave
> Sister (woman speaking):   Taina

In New Guinea this Oceanic usage has been adopted in the vernacular (Pidgin English) in which natives communicate with Europeans, and resulting misunderstandings are frequent. The European is naturally surprised when a woman refers to another woman as her "barata", a corruption of "brother". In Pidgin English, of course, "barata" means "sibling of the same sex".

Special terms are employed in anthropology for different kinds of cousin. **Cross-cousins** are two persons so related that the mother of the one is sister to the father of the other, that is, an individual's mother's brother's children and father's sister's children. In other words, they are cousins related through parents who are siblings of different sexes. It should be noted that cross-cousins can never be members of the same clan, whether descent in the clan is patrilineal or matrilineal. **Parallel-cousins** are two persons so related that the father of one is brother to the father of the other, or that the mother of one is sister to the mother of the other, that is, an individual's father's brother's children and mother's sister's children. In other words, they are cousins related through parents of the same sex. The term **ortho-cousin** is sometimes used for parallel-cousins who belong to the same clan, that is, they are the children of two brothers when descent is patrilineal and of two sisters when descent is matrilineal. These terminological usages are diagrammatically represented in Fig. 9.

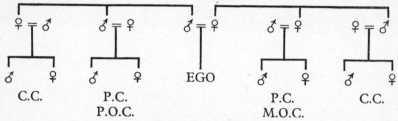

FIG. 9.—Types of Cousin

C.C.   = Cross-Cousins
P.C.   = Parallel-Cousins
P.O.C. = Ortho-Cousins under Patrilineal Descent
M.O.C. = Ortho-Cousins under Matrilineal Descent

5. *The Rights, Obligations and Restrictions of Kinship*

We have described in the last section some of the elaborations of primitive kinship terminology, which are apt to strike the European as unnecessarily complex. But there is a positive social reason for their complexity. In all human societies the kinship bonds of the family satisfy various needs of individuals—of men and women for socially approved sexual association and of their offspring for care during infancy. But human beings living in society have many other needs—for education, for assistance of a practical kind in economic tasks which they cannot undertake individually, and for care in time of illness or in old age. Furthermore, the family cannot fully serve its functions if one of the parents should become an invalid or die, and these functions must be, partially at least, taken over by other social agencies. In our own society there are institutions which serve functions to which the family is inadequate, or meet critical situations such as prolonged illness or death. Examples of such institutions are orphanages, schools, hospitals, specialized occupational groups (farmers, builders, manufacturers and so on), insurance companies or schemes of public insurance and homes for the aged.

In general, none of these specialized institutions exist in primitive society, their functions being served by systems of kinship. Orphans are adopted, the old and sick are cared for, and widows (if they do not remarry) are provided with a home by kinsfolk. A young man in Bantu society owns no cattle, and if he wishes to provide *lobola* must obtain the necessary beasts from his father and other kinsfolk, a service which he must in turn render to his own son at a later date. Under primitive conditions a man who wishes to build a house, a task too heavy to undertake alone, instead of employing professional builders, summons his kinsfolk to his assistance, and they in turn have similar claims upon his services. This is the explanation of the complexity of primitive kinship and of the classificatory system of terminology. For example, a man calls his mother's sister "mother" because she is a natural foster-mother if his own mother should die, and if the latter should have no sisters, the classificatory system equips him with a whole cadre of "mothers". The same applies to other kin. Thus, the mother's brother is usually a vitally important relative, owing all sorts of obligations to his sister's son, not only in matrilineal but also in patrilineal societies. If a man's mother has no brother, the classificatory system makes available other more remote kinsfolk who are expected to undertake his duties. To adopt a metaphor from the theatre, classificatory kin are the understudies of real kin.

But this is not the whole explanation of classificatory kinship. Under primitive conditions, as we shall see, groups of kinsfolk normally live together in such entities as the extended family. This means that a child's household includes other relatives, such as his father's brothers, mother's sisters or father's brothers' wives. These naturally have much more to do with him, and render more services to him, than the corresponding relatives in our own society. It is therefore appropriate that they should be designated by kinship terms which reflect patterns of behaviour. Thus, a boy must treat his father's brothers with respect as he does his own father, while an infant normally receives from its classificatory mothers, as from its own mother, all sorts of attentions, and occasionally even such intimate services as suckling.

The general use of classificatory terms, and to a large extent their differential applications in particular societies, can be understood if we realize that they reflect behaviour patterns similar to those existing in the primary kinship relationship, for example, between a woman and her own children. But we must again emphasize the fact that the primary relationship is always distinguished, and that the styles of classificatory behaviour patterned upon it become less significant and clear-cut as the genealogical distance increases. Thus, a boy treats his father and his father's brothers with respect, but a breach of etiquette towards the latter may be less severely regarded than an act of disrespect towards his own father. Finally, when we proceed outwards in the genealogy to very remote "fathers", the obligation ceases to be one of filial piety and becomes a mere formality, particularly where there is little disparity in age between the parties concerned.

The differences based on genealogical proximity are qualitative as well as quantitative. A man may expect constant care and solicitude from his own mother's brother, while the obligations of remoter kin of the same kind may be limited to ceremonial observances, such as attendance at his initiation or marriage.

It will help to clarify these aspects of the classificatory system if we reflect that we ourselves use certain kinship terms for purposes other than defining genealogical relationship, for example, the use of the term "sister" in hospitals or "brother" between judges. A good example is the practice of using the term "father" for a priest in the Roman Catholic religion, where other kinship terms are likewise employed in religious orders, as they are in other religious faiths in various contexts. Archaic kinship terms are, or have been, employed in a similar way—for example, "sire" and "matron". Colloquial speech and slang provide other examples, as when a man seeks to impress his authority on a strange boy by calling him "son" or "sonny", or in the slang description of the pawnbroker as "uncle", reminiscent of the financial and other benefits which one expects from this relative during childhood. In all these usages, some element of the primary kinship relationship, whether it be partial social identity ("brother"), authority or dependence (or both reciprocally, as in the case of "Our Father"), or financial inadequacy, is stressed in a relationship of a non-genealogical kind. The same sort of principle underlies classificatory usage in primitive society though here it is more extensively and systematically applied, and is infinitely more important in determining human behaviour.

This enables us to understand why Malinowski has based his explanation of the classificatory system on what he calls the *metaphorical extension* of kinship terms. These are first learned by the child in the immediate circle of relatives among whom it is born and spends its infancy, in the *initial situation of kinship*. They are subsequently extended and redefined so as to embrace a very much wider circle of kinsfolk, whose significance will be apparent from what was said at the beginning of this section.

We are now in a position to appreciate the importance, in primitive society, of the rights and obligations of kinship, though the precise nature and incidence of these vary enormously from one primitive society to another. Among the culturally pre-scribed obligations of kinship are: care and assistance in times of distress or difficulty; respectful or deferential behaviour; the giving of gifts; support in quarrels; day-to-day co-operation, and participation in ceremonial connected with such events as births, initiations, marriages and deaths. In addition there are certain special usages, particularly connected with marriage and the family. We shall constantly meet examples of the rights and obligations of kinship in subsequent chapters, since kinship per-vades every aspect of native life.

The obligations of kinship include rules of a negative order, which prohibit certain types of behaviour between specific kin. Among these the most important and widespread are the rules prohibiting **incest**, that is, sexual relations between near kin. All primitive kinship systems have such rules in some form or other, though their nature and incidence vary from one com-munity to another. Universally sexual relations between members of the individual family (except husband and wife) are pro-hibited. Exceptions are found in ancient Egypt, Hawaii and among the Incas of Peru, where brother-sister marriages occurred, but *only in the case of the ruling families*. These isolated and limited exceptions contrast with the overwhelming majority of human communities in which the rules of law, morals and religion insist upon a rigid exclusion of sexual relationships—with the exception of that between husband and wife—from the family.

The conception of incest, however, goes beyond the individual family. Most primitive societies extend it to other kinsfolk, often to relatives whom we should not regard as "near" kin. It may even apply to all members of an individual's group (for example, a clan) irrespective of genealogical relationship. This, of course, precludes marriage within the group, which is said to be **exogamous** and the rule is termed **exogamy.** The opposite rule is **endogamy,** whereby a man *must* marry within his own social group (for example, caste), which is then termed **endogamous.** Exogamous and endogamous groups may co-exist in the same society.

Two points must be emphasized in order to clarify the meaning of the terms mentioned in the preceding paragraphs. In the first place the term "incest" refers primarily to sexual association (though the prohibition of this automatically rules out marriage also) in the case of individuals between whom a particular genealogical relationship exists. Exogamy refers primarily to marriage between individuals on the basis of their membership of a social group, irrespective of genealogical connection. Sexual relations between such individuals are normally prohibited or socially disapproved, though not so severely as in the case of incest. Such relations within the clan are described as *clan incest*. In the second place the rules both of exogamy and endogamy are prescriptive and proscriptive, never permissive. It is therefore quite incorrect to say that a certain group is endogamous if we merely mean that marriages within the group are permitted. We can only use the term if such marriages are obligatory. Similarly exogamy can only refer to the rule that a man must marry outside his group, and not to the permitted or merely customary occurrence of such marriages.

As regards the prohibition of incest so far as it affects kin not closely related by blood and also as regards the rules of exogamy in the case of such kin, it should be noted that these are not universally obeyed or enforced. Liaisons may be carried on *sub rosa* and even marriages are occasionally tolerated. They are usually condemned by public opinion, though sometimes with little vehemence or sincerity, or they may be regarded as regrettable necessities. Thus, irregular relationships crop up from time to time. In a certain Chinese village it is recorded that several men lived for a time at least with women in incestuous relationships; in one case a widower had a liaison with his own daughter, and though the couple were condemned by public opinion, nothing was done to put an end to the relationship. Again, Malinowski has shown that in the Trobriand Islands, although clan incest is officially prohibited and morally condemned, liaisons of this kind not only occur, but are actually regarded by the young men as specially creditable achievements—on the same basis as the young in most societies take pride in flouting convention. But in the Trobriands these liaisons cannot continue if they become a public scandal. If someone, such as a jealous rival, publicly denounces the culprit, the situation of shame in which the latter finds himself is so acutely felt that he has no alternative but to commit suicide by jumping from the top of a palm tree or by taking poison. Finally, we have referred to the elaborate prohibitions, based on real or classificatory kinship, connected with marriage in Australia. These often mean that the majority of the women in a particular tribe are prohibited as mates to any given man who may be unable to find a wife of the correct relationship. In such cases he usually marries a woman of an inappropriate relationship, either with the reluctant approval of public opinion or in defiance of it.

We must now consider various explanations of the prohibition of incest which is universal, and of the rules of exogamy which are common, in primitive cultures. Several unsatisfactory explanations of the phenomena have been suggested, and because of their simplicity have gained wide currency in popular discussions of primitive society. One such explanation attributes them to a need, whether consciously recognized or not, to prevent the alleged evil effects of in-breeding. Now quite apart from the fact that biologists are by no means agreed on the deleterious effects of in-breeding, many incest prohibitions preclude sexual relationships between individuals who are unrelated biologically, for example, between a man and his son's wife. And while this explanation is not inconsistent with the prohibition of incest within the family, it becomes ludicrous when applied to the rules of exogamy. For example, where these rules are based on matrilineal descent, they would permit marriage between a man and his mother's brother's daughter but would forbid him to marry his mother's mother's mother's daughter's daughter's daughter, and also women of his clan with whom no genealogical relationship could be traced.

Other explanations attribute the prohibition of incest to an alleged "natural" or "instinctive" aversion to intercourse with near kin or to the dulling of sex-appeal by prolonged intimate association from infancy onwards. As with the theory previously mentioned, these explanations do not take into account the actual incidence of incest prohibitions, which often apply to relatives who are only related by fictional kinship, with whom no biological or genealogical relationship can be traced, who are regarded by the natives as by ourselves as distant kin, and who may even be complete strangers to each other. Furthermore, such interpretations, which assume a spontaneous mental process as a basis for incest prohibitions, do not take account of the widespread sanctions designed for their reinforcement. In all societies incest is morally condemned, and in some this condemnation is backed by powerful legal sanctions; in others it is believed to lead to terrifying supernatural punishments—misfortune, illness or death. Why should the most powerful forces of human society be mobilized in this way to prevent the individual from performing an act towards which he feels "natural" indifference or even aversion? We must look to the biological and social conditions of family life, rather than to spontaneous psychological processes, for an explanation.

In view of what we have said earlier about the extension of kinship obligations, the reader may have guessed that the prohibition of incest and exogamy are capable of similar explanations, the latter being an extension of the former. This is in fact the case. Let us commence with the problem of the prohibition of incest.

Because of its importance in human evolution, sex is a powerful force, but one whose frustration lets loose the most disruptive of human passions. On the other hand, these passions must be controlled in the interests of social order. Nowhere is this so true as in the family, whose intimate system of domestic and economic co-operation necessitates harmonious relationships between its members. Paternal love and filial respect cannot be maintained if father and son are rivals for the sexual favours of the same woman. Family life would be impossible if brothers were always quarrelling, as they would be if they were allowed access to their sisters. The same interpretation applies to wider kinship groups such as the clan. Here, again, the need for harmonious co-operation in economic, political and religious activity is threatened by the disruptive forces of sex, and this leads to the rules of exogamy and the prohibition of clan incest. This is one of the extensions of family sentiments, in this case of a negative order, which lie at the base of the classificatory system of relationship.

For example, by calling all female members of his clan "sister", a man establishes a relationship of fictional kinship with them which precludes, ideally at least, marriage or sexual intercourse.

That the above explanation of the prohibition of incest does not rest merely on assumption and *a priori* argument will be seen from a vivid account of the tension and finally disruption actually caused in a household group by one of the cases of incest in a Chinese village mentioned earlier in this section. The case in question was that of a farmer who lived in an extended family group consisting of nine members. Only the eldest son was married, and this man's wife entered into an incestuous relationship with her husband's father. Professor Hsu (1) describes the consequences as follows:

"At first his son only learned vaguely about the father's liaison with his wife. One day, there was a witch doctor curing some illness . . . next door. All the members of . . . (the) family, except the father and daughter-in-law and her two months' old child, went out to watch the proceeding, which was always fascinating. Unfortunately, the son came back alone earlier than the others, and to his vexation, he found his father having sexual intercourse with his wife. I did not know exactly what they said to each other at this moment, but when the rest of the family and some relatives returned to his house (I was among them), we found a great drama: the daughter-in-law was trying to commit suicide publicly by drinking a bowl of distilled salt. This was at once stopped by relatives. The son then dashed out of the room and loudly abused his father with the worst language. The father at first pretended that he did not hear, but when the abusive language continued for some time, he jumped up and attempted to whip his son. This was again stopped by relatives. After that time there was a wide gap, with mutual suspicion, between the son and the father. They could never get along with each other as they did before. The father's wife also bore a grudge against her husband. Thus, the authority of the father was greatly shaken. He also felt as if he had not much face to meet others. Soon after that there was talk about division of the family, but this did not occur until three years later because of the son's economic inability."

In conclusion, it should be mentioned that although the prevention of conflict within closely-knit groups appears to be the primary function of the rules prohibiting incest and those of exogamy, such rules also play a more positive part in social life. They ensure that smaller social units shall be bound to one another by ties of affinal kinship, and so conduce to the integration of wider social groups.

The explanation of the rules of endogamy, which is far less common than exogamy, is much easier for the European to appreciate because of its occurrence, *de facto* if not as an absolute rule, among royal families and aristocratic classes in modern times. Everyone is familiar with the abdications and other drastic consequences which have resulted from failure to observe it, as with the morganatic marriages which attempt to reconcile the wishes of individuals with the endogamic principle. In many primitive societies endogamy is similarly correlated with the existence of hereditary social classes, whose economic, political and social privileges it serves to maintain by preserving the conception of purity of blood. It thus gives offspring a double claim to power or economic privilege, while preventing any association between them and members of the lower classes. It may be mentioned that the brother-sister marriages of the Incas,[1] Hawaiians and ancient Egyptians should be regarded as exceptional extensions of the principle of endogamy rather than as negating the universal significance of the prohibition of incest.

The rules of endogamy are not only less common than those of exogamy, but are in general less rigidly defined. Sometimes, as in Indian caste systems generally, the group within which a man must marry is clearly circumscribed. But in other societies, for example, in the aristocracies of Polynesia as in modern Europe, the highest ranks shade off into those of the lesser nobility, so that no hard-and-fast line can be drawn between them.

We may conclude the discussion of the rights and obligations of kinship by reference to two types of standardized behaviour found sporadically in primitive society, namely, avoidance and the joking relationship. The rule of **avoidance,** in its most extreme form, means that individuals who stand in a particular relationship must, as far as possible, ignore each other's existence and must refrain from social intercourse. They may not speak to each other, and if they meet on a path, one must stand aside or

[1] An interesting speculation has been put forward to account for the incestuous marriages of the royal Incas. The Inca empire apparently embraced many different peoples, some of whom were patrilineal and others matrilineal. At the head of this empire was a personage who was the legitimate successor to the title under either system, and who would therefore be acceptable to all his subjects.

make a detour. Sometimes they may not even mention each other's names.

The most common relationship in which avoidance is enjoined is that between a man and his wife's mother, commonly called "mother-in-law avoidance".[1] But the custom may be observed with other kinsfolk also, particularly other affinal kin, and also between brothers and sisters. In most of these instances avoidance does not take the extreme form described above, and would be better described as restrained behaviour. All degrees of restraint are found, from complete avoidance to mere limitations on speech, certain words or allusions being prohibited between specific relatives who, in other respects, may associate freely and co-operate socially. Commonly such verbal restrictions apply to references to sexual matters. For this and other reasons avoidance has been explained as a mechanism for the prevention of sexual intercourse, the significance of which will be apparent from our discussion of incest. But this is at best a partial explanation, for it does not account for cases of avoidance between relatives of the same sex, for example, between a man and his wife's father. These occur in some primitive societies, though they are neither so stringent nor so widespread as avoidance between kinsfolk of different sexes.

The **joking relationship** refers to the custom whereby specific relatives may or must joke with or tease each other when they meet. The joking relationship is commonly found between affinal kin. As with avoidance, there is a great range of variation in the actual usages described by the term. Sometimes joking is obligatory, sometimes optional. It may be symmetrical, both parties making jokes at each other's expense, or one party may be expected to take the jokes of the other in good part without retaliating. It may or may not be accompanied by horseplay, and the inclusion or otherwise of obscene references in the jokes is also variable.

[1] The operation of this custom is illustrated by an incident which occurred while I was working among the Karadjeri. A missionary, travelling in his car with a party of natives from a distant tribe, stopped for the night at Lagrange Bay. In the evening the visiting aborigines gathered at the camp of the Lagrange Bay natives for a "corroboree", a colloquial expression in Australia for singing and dancing, particularly around the camp-fire at night. As I passed by the missionary's car, I noticed one of the visiting natives sitting alone on the running-board smoking his pipe. When I asked him why he had not joined in the festivities, he replied that there was a classificatory wife's mother of his among the Lagrange Bay people, and he could therefore not join the group. The fact that he came from a place some two hundred miles away illustrates very well the ramification of Australian kinship relationships.

Strange as it may seem, the two contrasting customs of avoidance and the joking relationship appear, in certain cases at least, to be capable of a similar explanation. All kinship relationships entail expressions of goodwill and mutual services between the kinsmen concerned. But in many of them, particularly between affinal kin, this is tinged by a feeling of tension and even by the possible hostility which may arise from the failure of one party to honour his or her obligations. The terms *solidarity* and *opposition* [1] have been used to describe these contrasting aspects of kinship relationships, and more recently Professor Radcliffe-Brown has suggested the terms *conjunction* and *disjunction*. The psychological term *ambivalent* might be used to describe relationships in which both of these contrasting aspects occur, but in the present context without the implications of violent emotion and the process of repression involved in the psycho-analytic use of the word. Whatever terms we use, it is clear that certain relationships between kin entail contradictory feelings and patterns of behaviour, which may produce situations of tension and embarrassment. One way of preventing the occurrence of such situations is to enjoin complete avoidance, or to impose formal restrictions on mutual behaviour. But the sort of contradictory relationship we have described can also be expressed by joking. On the one hand laughter expresses a certain mild hostility, and there is a feeling that to make a joke at someone's expense is a way of "scoring off" them. This is reflected (and over-emphasized) in Hobbes' attribution of laughter to a feeling of "sudden glory", a view which has been taken up and elaborated by many subsequent writers.[2] On the other hand, laughter and joking do not express unmitigated hatred—one does not joke with deadly enemies. It might be said that mutual jesting implies friendly hostility. Consequently, the joking relationship avoids tension between kinsfolk by enabling them to express both aspects of their ambivalent relationship at the same time.

[1] These terms have been extensively employed, particularly by French sociologists, to refer also to social relationships other than those founded on kinship. They are useful in a general way as stressing the fact that no relationship between individuals or between social groups can be completely and permanently harmonious. But they are apt to obscure the specific character of the relationships concerned. The forms of solidarity existing between husband and wife, between comrades-in-arms and between boon companions are radically different in terms of feelings, obligations and social functions. The same applies to the forms of opposition existing between protagonists in a scientific controversy, between pugilists in the boxing ring and between nations at war.

[2] For a critical review of theories of laughter, see Piddington (3).

6. Marriage Observances

The social bond of marriage is recognized and regulated in various ways in different primitive societies. Many of the usages connected with marriage depend upon the fact that each of the two parties is a member of a distinct family group, through which they both possess a set of wider kinship bonds. With the general significance of such bonds we are already familiar. Their importance here lies in the fact that marriage links together, not only two individuals, but also their respective kinsfolk. While this is true in all societies, it is of paramount importance in primitive cultures, where there usually exist elaborate social arrangements to regulate the relationships between affinal kin.

Among the most important of these is the widespread practice of **bride-price**,[1] the transfer at marriage of gifts from the bridegroom and his kinsfolk to those of the bride. The nature of the possessions given in this way is variable—cattle (and also hoes and other subsidiary forms of wealth) among most Bantu and other African pastoralists, pigs or shell currency in parts of Melanesia, and reindeer in the case of the Tungus *turi*. In some communities the whole bride-price is handed over at one time, either before, or immediately after, the couple begin to co-habit; but in others payment may be deferred, or may take the form of a prolonged series of presentations. Thus an Australian aborigine from time to time sends material possessions—tools, weapons, ornaments, or articles of clothing—to the family of his wife, an obligation which continues throughout the whole of his lifetime.

There are various principles underlying the practice of bride-price. The incidence and relative importance of these vary from one community to another. The most general principle rests upon the economic value of women in primitive society. Because of the economic division of labour between the sexes, young girls are most useful to their parents, helping in the production of food as well as in domestic tasks. The loss of such services demands some compensation, which may take the form of bride-price, or

[1] Exception has been taken to the use of this term, because it may imply, and has often been held to imply, that the woman concerned is a mere chattel. As we shall see, this view is totally incorrect, and because of the misunderstandings which have occurred, the alternative term *bride-wealth* has been proposed, but has not gained universal currency. There should be no objection to the use of the term *bride-price* if we remember that we often use the word "price" in a metaphorical and non-mercenary sense, for example, "The price of freedom is perpetual vigilance."

alternatively of the rendering of actual services by the husband to the family of his wife, as among the Bemba.

But the loss which a family suffers at the marriage of one of its young women is not merely economic. Because of the bonds of personal affection and loyalty existing within the family there is also a social or spiritual loss. On the other hand, the husband receives more than merely economic services from his wife—she is also his companion, his sexual mate and the person who bears and cares for his children. The partial transfer of a woman's allegiance and companionship from her family calls for some compensation, so that the balance achieved by bride-price is social as well as economic. This reciprocal character of primitive marriage arrangements is clearly seen in the occasional practice of **sister exchange,** which may take the place of, or supplement, bride-price. In this case two men marry each other's sisters, so that the loss of one woman by each family is offset by the acquisition of another.

Since the payment of bride-price is essential to the bond of marriage in certain communities, it also establishes the legitimacy of the offspring of the union—according to one Bantu saying: "Cattle beget children". It is the *lobola* payment which establishes the claim of a father to his children and their membership of his patrilineal group. This is most clearly seen in certain Bantu groups where, in case of divorce, the children remain with their father unless the original cattle handed over at marriage are returned, in which case the children belong to the group of their mother. This rule is summed up in the native saying: "The children are where the cattle are not".

Certain important subsidiary functions are served by bride-price in different primitive communities. Where there is an elaborate political organization, the payments are usually much more lavish in the case of chiefs and men of rank than among commoners, and this serves to support their authority and prestige. Again, the need in Bantu society for a man to obtain the necessary *lobola* cattle, which are mainly provided by his father, is an indirect means of supporting parental authority. Finally, it must be emphasized that the custom of bride-price does not stop with one transaction. The cattle or other wealth obtained in return for a woman are very frequently used at a later date to obtain a wife for her brother, and a progressive series of such transactions links together a whole series of individuals and groups in a complex network of social relationships which is characteristic of primitive society. This process has been graphically described by Mr. Cullen Young in his discussion of bride-wealth: "To those who, whenever they read the new phrase, see at once the little bunch of cattle setting out from one group-settlement to another, and see simultaneously the maiden setting out in the opposite direction and, so to say, passing the animals on the way; who see also those beasts kraaled and tended till a later day, when they again set out from the settlement that had in the first instance been that of a receiving wife-group but has now become that of a paying husband-group, as a young male in the family has reached the stage of taking a wife; who see this process going on endlessly and these cattle always when they set out equating with a maiden likewise setting out to meet and transfer for them; to those alone has the phrase 'bride-wealth' its real meaning ".[1]

In view of the reciprocal character of relationships set up between different groups of kinsfolk by marriage, the custom of bride-price usually co-exists with obligations on the part of the kinsfolk of the bride to make complementary gifts to those of the bridegroom. These are usually of less value, and are often mere formalities having little economic significance. The term *dowry*[2] should not be used for such purely ceremonial gifts, but should be reserved for major payments in communities where unmarried women are, to some extent, a liability. As we have seen, the contrary is generally true in primitive society. Consequently, where dowry gifts are the custom, they are usually offset or outweighed by bride-price, as we have seen among the Tungus. In Samoa the reciprocal payments are of approximately equal value, the kinsfolk of the bridegroom providing *oloa* (food, tools, weapons and ornaments), while those of the bride return *tonga*, consisting primarily of fine mats. The whole exchange is made publicly, and is an important ceremonial event.

In other societies, also, marriage is marked by ceremonial, feasting, or various rites designed to reflect symbolically the new union between the man and woman concerned—for example, sitting together in public, joining hands, sharing a meal or even a semi-public consummation of the marriage. Sometimes the provisioning of feasts and ceremonies is a heavy economic burden on

---

[1] Cullen Young (2), p. 69.
[2] This word is sometimes used, quite incorrectly, to refer to bride-price, of which it is the antithesis.

the families of the bride or of the bridegroom, as it is in many Indian and Chinese peasant communities. It is important to note that in most primitive societies wedding ceremonies are not religious in the sense in which they are among ourselves. Sometimes there are magico-religious rites to ensure prosperity, the health and abundance of offspring and good fortune generally, but these are practical in their intention and do not sanctify the marriage. The secular character of primitive marriage is reflected in the fact that there is generally no religious or legal bar to divorce. This does not mean that the marriage relationship is unstable. There are many social and practical obstacles to divorce, such as the shame implied in the suggestion that one party has failed to honour their marital obligations and the economic complications connected with bride-price, which we have touched upon in connection with *lobola*.

A dramatic custom known as **marriage by capture** is found sporadically among primitive peoples. This means the forcible abduction of the bride by the bridegroom, usually accompanied by some show of resistance by her relatives. Usually, though not always, this is a purely ceremonial affair, the match having been agreed upon beforehand. In view of what has been said above, the reader will appreciate the significance of this custom which has frequently been misinterpreted as a "survival" of a stage of society when all marriages were based upon abduction of the bride against the will of her family. Actually, of course, it is a ceremonial reflection of the socio-economic loss sustained by the latter, and of the substratum of hostility inherent in affinal relationships.

Because of the ramifications of kinship systems, marriages between kinsfolk are common in primitive society. The extreme form of this is found in Australia, where it will be clear that a man *must* marry a kinswoman, since he is related by bonds of kinship, real or classificatory, to everyone with whom he comes into contact. While this is not true in other primitive societies, many of them do prescribe certain relatives who are preferable as mates. This custom is known as **preferential marriage.** The commonest unions so prescribed are those between cross-cousins, particularly between a man and his mother's brother's daughter. This is the preferred type of marriage among many Bantu peoples, though others enjoin marriage with father's sister's daughter. In some Australian tribes cross-cousin marriages are not only preferential but obligatory. For the different varieties of such unions the following terms are sometimes used:

Marriage with either of a man's cross-cousins: *Bilateral cross-cousin marriage.*

Marriage with mother's brother's daughter: *Matrilateral cross-cousin marriage.*

Marriage with father's sister's daughter: *Patrilateral cross-cousin marriage.*

But cross-cousins are by no means the only kin preferred as mates. Mohammedan law encourages marriage between parallel cousins, and in other communities even more remote kin are regarded as the most suitable or as the only possible mates, as in the Australian examples given in Chapter III, Section 9.

In connection with preferential marriages, we must refer to two terms which correspond to widespread types of marriage, namely, the levirate and the sororate. Under the **levirate,** when a man dies his widow becomes the wife of one of his brothers. In some communities a man *must* marry his deceased brother's wife, in others he may waive the right if he does not want the woman. The children of such a union are sometimes regarded socially as the children of the dead man. In this case the second husband "raises up seed" to his deceased brother. When the duty or privilege of marrying a deceased brother's widow is restricted to his younger brother, the custom is known as the *junior levirate.*

The term **sororate** is a somewhat ambiguous one, being used in three different senses by various writers to refer to: (*a*) the rule whereby a man who marries a woman has a pre-emptive right to marry also her younger sisters as they reach maturity; (*b*) the rule whereby if a man wishes to marry more than one wife, the subsidiary wives must be sisters of his first wife; (*c*) the rule whereby if a man marries and his first wife dies, then his wife's kinsfolk are under an obligation to provide him with another wife, particularly if the first wife has died childless. The last of these uses of the term is analogous to the levirate.

Both the levirate and the sororate serve useful social functions in the communities in which they occur. The former provides for the disposal of widows. Owing to the sexual division of labour in primitive society, a woman who lacks the co-operation of a man cannot lead an independent existence. She can and sometimes does return to her own people, where she relies on the co-operation of her male consanguineous kin. But it is more satisfactory that she should re-marry, and the levirate ensures that this shall occur with the least possible social friction and disruption of the kinship system. Furthermore, when a man dies childless, the levirate often ensures the continuity of his line, since the community may regard subsequent children as his. This is frequently connected with ancestor worship, and the feeling that every man should have descendants who will make offerings to him and perform ceremonies in his honour after his death. On the other hand, the sororate (in the last of the senses mentioned above) ensures that a man who has handed over bride-price shall have the privileges to which this entitles him—the services of a wife and descendants to assist him during life and pay homage to him after death. Where the term "sororate" refers to marriage with sisters who are alive at the same time (the first two meanings given above), this custom, which is often observed in practice even when it is not obligatory, means that a man's wives are sisters to each other. This reduces the tensions and conflicts which are always apt to arise between co-wives in polygynous societies.

7. Extended Kinship Groupings

In all societies the family is the basic unit of kinship structure, and in the case of any individual, kinship relationships are traced through both parents whatever may be the system of descent. For example, we have referred to the importance of the mother's brother in patrilineal societies. But for purposes of social continuity one or other parent only is usually regarded as relevant, according to whether descent is patrilineal or matrilineal. The fact that this is consistently applied in all families in a community leads to the formation of *extended kinship groupings* founded on unilateral descent either through males or through females.[1] The first of these to be considered is the lineage.

A **lineage** consists of a group of males and females who trace descent from a common ancestor or ancestress [2] in the patrilineal

---

[1] As we shall see, a few societies have extended kinship groupings in which descent through both parents is recognized.

[2] In view of what was said in Section 3 regarding the exercise of power by males in matrilineal societies, it must be emphasized that in such societies it is often the brother of an ancestress, rather than the ancestress herself, who is emphasized. Thus the effective head of a matrilineal lineage is usually its senior living male member, while among dead forbears it is often the brother of an ancestress, rather than the ancestress herself, who is emphasized in religion and mythology. But the matrilineal principle is strictly observed—the individual in question owes his importance to his relationship through a female to the lineage as a whole.

or in the matrilineal line. Usually most of the members of a lineage are dead, but this does not affect the structure of the unit. A large lineage is often subdivided into subsidiary units of the same type but of smaller size, and for these certain special terms have been suggested. The term *maximal lineage* refers to the largest group of kinsmen who can trace descent from a common forbear. This may consist of two or more *major segments*, which may again be subdivided into *lesser* segments and so on until we come to the *minimal* lineage, in a patrilineal society, of a man and his children.[1]

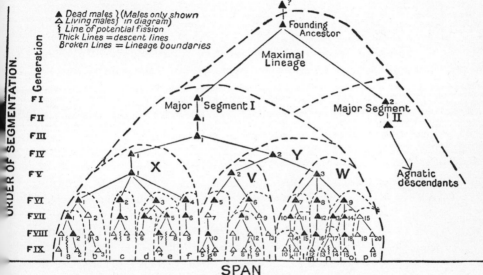

FIG. 10.—Paradigm of the Lineage System of the Tallensi

A paradigm of the hierarchical lineage structure of the patrilineal Tallensi is given in Fig. 10. It should be noted that this diagram is schematic only, and omits females who are sisters of male members of each lineage and who also belong to it. The term *agnatic* which appears in the diagram is, in the context, equivalent to what we would call patrilineal kinsfolk.

In the lineage each individual can trace explicitly his genealogical connection with the forbear upon whom the lineage

---

[1] The unit to which the term *minimal lineage* might be applied in a matrilineal society is open to question. If we follow the analogy from patrilineal descent, it should consist of a woman and her children. But in view of the legal and economic position of the mother's brother of the children in such societies, he should probably be included, since he is essential to the social functioning of the unit.

depends for its existence. In other words, he can name all the individuals in the intervening generations through whom descent is claimed. But there are other unilateral units in which the kinship of members is fictional. It may be attributed to descent from a common ancestor with whom explicit genealogical relationship cannot be traced, or individuals may claim fellow-membership of a group simply because their relevant parents belonged to it. The best known of such units is the clan. A **clan,** sometimes called a *sib* or *sept,* is an exogamous social group whose members regard themselves as being related to each other, usually by fictional descent from a common ancestor. Clans may be patrilineal or matrilineal, and the two types occasionally co-exist in the same community.

The above definition by no means corresponds with the many different senses in which the word "clan" is used by various writers. These differences in usage are apt to lead to confusion, and some discussion of them is therefore necessary. Thus the term "clan" is often used for units whose members can trace explicitly their descent from a common ancestor, and which would therefore be better termed lineages. It has also been applied to aggregations of individuals who have nothing in common except the rule of exogamy prohibiting intermarriage between them. Thus, in the classical legal code of China, people having the same surname were not allowed to marry, though apparently little attention is paid to this rule nowadays. Chinese individuals having the same surname have therefore sometimes been referred to as a "clan", a usage which is highly questionable in view of the fact that they were scattered over the whole country and never functioned as a group. On the other hand, Professor Firth uses the term to apply to the four component units of Tikopia society, for although they are not exogamous, they function in other respects as clans. There can be little objection to such usages provided that the writer makes clear exactly what he means when he speaks of a clan, but unfortunately this is not always the case in ethnographic records. A usage which is quite unjustifiable is the employment of the term "clan" of the extended family, to be described presently, which includes affinal kin. The very essence of the clan is consanguineous kinship, whether genealogically definable or fictional.

In connection with the Tikopia usage, it should be noted that the original Scottish clan does not correspond with the above definition, since it has never, so far as we know, been exogamous. The adoption of the Gaelic term with the specialized meaning usually given to it by anthropological writers is resented by some Scotsmen, and undoubtedly adds to the confusions surrounding our use of the word. But as the criterion of exogamy is generally observed in the mass of existing anthropological literature, it is better to adhere to it as closely as possible. Finally, we must mention the fact that the terminology used by certain American writers in speaking of "clans" varies from that employed in Great Britain according to the following table of equivalence:

British Terminology	American Terminology
Clan	Sib
Patrilineal clan	Gens
Matrilineal clan	Clan

The bonds of fictional kinship which unite fellow-members of the group to which the term "clan" is usually applied are reflected in close social solidarity and binding obligations akin to those we have mentioned in connection with kinship. Fellow-clansmen support one another in quarrels with members of other clans, and they co-operate in practical day-to-day activities, such as house-building or major economic undertakings, though frequently such co-operation is limited in practice to those clansmen who are also bound together by bonds of individual kinship or neighbour-hood. The clan is frequently a political and war-making unit. Finally, clan membership is frequently sanctioned by religious observances, such as the worship of a common ancestor [1] or the possession of a common totem or totems (see Chapter V, Section 5). Often the members of a small clan inhabit a common territory, apart from those who have left the clan territory at marriage. The social, economic and political implications of clan-membership in a primitive society are well exemplified in the material from Wogeo which we shall examine in a later chapter.

Sometimes two or more clans are linked together to form a wider group which is also exogamous. Such a group is termed a **phratry**.[2] Thus, among the Chenchus there are several patrilineal clans, the occurrence of which varies from one Chenchu area to another.

[1] When a clan or other social group actually bears the name of the man from whom its members believe themselves to be descended, this man is called the **eponymous ancestor** of the group concerned.
[2] Sometimes the terms *clan* and *sub-clan* are used instead of *phratry* and *clan*, but this is impossible where the larger groups are not named.

In one district ten clans are found, and these are grouped together into four larger units as follows:

1. Menlur, Daserolu.
2. Sigarlu, Urtalu.
3. Tokal, Nallapoteru, Katraj.
4. Nimal, Eravalu, Pulsaru.

These wider groups are phratries, since a man of the Nimal clan, for example, is prohibited from marrying, not only a Nimal woman, but also any woman of the Eravalu or Pulsaru clans.[1]

In communities where two exogamous groups exist, such groups are termed **moieties,** and the community is said to possess a *dual organization.* In some societies the moieties are the only exogamous unilateral groups. In others each moiety is composed of several component clans. Such moieties are structurally equivalent to phratries, and are sometimes so called by American writers.

Because of its size, the moiety can never be a closely co-operating unit as is the clan, though particular members of the two moieties are often aligned *vis-à-vis* one another in a complementary manner in practical undertakings and ceremonial affairs, as we have seen to be the case among the Haida. In other communities the interrelationships between members of the same or different moieties are confined to limited ceremonial and more or less formal observances, as in the matrilineal moieties of Wogeo.

We have so far considered groups founded on unilateral consanguineous kinship. But certain important groupings depend upon bilateral and also affinal kinship, and are frequently associated with common residence. The best known and most widespread grouping founded on kinship is the **extended family,**[2] sometimes called the *joint family* because of their common claims to land and certain kinds of property. The extended family is a group founded on kinship and locality, and resulting from the rules of patrilocal or of matrilocal marriage. It is a socially recognized group of individual families living together in close association, which are bound together by the fact that either:

[1] The Chenchu phratries are not named, and the people themselves have no very clear conception of their structure. Every Chenchu knows the clans into which he may not marry, but informants are apt to become vague when discussing the possibility of intermarriage between clans other than their own.

[2] The German term *Grossfamilie* is sometimes used to denote this type of grouping.

(*a*) The men in each of the individual families are genealogically related in the male line (the patrilineal or patrilocal extended family); or

(*b*) The women in each of the individual families are genealogically related in the female line (the matrilineal or
matrilocal extended family).

The relationship is traced to a grandparent or more distant forbear. The core of an extended family is thus a patrilineal or matrilineal lineage (or rather segment of a lineage), *plus* males or
females who have joined the extended family at marriage *minus*
males or females who have left it at marriage. It also differs from
the lineage in the greater emphasis placed upon living as opposed
to dead forbears.

The extended family must be carefully distinguished from the
clan, with which it is often confused. The following are important
differences:

Extended Family	*Clan*
Always an economic unit.	Frequently an economic unit, but not always so.
Always a local group.	Members may be scattered over a wide area.
Includes affinal kin.	Does not include affinal kin.
Genealogical relationships can be traced between all members.	Genealogical relationships between members not necessarily definable.

The kinship relationships within the extended family are
founded on the bilateral principle. For example, in a matrilocal
extended family, an unmarried man's father is also a member,
although he is not, under matriliny, a consanguineous relative,
and the same applies to other men who have married into the
group.

So far as the extended family is concerned, *group* relationships
(as distinct from individual kinship bonds) are not extended
beyond the group of kin who reside together. But bilateral groups
of a non-residential kind are occasionally found in primitive
society. Such groups are often referred to by the term **kindred**,
but no exact definition of this word is satisfactory, because the
types of grouping of which we are speaking vary enormously in
the importance which they attach to different kinds of kinship
(patrilineal or matrilineal, consanguineous or affinal), in the
range to which the recognition of kinship extends, and in the

lateral as against the vertical extension of recognized relationships.

The best example of a bilateral non-residential grouping is the
kano a paito of Tikopia. This is a body of relatives composed of an
individual's kinsfolk on both the father's and the mother's sides,
as well as some affinal relatives. It is an ill-defined group, membership of which depends upon such factors as proximity of residence
and rank. Thus, when a man falls ill, his *kano a paito* assemble as
an act of sympathy. The most important members are the close
relatives of the sick man's mother and father. When we come to
more distant relatives, attendance is to some extent a matter of
individual choice, since membership of the *kano a paito* is not
rigidly circumscribed or clearly defined. It is also most important to recognize that this group is not an autonomous unit in
the social structure, distinct from other units of the same type.
It is constituted with reference to a particular individual. That this
is a necessary result of its bilateral constitution will be realized
when we reflect that if it were otherwise in a small primitive
community, everybody would sooner or later belong to all the
bilateral groups in the society, and these would thus lose their
identity. The best analogy with such a bilateral grouping which
can be found in our society is in what we term a "family gathering", using the term in a non-anthropological sense. The individual families of the Smiths and the Browns are distinct social
units, but a Christmas gathering at the home of the Smiths may be
attended by members of the Brown family if they are related to
each other by marriage or by descent in either the male or female
line. As with the primitive kindred, the actual working of such
groups depends upon a number of factors, such as residence, rank
and customary usage in different social strata.

We have discussed various types of extended grouping found in
different primitive societies. The relationships of kinship and
locality upon which these are founded may be clarified by reference to Fig. 11. It must be emphasized that this diagram[1] is
schematic only. On the one hand, all the groups mentioned
could not co-exist in any given primitive society. On the other
hand, the diagram represents a simplification and attenuation

[1] Readers who find difficulty in following the diagram in its existing form may be
helped by copying out the symbols and substituting underlining with different-coloured
pencils for the letters which indicate various relationships. Thus, patrilineal kinsfolk
could be underlined in red, matrilineal in blue, and so on. Such a diagram gives a
much more vivid impression of the relationships concerned.

of the relationships actually recognized. Thus many affinal relatives are omitted, while the diagram gives a misleading impression of the numbers of individuals who may constitute a maximal lineage, as will be seen by comparing it with Fig. 10.

The relationships indicated by various letters are given in the key. To these it must be added that a bilateral non-residential kinship unit of the kindred type would be composed of some or all of the patrilineal and matrilineal kinsfolk and also other consanguineous kin and, in the case of the *kano a paito*, affinal relatives. The kinship relationships indicated are not necessarily mutually exclusive owing to the types of preferential marriages mentioned in Section 6. Finally, as regards the extended family, it must be pointed out that the diagram does not represent a stable state of affairs. Thus, in the first descending generation the siblings of one or other sex would leave the extended family at marriage.

Before concluding our discussion of extended kinship groupings, it is necessary to refer to certain exceptional or atypical forms. The first of these is the Maori *hapu*, which has been described as *ambilateral*. The Maori were organized into extended families, and as one of these expanded it might develop into a *hapu*, consisting of several hundred people. Usually such a unit inhabited a single village, though a large village might be shared by several *hapu*, while a small one might contain only a section of a *hapu*. A man might marry either within or outside his *hapu*. When parents belonged to different *hapu*, their children belonged to either, and claims to membership might be exercised for two or three generations either through males or females, though patrilineal affiliation was preferred. Such inherited claims were conditioned by residence. Thus, if a man from *hapu* A came to reside with *hapu* B and married a woman there, and their descendants continued to reside with *hapu* B for several generations, their claims on *hapu* A in matters of residence and land ownership became, in the native idiom, "cold" unless such claims were kept alive by occasional periods of residence with *hapu* A. Thus, residence as well as descent conditioned membership of the *hapu*.

While the vast majority of primitive peoples stress either patriliny or matriliny in tracing descent, some of them have two sets of groups based on different principles. Such a condition prevails among the Yakö and in other West African communities.[1]

Every individual in a Yakö village belongs to both a patrilineal

[1] For example, in Ashanti, though the information for this area is not fully adequate.

clan and a matrilineal clan, which we may call *pun* and *jima* respectively.[1] The rule of exogamy prevails in both, but is less strictly enforced in the *jima* than in the *pun*. Membership of each group implies a different set of rights and obligations. Marriage is patrilocal, so that male members of a *pun* form a residential group within the village and also cultivate tracts of farm-land adjoining it. Each *pun* has a priest, who performs ceremonies at a special shrine for members of the group and also arbitrates, together with the elders of the *pun*, in internal disputes. Claims in regard to dwelling sites, forest resources, farm-lands and co-operative labour in the annual clearing of the land are exercised through, and inherited by, members of the *pun*.

The *jima*, on the other hand, are necessarily non-territorial units, in view of patrilocal marriage. The most important rights and obligations arising from membership of a *jima* are those relating to inheritance of livestock, currency and other movable property, as distinct from land. When a woman marries, most of the bride-price [2] goes to members of her *jima*, who are correspondingly responsible for its return if she should subsequently leave her husband. On the other hand, members of a man's *jima* provide a considerable share of the bride-price which he pays to members of his bride's *jima*. Members of the *jima* are also responsible for debts incurred by a kinsman, and can claim recompense for injuries done to him. Though, as we have said, most land rights and claims to natural resources are exercised through the *pun*, the *jima* also have certain limited and specific rights, for example, in regard to wine collected from oil palms.

The *jima* also have their own shrines, where spirits of fertility connected with the *jima* are invoked by special priests in connection with agricultural ritual. To these shrines each woman of the *jima* is brought during her first pregnancy with offerings to secure the welfare of her unborn child and her own future fertility. A corresponding rite is often performed at the father's *pun* shrine, but this is regarded as less important. The supernatural power of the *jima* priests is a sanction for law and order in the village as a whole (as distinct from disputes within the *pun*), because they can enforce the wishes of the village council by appeal to the beneficent or destructive powers of the *jima* spirits.

---

[1] These are abbreviations of the terms employed by the natives, who actually use the words *kepun* and *lejima* (singular) or *yepun* and *yajima* (plural). But our omission of the prefixes will simplify reading of the following text.

[2] This consists traditionally of specified amounts of native currency, food and wine.

C.
.C.
C.

C.P.

C.M.

F.P.

F.M.

Q, R
y, z

c
A

c
l

II.

This brief summary indicates the differential rights and obligations of patrilineal and matrilineal kinship respectively in such diverse fields as economics, law and religion. These are complementary to each other and do not normally conflict. The natives sum up the position by saying that a man eats in his *pun* and inherits in his *jima*. But it must be emphasized that though some of the rights concerned operate through group membership, others, such as those pertaining to bride-price, are exercised through individual kinship and not by the group as a whole.

Though the social structure of the Yakö is atypical for primitive societies, it must not be regarded as contradicting the general principles which are operative. Though the functions—economic, legal and religious—corresponding to those we have mentioned are more commonly discharged either by patrilineal or by matrilineal groups, we have seen that in all societies kinship through both parents is important. We should therefore think of the majority of primitive societies as being predominantly, rather than exclusively, either patrilineal or matrilineal. In these terms the unusual situation found among the Yakö represents merely a consolidation into group relationships of the bonds of individual kinship through both father and mother which are found in all societies.

8. The Family Reconsidered

The preceding sections have indicated the important ways in which primitive systems of kinship differ from our own and from one another. But emphasis on such differences is apt to obscure, and has often in fact obscured, the universal basis of kinship— the individual family. This unit is founded basically upon the bio-psychological characteristics of the human organism. In all communities men and women experience sexual desires towards each other, and owing to the capacity for habit-formation which is related to the structure of man's cerebral cortex, such desires tend to crystallize around a special individual or individuals. This, together with economic motives and considerations of convenience, leads to the permanent association of men and women in domestic units. In all human societies, women suffer the trials of pregnancy and childbirth, and everywhere the children so produced require care and attention during the early years of their lives—they must be suckled, cleansed and prevented from injuring themselves. In the course of these profoundly significant experiences are formed the sentiments of love, tenderness and mutual dependence which are the foundation of the family.

But the family also has other functions. Because of the need for domestic co-operation and sexual division of labour in the economic field, and also because of the wider bonds of kinship— real, classificatory and fictional—beyond its bounds, it is essential that every child born into a society should have two parents.[1] This is everywhere recognized, even though in certain communities the stigma attaching to illegitimacy may be relatively slight and the social bond of marriage may not be very clearly defined, or may be, in many individual cases, impermanent. The basic unit of all human societies is the group of man, woman and children living together in an association which is regarded as right and proper, and which is not inconsistent with the need for establishing wider bonds of kinship, particularly those connected with descent, succession and inheritance.

All this may appear trite to the reader who is not familiar with the evolutionary controversies which raged around the subject of the family during the late nineteenth and early twentieth centuries. Some of the theories expounded denied the existence of the family either in contemporary primitive communities or in the hypothetical conditions of early social life in the distant past. They asserted that the functions of the family were originally discharged by a wider unit, such as the matrilineal clan, to the constitution of which paternity is not necessary. Such theories often referred to the fact that the natives of the Trobriand Islands and the Australian aborigines do not know of the connection between sexual intercourse and childbirth, and are therefore ignorant of physiological paternity.[2] It was inferred that no such thing as fatherhood could exist in such communities. A refutation of this assertion is provided by reference to data obtained by modern methods of field-work.

[1] The emphasis upon the bilateral character of the family has been called the *principle of legitimacy*.

[2] It is important to stress the fact that the Trobriand Islands and Australia are the only well-authenticated instances of the absence of knowledge of any connection between the two events. Other primitive communities recognize some connection, though their accounts of the physiology of reproduction are always superficial and frequently inaccurate. More important still, the biological facts, so far as they are known, may not be regarded as socially relevant. In this connection recent research has indicated that among some Australian tribes certain individuals are aware of the relationship, but this is not important, since paternity is socially established in other ways. The theoretical implications of the Australian and Trobriand data, particularly the misleading implications in regard to social evolution and native intelligence which have been attributed to them, will be dealt with in Volume II.

We have seen that in the Trobriand Islands many of the duties carried out by the father in our own community are discharged, not by the father, but by the mother's brother. It is the latter who disciplines the child and who gives him his place in the community, for a man inherits wealth, magical knowledge, status and rank, not from his father, but from his mother's brother. A child, its mother and its mother's brother all belong to the same clan, while the father belongs to another, owing the obligations which we have mentioned, not to his own children, but to those of his sister.

If, then, society excludes the father from this social scheme, where does he enter into family life? Stripped of the functions which we attribute to him, can the "father" be said to exist in such a community, and, if so, in what sense? The answer is to be found in the facts of family life. The father is, first and foremost, the consort of the mother, her sexual partner, her protector and helpmate. This establishes an indirect bond between the father and child through the mother. But when the child is born, a very direct relationship is established; it is the father who cares for the child during its early years, who carries out menial service for it, and who lavishes upon it all the blessings of paternal affection. These experiences of early care establish between father and son sentiments of affection which are just as real as our own; if a Trobriander is asked why a father loves his child, he will reply: "Because his hands have been soiled with its excrement", a vivid way of expressing the intimate services which a father carries out for his child. So effective is this in establishing parental love, that a father will often try to evade the rules of mother-right, and seek to secure for his own children privileges which belong by right to his sister's children.[1]

Even a superficial survey of the ethnographic material indicates the absurdity of suggesting that the clan can ever have discharged

[1] One perfectly legitimate means by which a Trobriand father, if he is a chief or other man of wealth and position, may secure benefits for his son is by betrothing this son in infancy to his (the chief's) sister's daughter. The implications of this may be clarified with reference to Fig. 12. Let us suppose that A is a chief who betroths his son C in infancy to b. While B is the legitimate successor to A and inherits his wealth, C has nevertheless economic claims on B through the system of *urigubu* gifts. He is also in a privileged position in other respects and his own son D is a possible successor to the chieftainship. The strict rules of matriliny, so far as they conflict with paternal affection, are thus to some extent circumvented. A similar expedient is adopted in other communities. Thus, among the Yakö a man of substance sometimes arranges a similar marriage for his son, so that the movable wealth inherited in the matrilineal line reverts, after a lapse of one generation, to a patrilineal kinsman of the original owner, that is, to his son's son.

the functions of the family. A clan cannot wash a baby or perform the intimate services referred to in the Trobriand saying quoted above.

Though the phenomenon known as the "ignorance of physiological paternity" is confined, so far as is at present known, to the two societies mentioned, the *irrelevance* of physiological paternity is far more common. It clearly occurs in polyandrous societies and in those instances of the levirate in which a man "raises up seed" to his dead brother. Again, it is obvious that little importance can be attached to it in those communities which allow or prescribe extra-marital sexual intercourse. Furthermore, what has been said of paternity can also be said, to some extent, of maternity. In the latter case the physiological bond is more apparent and more intimate. But in some patrilineal societies the

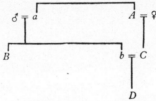

Fig. 12.—Trobriand Cross-cousin Marriage

woman is regarded merely as the soil in which the seed of the father germinates. This, again, does not negate the reality of maternal affection or the socially recognized fact of motherhood. It merely means that the interpretation of the physiological facts of reproduction is different from our own. Finally, the widespread practice of adoption in various primitive societies indicates how readily family sentiments can be established irrespective of physiological relationships. In all these cases our own knowledge of, and emphasis on, the physiology of reproduction is a bar to understanding. We could appreciate primitive attitudes towards parenthood far more readily if we all believed in the stork.

Though the family is universal in human societies, we have seen that *some* of the functions normally discharged by one or other parent may be taken over by other individuals or agencies. Lest we should give a too rigid impression of family life, we may consider the extremely atypical form of family organization, described by Professor Evans-Pritchard, among the patrilineal Nuer.

The social bond of marriage is established among the Nuer by the performance of a sequence of ceremonies and by the handing over of cattle by the bridegroom to the kin of the bride, but it is not regarded as complete until after the birth of the first child. The simple legal family of the ordinary type exists among the Nuer, but is supplemented by other forms of union, including the levirate and an unusual type of relationship which has been termed *ghost-marriage*. Under the latter, if a man, married or unmarried, dies without male issue, it becomes the duty of one of his kinsmen to marry a wife on his behalf. The sons of such a union are legally the children of the dead man, and inherit social or ritual privileges which he would normally pass on to his sons. This custom of ghost-marriage is based on the feeling that a man should not lie in his grave unremembered. He needs male offspring to whom he can make his wishes known in dreams, and if his kinsmen fail in their duty to marry a wife for him, he may bring evil upon them.

The parenthood of a "ghost-father" is most important in the adult life of his sons. During their childhood they live with their mother and her pro-husband in a union superficially indistinguishable from simple legal marriage. The pro-husband has legal authority over the children and over the wife. This type of union is almost as common as simple legal marriage, owing to the number of men who die without male issue. In the past this was largely due to casualties in tribal fighting. And though this has now been prohibited by the administration, it is important to note that the system of "ghost-marriage" tends to be self-perpetuating. Thus, if a man who has married a wife for a dead kinsman himself dies without marrying a wife of his own, that is, a wife whose children would legally be his, the duty of marrying a wife on *his* behalf devolves upon the sons whom he has begotten physiologically, but who are legally the children of another man.

The types of kinsmen who normally marry a wife on behalf of a dead man are his brothers, sons, brother's sons and sister's sons. The latter type of union only occurs when the sister's son has obtained possession of his mother's brother's cattle, which may pass to him for the specific purpose of contracting the ghost-marriage in question. There is a definite rule that a man contracting a ghost-marriage must not belong to a generation senior to that of the dead man. Finally, it may be noted that a woman may sometimes contract a ghost-marriage with another woman on behalf of a dead kinsman.[1] The children of the second woman, begotten by some extraneous man, are legally the offspring of the "female husband's" dead kinsman.

The levirate is practised by the Nuer although a widow, particularly if she has borne children, has a considerable amount of freedom in her choice as to whether she will become the wife of her dead husband's brother or seek a partner elsewhere. In any case, any children which she may subsequently bear are legally the offspring of her dead husband. Leviritic marriage differs from ghost-marriage, in that there is no transfer of cattle to her kin, since this duty has already been carried out by the dead man. The procreative services of a woman belong, not merely to the man she actually marries, but to his group of near kin, who sometimes speak of her as "our wife". The Nuer do not use the term "marry" in connection with a leviritic union, but say that a man "has provided his dead brother's wife with a hut". The pro-husband has less control over the wife in a leviritic than in a ghost-marriage, though if she commits adultery he can claim compensation.

If the widow chooses to live with a stranger rather than with a kinsman of her dead husband, the children born of the union are still the legal offspring of the latter. While the union resembles marriage so far as domestic and economic co-operation is concerned, the man has no legal status in regard to either the woman or her children. She may leave him at any time and he cannot claim compensation for adultery. This type of union is described as "widow concubinage", since the man is not legally married to the woman—he is not even the legal representative of the father of her children, as is the pro-husband in leviritic and ghost-marriage.

The last type of union to be described is simple concubinage. Owing to certain circumstances—a flighty disposition or parental despotism in regard to marriage arrangements—some Nuer women never marry. But such women usually live in association with one or more men in a union which resembles normal marriage so far as domestic life is concerned. There are, however, no legal rights existing between the two partners in such a union.

---

[1] The custom of *woman marriage*, whereby one woman becomes legally the "husband" of another, who then has children by a cicisbeo, is not peculiar to the Nuer, but is found sporadically in parts of Africa as far apart as the Transvaal and Dahomey. In these cases the usual motive seems to be the desire of a barren woman to transmit to offspring her own social and economic privileges. The social implications of the practice are therefore different from those found among the Nuer.

Since readiness to live as an unmarried concubine often denotes a restless disposition, the male partners of unmarried women are not anxious to marry their concubines, though they are eager to acquire legal paternity in regard to their children. This they can do by payment of cattle as legitimatization fee. Such payments differ from ordinary marriage cattle in two important respects: they are given to the woman's father only, and are not distributed among her kin; and each payment legitimatizes one child only, not all offspring of the union.

The status of unmarried concubines and their children is not so high as that of wives, yet such women are often better treated than wives, since a woman living in this relationship is more free to leave her partner if he should prove unsatisfactory. On the other hand, a concubine cannot expect support from her kinsmen in the case of domestic disputes.

The actual incidence of the different types of union described above may be judged by reference to Professor Evans-Pritchard's statement of the marital position of thirty-three women in a typical Nuer village:

	Union of 33 women in 1936	Total unions of 33 women	Children of 32 women
Wives in simple legal marriage .	3	23	44
Female husbands . . .	1	1	—
Wives of female husbands .	3	3	5
Wives in ghost-marriage . .	5	5	6
Wives in leviritic marriage .	2	4	12
Widow-concubines . . .	6	14	36
Unmarried concubines . .	3	5	3
Women living in adultery .	1	—	3
Old women without mates .	9	—	—

The first column shows the existing domestic condition of the women concerned. The second column gives the different types of union in which these women are known, at one time or another, to have been partners. This corrects any distorted impression which might be created by the first. It shows the preponderance of the union of marriage, and particularly of simple legal marriage. Apart from the three unmarried concubines, all the thirty-three women have at some time or other lived in some form of marriage. In view of this, and of the custom of legitimatization mentioned above, it follows that the vast majority of the children have a legal father, living or dead.

How far does the Nuer material lead us to reformulate what we have said about marriage and the family? The main difficulty is to decide to which types of Nuer union or social unit these terms should be applied. If we stress sexual and domestic association, then we shall apply them to any type of existing domestic union which is not socially disapproved. If we stress the transmission from one generation to another of wealth, position and ritual privilege, we shall emphasize the legal bonds uniting a man, a woman and the woman's children, even though they may never have functioned as a biological or social unit. Though the former is more in line with our analysis of the family, neither usage is accurate, since among the Nuer the family *as we know it in our own society* exists only in simple legal marriage. But the same applies to other communities also—to matriliny and to other instances of the levirate in which the dead brother is the legal father of the children. Moreover, in many communities it is sometimes difficult to distinguish between legal marriage and other types of union.[1]

The difficulty is thus terminological rather than analytical. Evans-Pritchard's precise statement of what occurs among the Nuer enables us to appreciate the human relationships which actually exist. These are fundamentally not very different from those prevailing elsewhere in human society. They are merely more different from what we regard as the normal pattern of family life—if indeed the latter concept could be clearly defined. That social position among the Nuer should be transmitted by a dead patrilineal relative rather than by the man who functions as a father during the early years of childhood is no more surprising than the fact that it is so transmitted by the mother's brother

---

[1] Thus, in Scotland at the present time, a legal marriage may be established by "co-habitation with habit and repute". Its validity may be proved "by the co-habitation, or living together at bed and board, of a man and woman who are generally reputed husband and wife" (Gloag and Henderson, *Introduction to the Law of Scotland*, Fourth Edition, 1946, p. 574), without any religious ceremony or formal secular contract. The constitution of such a marriage is not affected by the fact that there may have been no intention of marriage at the beginning of co-habitation. A somewhat similar relationship, known as "common law marriage", is legally recognized in twenty-four states of the U.S.A., including New York State, and "notwithstanding criticism levelled at such informal marriages, they have been expressly repudiated in very few states; and in many states such marriages have been held to survive even in the face of elaborate regulations governing licensing and solemnization of marriages" (Information from Vernier, *American Family Laws*, Volume I, Section 26, communicated by Professor A. L. Goodhart). In the Scottish example, apart from the cases which have actually been disputed in the courts, it would be impossible to say at what point of time any given union changes from a liaison into a marriage, and children of the union automatically become legitimate.

under matriliny. Domestic units are unstable, though for different reasons, in Hollywood as in Nuerland. And various types of irregular union are no more a negation of the principles of family life in the Sudan than they are in Bloomsbury or Greenwich Village.

9. Conclusion

We have attempted in this chapter to give an indication of the major principles governing kinship organization in primitive society. These have been deliberately stated in a simple form in order to stress their nature and significance as organizing factors in primitive culture. But such simple formulations to some extent distort the reality of native life. There is a danger that the reader may gain a too rigid conception of how the rules governing kinship actually operate. To guard against this, four important points must be stressed:

1. The operation of principles founded on kinship is constantly modified by such other principles as those based on residence, rank and economic organization.

2. The incidence and degree of operation of these principles varies greatly from one society to another, for example, such a practice as patrilocal marriage ranges from a rigidly enforced rule to a situation where there is nothing but a general tendency for women to join their husband's groups at marriage, no pressure being brought to bear to force them to do so. Between these two extremes are a series of gradations in which patrilocal marriage is more or less customary, though matrilocal marriages sometimes occur, as we shall see to be the case in Wogeo. Similarly, principles which we have stated in connection with the prohibition of incest and the rules of exogamy vary from rigid proscription enforced by drastic legal or supernatural sanctions to a mere feeling that certain types of union are undesirable.

3. Even where certain clearly defined rules exist, they are constantly modified in the light of individual circumstances, such as rank, economic position, ritual privilege, popularity and other factors affecting the personal situation of a man or woman. A chief or priest may be able to "get away with" conduct which would be punished in the case of a commoner or layman, or alternatively may be expected to observe the social code more meticulously. A man of wealth may be

accorded privileges denied to poorer folk, but on the other hand is usually expected to be more lavish in discharging the economic obligations of kinship. A popular man may succeed in evading punishment for breaches of social custom, while a "bad lot" is sometimes heavily penalized for what we might term a technical offence. Personal hardship may also modify the rigid operation of kinship rules, as when an unmarried man is allowed to contract a marriage which breaks the rule of exogamy, when similar conduct would be severely condemned in the case of a man who already had several wives.

4. Finally, strength of individual character often means that certain individuals are prepared to risk the social consequences of evasion or breach of custom, and are sometimes successful in doing so.

A few examples of the operation of these modifying factors have been given and others will occur in subsequent pages, particularly in our discussion of primitive law. These will to some extent correct the somewhat rigid conception of social organization which may at times have been conveyed in this chapter. But the way in which the principles which we have enunciated actually work can only be defined with reference to each primitive community specifically, and correct impression of their incidence and operation can only be acquired by a further reading of good ethnographic records.

10. Bibliographical Commentary

The definition of social structure given at the beginning of this chapter may strike some anthropologists as an unjustifiable attempt to reconcile two different interpretations of the term. For a theoretical discussion of the problem, see Radcliffe-Brown (6).

There is no really adequate review of the phenomena of social organization in primitive society. Rivers (2) provides some useful discussions of terminology, but is written in the light of theoretical interpretations and ethnographic material which cannot be regarded as tenable and reliable today. Lowie (1) is largely concerned with criticism of Morgan's theory of social origins. This theory cannot be taken seriously in the light of modern research, and it should not be necessary for the reader to follow the ingenious arguments by which Lowie disposes of Morgan's evolutionary guesswork. The main value of Lowie's work is to be found in the light which it casts on the variety and complex interlocking of different types of social grouping in primitive society.

As stated at the end of Section 9, the best approach to the problem of social organization is through modern ethnographic records, particularly those dealing specifically with kinship. Some of these are mentioned in the bibliography. The fullest and most enlightening discussion of the place of kinship in a primitive culture is undoubtedly Firth (8). Valuable discussions of problems connected with kinship are contained in Deacon (1), Fei (1), Hoernlé (2), Hunter (2), Nadel (4), Raum (2) and Richards (2). A brilliant analysis of structural relationships founded on kinship is contained in Fortes (3), but the beginner will probably find this work somewhat difficult to follow.

Fuller statements on the material presented in this chapter on kinship among the Maori, Yakö and Nuer will be found in Firth (5), Forde (4) and Evans-Pritchard (5).

The relationships between the individual bonds within the family and wider kinship extensions are discussed in Malinowski (6 and 7) and, with special relationship to the place of sex in social life, in Malinowski (4). Some of the implications of the ignorance of physiological paternity among the Australian aborigines are discussed in Ashley-Montagu (1). There is a vast amount of material, mainly published in the journal *Oceania*, on Australian kinship. For the first systematic account upon which subsequent research on kinship in Australia has been founded, we are indebted to Radcliffe-Brown (2). An excellent example of the application of this approach to the kinship system of an Australian tribe is Warner (1). Finally, as an illustration of the principles stated in Section 9, reference should be made to Kaberry (1) to correct any exaggerated impression of the rigidity of Australian kinship which might be gained from writings which are primarily concerned with its more formal aspects.

CHAPTER V

SOCIAL ORGANIZATION (*Continued*)

1. Local Grouping

IN considering any primitive people, it is important to know how they are distributed in local groups over the territory which they occupy. This is termed their **local organization.** It varies greatly from one community to another; it reflects the adjustment to geographical environment; and it affects, and is affected by, the character of social institutions.

The largest unit of social organization usually recognized in social anthropology is the tribe, a term which is somewhat loosely employed. We may define a **tribe** as a group of people speaking a common dialect, inhabiting a common territory and displaying a certain homogeneity in their culture. The tribe is never exogamous; in fact, its members marry fellow-members more often than they marry outsiders. The tribe is not primarily or usually a kinship group, but in certain cases all members of a tribe claim descent from a common ancestor.

The tribe is frequently a political unit for purposes of the internal administration of justice and external relations, such as the prosecution of war. It will be noted that this is not essential according to our definition, nor is the actual numerical strength of the group concerned. Thus the Ibo tribe of south-eastern Nigeria numbers approximately four million people, who have no centralized political authority, being bound together merely by the fact that they share a common language, territory and culture. The latter part of this statement is also true of the very much smaller Australian tribe. An approximate estimate, which is little more than a guess, puts the size of the average Australian tribe in 1788 at about one thousand individuals, though some were considerably smaller. Nowadays, depopulation has rendered many Australian tribes extinct, while of others only a handful remain.

As we have said, the term "tribe" is loosely employed, and this is to some extent unavoidable. For one thing, it is impossible to say exactly what is meant by cultural homogeneity. Most large tribes exhibit cultural variations from one area to another, and in politically organized tribes some measure of political authority is usually delegated to smaller component units. It is often doubtful whether such units should be regarded as **sub-tribes** or as tribes in their own right. Sometimes the criteria of territorial, linguistic and cultural unity do not coincide. Thus the Nupe people of Central Nigeria are composed of several groups having marked variations in culture and dialect, but these cannot be regarded as distinct tribes, since they overlap and intermingle territorially, and moreover, their members have a sense of unity extending beyond the bounds of their particular sub-groups—they all speak of themselves as "Nupe", as distinct from neighbouring peoples who speak practically the same language but are regarded as merely "relatives".

Whatever the size and territorial extent of the tribe, it is always subdivided into smaller groups based on neighbourhood, known as *local groups* or *residential aggregates*. Such groups inhabit the same or adjoining dwellings, co-operate in economic activities and are usually bound together by ties of kinship. The size of such group-ings again varies very greatly, particularly in relation to type of economy. Thus hunters and food-gatherers are usually nomadic,[1] and their settlements are therefore rude and temporary shelters of no very great extent, as we see among the Australians, Semang and Bushmen. Only where natural resources are exceptionally plentiful can a hunting and food-gathering economy support permanent villages, but this occurs among the Haida and other tribes of the North-West Coast.

Pastoral peoples also tend to be nomadic, and their settlements are therefore often found to consist of temporary or light movable habitations. Only where pastoralism is combined with agri-culture do we normally find permanent or semi-permanent villages, surrounded by common pastures and agricultural land, as among the Nyakyusa (Fig. 19, p. 302).

The nomadism of hunters and food-gatherers and also of pastoralists is frequently seasonal, as we have seen to be the case among the Eskimo, the Kazaks and the Tungus.

Among peoples who are exclusively or primarily cultivators we

[1] Or more correctly semi-nomadic. The small hunting bands which form the economic units of such societies do not wander indiscriminately, but over defined areas of territory. In Australia this practice is sanctified by mythology and magico-religious ritual.

again find considerable variation. Under shifting cultivation village sites may be moved if necessary after several years, when the neighbouring land has been exhausted. But where the latter is plentiful, or where rotation of crops or mixed farming is practised, the village is usually permanent.

The size of the local group among communities which subsist by cultivation is extremely variable. At one extreme we find in New Guinea areas where the steep hillsides do not provide sufficient flat ground for the formation of villages, and the local unit consists of tiny clusters of houses perched on the top of steep

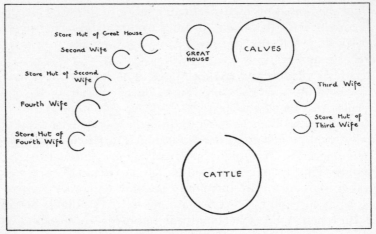

FIG. 13.—Plan of one type of Pondo *umzi* (after Hunter)

ridges, accommodating perhaps not more than three or four families. At the other extreme are the densely packed Pueblo settlements of the south-western U.S.A. One of the largest of these, the Pueblo Bonito of New Mexico, contained about five hundred rooms, and might have accommodated over two thousand people. Intermediate between these extremes are a number of varieties of village organization and scattered settlements. Thus the Pondo live in groups of huts called *imizi* (singular: *umzi*), as shown in Plate IV, each cluster of huts housing a patrilineal extended family. The ground-plan of the *umzi* varies according to the constitution of the household. That of one type is shown in Fig. 13. The distance between *imizi* varies from about fifty yards to a mile. This may be compared with a different type of Bantu settlement, the Bemba village shown in Plate V.

PLATE IV

PONDO *IMIZI*

The size of the buildings in which members of a local group reside is also variable. In many polygynous societies each wife has her own hut, the husband residing with or visiting each wife in turn. Sometimes a polygynous household shares a common habitation, a defined area of which is assigned to each wife. In other communities a single building sometimes houses the whole of a local group, as in the Long House of the Iroquois. Similar structures are common in Malaysia, for example, in parts of the Philippines there are buildings of hardwood timber measuring up to 400 yards in length. One or two of these accommodate the whole population of a village. As with the Iroquois, they have a central corridor, flanked by separate compartments for individual families.

We have mentioned only a few of the many types of local grouping found among primitive peoples. The real importance of such groups lies, not in mere demographic or cartographic description, but in the study of the relation of local grouping to social institutions. Thus, if we compare two types of Melanesian village, one from the Trobriand Islands and the other from Wogeo, we can discern at once the relation of village-plan to political and economic organization. In Omarakana (Fig. 14) we see the chief's hut, and even more important his yam house, dominating the scene, while in Wogeo (Fig. 17, p. 291) it is the *niabwa* which is the most imposing structure and is the central feature (both topographically and socially) of the village. The significance of this comparison will be obvious from the sociological data from the two communities given elsewhere in this book.

Among the institutions which often affect the local grouping of a people, one of the most important is warfare. The need for defence against attack has often led to the construction of more or less inaccessible settlements. Thus the Maori had two types of village, the ordinary unfortified village (*kainga*)[1] and the hill fort, or *pa*. The latter type of settlement, which was virtually confined to the North Island, was usually built upon a hill or ridge, or was protected on one or more sides by a cliff, a stream or the sea. Though the selection of a site for a *pa* was determined primarily by the need for defence, the proximity of economic resources—fertile agricultural land or fishing grounds—was also taken into consideration. The natural defences of the *pa* were

---

[1] This is the only type of Maori village found in New Zealand today.

supplemented by artificial fortifications, such as earthworks and stockades built of heavy timber. The *pa* was not merely a temporary refuge, but was the permanent residence of members of the village, the sections occupied by its component families being frequently partitioned off from each other. In

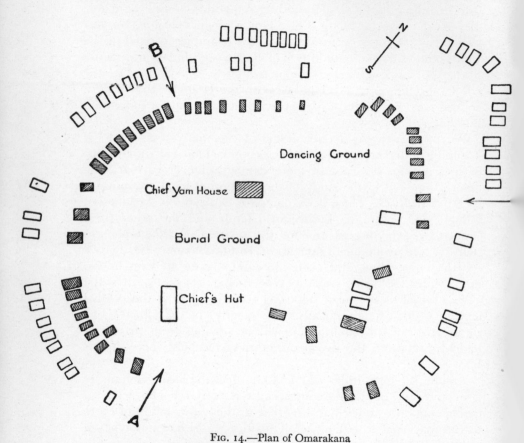

FIG. 14.—Plan of Omarakana

addition to dwellings, there were storage huts, particularly important in time of siege, while the whole village was dominated by a sort of citadel, composed of the houses of the chief and his principal relatives. Thus the structure of the Maori *pa* was not only based on the need for defence—it was related to the other activities of the people, domestic, economic and political.

PLATE V

A BEMBA VILLAGE

2. Sex Grouping and the Place of Women in Primitive Society

In all cultures the biological differences between men and women imply differences in their respective social rôles, but the precise character and degree of such differentiation are largely variable.

The most important difference, which all cultures must recognize, lies in their respective physiological rôles in the production and rearing of children. But this generally leads to certain secondary forms of differentiation, of which the most important is the sexual division of labour. Very broadly, there is a tendency to allocate dangerous tasks and those requiring strenuous and concentrated physical effort for comparatively short periods to men, while relatively safe work, which calls for more prolonged but less concentrated effort, is usually the province of women. A good example of this contrast is to be found in the fishing of Oceanic communities. Deep-sea fishing, with its intermittent demands for violent physical effort, is the work of men, sometimes sanctioned by taboos on women embarking in sea-going canoes; on the other hand, fishing from the shore and the gathering of sea food from lagoons and rock pools tend to be the work of women. Again, among the Australian aborigines the men do the hunting while women gather edible plants, fish, or collect goannas and other small game. Hunting an emu or kangaroo with dogs makes heavy demands on physical stamina, as the author can testify, while collecting oysters or digging up ants calls for patient periods of prolonged effort which is never very strenuous and can be interrupted at any time.[1]

In the last sentence we have the clue to this feature of the sexual division of labour. Most women become pregnant on one or more occasions during their lives, and are subsequently encumbered with young children who are dependent on them for nourishment and attention. Consequently, their work is such as is not jeopardized by these necessary biological responsibilities.

Similar observations apply most forcibly to warfare. This is, indirectly, an important aspect of economic life in those agricultural and pastoral communities who are constantly subject to raids by other groups seeking to acquire land or cattle, or who

---

[1] The same considerations apply to the carrying of burdens. When an aborigine group is on the move, most of their scanty baggage is carried by the women, since the men must not be encumbered in making their specific contribution to the food supply.

themselves subsist by such activities. Thus, among the Bedouins
and many Hamitic and Bantu peoples, the men must always be
ready to repel attack, or alternatively to be absent for some time
on aggressive enterprises. Therefore in such communities we find
that most of the "work", in the limited sense, is done by women,
a situation which often calls forth the contempt or condemnation
of Europeans with whose traditions of chivalry it is inconsistent.
But chivalry is a matter of minor importance when survival itself
is at stake.[1]

The above explanation does not account for all differences in
the sexual division of labour. Thus, it is hard to see why the
making of pottery should in some communities be done exclusively by men, whereas in others it is the province of women.
Again, the respective magico-religious functions of men and
women are defined in various ways by different communities.
Whether one or other sex participates in, or is excluded from,
specific forms of religious or magical ritual cannot be explained
in biological terms. It can only be interpreted in terms of the
particular cultural institutions and values of the community
concerned.

What we have said about warfare is also true, though to a lesser
extent, of the exercise of political power which, it may be noted,
is often identical with leadership in war. Only very rarely do we
find women actually exercising administrative functions, although,
as among the Bemba, Ganda and the aristocratic cultures of
Polynesia, we often find specific relatives of the chief—mother,
sister or Great Wife—occupying a privileged ceremonial position.
Such women, particularly if they have strong personalities, can
often exert a considerable influence on social life. The unusually
active part played by women in tribal affairs among the Iroquois
has already been mentioned, but it must again be emphasized
that this is quite exceptional. Normally, women play little or no
part in political affairs, nor do they usually display any inclina-
tion to do so.

When we come to the magico-religious sphere, the data are
less consistent. In Australia women are rigidly excluded from the

---

[1] An interesting sidelight on what has been said is cast by the quite exceptional
organization of "Amazons" in Dahomey. These were a cadre of specially selected and
trained women who fought fiercely in battle, and in peace-time administered the
women of the king's household. They did not, however, form part of his harem, and
were rigorously segregated from men at all times. This reflects the inconsistency
between military duties and the biological responsibilities of women.

sacred ceremonial of the men, though they carry out other less spectacular rites of their own. In Melanesia, too, we usually find that women play no part in the more important magico-religious ceremonies, which are the exclusive province of the men. Among Amerindian tribes, on the other hand, the situation is quite different. Thus, membership of the important Tobacco Society of the Crow was open to both sexes, and women feature at least as conspicuously as men. In many American tribes we find both male and female shamans, and even where men occupy a dominant position in religious ceremonial, women also have their own religious societies and carry out forms of ceremonial peculiar to them. Much the same situation exists in many parts of Africa, for example in Sierra Leone, where the men's society (*poro*) finds its counterpart in the women's association (*bundu*), each sex being excluded from participation in the ceremonial activities of the other.

To sum up, we may say that generally men play a more important part in magico-religious ceremonial than women, but this is frequently offset by the admission of women on equal terms to religious organizations, or alternatively by a definition of different types of religious ceremonial as appropriate to each sex, even though that of the women may be less spectacular than that of the men.

Though it will be apparent that it is highly dangerous to generalize about the position of women in primitive societies, something must be said on the subject, because of the many misinterpretations which have been put forward. At one extreme is the view that women occupy, or once occupied, the dominant position associated with the term "matriarchate", a conception which nobody would seriously defend today. But the contrary view that women in primitive society occupy an utterly degraded and menial position, being regarded as mere chattels, is still frequently put forward. Here it is important to distinguish between theory and practice. In terms of explicitly formulated legal rules, it is true that women often appear to occupy a subordinate position. But as we shall see, this is offset by other considerations.

The view that women occupy a degraded position in primitive society is often supported by superficial observations and spurious arguments. Those connected with bride-price and the sexual division of labour we have already mentioned. In addition, it is often pointed out that marriages are often arranged by relatives, sometimes during the infancy of the parties concerned, and that kinsfolk often bring pressure to bear to maintain a marriage against a woman's will. This is said to imply that the woman is therefore a mere pawn in a game determined by motives of greed and ambition.

In the first place it must be noted that such restrictions on individual liberty affect men as well as women. And even if it be admitted that they operate differentially to the detriment of the latter, there are still certain important considerations to be taken into account, considerations which affect the more general question of the place of the individual in primitive society.

The question of individual choice in marriage is one on which much confusion has arisen. In some primitive societies courtship is by individual choice, though perhaps restricted by such influences as the wishes of relatives and considerations of rank, as it is to some extent among ourselves. Even where marriage is said to be "arranged by the relatives", the arrangements are often influenced by the wishes of the parties concerned. Furthermore, owing to the homogeneity of cultural standards, the advantages of a particular choice made by relatives are likely to be the same as those valued by the parties concerned; in particular, industriousness and proficiency in the day-to-day work appropriate to the sex concerned. The social value attached to this was reflected by the derisive songs sung by young people of each sex against the other among the Maori:

> *"Who will marry a man*
> *Too lazy to till the ground for food? . . ."*

> *"Who will marry the woman*
> *Too lazy to weave garments?"*

Such practical considerations receive, in general, more attention in primitive society than "personality". Marriage is more practical and less "romantic" among primitive peoples than among ourselves. It might be said, very generally, that in our ideology of marriage, two people come to love each other first and then marry, whereas the primitive conception reverses the order. Thus, when Dr. Richards, working among the Bemba, asked about a newly married man: "Is X very fond of his bride?" her informant replied, with some surprise: "How can he be fond of her? How can he know what her heart is like until they have grown old together?"

This does not imply that genuine affection is absent from primitive marriage. On the contrary, the field-worker is constantly brought face to face with examples of it, particularly in times of crisis such as illness or death. The personal feeling between husband and wife is no less real because it is not surrounded by an aura of romantic conceptions peculiar to civilized society, and is often obscured by customary restrictions, restraints and taboos on its public expression.

Although the more homogeneous pattern of social values found in primitive society gives less scope for the development of personality, it also minimizes the sexual and personal maladjustments which, in our own society, provide a living for novelists, playwrights, psychiatrists and divorce-court lawyers. Marriages arranged by relatives tend to be accepted by the parties directly concerned as a matter of course. In particular, in the case of infant betrothal, each party has grown up from infancy regarding the other as his or her destined mate, in a community which regards infant betrothal as the right and proper avenue to marriage. In the majority of cases the individuals concerned would no more think of objecting than we would think of protesting because we were not given a choice of parents, brothers or sisters.

The important part played by kinsfolk after, as well as before, marriage has also advantages and disadvantages so far as both men and women are concerned, but the general effect of its operation is probably beneficial. It serves as an important mechanism of validation for the rights of individuals. A partner who is badly treated can rely on the support, moral and practical, of a whole cadre of kinsfolk; while the partner who is in the wrong can usually expect, at best, tepid sympathy and grudging assistance, since by failing to discharge the obligations of marriage, he or she has ruptured a number of social and economic relationships in which his or her kinsfolk are directly involved.

But the influence of kinsfolk is by no means the only stabilizing factor in primitive marriage. Because of the importance of public opinion in primitive societies, the attitude of neighbours and society at large has an important influence. Last, but by no means least, is the system of reciprocity between husband and wife—the obligations connected with economic production, domestic duties and conjugal rights. As with other systems of reciprocity, failure to honour obligations may lead to direct retaliation in the refusal of the wronged partner to discharge some of his or her obligations, leading in extreme cases to a complete rupture of the marriage bond.

Formal statements regarding the rights of individuals, and of women in particular, must be considered against the background of these complementary and interlocking factors in primitive marriage. The operation of these factors in a specific tribe is described elsewhere (p. 304). The important thing to recognize is that they affect both partners in the relationship and are essential to the satisfactory functioning of the family as a social institution.

The widespread practice of polygyny has often been cited as an example of female inferiority. But it is certainly not felt as such by native women. Polygynous households generally run fairly smoothly, at least more so than we would expect them to do, because the rights and obligations of the various parties concerned are socially recognized. The satisfactory working of a polygynous household is greatly facilitated where, as very commonly, the wives are sisters to each other. But we must not build up an idyllic picture of polygynous marriage. In spite of all that has been said, quarrels and clashes of interests between co-wives are far from uncommon, and produce from time to time both social disruption and individual unhappiness. This, however, is at least partially offset by the fact that, broadly speaking, no marriageable woman is ever without a helpmate or an opportunity to raise a family. Furthermore, in a number of cases, co-operation and even genuine affection exist between co-wives, while sometimes a woman will actually ask her husband to take another wife in order to lighten her domestic and economic tasks.

The above considerations should lead us to examine very carefully any data brought forward as evidence of female inferiority in primitive society. Though their social rôle is in general less spectacular than that of the opposite sex, women have their own "spheres of influence", from which they derive satisfactions and rights which are definitely validated in social custom and usage. While it would be rash to make any general statement as to whether women are happier or more contented than under civilized conditions, it is absurd to speak of their "degradation" in primitive society generally.

We mentioned at the outset that the physiological differences between men and women are recognized by all cultures. Such recognition is expressed in differences in dress and ornament, as well as in the specialized rôles of the two sexes in social, economic and ceremonial life. But these rôles are not always and for all individuals defined in terms of physiological differences. We have already mentioned the African examples of "woman marriage", in which a woman undertakes socially the rôle of a man. Several Amerindian tribes provide us with examples of an analogous social process whereby certain men assume the social position of women. Under this practice, termed *berdache* by the early French travellers, a boy or young man might assume the clothes and occupations of a woman, sometimes becoming married to and living with another man. The *berdache* was frequently regarded as exceptionally able and often achieved a fortunate position in religious and economic affairs. Thus the Dakota would praise a woman's household possessions by comparing them with those of a *berdache*.

The place of homosexuality in such cases of changes of sex is difficult to state, particularly in view of the reticence of the early observers and their readiness to express disgust rather than to investigate the matter thoroughly. It is clear that many if not most of the *berdaches* were either homosexuals or persons of inadequate sexual endowment. On the other hand, the social and economic advantages must not be forgotten. In the African examples of woman marriage, as we have seen, these are the dominant factor, though it is possible that the social practices sometimes provide an outlet for the emotions of homosexual women.

3. Age Groups, Initiation Ceremonies and Primitive Education

As with sex differences, so the physiological differences between individuals of different ages are recognized in all cultures by variations in dress, prescribed behaviour patterns and differential social status. In most, though not all, primitive societies there are also **initiation ceremonies**, which mark stages of growth, particularly the transition from childhood to adult life.[1] In con-

---

[1] In addition to these ceremonies, which have been termed ceremonies of *general initiation*, there are also rites of *specific initiation* which introduce individuals to secret societies, priesthoods, trade guilds and other specialized groups within a community. The latter rites are far less common than rites of general initiation. Usually they display formal characteristics (the infliction of pain or physical discomfort, secrecy and the observation of taboos) similar to those which we shall mention in connection with ceremonies of general initiation.

formity with the less spectacular place of women in ceremonial life, such ceremonies for males are far more common, and usually more elaborate, than corresponding rites for females. In some communities initiation consists of a single simple rite or sequence of rites taking place usually at or about puberty. In other cultures the stages of individual growth are marked by an intermittent series of rites covering a considerable span of the life-cycle of the individual, as we have seen among the Karadjeri. In many African tribes, gradations of age are even more highly institution-alized, and we find the male population divided into a series of **age-grades.**[1] These consist of a number of males of approximately the same age who undergo initiation at the same time and form groups having specific rights and duties. The best-known example comes from the Masai, where adolescent youths undergo a period of initiation, which includes circumcision by special operators of the Dorobo tribe. At intervals of about ten years or more, all such youths have their heads shaved at the same time, and this admits them into the class of warriors, where they form a special "age regiment" having a specific name. The members of such a group fight, camp and perform ceremonies together, and they also owe obligations of help and hospitality towards each other. Promotion in, and retirement from, the warrior class is determined by a com-plicated set of rules. When members retire from this class and become elders, membership of their age-group still affects their social status. The Nuer have a similar system of age-grades, but these have no corporate activities and lack the military and cere-monial functions of those of the Masai. They are primarily a means of establishing relative seniority between male members of the tribe, and in this way determine their relationships to each other in social and ceremonial affairs. Other types of age-grade occur elsewhere in Africa, among certain Amerindian tribes and in parts of Melanesia. In the latter area they shade off into secret societies (Section 6) based on voluntary membership and the pay-ment of membership fees.

Initiation ceremonies, whether single or multiple, whether correlated with age-grades or not, display certain common characteristics among primitive peoples in all parts of the world, though among specific peoples some of them may be absent. A well-nigh universal feature is the subjection of the novice to some form of painful ordeal or physical discomfort. This is frequently

[1] Also called *age-sets* or *age-classes*.

regarded as a test of his manhood, and he is required to bear pain and discomfort with fortitude. Sometimes the ordeals are transitory, consisting of such trials as whipping, being choked by smoke, or bathing in ice-cold water. More frequently they are such as to leave a permanent mark—thus, among the Nuer, boys are initiated by cutting the flesh of the forehead to the bone, thus making six horizontal scars, extending from ear to ear, which are plainly visible for the remainder of the individual's lifetime. Elsewhere in Africa, and in other parts of the world, deep cuts are made in the flesh of the body, usually according to some culturally defined pattern, and ashes or other foreign substances are rubbed into the wounds so as to produce protuberant weals.[1] But by far the most common form of marking at initiation is that resulting from **circumcision.** This operation is sometimes confused with the less common practice of *subincision* (slitting the urethra),[2] and an operation which consists of making a longitudinal slit in the upper surface of the prepuce and which is variously known as *incision, supercision* and *superincision.* The latter is the physical ordeal connected with initiation in Tikopia and certain other Polynesian societies, while subincision is practised by many Australian tribes in addition to the more common rite of circumcision.

The widespread occurrence of circumcision in areas as widely separated as East Africa and Australia probably depends upon the fact that, since it modifies the shape of the male genitalia, it is one which is particularly well suited to mark off the initiate both from women and from uninitiated boys. But this explanation must not be pressed too far. Circumcision is merely one of the ordeals of initiation which vary widely from one community to another. Even in a fairly homogeneous cultural area such as Australia, we find not only circumcision and subincision but also the knocking out of a front tooth, cicatrization, the tying of tight ligatures around the arms and the plucking out of hairs from the face and body practised as part of initiation ritual. The character of the ordeal to which the initiate is subjected varies from tribe to tribe, and sometimes we find two or more co-existing in the same area, as among the Karadjeri.

The painful character of primitive initiation ceremonies has often aroused the sympathy or indignation of European observers.

---

[1] This custom, known as **cicatrization,** is sometimes carried out for purely æsthetic reasons, and does not form part of the ritual of initiation.

[2] The attribution of a contraceptive purpose to this operation is entirely erroneous.

Undoubtedly the ordeals are often extremely trying, but it is probably true that the sensitivity to pain of primitive peoples is less than among ourselves, not of course owing to any biological differences, but as a result of the relatively low social value attached to pain in primitive society. It is impossible to support this statement by reliable evidence, but field-workers who have administered first-aid to natives, and who have observed their reaction to painful ordeals, have been impressed by the stoicism which they display. Furthermore, in the case of the initiates, the pain experienced is largely offset by the social advantages and prestige which it confers on them, and they are usually willing and even eager to undergo the ordeals of initiation prescribed by their culture.[1]

In addition to trying ordeals, initiation ceremonies often include a systematic teasing of the novice, reminiscent of "ragging" in schools or colleges. The novice is usually secluded from social life for a time, and sometimes this is metaphorically expressed as death and rebirth—the initiators say that they will take the novice away from the womenfolk and kill him. Of course everybody knows that this is a fiction, and that the person who returns after initiation is the same individual as before. But in a social sense he has died and been re-born, since he has ceased to exist as a child and has become a man. In addition to seclusion, the novice is usually forced to observe taboos on eating and other types of social activity.

A prominent feature of initiation ceremonies is the part played in them by the kinsfolk of the novice. These often mutilate themselves, weep and play specific rôles in the prescribed ritual. In many communities such ceremonies are among the most spectacular ways in which kinship bonds are expressed.

Initiation ceremonies usually have an important magico-religious background, consisting generally of a myth or cycle of myths telling of the institution of the ceremonies by some legendary figure in the distant past. Often the ritual re-enacts the dramatic episodes recounted in the mythology. This aura of sanctity which surrounds initiation ceremonial, and the spectacular character of the rites, serve to impress upon novice and upon

---

[1] We have said initiation rites for females are less widespread and less spectacular than those for males. They are also in general less trying, and consist for the most part of a temporary seclusion or the observation of certain taboos connected with the first menstruation. But in parts of Africa a rite known as *clitoridectomy* or "female circumcision" is practised in connection with the initiation of women.

the community at large the significance of the change from childhood to adult status.

Initiation is often accompanied by instruction of the novice in the secret lore of the ceremonies, and also the obligations of tribal morality, particularly those connected with respect for elders and with sexual behaviour. For this reason they have often been described as a primitive form of education, but this statement requires qualification. Apart from its secret aspect, the instruction given generally concerns rules which are already known to the novice, and its importance lies, not so much in its content, as in the impressive circumstances under which it is given. It hardly ever includes matters of practical knowledge and technical skill. A knowledge of these is gained in the more mundane context of day-to-day life. As this process is apt to be obscured by the more spectacular character of initiation ceremonies, we must now turn to the more general subject of primitive education, in which initiation plays only a limited and specific part.

Education, as the anthropologist understands it, is a very much wider process than anything corresponding to "schooling" in our own community. It covers all the cultural influences which are brought to bear upon the individual during the early years of his life, and by which the helpless and immature infant eventually becomes an adult member of the community equipped with all the knowledge, skill and social sentiments which membership of that community entails. The process of education thus defined may be considered from two points of view—the sociological and the psychological. The *sociological* function of education, that is, the part it plays in the life of the community, is to transmit cultural equipment, knowledge, skills, values and sentiments from one generation to the next. Its *psychological* function, that is, its effect upon each member of the community, is to mould the growing individual in accordance with the cultural standards to which he is heir. These are, of course, merely different aspects of a unitary cultural process.

Education in primitive society, though its actual operation varies greatly from one culture to another, contrasts in a marked way with the corresponding system in civilized communities in regard to (1) methods, (2) personnel, (3) content and (4) the motives and attitudes underlying the educational process. We shall consider these four aspects of primitive education in turn.

1. In regard to the *methods* of education, those of primitive

peoples are characterized by the fact that the training of children tends to be a by-product of other activities rather than a specialized cultural process, and is effected by the progressive participation of the growing individual in adult pursuits. Thus a small boy will watch his father and other male relatives making a canoe, and will play about with adzes and other tools, being from time to time advised and corrected by his elders. At length, by a series of such acts of imitation of, or participation in, the technical activity concerned, he finally becomes a skilled craftsman. Here the activity of building a series of canoes is determined by the economic needs of the community at large and is not consciously directed to the education of children, though it achieves this result incidentally. It follows from this that education in primitive society differs from our own in that it lacks in general the distinction between informal education, for example that which occurs in the home, and formal education at a school, technical college or university. Where specifically educational institutions exist in primitive society, they are generally limited to certain highly specialized crafts, to the esoteric spheres of magic and religion, and to the limited types of instruction mentioned above in connection with initiation ceremonies.

Most of what a child learns in primitive society is acquired in a context of real as opposed to artificial training situations; that is to say, it does not occur in situations specially designed for educational purposes. It follows that there exists in primitive education a temporal and local continuity in the educational process. A child learns in or near the village, in the fields, or by accompanying adults on hunting or fishing expeditions. These are carried out at places and at times determined by the needs of the community, their geographical environment and their specific types of economy. Such a process contrasts with our own procedure of setting aside special times and places for lessons. In the same way knowledge acquired in the educational process is not divided into compartments or "subjects" independently taught. Because a child learns by progressive participation in adult activities, the selection of activities to be learned is largely determined by the child's own inclinations, and what is learned is not conceived by adults or by children as belonging to distinct compartments of knowledge.

It follows that our own distinction between play and education is difficult to draw in the case of primitive communities. As we know, play is biologically and psychologically a preparation for adult life, and this is more marked in primitive society where the play of children may more often be regarded as adult institutions in embryo. For example, when a boy uses artefacts such as a hoe made for him by his father, it is sometimes difficult to say whether the object concerned should be called a toy or a tool. For obvious reasons it is made on a smaller scale than its adult counterpart, but it is nevertheless adequate to achieve practical and useful results on a small scale. This is not in general true of the toys of our own children.

In many primitive communities play forms part of, or is carried on side by side with, responsible tasks. Among the Chaga, for example, young boys when tending cattle organize themselves into play groups, elect one of their number as "Chief of the Pasture", and carry out battles in imitation of the adult institution of warfare. The play of such children is thus integrally linked with the essential economic activity of caring for the herds. Children's play, like their more serious tasks, is taken over directly from the adult world rather than being a set of artificial situations specially arranged by adults for children.

There is, in primitive education generally, no punishment for incompetence or backwardness, success or failure providing the necessary sanctions. But discipline in matters of social custom forms part of many primitive educational systems, although its severity or laxity is very variable. Thus in Samoa we find that adults allow a considerable amount of latitude to children, while in other communities, such as the Chaga, correct behaviour is enforced by strict discipline, including severe forms of physical punishment. As regards the latter, its incidence in primitive society has been greatly under-estimated in ethnographic records. It is true that in a few primitive societies physical punishment is never inflicted upon children. But in most it definitely occurs, even in cases where its occurrence is denied in superficial ethnographic records. As Dr. Raum has pointed out, such denials are likely to arise, because primitive peoples, like ourselves, refrain from punishing their children in the presence of strangers, a category to which many of the early ethnographers definitely belonged.

As regards the infliction of physical punishment, however, there is a very important distinction in the spirit in which it is administered. Primitive peoples would agree with Bernard Shaw's saying that a child should never be punished except in

anger. Hogbin records an instance of a man building a hut while
his small son played nearby. The child persisted, after several
warnings, in untidying a neat pile of thatching which the father
had arranged. Finally, the father struck the child with the words,
"You interfere with me, I interfere with you". This, it will be
seen, represents an entirely different idea from that of "punishing
a child for its own good". It emphasizes, not an abstract moral
code, but the principle of reciprocity, the importance of which in
primitive morality will become apparent later. To this it must be
added that training in the observation of taboos is often a disciplinary matter, but also differs from our own conceptions of
moral education. It is largely a matter of protecting the child
from putative dangers of a practical kind, rather than "character
training".

2. *Personnel.*—The personal agents in the primitive educational
process are primarily kinsfolk and neighbours, and also older playmates who often take charge of younger children. This contrasts
with our own system, in that there is in general a lack of professional teachers who are otherwise strangers to the children and
who may have no social relations with them outside the class-
room. This aspect of primitive education is correlated with the
lack of economic specialization in primitive society, where almost
everybody, apart from very young children, the aged and invalids,
does the same kind of work (for example, hunting, cultivating,
fishing, cattle-tending and house-building), subject only to the
sexual division of labour mentioned above. It follows that all
adults are capable of instructing their own children or those of
near relatives in the basic technical activities of the community.
Thus, children acquire most of their technical knowledge and
skill from close kinsfolk and neighbours.

In connection with the sexual division of labour, it is important
to note the early differentiation of the interests and activities of
boys and girls respectively. The former tend to adhere to their
male kinsfolk and the latter to their female kinsfolk, each sex thus
acquiring specialized interests and skills appropriate to it. Such a
differentiation exists among ourselves in the sphere of play; for
example, boys play with trains and girls with dolls; but it is
almost completely lacking in formal education.[1]

[1] This has a bearing on the question of the relative status of the sexes in primitive
society which we discussed in the preceding section. It should be noted that the question of sex equality can only arise when there is a possibility of members of both sexes
being subjected to the same educational process and carrying out the same types of

It follows from what has been said above that learning in primitive society is an active process—the interests of children themselves make them active participants in the educational process rather than passive recipients. Primitive education consists rather of learning than of being taught. This is correlated with the fact that children are regarded as immature adults rather than as a separate group with interests divergent from those of adults. The simple economic activities of primitive peoples are readily understood by intelligent children, in a way which does not occur in our society. A doctor, lawyer, or technician could not possibly explain the techniques of his profession or trade to his young children. The understanding of these techniques necessitates a long and highly specialized period of training. In primitive society, on the other hand, children can participate increasingly in adult activities, and are gradually drawn into the social framework of the adult community without any abrupt transition, except in so far as initiation ceremonies are concerned; and, as we have seen, these are mainly concerned with social and religious status and not with the acquisition of technical skill.

In everyday life in primitive society children play a useful part in adult activities at a very much earlier age than amongst ourselves. This means that children think of themselves at a very early age as members of a community to whose vital activities they are progressively making a greater contribution as they grow up. This difference, like several others which we mentioned, is a relative one, but is none the less significant. It is true that children, particularly girls, are occasionally useful in our society (especially in rural communities), and are conscious of the contributions which they make. But the earlier and more full participation of children in adult pursuits in a primitive educational system is clearly seen in the following table. This synoptic view of education among the Tallensi also brings out very clearly the

activity in adult life. Thus, in our own society the emancipation of women in such spheres as higher education and membership of learned professions has only progressed because members of both sexes can in fact undergo the same types of education and follow the same lines of adult activity. A woman journalist, lawyer or doctor is not precluded from following her career by occasional pregnancies and the care of young children, since the latter may be largely delegated to nurses and schoolteachers. The same is not true of male activities, such as hunting and warfare, in primitive society, and therefore the question of sex equality simply does not arise. Consequently, although the work and life of women may be more arduous and from our point of view less dignified in some primitive societies than those of men, they are not conceived in this way by natives of either sex. They are accepted without question as part of the cultural situation into which the individual is born.

close integration of play with more serious activities, the importance of which was stressed earlier in this section.

SYNOPTIC CHART OF EDUCATIONAL DEVELOPMENT AMONG THE
TALLENSI[1]

BOYS

Economic Duties and Activities	*Play*
	3–6 years
None at first. Towards end of this period begin to assist in pegging out goats; scaring birds from newly sown fields and from crops; accompany family sowing and harvesting parties; using hoe in quasi-play to glean ground-nuts in company of older siblings.	Exuberant motor and exploratory play. Use mimetic toys (bow, drum, etc.) in egocentric play. Towards end of period social and imaginative play with "cattle" and "house-building" commences, often in company of older children of either sex, as well as recreational games and dancing.
	6–9 years
These duties now fully established. Help in house-building by carrying swish. Assist in sowing and harvesting. Towards end of period begin to go out with the herd-boys, and to care for poultry.	Imaginative "cattle" and "house-building" play common, the latter often reflecting current economic activity of adults. Practice with bow and arrow in marksmanship competitions, and "hunting" with groups of comrades begun. Recreational games and dancing established. Modelling clay figures and plaiting begun. Ritual play begun.
	9–12 years
Fully responsible cattle-herding. Care for poultry. Assisting parents in hoeing and care of crops, but without responsibility. Farming own small plots and ground-nuts, but in quasi-play. Sons of specialist craftsmen assist fathers in subsidiary capacity—"learning by looking".	Further development of preceding forms of play, especially of ritual play. Clay-modelling and plaiting established. Recreational games and dancing more skilful. Quasi-play farming.

Sexual dichotomy in work and play established.

---

[1] This chart is reproduced by courtesy of the International African Institute, from Fortes, "Social and Psychological Aspects of Education in Taleland", Supplement to *Africa*, Vol. XI, pp. 62–4.

12–15 years

Duties as in preceding period, but more responsible. Responsible care of poultry, sometimes own property. Leaders of herd-boys. Real farming of own plots and in co-operation with older members of family established by end of period. Sons of specialists experimentally making things.

Imaginative play abandoned. Dancing the principal recreation. Ritual play abandoned. Modelling gradually abandoned. Plaiting for personal decoration mainly. Regular sweet-hearting commences.

GIRLS

Economic Duties and Activities

Play

3–6 years

None at first. Towards end of period the same duties as small boys. Frequent nursing of infants. Accompany mothers to water-hole and begin to carry tiny water-pots. Help in domestic tasks such as sweeping.

Exuberant motor and exploratory play. Attached to older sisters and drawn into their "housekeeping" play. Towards end of period begin to take active social part in the latter, and begin recreational play and dancing. Often found in mixed sex groups.

6–9 years

Duties of previous period established. Responsible co-operation in water-carrying and simpler domestic duties. Help in cooking and in activities associated with food-preparation, such as searching for wild edible herbs. Accompany family parties at sowing and harvesting, giving quasi-playful help. Carry swish at building operations and assist women in plastering and floor-beating, but still with a play element.

"Housekeeping" play usual. Recreational play and dancing established. Begin to learn plaiting. Participate in "building" play of boys, mimicking current women's activities, e.g. plastering.

9–12 years

All domestic duties can be entrusted to them by end of this period—water-carrying, cooking, care of infants, etc. Assisting in building and plastering, etc., more responsibility. Often sent to market to buy and sell. Help in women's part of the work at sowing and harvest times.

"Housekeeping" play continues, gradually fading out at end of this period. Dancing becomes principal recreation. Plaiting both for decoration and use established. Begin to have sweethearts, but not yet with serious intent.

Sexual dichotomy in work and play established.

12–15 years

Responsible part in all domestic duties of everyday life, and of those associated with ceremonial occasions. Go for firewood and collect shea-fruits in the bush, and help to prepare shea-butter. (Marriage a very near prospect.)

Note.—Care of infants and children is a duty of girls at all ages. Boys also are frequently entrusted with this task.

Imaginative play abandoned. Dancing the main recreation. Courtship and hetero-sexual interests occupy a great deal of time and attention. Actively participate in the social side of funeral ceremonies, etc., in the rôle of marriageable girls.

3. In regard to the *content* of education, that is, the things learned by the growing individual, we have already pointed out that these include knowledge and skills on the one hand and sentiments and values on the other. The former are necessary to economic pursuits, practical life and adjustment to geographical environment. The latter are concerned with the individual's adjustment to his social environment—he must acquire the social sentiments and moral values associated with his kinship obligations, his sexual behaviour and his conformity with tribal traditions generally.

We have already emphasized certain ways in which primitive technical education differs from our own. In the sphere of moral education the differences are even more striking. The most salient difference is that in primitive society generally no knowledge is withheld from the child except that connected with esoteric law and ritual. This is especially important in regard to the facts of life and death. Primitive peoples are, by our standards, extraordinarily frank in discussing such matters.[1] This is not a matter of deliberate "sex education", but a more or less necessary consequence of life under primitive conditions. Privacy in family life hardly exists where the whole family shares the same sleeping accommodation; and where domestic animals are kept, primitive children acquire at an early age a knowledge of the facts of reproduction. In the same way the facts of death, from which we are apt to shield our children, are regarded in a much more matter-of-fact way by primitive children. Most of them have at some time or other seen a corpse, sometimes under conditions which we should regard as quite unsuitable for children, as in Samoa,

---

[1] Apart from specific taboos connected with particular kinship relationships, for example, reticence often enjoined between brothers and sisters.

where they may witness a magical autopsy on a woman who has died in childbirth. The relative lack of concealment, both in speech and behaviour, of the fundamental facts of human existence leads children to acquire a more realistic attitude towards them, and minimizes the morbid fears and other psychopathic developments which are apt to become associated with them in civilized society. Furthermore, children acquire in this way an early appreciation of their destined biological rôle. Thus a little Tallensi girl of nine or ten years was asked why she did not eat some of the meat distributed in connection with a certain sacrifice. She replied by pointing out that the Tallensi believe that a woman partaking of such meat will be rendered sterile: "Am I not a woman? Who wants to be sterile?" It is clear that such a child could never experience the anxieties often associated with reproduction in the case of sensitive young women in our own society. Not only the simple facts of reproduction, but also their social implications are appreciated at a very early age by children. Another example from the Tallensi explains why small boys of six or seven are always anxious to own a hen. Such a boy will explain his ambition in the following terms: " 'If you have a hen it lays eggs, and you take the eggs and breed chicks, then you can sell the chickens and buy a goat, and when the goat breeds you can sell its offspring and buy a sheep, and when the sheep breeds you can sell its offspring and buy a cow, and then you can take the cow and get a wife.' "[1]

The conditions of primitive education thus conduce to an early acquisition of adult outlook and values and also minimize sources of psychological conflict. But the rôle of mere frankness in the latter case can be exaggerated. An even more important factor is probably the fact that social sentiments are acquired as a part of a unitary and homogeneous set of cultural values. In our own society every child is subjected to a number of divergent and often violently contradictory cultural values. In the home the parents may disagree on questions of religion, morality or politics; when the child goes to school, it is subjected to different influences from teachers and playmates; and the transition to the workaday world, and to membership of all sorts of clubs, societies and associations, together with the influence of various forms of political, moral and religious propaganda, subject the growing individual to a number of cultural influences which conflict

[1] Fortes (1), p. 11.

with one another and often with those which have been operative in home and school.

In primitive society, on the other hand, everybody is in general agreed as to what is right and wrong. As we shall see in dealing with primitive law, this does not mean that everybody conforms to social custom. It merely means that nobody challenges it as a matter of moral principle. Individuals may evade their religious obligations or pay little attention to dogma, but there are, in general, no heretics or atheists. Though it is true, for example, that a child's parents may belong to different totemic clans or worship different ancestors, the two types of observance are similar and each agrees that the other is right in following his or her cult, and that the child should adopt one or the other according to whether descent is patrilineal or matrilineal. In the sphere of politics, the people may combine to depose an unpopular or autocratic chief, but only to replace him by someone more acceptable; nobody challenges the institution of chieftainship, or advocates social and economic equality. In war-making societies, individuals experience a natural fear of the dangers of battle, and sometimes succumb to it; but they are not torn in opposite directions by the conflicting ideals of patriotism and Christianity as are many pacifists in our own society. All these features of primitive life exert their influence on the mind of the growing individual. He may and often does assert his own individual desires against the dictates of custom, and sometimes experiences conflicts of personal loyalty. But he is not usually subjected to the intense moral conflicts which come with civilization. Primitive communities include individuals who are actually or potentially maladjusted psychologically, but they do not flourish like the green bay tree, as they do in our own society.

4. It may be inferred, from what has been said, that the *motives and attitudes* underlying the educational process display certain characteristics peculiar to primitive society. There is far more sharing of interests by adults and children. This is because the interests of the adult community are more obviously relevant to the welfare of children. Among ourselves, the young are incapable of appreciating the practical difficulties and financial worries of their parents. Primitive children know all too well, often from bitter experience, the meaning of a bad harvest, a hurricane, a drought, or a plague of locusts. Consequently, their interest in, and desire to acquire knowledge of, the ways, both

practical and magico-religious, in which their community meets its problems are very much more keen than among our own children, who live in a world largely isolated from that of adults. The principles and goals of education are thus appreciated by primitive children, and are not taken on trust or imposed by adult discipline. As they learn, they realize the importance of what they are doing, and their progressively greater participation in adult affairs gives personal satisfaction through increasing skill and the acquisition of reputation in activities vital to community life. The place of "prizes" is taken by real rewards, material and social, for real tasks successfully accomplished, and this again conduces to an early acquisition of the adult outlook, skill and values.

4. Political Organization and Social Status

In all primitive communities differences in the social status of individuals are recognized. Even among such peoples as the Eskimo and the Australian aborigines, proficiency in hunting and old age respectively serve to mark off superior individuals from the remainder of the community, and this is expressed in a number of privileges, both social and material. Usually, social status co-incides with the exercise of power in the economic and political fields, but sometimes they are differentiated, as among the Haida.

The standards of social superiority vary extensively. Hereditary rank, success in economic pursuits, wealth, military prowess, old age, magico-religious status or power, and even proficiency in games and entertainment—all of these may operate as criteria of social status in different primitive societies. Usually two or more of them are operative in any given community, either in reinforc-ing the position of the same individuals or groups or by differen-tiating various individuals or groups according to their respective powers and claims to fame. For example, members of despised classes may be held to possess extraordinary magical powers, as in parts of India, or may be specialist craftsmen, as among the Banyankole.

But such examples are exceptional. More commonly the various criteria of social status reinforce each other. The commonest example is the reciprocal relation between hereditary rank and wealth. Where the hereditary principle, either patrilineal or matrilineal, is operative, it is usually reinforced by inheritance and by the payment of tribute. As we shall see, this is not simply a matter of economic autocracy. The wealth of men of rank is constantly redistributed in the form of gifts, feasts and the provision of entertainment, or is kept as a reserve to meet the needs of the community in times of crisis or when large-scale corporate hospitality must be offered to other communities.

Magico-religious factors also serve to support political authority in the majority of primitive communities, either through the belief that the chief or headman has peculiar supernatural powers or attributes, or by the fact that by virtue of his wealth and position he can command the services of priests or sorcerers. We shall meet many examples of the interrelationships of wealth, political authority and magico-religious status and power, and of the different ways in which these interact in various primitive communities.

Apart from the individuals, classes, castes, councils of elders and other authorities which exercise political power, there exists an important distinction in regard to the size and structure of the groups over which such power is exercised. Primitive peoples may be broadly divided into those in which political organization is stratified and those in which it is segmented. As usual, borderline cases can be found, but the distinction can nevertheless be drawn in most cases, and is absolutely vital, not only to the theoretical discussion of political organization, but also to practical problems of native administration.

Stratified societies are those in which there exists a centralized authority, a complex mechanism of administration, and usually also some form of specialized legal institutions. Such an organization is found in most Bantu tribes, where there exists a hierarchy of chief, sub-chiefs and headmen with an accessory establishment of courtiers, councillors and deputies, as well as executive and legal officials. The duties, privileges and powers of the various authorities in such a system are clearly defined in relation to one another and to the supreme authority. Similar types of political organization are found among many Amerindian tribes and in Polynesia.

A typical example of a stratified political system is found in the traditional organization of the Hehe of Tanganyika. Though this organization, as described here, has been successively modified by German and British occupation, the system as a whole is still active, and provides the judicial and administrative institutions by which the tribe is governed under the British mandate.

The legends of the tribe record that until the middle of the last century the Hehe people consisted of a number of small tribes. These small tribes were welded together by two able men, from whom the present line of chiefs is descended. The tales still told of their conquests were a charter for the authority of the chief, and for the right of the chiefly family to rule. In addition to the chief there were sub-chiefs and local headmen.

The powers of the Hehe chief were judicial, legislative, administrative, economic and military. This unity of function descended throughout the whole tribal hierarchy, even to the headmen. But in spite of his very extensive powers, the Hehe chief was not in fact an autocrat. He was assisted by a tribal council, whose members were chosen by himself on a basis partly of friendship and partly of skill in political matters. Generally, it was the council as a whole which reached a decision, and the chief only opposed his councillors in very exceptional circumstances.

Within limits the chief could change the law. This he did, firstly, by his decisions in court which established a sort of "case law"; and secondly, by making proclamations at large public gatherings. Such decrees were connected with such matters as military levies, taxation and emergency measures against famine.

The chief was a rich man. His wealth came from several sources. He had large herds of cattle, which were augmented from time to time by raiding the herds of neighbouring tribes. Many of the captured cattle were distributed by the chief to warriors who had taken part in raids, but the chief kept a generous portion for himself. Furthermore, the chief could confiscate the cattle of any commoner who was held to own possessions above his station—the privileges of chiefs and men of authority in such matters were jealously guarded. In theory all cattle were the chief's to requisition in peace or war, but there is no evidence that this privilege was abused. The chief could demand forced labour for the building of his house and could also claim tribute. Each headman was responsible for a communally cultivated garden, the produce of which went to the chief, who could also exact a levy on the harvests of commoners.

Finally, the chief had a monopoly of the ivory trade. All tusks were brought to him, and he paid for them with guns, ammunition and cloth which he obtained from traders. He was thus the focus of the ivory trade, and if this was a source of profit to him, it was also an advantage to the people. In fact, the wealth of the chief in general was a source of advantage, not only to himself, but also to the community. Thus his accumulation of cattle and grain was used as an emergency store in case of famine, for the rewarding of men who had performed useful services and for the feeding of warriors at war.

In addition to the economic basis of the chief's authority, this was supported by magico-religious beliefs and practices. The chief acquired a number of "medicines", the object of which was to produce magical results—to protect warriors going into battle, to drive away enemies, and to protect the chief and his family against danger. His authority was also supported by the system of ancestor worship. Among the Hehe each family invoked its own ancestors, and the only tribal gods were the souls of dead rulers. These, of course, could only be invoked by the chief, on whom the people were thus dependent for prayers in connection with war, droughts and other matters of public concern. It may be noted that sub-chiefs and headmen could invoke their own ancestors for rain, but only with the chief's permission.

The chief had many ceremonial privileges. He had a vast retinue, including guards, messengers and slaves. The latter were either prisoners-of-war or men drawn from a special hereditary class called *va-fugwa*. Even today it is a serious insult to call a man a *mufugwa*. This class of slaves did the menial work and also provided children to act as human sacrifices when chiefs and members of their families were buried. The chief also had many wives, both at his own residence and scattered throughout the tribal territory. He had a special decorated stool on which he alone could sit, and a special term of respect, *atse senga*, was used when addressing him.

The Hehe sub-chiefs, of whom there were about thirty, held a somewhat similar, though subordinate, position. At the time of the unification of the Hehe, most of the original chiefs of component tribes were retained as sub-chiefs, their titles being hereditary. Some, however, were nominees of the chief. There was no hierarchy among the sub-chiefs—no one of them was responsible to another, though they were all subordinate to the chief. The sub-chief had a small retinue and some wealth in cattle, depending on his station. He acted as local war leader and as judge. His judgments were generally accepted, though there was a right of appeal to the chief.

The headmen exercised similar functions on a smaller scale, and in addition had control over land. If a man from another district wished to settle in an area, it was to the headman, not the chief, that he would appeal. Permission was normally given, except when land was scarce or the applicant a notoriously bad character.

The headman's court served a useful function in dealing with such matters as marital and family disputes, petty theft, adultery, slander and abuse, fighting, and suits for debt. The headman acted more as arbitrator than as judge. He listened to the opinions of the assembly, and his decision was not so much his own judgment as the consensus of opinion of the whole gathering. The meetings were less formal than in the larger courts, and thus made possible the airing of grievances and amicable settlement of disputes. In fact, litigants would often renounce compensation once they had ventilated their grievances and been vindicated by public opinion.

The system of the Hehe illustrates very well the working of primitive political and legal institutions. The power of chiefs and others in authority was great, and in some fields absolute. It was supported by economic obligations, magico-religious beliefs and ceremonial observances. On the whole, however, it was not abused. Apart from the chief's sense of responsibility towards his people, there were other factors of restraint: public opinion, the fear of revolt or secession, and the fact that the chief was himself largely dependent on the people for tribute, gifts and support in war. In the case of subordinate officials, power was also limited by the possibility of appeal to the chief. The people were likewise dependent on their rulers for leadership in war, the administration of justice, prayers to the gods on matters of public concern, and the expenditure of wealth for public purposes. The relations between rulers and people were thus essentially reciprocal. They were personal in character, thus ensuring, on the whole, a harmonious and just administration.

An almost universal concomitant of social and political stratification in primitive society is the rule of endogamy, which ensures that men and women of certain classes or castes must intermarry. Occasionally, it is laid down that a man of rank must marry, not merely any woman of his own class, but a particular kinswoman. A highly specialized example of this is found in Tonga, where the sanctity and secular authority of various members of the aristocracy were reinforced by the kinship relationships existing between them. As we shall see, the whole political structure of Tongan society was based upon certain fundamental characteristics of the kinship system.

The domestic unit in Tonga consisted primarily of a man and his wife, together with their own and adopted children. But this household was often augmented by polygyny, and by resident consanguineous and affinal relatives; and also, in the case of chiefs, by a number of kinsmen of inferior rank, who acted as servants and attendants. Within the kinship organization, rank was determined by two factors, age and sex, the latter being the more important. A woman was always superior in rank to her brother, and the same relative status obtained between their respective children. After sex, age was the important determinant of status.

The father was the head of the household, and towards him and his brothers the children preserved an attitude of respect. But they showed an even greater respect towards his sister, an attitude which was extended to her husband. This whole system depended, of course, upon the superiority in rank of the father's sister over her brother.

The attitude of restraint, respect and obedience towards the father and the father's sister contrasts in a most marked way with the attitude adopted towards the father's father and mother's father, towards whom a considerable amount of liberty was allowed—a youth might wear his grandfather's clothes or eat his food. But this free attitude found its greatest development in the relationship towards the mother's brother; this was described by saying that the sister's son was *fahu*[1] to his mother's brother. The *fahu* relationship was expressed concretely in a freedom of restraint in behaviour towards the mother's brother, together with a number of claims to his property, and to that of his children. This arrangement was non-reciprocal, for the mother's brother had no corresponding claims upon the property of his *fahu*, his only compensation being his corresponding *fahu* rights towards his own mother's brother. Though the sister's child was the "great *fahu*", the grandchildren of a man were also *fahu* to him in a lesser degree, as were his classificatory sister's children.[2]

---

[1] This term has been translated "above the law". The relationship to the mother's brother which it embodies has been given a specific interpretation by Professor Radcliffe-Brown. (See A. R. Radcliffe-Brown, "The Mother's Brother in South Africa," *South African Journal of Science*, Vol. XXI, pp. 542–55.)

[2] The *fahu* relationship was not a mere kinship formality; apart from socially defined ceremonial rights, the *fahu* did in fact very often exercise his rights over the property of his mother's brother, though too great an abuse of the privilege seems to have been prevented by the force of public opinion.

This very brief reference to kinship relations in Tonga is necessary as a prelude to the discussion of chieftainship. The highest Tongan chiefs were the heads of patrilineal lineages called *haa*, of which there were about thirteen. The highest lineage of all was that of the Tui Tonga, which was not called *haa*, but *sinae*, a special term designed to emphasize the Tui Tonga's transcendent rank. In order to clarify the highest ranks of Tongan aristocracy, it will be well to list briefly its more important titles.

1. *The Tui Tonga.* — The higher ranks in Tongan society all centred around the "sacred king", the Tui Tonga. The most striking thing about the Tui Tonga was his extreme sanctity on the one hand and his lack of secular power on the other. The first Tui Tonga was of divine descent, being sprung from the god Tangaloa, and the sanctity of the office was expressed in a number of taboos and ceremonial observances surrounding it.

2. *The hau.*—While sanctity resided in the Tui Tonga, administrative power was exercised by the *hau*, or secular ruler. According to tradition, the two functions were once merged in the Tui Tonga, until the twenty-third of the line was assassinated; his son Kauulufonua I pursued his father's murderers throughout the neighbouring islands, finally exacting vengeance upon them at Uvea. After this, through fear of assassination of himself and his descendants, Kauulufonua delegated his administrative power to his younger brother, who was given the title of Tui Haa Takalaua, and who thus became the eponymous ancestor of the lineage called Haa Takalaua. The Tui Tonga still retained his exalted status, his claims to tribute and to women of high rank in marriage, while the duties of administration were taken over by the Tui Haa Takalaua. This state of affairs persisted for some time, until the sixth Tui Haa Takalaua appointed his son Ngata as the first Tui Kanokupolu. Thereafter the Tui Kanokupolu tended to assume the office of *hau*, and though the line of the Tui Haa Takalaua seems still to have exercised a considerable amount of power, this passed in time mainly into the hands of the Tui Kanokupolu.

3. *The great royal wife of the Tui Tonga.*—The Tui Tonga had a number of wives, but there was always one, referred to as *moheofo*, who was the mother of the succeeding Tui Tonga. The *moheofo* was always a woman of high rank. Several of the earlier *moheofo* came from other islands, two of them being Samoans. But in later times there emerges what appears to be a stylization of the relationship. Of the sixteen *moheofo* listed by Gifford, the seventh,

eighth and ninth were daughters of the Tui Haa Takalaua, the first of these marriages taking place a short time after the institution of the first Tui Haa Takalaua. Again, the inauguration of the office of Tui Kanokupolu was followed by a series of marriages, in which five *moheofo* were daughters of the Tui Kanokupolu, and one his son's daughter. These cases support the statements of several observers that marriage between the Tui Tonga and the daughter of the Tui Kanokupolu was obligatory. The record of actual instances is of course incomplete, there being only sixteen *moheofo* recorded as against thirty-nine Tui Tonga, but it does suffice to show a tendency for the Tui Tonga to have as his *moheofo* the daughter, first, of the Tui Haa Takalaua and later of the Tui Kanokupolu.

4. *The Tui Tonga Fefine.*—The female Tui Tonga (Tui Tonga Fefine) was the oldest living sister of the Tui Tonga. As such, she was senior to the Tui Tonga and to his son, which will be clear from what we have said above concerning the brother to sister and brother's son to father's sister relationships.

5. *The Tamaha.*—The daughter [1] of the Tui Tonga Fefine was the Tamaha, and was the person of highest rank in all Tonga. As the great *fahu* of the Tui Tonga, she commanded his respect, which was expressed in acts of abject obeisance and in the humble presentation of offerings.

In the above brief account of the high titles of Tongan society, we can see the importance of kinship in political organization. In the first place, the high chiefly lineages of the Tui Haa Takalaua and the Tui Kanokupolu derived their sanctity from the lineage of the Tui Tonga, and ultimately from Tangaloa. Sanctity was a relative matter, and the other high lineages derived it from the fact that they were collateral branches of the dynasty of the Tui Tonga. But apart from renowned and divine descent, the system just described was reinforced by affinal relationships which at the same time organized political structure on the basis of kinship, and also set a pattern of kinship relationships which ran right through Tongan society from the highest to the lowest.

The ideal scheme of affinal relationships centring round the Tui Tonga is represented by Professor Radcliffe-Brown [2] as follows:

[1] The title of Tamaha might be held by a sister's son of the Tui Tonga, but it belonged primarily to his sister's daughter, in accordance with the seniority of sisters over their brothers.

[2] Unpublished notes by A. R. Radcliffe-Brown communicated to R. W. Williamson.

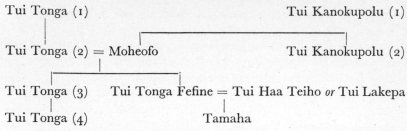

The most important feature of this table is the marriage of the Tui Tonga to the daughter of the Tui Kanokupolu. Radcliffe-Brown states that "when the rank of Tui Kanokupolu was first established, the Tui Tonga laid it down that it was the duty of the Tui Kanokupolu to give his daughter to the Tui Tonga as his wife"; and certainly, from the time of the thirty-fourth Tui Tonga and the fourth Tui Kanokupolu onwards, this seems to have been the general practice.

In connection with this, Radcliffe-Brown notes several points for consideration. In the first place, there is the seniority of a sister over her brother, to which we have referred above. Though descent and inheritance were patrilineal, rank was determined to a greater extent by the mother than by the father. This is clearly seen in the custom of regarding the "half-chiefs" who were sons of women of chiefly rank and commoners more highly than those whose parents were male chiefs and female commoners. For this reason the daughter of the Tui Kanokupolu would be of higher rank than his son, that is, the succeeding Tui Kanokupolu.

Secondly, in Tonga the grandchildren occupy a very favoured position, a daughter's son ranking above a son's son. In olden days a number of respectful observances towards the daughter's son (who was a "lesser *fahu*") gave expression to this principle. This would mean that, in terms of the diagram, the Tui Kanokupolu (1) would occupy this position in relation to his daughter's son, the Tui Tonga (3). The Tui Tonga, being generally either the sister's son or the daughter's son of the Tui Kanokupolu, was thus entitled to the respect generally accorded to these relatives, and the whole system is thus seen to emphasize the seniority of the Tui Tonga lineage over that of the Tui Kanokupolu.

The significance of this thesis of Professor Radcliffe-Brown is that the adoption of a standard of kinship relationships between the highest members of the aristocracy served to define those relationships in a manner consistent with the political system, which was thus reinforced. The sanctity of the Tui Tonga, established in the first place by his divine origin and the legendary accounts of the illustrious deeds of his ancestors, was still further emphasized by his kinship relationship to the secular ruler, to whom he was nominally senior, and upon whom he exercised certain claims defined by the affinal relationship existing between them.

As we have said, the rule of endogamy is almost universal in stratified societies. But there are one or two atypical examples in which the rule of *exogamy* is operative, the best illustration being the political system of the Natchez. This tribe was divided into three grades of nobility and one of commoners. The former, in order of superiority, were referred to as Suns, Nobles and Honoured Men (or Women). The Suns were the highest grade of nobility, and among them the Great Sun was the high chief. The commoners were called *Puants* by the early French observers, a word which has been translated "Stinkard". The curious feature of Natchez social organization was that members of the three noble classes married Stinkards, though the latter also married among themselves. Children of *women* of the nobility who married Stinkards belonged to the class of their mother. Children of men of the nobility who married Stinkard women belonged to the social class immediately below that of their father. Swanton gives the following representation of the constitution of Natchez society:

NOBILITY
- *Suns:* Children of Sun mothers and Stinkard fathers.
- *Nobles:* Children of Noble mothers and Stinkard fathers, or of Sun fathers and Stinkard mothers.
- *Honoured People:* Children of Honoured women and Stinkard fathers, or of Noble fathers and Stinkard mothers.

STINKARDS: Children of Stinkard mothers and Honoured men, or of Stinkard fathers and Stinkard mothers.

The actual operation of the Natchez system was probably less rigid than this representation would suggest, since individuals could apparently change their class to a limited extent. Thus a Stinkard who possessed superior social qualities could raise himself to the grade of Noble. Unfortunately, the original records are inadequate and to some extent contradictory, and it is impossible to discern exactly what variations existed within the rigid system outlined above. But the general pattern of the system is clear, and is interesting as a striking exception to the general rule of endogamy associated with stratified societies.

In contradistinction to stratified political systems, such as those just described, many peoples of Africa and America, as well as the majority of those of Melanesia and all Australian aboriginal tribes, are organized as **segmented societies.** Here each small local group, whether static or nomadic, forms an autonomous political unit. The segmented societies of Melanesia are exemplified by those of Malaita and Wogeo. In Australia it is the local horde governed by its older men which is the only unit of political organization. Most of the Amerindian tribes of the Area of Wild Seeds were likewise organized into small autonomous local groups. Thus the nomadic hunting and food-gathering bands of the Paviosto numbered only about a hundred individuals, each band being politically autonomous. In Africa there are many segmented societies, of which the Nuer and Tallensi may be cited as examples.

The component autonomous political units of segmented societies may combine on occasion for purposes of war, but they owe no allegiance to any centralized authority. Political power is exercised by hereditary headmen, by councils of elders or by men of wealth in the community whose authority may cover only a village or other small local group. In such communities the bonds based on kinship—for example, in the lineage or clan—are of paramount importance. The small local group is usually held together by the relations of kinship or clan membership which unite the various individuals composing it. In stratified societies such bonds exist, and are indeed extremely important in the functioning of the smaller segments of the political structure, and also, through the rule of endogamy, in maintaining the solidarity and privileges of the ruling classes. But so far as the political organization of the whole community is concerned, the bonds of kinship are secondary to those based on habitation of a common territory, community of culture and common allegiance to higher political authorities.

This distinction, however, must not be pressed too far. The forces of kinship, clanship and membership of small local groups may also be extremely important in stratified societies. Thus, even in the highly developed political organization of Ngonde, the paramount chiefs played little or no part in maintaining the

common law, which was administered by local chiefs and headmen, while disputes relating to marriage were normally settled
by the kinsfolk of the two people concerned, just as such matters
are normally dealt with in segmented societies. Again, in the
kingdom of Ankole the supreme judicial power of the Mugabe
was limited in cases of murder to granting the right of blood
revenge, which was carried out by the kinsfolk of the dead man.

5. Totemic Groupings

Among many primitive peoples there are found various forms
of association between human groups on the one hand and species
of animals, plants or natural phenomena on the other. Such an
association is known as **totemism,**[1] though there exists a considerable variety of opinion as to the proper definition of this
term and as to whether certain atypical and unusual practices
should be classed as totemic. In the vast majority of cases totemic
groups are unilateral descent groups, such as clans or moieties.
Each clan or moiety in a totemic society regards itself as being in
some way associated with its totem, which is usually some
species of animal, bird, plant or other living thing.[2] Sometimes a
totemic group has two or more species as its totems, in which
case the practice is known as *linked totemism,* or *multiple totemism.*

The actual beliefs and observances associated with totemism
vary enormously from one community to another, but certain
characteristics are widespread:

(*a*) It is common for the human group to be called by the name
of the totem.

(*b*) The totemic association usually has a legendary background, consisting of one or more myths which link the
human group with its totemic species. Very commonly this
takes the form of a belief in descent from a totemic ancestor,
that is, from some being who was partly human and partly
animal, bird, fish and so on.

(*c*) There is often some form of religious ritual connected with
the totem. This ritual frequently re-enacts dramatically the
mythological events which are believed to account for the
origin of the totemic relationship. A specialized type of

---

[1] This term is derived from a Chippewa word, variously rendered as *dodaim, too-
daim, ototeman* and *ododam,* which has been adopted into the English language in the
form *totem.*

[2] Very occasionally a totem may be an object of material culture or some inanimate
natural phenomenon or force such as wind, moon, thunder and so on.

totemic religious ritual is found in the increase ceremonies of the Australian aborigines.

(d) The religious observances connected with totemism commonly include prohibitions against members of the totemic group killing or eating the totemic species.

(e) Since totemic groups are usually clans or moieties, totemism is usually found to be associated with the rule of exogamy.

(f) It is common for the totemic species to be represented by some kind of carving or symbolic design, which forms an emblem or crest with which the totemic group feels itself to be associated. The most striking example of this is found in the famous "totem poles" of the north-west coast of America.

While the above characteristics are common features of totemism, it must be emphasized that in any given totemic system, one or more of them may be absent and that they receive differential emphasis from one community to another. This becomes clear if we review briefly the characteristics associated with several totemic systems, characteristics which may be compared with those of the Karadjeri system described in greater detail in Chapter III, Section 10.

In Tikopia, each of the four clans is associated with one of the major types of vegetable food as follows:

> Yam—Kafika clan.
> Coco-nut—Tafua clan.
> Taro—Taumako clan.
> Breadfruit—Fangarere clan.

The clans are not named after their totems, but the vegetable food concerned is said to "obey" or "listen to" its associated clan, and particularly the chief of the clan. The chief of the Tafua clan performs no ceremonies in connection with the coco-nut, but the other chiefs have important ritual duties (which vary between the clans) in connection with the planting or harvesting of their respective totems. There is no taboo on the eating of the totemic food, and the only trace of ritual prohibition occurs in the case of members of the Tafua clan, who are required to open a coco-nut by piercing the eyes and not by cutting, as is commonly done by members of other clans. Each of the four totemic foods is associated with the principal deity of its clan, and the ceremonies performed are designed to maintain the food-supply by invoking this deity. There is also a general myth, given in Chapter X, Section 4, which accounts for the origin of the totemic system. Finally, since exogamy is not a feature of the Tikopia clans, this characteristic is absent from Tikopia totemism.

Among the Baganda we find a variety of linked totemism. The Baganda had approximately thirty-six exogamous patrilineal clans. Each clan was named after a totemic species, and also had a secondary totem. There was a taboo on killing or eating either of the totems, and the unpleasant consequences which were believed to follow a breach of this rule were more drastic in the case of the secondary totem. There were, however, no ceremonies to ensure the fertility of the totemic species.

The totemism of the Iroquois was of an entirely different kind, and varied slightly in character between the tribes composing the League. Among the Seneca, each of the matrilineal moieties was divided into four matrilineal clans, which derived their names from totemic species. The totems, however, were not the subject of any religious ceremonies, nor was there any taboo on killing or eating the totem.

On the north-west coast of America we find a highly specialized variety of totemism, in which the representation of the totemic creature, in the form of a mask or carving, was far more important than the totemic species itself. Clans and other unilateral exogamous groupings took their names from their totems. Although there were many food taboos and rites designed to ensure the supply of natural species in this area, these were in no way connected with totemism. There was, however, a system of mythology which linked the totemic group with its totemic species, and sometimes implied descent from the totem.

The above brief summary indicates how variable are the social systems to which the term "totemism" is applied. This emphasizes the fact that, though we have listed the common characteristics of totemism, in any given totemic system we find some, but not all, of these characteristics present. Moreover, the totemic systems of certain peoples are not internally consistent. In some societies certain practices connected with totemism may be observed by some totemic groups but not by others, as we have seen to be the case in Tikopia. Again, among the Hopi, some clans refrain from killing their totems, but others do not.

We have so far dealt with the forms of association between unilateral descent groups and natural species which are most commonly referred to as totemism. But other types of grouping may be similarly associated with totemic species. In parts of eastern Australia members of each sex have a particular species of animal or bird as their totem, a practice which is known as *sex totemism*. Thus among the tribes of the Hunter River, New South Wales, the woodpecker was sacred to the women and the bat to the men. Not only did each sex respect its own totem, but quarrels broke out if a man injured a woodpecker or a woman injured a bat. Again, secret societies or other forms of voluntary social grouping are sometimes associated with a natural species in a manner which might be described as totemic. In many communities a particular individual, usually a shaman or other person endowed with unusual supernatural powers, sometimes enters into a special relation with a natural species. This custom is sometimes referred to as *individual totemism*. Finally, an atypical form of totemic organization is found in the *conceptional totemism* of the Aranda. Here, membership of a totemic group depends upon the existence of sacred totemic centres. A child belongs to the totemic centre nearest to the spot where its mother first became aware of her pregnancy, or, in native belief, where a totemic spirit from the centre first entered her body. Since men normally live in the vicinity of their totemic centres and their wives reside with them, it usually happens that a child belongs to the totem of its father, though this is not necessarily the case.

It will be seen that the term "totemism" has been applied to a bewildering variety of relationships between human beings and natural species or phenomena.[1] For this reason it is impossible to reach any satisfactory definition of totemism, though many attempts have been made to do so. Frazer's monumental work on the subject [2] opens with the words: "A totem is a class of material objects which a savage regards with superstitious respect, believing that there exists between him and every member of the class an intimate and altogether special relation"; but this formulation is inapplicable to many Amerindian forms of totemism in which the magico-religious element is lacking. On the other hand, Goldenweiser's definition of totemism as "the tendency of definite social units to become associated with objects and symbols of emotional value" is too vague and general—it would apply, for example, to the flags of modern nations or badges of clubs or

---

[1] In Australia alone, Professor Elkin distinguishes six different varieties of totemism, namely, individual totemism, sex totemism, moiety totemism, section and subsection totemism, clan totemism and local totemism.

[2] *Totemism and Exogamy.*

societies, whereas primitive totemism is in general concerned
with natural species or phenomena, even when the symbolic
representation (crest or emblem) is more significant than the
species or phenomenon itself. All definitions of totemism are either
so specific as to exclude a number of systems which are commonly
referred to as "totemic" or so general as to include many
phenomena which cannot properly be referred to by this term.

Although we cannot arrive at any really satisfactory definition
of totemism, Professor Radcliffe-Brown's formulation, with
specific reference to Australia, comes as close as possible to a
satisfactory statement of the position: "Throughout Australia we
find, with many local variations, a system of customs and beliefs
by which there is set up a special system of relations between the
society and the animals and plants and other natural objects that
are important in the social life. Some of these customs and beliefs
it is usual to include under the term 'totemism'." [1] This statement
emphasizes the fundamental character of totemism as a relationship between social organization on the one hand and geographical environment (particularly the natural species inhabiting it) on the other. All human societies are divided into various
types of social groupings, described in this and the preceding
chapter, and all societies likewise live in a culturally defined
relationship with their natural environment, a relationship which
is far more intimate and significant among primitive peoples than
among ourselves. Where these two principles become integrated
into a single system, where human groups are classified in terms
of natural species, and where the significance of natural species is to
a large extent interpreted in terms of their relationship to human
groups, we may speak of totemism. This implies a segmentation
of society and a parallel segmentation of natural species, or
some of them, which may be graphically represented as follows:

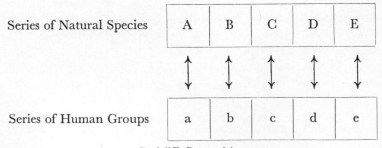

Series of Natural Species	A	B	C	D	E
Series of Human Groups	a	b	c	d	e

Radcliffe-Brown (2), p. 29.

Similar synoptic diagrams for specific totemic systems are given in Fig. 15. The arrows, indicating the relationship between human groups and their totems, may stand for any of the beliefs and customs listed on pp. 201–2. Very broadly these beliefs and customs may be classified as either social or religious, and some writers have stressed the distinction between social totemism and

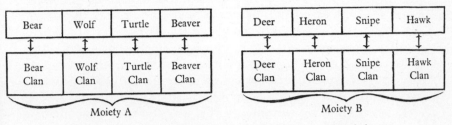

(a) Totemism of the Seneca Tribe—Matrilineal Clans and Moieties.

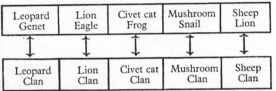

(b) Linked Totemism of the Baganda. This diagram is incomplete, as the Baganda have about thirty-six patrilineal totemic clans.

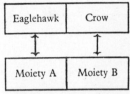

(c) Moiety Totemism, as found in parts of South-Eastern Australia.

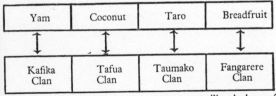

(d) Totemism of the non-exogamous patrilineal clans of Tikopia.

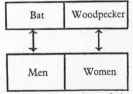

(e) Sex Totemism of the Hunter River Tribes, Eastern Australia.

FIG. 15.—Some Varieties of Totemism

cult totemism, according to whether the integration of the social groups concerned, or their ritual relationship to natural species, receive more emphasis in native belief and custom.

While a relationship based on segmentation is the commonest and most general basis of totemism, there naturally occur certain marginal or atypical forms, for example, individual totemism (where the totem is not common to a group) and the

totemism of secret societies (where non-members have no totem).
The term "totemism", however, should not be applied to instances
where the community as a whole bears a relationship to a particular species or animal emblem (for example, the British lion), or to
cases where only one creature, and not the species as a whole, is
the subject of special observances, as in the case of a special white
crocodile which is held sacred by the Yoruba. But once again it
must be emphasized that no hard-and-fast line can be drawn
between usages which are totemic and those which are not. Thus,
with specific reference to ritual to secure the fecundity of nature,
we find cults of varying degrees of specificity, from the undoubtedly totemic increase ceremonies of Australian tribes to generalized nature cults, fertility rites and other magico-religious rituals,
such as rain-making ceremonies. Though these are not totemic,
they reflect the same dependence of man on nature as lies at the
basis of true totemism, in which this dependence is interpreted in
terms of the social organization of the community.

6. Voluntary Associations

We have so far dealt mainly with social groupings to which any
given individual is obliged to belong, either through biological
necessity or social custom. As we have said at the outset, these are
by far the commonest types of grouping in primitive society,
which in this respect contrasts in a striking way with our own.
But in a limited number of primitive communities there exist
societies based on a voluntary membership, and these are usually
referred to as **associations.** Professor Lowie uses this term in a
much wider sense to describe "social units not based on the kinship factor", but the criterion of voluntary membership seems
preferable to this negative definition. It should be noted, however,
that the term "voluntary" in this context is a relative one, and
that, in the case of many primitive associations, social or economic
pressure upon the individual is often sufficient to make membership obligatory, de facto if not de jure. This was apparently the case
in some of the Melanesian associations which we shall mention,
but even in these cases there were certain individuals who preferred to abstain from joining, a situation which could not arise in,
for example, kinship groupings or the ordinary type of age-grade.

Since members of associations in primitive society feel themselves to be a group distinct from the community at large, their
activities are frequently kept secret from non-members. Associa-

tions in which this occurs are known as **secret societies,** but it must be noted that these differ from the corresponding organizations of modern society in that *membership* of the society is usually not secret—on the contrary, the component individuals are proud to have it known that they belong to the society. It is only the actual proceedings of the society which are carried out in secret, and in some primitive associations, such as the *arioi* of the Society Islands, no element of secrecy is involved.

Secret societies are common, though by no means universal, in Melanesian cultures. In the Banks Islands there were two distinct sets of such associations. There were societies called *sukwe*, whose habitats were long village club-houses or buildings called *gamal*, and others called *tamate*, whose meeting-places were buildings or open spaces in secluded places in the bush, called *salagoro*. The *sukwe* were men's clubs, divided into a number of divisions or ranks, each having its distinctive name, and eating and sleeping in a separate compartment of the *gamal*. Since almost every man was a member of the *sukwe*, the *gamal* served to a considerable extent for public services. Initiation into the *sukwe* could take place at any period of a man's life, from infancy to old age, but the presumed time was the period of commencement of puberty. Prior to initiation, he had to feed with the women. There was a ceremony on initiation into the *sukwe*, and a ceremony on the occasion of each transition from a lower to a higher rank. Each of these ceremonies involved costly presents to the members of the *sukwe*. It was not necessary for a member to pass through all the ranks beginning at the lowest. He could, on his first initiation, pass directly into any of the other ranks; but the extent to which this could be done was limited by considerations of cost. The great mass of the people never rose above the middle rank and many did not even reach that. Each rank of the *sukwe* had a distinctive hat or mask connected with it, and membership of the higher ranks involved special privileges, for example the right to drink kava. There appears to have been very little element of secrecy connected with the *sukwe* or its performances, and the *gamal* was the general meeting-place of the village.

The other type of Banks Islands association, the *tamate* societies, were very numerous. Membership was in nearly all cases confined to men. A youth who did not become a member of one of them did not take a position of social equality with those who did, and would probably not marry. Secrecy was an essential and fundamental feature. The meeting-places of these societies, hidden away in the bush, were taboo to the uninitiated and to women; their masks (also called *tamate*) might not be seen by women or the uninitiated, except when the members were going about the island, and the masks would not be closely observed. Some of the societies had a practice of robbing the gardens and chasing or terrifying the uninitiated. Others did not do this, but merely came out to show their finery and dance in public. Initiation was a subject of ceremony, and was in some cases followed by a period of seclusion; but apparently no instruction was given to the initiate beyond the disclosure of the modes in which the dresses and masks were made and the mysterious sounds produced, and the teaching of songs and dances. In most of the *tamate* societies the neophytes had not to undergo any tortures or even hardships. The Banks *tamate* societies had badges, used by their members as taboo signs, to protect their gardens and property.

The *sukwe* and *tamate* were connected with each other. For example, no one could pass above a certain rank in the *sukwe*, unless he had been initiated into the most important of the *tamate* societies. There were also certain *tamate* societies which were only open to persons who belonged to the *sukwe*. One of the most important features of the *sukwe* and *tamate* societies was that the determination of social rank and importance was largely dependent on them. A chief who was not a member of both societies would possess little authority or importance in comparison with one standing high in these organizations.

Another type of Melanesian association was the *dukduk* society of New Britain. Its activities were of a seasonal character, commencing in a period of the year when it was supposed to be born, and ending with its illness and death in another period. Most of its members were males, though apparently there were a few old women connected with it. There were very few adult males who were not members, whilst many boys as young as four or five years were members. Membership was requisite for recognition of manhood and the uninitiated were laughed at and spoken of as women. *Dukduk* was a secret society, and had its secret enclosure called *taraiu* in the seclusion of the thick bush. In it were a few houses which were used by the members, and in which the masks were hung. The members had their feasts, dances and songs; and during the period of their activities they used to live in seclusion. From time to time parties dressed up in their fantastic garments and masks went about the country whooping and dancing, terrifying the women and uninitiated, and thus extorting gifts from them, the belief being that these terrible-looking creatures were spirits from the bush. The initiation of new members was a source of great expense to the relatives of the initiates. The lads had to submit to the terrors of armed attacks upon themselves, painful strains upon their strength and powers of endurance and other discomforts and annoyances. Here, as in the Banks Islands, the initiates seem to have been taught nothing more than the deceptions involved in the terrifying performances of the society and the steps of their dances, concerning all of which strict secrecy was enjoined.

Voluntary associations are also found among several Amerindian tribes, the Tobacco Society and secular clubs of the Crow being the best-known examples. Membership of the Tobacco Society was acquired by securing a sponsor who was already a member, to whom a substantial fee was paid, and to whom the novice subsequently referred as "father". In addition, special fees were paid for the acquisition of particular "medicines" or ornaments connected with the society and for specific privileges, for example, the right to occupy a position of honour in the ceremonial proceedings of the society. The original founder of the society was believed to have been "fathered" into it by a supernatural being, who instructed him to plant tobacco, this being the main privilege of membership of the society. The ceremonial planting of tobacco was believed to promote the welfare of the tribe, hence the social distinction which it conveyed. In addition, members of the society performed special songs and dances. Novices were instructed in these during initiation, but no pain or hardship was inflicted upon them. The Tobacco Society included numerous "chapters", among the members of which the fees paid by novices were shared. A notable feature of this society was that it included both men and women, and it was common to initiate a man and his wife at the same time.

In addition to the religious association of the Tobacco Society, the Crow had a number of secular clubs, all of which shared the right to perform a particular dance. There was no formal initiation, nor were membership fees exacted—in fact, as all these clubs were anxious to increase their membership, individuals were sometimes solicited to join by means of substantial gifts. Unlike the Tobacco Society, they were not religious associations.

Their functions were partly military and partly economic. They sought to gain renown in battle and carried out in rotation duties analogous to those of a police force; for example, the tribal chief each year assigned to a particular club the duty of maintaining order during the communal buffalo hunt. Because of the military character of these clubs, membership was in general confined to men, though women might occasionally be admitted. The economic obligations of membership of the Crow clubs included mutual assistance in communal labour and the raising of subscriptions to enable one of their members to join the Tobacco Society.

Social groupings founded on voluntary membership find their highest development in the secret societies which are still common in West Africa, though many of their original functions have disappeared as a result of European influence. One such organization was the Poro (or Porro) society found in Sierra Leone and Liberia, particularly among the Mende. The Poro was essentially a men's society [1] and women were admitted only under exceptional circumstances and even then only into the lowest grades. The Poro is believed to have had a supernatural origin, though there are different legendary accounts of how it came to be founded. The Poro had no centralized organization, but consisted of a series of local lodges, each with its own officials. Each lodge met at a special place, colloquially known as the Poro "bush", usually adjacent to a town. Here was situated the grave of the founder of the lodge, and those of other notable past members. This spot was strictly taboo to women and non-members, the direst penalties being exacted for trespass. Members of the Poro spoke through a horn, producing a harsh nasal sound, and this was explained to non-members who heard it as the voice of "devils". The Poro had a special sign, a spiral of ferns, an elaborate paraphernalia, including drums, medicines and masks, and a series of esoteric sayings and pass-words known only to members. These, and the details of the proceedings of the society, were a matter of the strictest secrecy. Each new member was obliged to take an oath of secrecy, and failure to honour this obligation was believed to lead to illness or even death.

Membership of the Poro was essential to the attainment of full

---

[1] A corresponding organization for women, the Sande or Bundu, also existed and served analogous functions. Like the Poro, the Sande is still active today, though in a somewhat altered form.

adult male status, and young men were not allowed to marry or
have sexual intercourse until they had been initiated. Before
joining they had to be circumcised, but this did not admit them
to the Poro, which had its own initiation rites carried out at the
Poro "bush". The novice paid a fee to members of the society on
joining, and was taken to the bush, where marks were cut upon
his back with a razor to indicate membership of the society. In
this and other hardships which he was forced to undergo he was
expected to display fortitude and self-discipline. He was instructed in the esoteric practices of the society, in tribal custom,
in recreational activities such as singing and drumming, and
sometimes in native crafts. At a later stage he might undergo a
further course of training and, by the payment of the appropriate
fees, move up into higher grades of the society.

The Poro served important functions among the Mende and
other West African tribes. It was a mechanism for the indoctrina-
tion of youths in tribal standards, and linked together members
scattered over a wide area, irrespective of their local and kinship
affiliations. It was important politically, and no man could hope
to attain political power unless he were a member of the society,
which played a leading part in the selection of chiefs and arbi-
trated in disputes between important members of the community.
The officials played a leading part at civil ceremonies connected
with the inauguration, illness and death of chiefs. The chief was
expected to preserve the interests of the Poro society, and in
return received customary presents and also services from its
junior members, such as help in the cultivation of his rice farm.
The Poro was also important economically, regulating trading
practices over a wide area and fixing fair prices for commodities
and services. In the discharge of all these political and economic
functions, the authority of the Poro was supported by the belief
in its supernatural significance, that it was in direct contact with
the spirit world, and by the punishments, both real and supernatural, which followed from a breach of Poro rules.[1]

A voluntary association of an entirely different kind was the
arioi of the Society Islands. This was an association of men and

[1] The cultural significance of the Poro in pre-European times is reflected in the
way in which its major political and economic aspects have largely survived up to the
present, while modern conditions have led it to assume new functions in spite of
Government opposition, the hostility of Moslems, and the general breakdown of
tribal custom. It is still the main agency in preserving indigenous social codes and in
uniting individuals of different groups, scattered over a wide area, by the possession
of a common cultural tradition.

women whose principal function was to provide entertainment. Highly organized and numerically very strong in ancient times, it decayed rapidly under the influence of missionaries, who were from the first violently antagonistic towards the whole institution, mainly because of the sexual practices and the rule of infanticide associated with it.

The *arioi* society was organized into a hierarchy composed of eight orders, marked off from each other by the different tattoo marks and decorations of their members. Initiates were first introduced into the lowest order with elaborate ceremony, and passed successively through the various grades, though few reached the highest rank of all, a privilege which could only be bestowed by the high chief. Each transition from one grade to another was ceremonially celebrated.

Statements as to the qualifications for membership are conflicting, some observers stating that membership was restricted to people of high rank and others that members of the lower classes might be admitted. Probably the reconciliation of these two opinions is to be found in the statement of one observer that membership of the *arioi* was an expensive matter, which would mean that, though there might not be any rigid ban upon membership for people of the lower orders, it would be restricted *de facto* to men of wealth and rank. But the essential qualifications for membership were that the initiates should be childless, and that they should be under the inspiration of the gods.

Membership of the *arioi*, and particularly of its upper grades, was a high honour, and a perfect knowledge of its poems and songs made its members sacred and favourites of the gods. Even after death an *arioi* could expect pleasures for which few others could hope.

The principal function of the *arioi* was to provide public entertainment. They wandered about the islands presenting performances for the delectation of the populace at large, being supported at the public expense. Their entertainment consisted of songs, speeches, recitations, dramatic presentations, dancing and sports. In these they were allowed to ridicule chiefs and other people of high rank with impunity. Many of their performances were, by European standards, extremely obscene, and free sexual practices were associated with their activities.

An interesting feature of the *arioi* society was its rule of infanticide. The killing of newly born children was practised fairly generally throughout the Society Islands, but in the case of members of the *arioi* it was obligatory, and failure to observe the rule meant ignominious expulsion.

The *arioi* was such an unusual and highly specialized institution that the interpretation of its functions is not easy. Organized in the first place to provide public entertainment, it seems to have been a powerful integrative force in the community. Each important district had its *arioi* house and its *arioi* "comedian", and these served for the entertainment of visitors. Their roving habits, together with the freemasonry which existed among them, did much to cement bonds between distant districts and to promote goodwill generally, while their right to lampoon the chiefs allowed of criticism which would otherwise have been impossible. Moreover, the feasting, sexual gratification and inversion of ordinary modes of life associated with their practices probably provided a relief from the humdrum round of orderly existence.

It seems probable that the explanation of their rule of infanticide is to be found along this line, the responsibilities of parenthood being inconsistent with a life concentrated upon enjoyment, relaxation and self-indulgence, which would provide the populace at large with entertainment as well as a sort of vicarious satisfaction for their anti-social tendencies.

In spite of its frivolous character, the *arioi* society had an important magico-religious aspect. Its patron deity was Oro, god of war. But when associated with the society he was referred to as Oro-i-te-tea-moe (Oro-of-the-spear-laid-down), and was represented by an emblem formed by three spears so placed as to form a triangle. The legendary origin of the *arioi* is attributed to Oro and members of the society performed religious ceremonies invoking this god. These ceremonies were carried out on the admission of a new member, on setting out on an expedition, upon arrival, and upon returning home again. In addition to this, the *arioi* appear to have served specific religious functions in perpetuating the legends of the cosmogony and of the gods, which they translated into songs and dramatic scenes; and they seem on occasion to have invoked the gods to obtain fertility in times of dearth. Their members, as we have seen, were specially favoured by the gods, and entered the society under their inspiration. Altogether, it cannot be doubted that, in addition to its functions as an institution for public recreation, the *arioi* society possessed a profound religious significance.

Before concluding our discussion of the principle of voluntary association, we must refer briefly to a type of "grouping" which consists of only two individuals, the relationship between whom is described either as **blood brotherhood** or **bond friendship** according to whether the relationship is regarded as one of fictional kinship or merely as an institutionalized form of friendship. Thus, among the Baganda, every man had from one to six blood-brothers, either found for him by his father or chosen by himself. At the ceremony establishing the relationship, each man ate a coffee bean anointed with the blood of the other, and this was believed to remain in the stomach, and to swell up and kill the individual if he should break the compact. Each of the two men then took a spear and a knife, which he placed behind him, to indicate his readiness to protect his blood-brother from violence, and the ceremony concluded with a feast. This ceremonial did not admit a man to full membership of his blood-brother's clan, but he was partly assimilated to it and observed its totemic taboos and rules of exogamy. Moreover, members of the clan addressed him by the same kinship terms as they applied to his blood-brother (that is, their own clansman) and admitted him to clan ceremonies. Blood brotherhood implied mutual aid and support, which in some cases was even more marked than in the case of actual kinship—for example, a murderer could count on finding refuge with his blood-brother, even if the latter were a relative of his victim.

In Tikopia a somewhat similar kind of relationship exists, but it is not interpreted in terms of kinship, nor is one partner assimilated to the clan of the other. The Tikopia relationship is therefore best called "bond friendship", in fact, the native term for it is *tau soa*, that is, people linked together as friends, or *soa*. Bond friendship is established voluntarily by two young men who ritually chew betel together, a single nut and leaf being divided between them. This expresses symbolically the obligation between bond-friends to share their possessions with each other—as the Tikopia say, "*soa* eat equally". There is no magico-religious sanction for bond friendship in Tikopia—the relationship is maintained by the mutual benefits which arise from it. Bond-friends exchange gifts and visits from time to time, they assist each other in economic affairs and give mutual protection in situations of danger. Finally, a man confides his love-affairs to his bond-friend, who assists him by denying any scandal which might arise—for example, if a young man is accused of having spent the night with a girl, his bond-friend will say: "Oh no! He and I slept together." A bond-friend in Tikopia, however, does not act as a go-between in his partner's love-affairs, as does the *soa* in Samoa.

7. *The Integration of Social Groupings*

We have now dealt with the major types of social groupings found in primitive societies, with the exception of those based on economic and on magico-religious functions, which will be discussed in Chapters VII and X. In conclusion, we must refer to some more general characteristics of social organization in primitive communities. In the first place, we have separated the different types of social groupings for descriptive purposes according to the principles of organization upon which they are founded— kinship, age, sex, locality and so on. But it must be emphasized that two or more of these principles may be operative in the constitution of any given social group—thus, in the Tongan aristocracy the principles of kinship, political authority and religious status are all operative in determining the rights and obligations of different individuals and groups within the community. Similarly, the solidarity of the Australian horde is founded, not only upon common residence, but also upon bonds of kinship, common economic pursuits within the horde territory, and joint participation in such magico-religious rituals as increase ceremonies. Furthermore, it is often difficult to classify precisely any given form of social group according to the principles which we have outlined. This is particularly true of voluntary associations. Thus the Tobacco Society of the Crow might be classified as a religious grouping, in view of the important magico-religious implications of the planting of tobacco, while the secular clubs might be classified either as economic, political or recreational groupings according to the various functions which they subserve. Again, in the case of the Poro, there is an increasing tendency for all males to be initiated, and the fact that non-members are forbidden to marry indicates that the term "voluntary association" can only be applied to this organization with some qualification. Finally, the Yakö have secret societies similar to those found elsewhere in West Africa, but membership is hereditary [1] and obliga-

---

[1] In conformity with the system of double unilateral descent of the Yakö, a man may inherit membership of a secret society in either the patrilineal or the matrilineal line.

tory, so that the principle of voluntary membership is here replaced by that of kinship affiliation.

Finally, we must emphasize the integration of social groupings and of principles of social organization, that is, the manner in which they overlap and interlock in such a way as to define the conduct of the individual in any given social situation. We referred in Section 3 to the homogeneity of cultural standards in primitive society. This is correlated with the fact that the obligations entailed in membership of different social groupings tend, in general, to reinforce one another. It is true that conflicts of loyalty do occasionally arise, for example, between obligations towards consanguineous kin on the one hand and affinal kin on the other, or between the demands of voluntary associations against those of kinship groupings. But these instances are of minor importance compared with the vast majority of cases in which different principles of social organization reinforce each other—for example, in the complementary character of political authority and wealth, in the support given to political power by secret societies, and in the strengthening of kinship ties by common residence in such groupings as the extended family.

8. Bibliographical Commentary

As a general discussion of social grouping in primitive communities, Lowie (1) may again be cited. For surveys of particular areas in Africa see Schapera (1), Hambly (1), Seligman (1), and for Amerindian peoples Wissler (2), Hodge (1, article on "Social Organization"), and relevant sections of the chapters in Steward (1 and 2). Elkin (3) and Radcliffe-Brown (2) provide material on Australia, while Firth (5 and 8) and Hogbin (2) give descriptions of different types of Polynesian social grouping. For Melanesia see the various works on the Trobriand Islands by Malinowski, but it must be remembered that this culture is in several respects atypical for Melanesia (p. 74), and reference should also be made to Blackwood (1), Hogbin (5 and 7), Deacon (1), Powdermaker (1), and Kaberry (2).

There is no detailed survey of local organization as such, but most modern field records contain maps, plans and photographs which convey a vivid impression of the character of local grouping. Reference should also be made to Forde (1) for a wide comparative study of the territorial and geographical implications of different types of social grouping. For a valuable discussion of terms such as "tribe" (in which a conclusion somewhat different from that adopted here is reached), see Nadel (4). On the Maori *pa* as a specialized type of local grouping, see Firth (4).

The best available discussion of the place of women in a primitive society is Kaberry (1), and though this deals with one culture only, it disposes incidentally of many popular fallacies regarding the place of women in primitive society. See also Hunter (1), Little (2), Thurnwald, H. (1), and Wedgwood (4). Though the first two of these deal primarily with the effects of culture contact, they provide incidentally an indication of the position of women in the indigenous cultures.

There is no comprehensive discussion of initiation ceremonies as such, but descriptions of these rites among particular peoples are contained in a number of field records, notably Firth (8), Evans-Pritchard (3), Deacon (1), Elkin (3) and Piddington (2). The best available descriptions of primitive educational systems are Fortes (1) and Raum (2). Reference may also be made to the more superficial accounts given in Mead (2 and 3).

The best comparative survey of political institutions is the collection of essays by various writers in Fortes and Evans-Pritchard (1), the preface to which contains a valuable discussion by Professor Radcliffe-Brown of the principles of segmentation and stratification in primitive political organizations. Among other field records which pay particular attention to political organization are Nadel (4) and Wilson (3). On the relation between wealth and prestige in various primitive societies, see the descriptions of the Potlatch given in Goldenweiser (1), Murdock (1) and Forde (1) and the critical review contained in Barnett (1). For studies of other communities in which wealth is closely related to prestige and political power, see Hogbin (5) and Stevenson (1).

A valuable account of certain aspects of political organization among the Mende is contained in Hofstra (1). On the political organization of the Hehe, consult Brown and Hutt (1). The material on Tonga in this chapter is founded mainly upon unpublished notes communicated by Professor Radcliffe-Brown to the late R. W. Williamson and also upon Gifford (1); the Tongan material is more fully discussed in Piddington (4). On the political organization of the Natchez, consult Swanton (1), Macleod (1), and for a critical review of certain apparent anomalies in the system see Hart (1).

There is no modern comparative survey of the phenomena of totemism. Frazer (1) contains much material from the older field records, while Goldenweiser (2) contains a valuable essay, "Totemism, An Analytical Study", which is, however, more significant in its destructive criticism than in its positive contribution. A most valuable comparative study of totemism in a particular ethnographic province is Elkin (2) and the shorter account in Elkin (3). The totemic systems specially mentioned in this chapter and elsewhere in the present book are described in Firth (7), Roscoe (1), Mair (3) and Piddington (1). Valuable incidental references to different varieties of totemism are contained in Murdock (1).

On various types of secret society and other forms of voluntary association, consult Humphrey (1), Lowie (1), Little (1), Piddington (4), Wedgwood (1), and Williamson (2). On blood brotherhood and bond friendship in different primitive societies, see Evans-Pritchard (1), Mair (3) and Firth (9).

On the observations contained in Section 7, no specific reading can be prescribed. Only by the perusal of several modern ethnographic records can the reader gain an idea of the many ways in which different types of social grouping interact and interlock in various primitive societies. In this connection, special reference may be made to Firth (8, 10 and 11), Evans-Pritchard (3) and, though the problems dealt with are somewhat advanced for the beginner, Fortes (3) and Nadel (4).

CHAPTER VI

THE PRINCIPLES OF CULTURAL ANALYSIS

1. The Instrumental Function of Human Culture

HAVING surveyed briefly and superficially some of the types of culture and forms of social organization found among primitive peoples, we may now turn to the more detailed scientific analysis of culture. We saw in Chapter I that culture is essentially an adaptive mechanism, making possible the satisfaction of human needs, both biological and social. It is not a thing of shreds and patches, or an agglomeration of beliefs and customs unrelated to one another. A mere catalogue of items of culture tells us nothing of their dynamic functions in relation to the needs of any given community or of the complex interrelationships existing between them. The study of these constitutes the real task of scientific social anthropology.

The first principle of cultural organization is the constitution of the human organism. The conception of man as an animal is essential to the study of his culture, because all cultures have a common basis in the biological and psychological characteristics of man. Of special importance in this connection are:

1. The needs which man shares with other animals; and
2. Specifically human characteristics and needs arising from man's unique physical and mental constitution.

In the first group of needs, the most important are for food, self-preservation and the reproduction of the species, together with other physiological requirements associated with breathing, sleep, the slaking of thirst and so on. Such requirements are known as *primary needs*.

As regards the second group, we have already referred in Chapter I to the importance of physical anthropology in describing the features which distinguish man from the lower animals, and particularly from those most closely related to him, namely, the anthropoid apes and other sub-human primates.[1]

---

[1] A useful classification of the Primate Order is as follows:
  1. Man.

The most important physical aspects in which man differs from the apes and other sub-human primates are:

1. He has attained a fully erect posture.
2. His foot is designed to support rather than to grasp, while his hands are specialized for manipulation.
3. His brain is larger and more complex. Thus the human brain is about three times the volume of that of the gorilla.

At some stage in man's ascent, his tree-dwelling ancestors, whose hands had gradually assumed a manipulative function, exchanged an arboreal life for a terrestrial one, and this was correlated with the adoption of the erect posture. The feet likewise became specialized for support and locomotion, and the hands could then be devoted wholly to the delicate movements entailed, for example, in the making of tools. A captive ape may use a stick to drag a banana into its cage, but it does not modify the shape of the stick or of any other material object to achieve its ends. Man is the only tool-making animal.

Man's brain, besides being much larger than that of any ape, is structurally more complex in those areas which are devoted to the functions of vision, speech, memory, imagination and the higher intellectual activities in general. The latter parts of the brain are known as the *association areas*, and make it possible for the organism to profit by experience. The difference is, of course, a relative one, but is nevertheless of the utmost significance. Man

2. The anthropoid (or man-like) apes, namely the Gorilla, the Chimpanzee, the Orang-Utan and the Gibbon. (The ordinary word "anthropoid", which refers to these apes only, must not be confused with the wider technical term *anthropoidea*, which covers man, apes and monkeys.)
3. The old-world monkeys, including baboons.
4. The new-world monkeys.
5. Tarsius.
6. The lemurs.
7. Tree shrews (?)

On the subject of man's relationship to the anthropoid apes, it is perhaps necessary to correct a popular misconception. Man is not descended from a primate closely resembling any of the present-day apes. Both arose from a common ancestral stock, from which they became differentiated in the course of evolution. The incorrect and correct formulations may be represented thus:

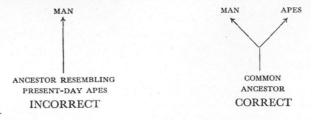

MAN   MAN   APES

ANCESTOR RESEMBLING PRESENT-DAY APES   COMMON ANCESTOR

INCORRECT   CORRECT

lives by acquired behaviour, that is to say, by habit based on memory, rather than by instinct, as do many lower animals. The ratio of acquired to instinctive behaviour is highest in the case of man.

This development of acquired behaviour means that young human beings reach maturity much more slowly than the young of other animals. They are for a long time quite helpless, and must, over a period of several years, learn the types of behaviour which will enable them and their community to survive.

Man alone among the animals possesses the power of speech, which is based upon special anatomical developments, not only in the so-called organs of speech, but also in the parts of the brain controlling such a function. This fact is vital to an understanding of human culture, since speech enables men to co-operate in common tasks, to give and receive orders, and to acquire the understanding necessary to action. It is also a medium for the passing on of cultural knowledge and tradition from one generation to the next.

The primary needs of man and the special characteristics and needs that have arisen in the course of human evolution make possible (indeed make necessary) the creation of culture, which is the specifically human form of biological adaptation. We therefore consider culture, not merely as a set of stereotyped traditional human reactions, but in terms of its *instrumental function* in satisfying the needs of man as a highly integrated type of organism.

2. *Primary Needs*

The satisfaction of the **primary needs** of the human organism, that is, the needs which man shares with other animals, assumes specific forms. Thus, man's *need for food* is not satisfied simply and directly, as in the case of the lower animals. Bodily, he is but poorly equipped for food-getting. But the endowment of culture which each human group possesses makes good this deficiency. Weapons for hunting, implements for agriculture, nets and hooks for fishing, and techniques connected with the tending of cattle are among the cultural responses produced by man's need for food in primitive society. In more advanced cultures improved techniques have enabled him progressively to increase his food supply until it rises well above the subsistence level, thus providing an economic surplus which makes possible the development of civilization and increased opportunities for intellectual, æsthetic and recreational development.

But the use of weapons and implements in food-getting by no means exhausts the cultural responses to the need for food. Collective food-getting activities occur in all cultures, together with some division of labour. Among a hunting and food-gathering people such as the Australian aborigines, collective food-getting often occurs from purely social motives. Women join together to gather food in small groups, not because it increases their efficiency, but merely from the desire for companionship and interest in common activities. But even in Australia we find types of communal hunting and fishing which necessitate organized co-operation between human beings. In agricultural communities, with their more systematized and planned ecology, this tendency is more marked, while civilized levels of human culture would be unthinkable without the economic specialization and interdependence which are invariably associated with them.

The collective production of food entails some regulation of its distribution, so that all members of the community, particularly those incapable of fending for themselves, shall receive a share. Thus, in the family, household and village we always find principles of distribution by which portions of the food supply are allocated to the component members of the group. Sometimes this system of distribution is highly formalized, as when specific portions of a beast or large fish or of the harvest are traditionally allocated to specific kinsfolk or functionaries. Even when the pattern of distribution is less formal, it is always socially significant. Food thus acquires a social value which is reflected in rules of etiquette, good manners and fair play, which govern its distribution and consumption. Finally, for reasons which will become apparent, in communities whose food supply is precarious (and this is more or less the case in the vast majority of primitive communities), there arise magical and religious observances designed to increase or maintain the food supply and to guard against the dangers, real or putative, connected with the production and consumption of food. The complex systems of knowledge, technology, sentiment, social practice and magico-religious usage by which the need for food is satisfied and regulated in any given culture has been termed the **nutritional system.**

Other individual physiological processes.—In addition to the need for food, other basic physiological needs must be provided for, as for example the need to breathe, to drink, to rest from time to time, and to eliminate waste products from the system. Biologically, these requirements are quite as imperative as the need for food, in that the organism could not survive if they remained unsatisfied. Culturally, however, they are less significant, because *under normal conditions* their satisfaction does not present a major cultural problem. Apart from accidents such as drowning or smothering, air is usually freely available under primitive conditions; in general this is also true of water, since completely arid areas of the world could never in any case be inhabited because of the lack of animal and vegetable food; the need for rest provides its own satisfaction, ultimately in the complete collapse of the organism from exhaustion; finally, the processes of excretion, in village communities ignorant of the principles of hygiene, do not require elaborate organization, though they are generally controlled by customary practices of decency and delicacy, and often by beliefs in magic.

Lest it should therefore appear superfluous to mention these basic physiological processes in connection with the analysis of culture, two groups of facts connected with them must be mentioned. In the first place, they may, *under certain circumstances*, assume cultural significance. The need for air becomes important when it is necessary to reconcile this with protection against the weather, that is, to secure at the same time both warmth and ventilation. The Eskimo winter house is a good example of such an adjustment in a primitive community. In our own society, such specific occupational groups as divers and airmen flying at high altitudes require special arrangements to make respiration possible; where water is scarce, such adjustments as wells, goatskin bags and the tapping of water-bearing trees are cultural adjustments connected with thirst; and congested urban conditions, especially when combined with a knowledge of the elements of hygiene and highly developed æsthetic standards, lead to elaborate systems of sanitation and sewerage.

In the second place, while special cultural arrangements are not absolutely necessary in order to provide for rest and sleep, they do occur to facilitate it, and variously take the form of beds, bunks, sleeping-mats and head-rests; in our own society the conditions of modern warfare lead to air-raid shelters and other provisions for rest under conditions of stress, while opiates and sedatives are employed to meet the needs of individuals under special conditions of bodily or mental ill-health. In regard to the other physiological processes mentioned, there are many examples of specific cultural adjustments which, while not essential to biological survival, nevertheless facilitate the satisfaction of the needs concerned, and harmonize this satisfaction with cultural standards—pragmatic, moral, æsthetic and magico-religious.

Defence against, and infliction of, bodily injury.—Anatomically, man is poorly equipped for conflict. This is particularly important when he has to cope with lions, tigers, wolves and other fierce and powerful adversaries. In most cultures he has to protect himself against attack from other human communities, and in warlike societies to devise mechanisms of aggression against them. This need is met by the manufacture of artefacts, such as armour, stockades, shields, spears, traps, snares, pitfalls, bows and arrows, by which he can protect himself against injury from other organisms or inflict injury upon them. In hunting communities the latter is an essential economic activity. Apart from purely material apparatus, cultural techniques of forest lore and principles of tactics and strategy arise in connection with the institutions of hunting and warfare respectively. Finally, both of these hazardous activities are invariably associated with a series of legal rules, ceremonial observances, taboos and other magico-religious beliefs and practices.

Protection against climate.—Man is the only organism which can survive in any climate which will provide a food supply, though this is also true of such animals as the dog and the rat in so far as they attach themselves to human habitations. Man can live in any environment, from the Sahara to the Arctic, only because of his heritage of culture, which is always adapted to the environment in which he lives. The specialized adjustments of the Eskimo and of the Australian aborigines provide striking examples of this, and of the way in which social activities, both economic and ceremonial, are adapted to seasonal variations in climate. It must be emphasized that, while the protection provided by habitations and clothing is not biologically essential in temperate and hot climates, they nevertheless usually occur, providing certain standards of comfort, decency and display as distinct from biological survival.

Sex.—While, from one point of view, the need for food is the most important requirement of man, and certainly determines the major part of his activities under primitive conditions, the emotions connected with sex have always played a vital, and at times dominant, part in human destiny. Fully consummated, sex produces the highest of spiritual experiences, both in its own gratification and in the joys of parenthood; frustrated, it leads to despair and neurosis, or brings out all that is base in human nature through the passionate destructiveness of revenge and jealousy. From time to time it bursts the flood-gates of social control and brings about far-reaching consequences in the destinies of human beings.

The reason for this is obvious, when we remember that man is an animal, in whose evolution the reproductive urge has played an essential part; but he is also a social being, whose headstrong passions must be curbed in the interests of social life. This is effected, on the one hand, by limiting the sexual impulses of the individual through the operation of laws, moral rules and æsthetic standards; and, on the other, by giving expression to these impulses through socially recognized channels, which draw upon the power of the sexual instinct for the creation of social institutions. Sex is not merely suppressed. It is actually harnessed in the interests of social life, and so comes to reinforce the very restrictions which limit its activity.

Thus it comes about that in all cultures we find social mechanisms for the satisfaction and restriction of the sexual impulse. Positively, this is allowed expression sporadically through such institutions as the bachelors' houses of the Trobrianders and the Kikuyu, through wife-lending, or by the *de facto* toleration of liaisons which are officially condemned. The sexual impulse universally finds expression in the relationship of marriage. On the negative side there exist rules prohibiting incest and adultery, as well as numerous special restrictions and taboos governing sexual relations at specific times or between specific persons.

Reproduction.—Biologically, sex is causally linked with reproduction, and it might be argued that both activities together form the basis of a single cultural system. But it is useful to draw a distinction between them, particularly in connection with communities which do not recognize the causal relation or who attach little importance to it. It cannot be too strongly emphasized that while copulation is a demonstrable physiological relationship between two individuals, culturally recognized as such, parenthood is essentially a social relationship depending upon a system of beliefs, social values and legal rules linking together the members of the individual family—father, mother and children. This is clearly seen in polyandrous communities such as

the Todas; here the performance of the bow and arrow ceremony establishes paternity as between the various husbands of a
woman, any one of whom may be the biological parent of the
child concerned. It is true that in most societies the physiological
relationship between father and mother is held to have some
relevance to parenthood, and is often the main criterion, as it is
in our own culture. But even in modern society, with its advanced
biological knowledge and emphasis upon sexual paternity, the
practice of adoption provides a legal and social basis for a form of
parenthood defined in purely cultural terms. This is even more
striking in the case of communities such as Manus, where the
practice of adoption is far more widespread.

Though the purely sexual aspect of reproduction may receive
little or no emphasis, the conditions of pregnancy and childbirth
are invariably connected with social observances and ritual
practices, determined partly by the dangers connected with them
and partly by their social importance. But childbirth is not the
end of the reproductive process in the human species. The young
require care and protection during infancy and childhood, and
from this fact emerge the rules connected with the care of the
infants and young children, as well as traditional arrangements
for the care of orphans.

Health.—Here we come to an entry which might be regarded
as a summary of the preceding ones. In its positive sense it implies
no more nor less than the full satisfaction of all the other primary
needs. But this is an ideal never attained in practice. The health
of individuals is menaced by the dangers of injury and disease,
and these always produce some form of cultural response.
Medical science in modern civilization is the most complex
example, and its multifarious medical and surgical techniques
illustrate how any physiological maladjustment may, under the
appropriate conditions, give rise to a specialized cultural response.[1]

---

[1] The developments of medical science during the past few decades suggest that
our statement that health is co-terminous with the full satisfaction of primary needs
might be extended to include also the social and spiritual needs of man. The growth
of the science of nutrition and of preventive medicine has increasingly stressed the fact
that biological health is essential to the most efficient functioning of a community.
Psychiatry has given an entirely new conception of mental ill-health, typified in the
transition from the straight-jacket to modern techniques of psychotherapy, techniques
which postulate the existence of psychological and social needs or drives, the frustration of which may lead to maladjustment. Finally, the development of social medicine
lays stress upon an even wider conception of health, which postulates as an ideal a
cultural environment in which individual organisms may develop their potentialities,
both biological and psychological, to the full.

In primitive society there is an almost complete lack of effective prophylactic and therapeutic measures; both the promotion of health and attempts to cure illness belong to the province of magic and religion. In this field, however, they play, as we shall see, a vital part in culture, specifically in their relation to the observance of social rules and moral codes.

3. Derived Needs

Our survey of the more important primary needs of man shows that they are always satisfied, regulated and evaluated in terms of cultural standards, social, ceremonial, legal and magico-religious. In all parts of the world human beings gather together in communities, whose activities are regulated by their peculiar form of cultural adjustment. Though man possesses basic biological needs comparable with those of the other primates, these nowhere find direct and indiscriminate satisfaction. The smallest biologically viable unit—the individual family—never occurs in isolation, as it does among the anthropoid apes. For one thing, it is incapable of adequate self-defence, and it could never develop and transmit human culture as we understand it. Even the smallest of communities, such as the nomadic bands of the Australian aborigines, differ from the gregarious groupings of primates such as baboons.

This is not a numerical difference, but one which concerns the whole determination of individual and group behaviour. Nowhere in human society is the sexual association of individuals regulated merely by dominance of physically powerful males—instead the regulations of marriage, and of other forms of sexual association, are rigidly laid down on the basis of culturally recognized status, rank, kinship, age or economic privilege. Food-getting, as we have seen, is never a matter of individual acquisition nor yet of casual sharing—it is always regulated by the economic and legal rules governing the production of food, which always entail a certain amount of co-operation and planning, and by culturally recognized systems of distribution and consumption. Under no circumstances do personal antagonisms lead to direct and unregulated physical retaliation as they do among the primates—the duel, the action at law or the milder sanctions of the frown or the sneer are cultural expressions of the impulse towards personal retaliation. Even where direct unarmed physical retaliation occurs, it is almost universally regulated by Marquess of Queensberry rules or similar social codes. Finally, the relations of individuals to each other are not merely a matter of individual instinct and habit—they depend upon the cultural recognition of individuals as occupying a specific position in a social structure. This position may, and in fact does, change from time to time—the boy becomes a man, the spinster becomes a wife, the layman becomes a priest. But such changes only become real, in a cultural sense, when they are recognized by society.

The specific character of individual relationships in human, as distinct from animal, communities is vividly exemplified by the fact of death. When a female baboon is killed in a "sexual fight", the males continue to quarrel over the body and to use it as a sexual object; a mother baboon or monkey will continue to carry the body of her offspring about for many days after death, sometimes until it is almost completely decomposed. She clings to the dead body, presses it to her breasts, picks through its hair, and treats it precisely as she did when it was alive, suggesting failure to recognize the fact of death. Contrast this with the elaborate cultural reactions to death in human communities—mortuary ceremonial, mourning, beliefs in immortality and ancestor-worship. Instances of cultural or metaphorical death should also be noted; for example, the fictional death and re-birth of initiates. Like all the biological characteristics of man, death is culturally interpreted and evaluated by every human community.

The fact that man can only survive and satisfy his biological needs through human communities regulated by human culture implies that man has certain **derived needs,** that is, needs which he does not share with the lower animals, but which are derived from the conditions of his collective life. Thus, we have referred to the long period of immaturity of the young. During this period they must learn to adapt themselves to their environment, geographical and social. This adaptation can only be achieved by assimilating culture, with its systems of technological and practical knowledge and its co-ordinated system of social sentiments and values. Since it would be impossible for any single individual in a lifetime to acquire this complex body of knowledge, belief and sentiment, the heritage of culture must be passed on from one generation to the next. Thus, the derived *need for the conditioning of the young and for the transmission of culture* invariably leads to an *educational system*, which is conditioned partly by the biological characteristics of man and partly by the conditions of his collective life.

The transmission of culture, as well as the day-to-day co-operation upon which man depends for his subsistence and welfare, would be impossible without some organized system of communication, some means whereby orders may be given, information imparted and types of behaviour approved or condemned. This *need for communication* is satisfied by man's power of speech, organized in the form of *language*, and also by other forms of cultural symbolism.

We have seen that man employs, in the satisfaction of such biological needs as nutrition, protection against the weather and self-defence, an equipment of artefacts which constitute the material substratum of culture. The creation of this is made possible by man's manipulative ability. Without it human communities as we know them could not exist, nor could they produce the surplus food necessary to the development of advanced levels of culture. The *need for material satisfactions*, which includes but goes beyond the merely nutritional requirements of man, produces the same types of cultural response as we have described in the case of nutrition: artefacts must be produced by standardized technological processes, involving human co-operation which, in its minimal form, is exemplified in the relation between teacher and learner; the proper use of artefacts and their cultural significance must be defined, whether the definition be purely utilitarian, ceremonial or magico-religious; finally, the distribution and ownership of material objects must be subject to legal and moral rules. Thus it is that the need for material satisfactions leads in every culture to a system of technology, knowledge and social evaluations embodied in the *economic system* of the community concerned.

The collective activities of man require organization. This is most clearly seen when we contrast them with the gregarious activities of the lower animals, which consist merely of the sum total of a number of individual reactions, instinctive and habitual, unregulated by tradition or by any system of common values and motives. Thus male baboons in a "sexual fight" may kill one of the females over which they are quarrelling. Contrast this with hostilities between human groups, whether in clan fighting, in a village brawl, or in the opposition of contending armies. Only by accident is damage done to individuals not directly concerned, and the whole procedure is governed by cultural standards of honour, loyalty and traditional antagonism. The same principles apply, as we have seen, to the organization of economic pursuits, as they do to all forms of human collective activity.

The *organization of collective activities* usually takes the form of *leadership* by special individuals or groups—chiefs, priests, technical experts or tribal councils. Such leadership may be validated by principles, such as hereditary privilege, respect for age, or magico-religious powers traditionally acquired. On the other hand, it may arise as a result of a more or less spontaneous reaction to the ability and skill of exceptionally intelligent individuals or forceful personalities.

But the term "leadership", in its generally accepted meaning, is too limited to cover all the cultural responses to the need for organization. Very often the organization of activities is inherent in the cultural definition of the activities themselves. An example from our own society will make this clear. In a relay race, the starter's pistol inaugurates the activity, but thereafter each member of the team knows precisely what to do, when and where to run, and how to inaugurate the activity of the member who follows him. The order of running may be decided by the ruling of a captain, but might equally well be determined by general agreement among members of the team. Here leadership plays a negligible part, the organization of the activity being secured by common knowledge of the procedure and rules of the game, as well as by a common desire to win.

The same sort of principle applies to many collective activities under primitive conditions. The ethnographer frequently witnesses a group of natives discussing alternative projects—whether to go fishing or hunting, when or where to hold a religious ceremony. The discussion proceeds, various opinions are expressed, and suddenly the group will break up, having decided upon a specific line of conduct without any orders having been given, and even without any formal expression of a consensus of opinion. While it is possible to observe that in such discussions the opinions of certain individuals appear to carry more weight than those of others, it is difficult to discern any form of leadership in the generally accepted sense, while the whole procedure differs radically from formal meetings in our own society with their stylized procedure of motions, amendments and points of order. Yet principles of organization exist, as is proved by the fact that subsequent activities are carried out in a systematic and efficient way, each individual playing a traditionally defined part. Too often the existence of this type of diffused authority has been obscured in the study of primitive communities by such negative statements as that "no form of leadership or authority exists".

In the domestic arrangements of the individual family, again, there is always a generally accepted definition of rights and obligations as between father, mother and children, reflected in the sexual division of labour and responsibility. Broadly speaking, in the care of children, the preparation of food and domestic arrangements, it is the woman who is primarily responsible for the organization and the inauguration of necessary activities; in the production of food, the respective rights and responsibilities of men and women are usually divided; while in political, ceremonial and magico-religious matters, it is generally the men who take the lead. It must be emphasized that such divisions of functions in the organization of collective activity are often not explicitly formulated. Since they are generally known and accepted by everybody, this is not necessary. They must be inferred from numerous individual observations of behaviour, and particularly of cases in which individuals are lax or incompetent in the discharge of their duties and the exercise of their authority. The woman who cannot or will not organize the home, the man who cannot or will not bring up his children in the way they should go, provide, by contrast, striking illustrations of the way in which informal, diffused, but culturally recognized authority is exercised.

We must not let the paucity of our terminology blind us to the fact that, even in the absence of explicit leadership, principles of organization exist in all collective activities. In fact, explicitly recognized leadership emerges only when these activities become complex; when alternative lines of conduct appear possible or desirable; when the interests of individuals or groups come into conflict; when, in short, overt decisions on matters of policy must be taken. There is a continuous series of forms of organization from the diffuse types of traditional authority implicit in the household to the explicit exercise of power in political systems, embodied in the formal edicts of chiefs, tribal councils, parliaments or dictators. These are but special examples of a universal social process whereby the *need for the organization of collective activities leads to traditionally defined systems of co-operation, to leadership and to forms of political authority.*

In certain limited fields of human activity, the observation of traditional rules of co-operation is ensured by the interests and convenience of individuals. Meal hours and the sequence of activities in daily life, which differ from one community to another, are observed because there is normally no particular urge to deviate from them; the provision of the household food supply is ensured by the fact that its individual members would otherwise go hungry; technological rules are observed because of the demonstrable results which they achieve in the production of efficient and valuable artefacts; and the banding together of the community for defence is dictated by the common danger to its component individuals.

But in most fields of human activity, culture from time to time makes demands upon the individual's capacity for altruism and self-sacrifice. Food is produced, not merely for the consumption of the household, hunting party or other food-producing group, but also for the making of gifts to kinsfolk, the entertainment of guests, and the provision of tribute for chiefs; the production of artefacts often calls for the expenditure of wearying or tiresome effort; warfare, and particularly aggressive warfare, calls for sacrifice and courage which do not subserve, but actually run counter to, the individual urge towards self-preservation. Whenever the demands of culture thus frustrate the aspirations or desires of the individual, and particularly when the compulsive human passions of lust, greed, vanity, fear and anger are involved, we always find some individuals who shirk, evade or flout the obligations imposed upon them by society. When breaches of law and custom occur in this way, there exist mechanisms of restraint and punishment, means whereby the wrongdoer is punished, others are deterred from similar action, and society expresses its horror, disgust or disapproval, thus affirming the moral sentiments upon which it depends for its existence. Society likewise provides rewards, both material and social, for conduct conforming to its particular set of cultural values. It is impossible to conceive of any society which could survive without sanctions of law and morality. Thus, the *need for social control* leads to the *sanctions of law and custom*, both positive and negative.

4. Integrative Needs

Our consideration of human needs derived from the conditions of man's collective life brings us to a group of needs which are more difficult to define. These needs differ from the others, in that they are not demonstrably essential to biological survival. Whether they are so in the last analysis is a problem for the solution of which no empirical evidence exists. But it is axiomatic that man requires, not merely to live, but to live well. It is also empirically demonstrable that all communities provide gratifications for their members over and above those which are essential to biological survival and the satisfaction of physiological appetites.

The existence of these gratifications justifies us in postulating a group of **integrative needs.** Nowhere are the rules of law and morals supported by the fear of punishment and the promise of rewards alone—there is always a set of common moral sentiments which postulate that certain lines of conduct are worth while, apart from material rewards or the fear of punishment. Concretely, the moral feelings of society are given linguistic expression in emotionally significant terms of praise and blame, in proverbs, maxims, myths and other moral tales which build up standards of social conduct in the minds of individuals. The very fact that these standards are not invariably observed shows their vital significance throughout the general run of human activities. The sharing of common tasks, the interdependence of individuals in systems of co-operation, and particularly the ceremonial and religious activities whose main function is the collective expression of optimism, grief, awe and other social sentiments—all these reinforce the individual's feeling of dependence upon his fellows and his respect for the traditional moral codes accepted by them as binding.

All cultures include a *magico-religious system* which, in part, satisfies the *need for the expression of collective sentiments,* and in part satisfies the individual's *need for a feeling of confidence,* of moral integrity and of optimism in the face of danger, disaster, bereavement and the frustration of human hopes. We shall see in Chapter X how primitive religion and magic satisfy these needs as well as the way in which they subserve other collateral functions by organizing and stimulating economic activity, by supporting authority and by reinforcing the rules of custom and law.

Finally, we come to a group of interrelated needs which produce cultural responses connected with man's *need for recreation and for æsthetic expression.* Like all the higher animals, the human organism, particularly when young, indulges in movements and sequences of activity which have no direct and immediate aim connected with the satisfaction of any of the biological needs previously mentioned. These movements provide for an overflow of surplus nervous energy. The tired organism does not play. But the movements concerned are not haphazard; they are demonstrably related to the behaviour patterns necessary to the survival of the species—for example, the series of predatory, aggressive and evasive movements in the play of a young puppy or kitten. Play thus serves the function of preparing the individual for adult life. In man this process is culturally standardized. Apart from the unco-ordinated movements and sounds of very young infants, play activity is usually organized on a collective basis, and, as we have seen, this plays an important part in the education of the young.

Akin to play are the activities which are related, albeit in a subtle and obscure way, to special patterns of sense impressions, visual, acoustic and kinæsthetic. Drawing, painting, carving, music, song and the dance are patterns of behaviour which take on different forms in various cultures. Whether there are any universally valid æsthetic standards is a philosophic question on which it would be unwise to be dogmatic. The music or representative art of primitive peoples often appears to the alien as meaningless, garish or insipid, while manifestly giving intense æsthetic pleasure to individuals reared in the community concerned and trained in its æsthetic standards. This is particularly true of narrative and dramatic art, which depend upon specific cultural standards and values. The mythology of the Australian aborigines is merely a tangled narrative of pointless events unless we can appreciate the value attached in Australian culture to the long-past "dream times", to the geographical environment, to the natural species which are of vital economic and social significance, and to specific standards of moral behaviour in relation to age, kinship obligations and the rules of sexual behaviour. On the other hand, the tragedy of Othello would appear meaningless to an unsophisticated Karadjeri native, since obviously the only rational conduct for the Moor would have been to demand a present of boomerangs from Cassio as compensation for the alleged act of adultery. Clearly the art forms of an alien people can only be appreciated by a full understanding of the complex of cultural values in which they occur. This seems to point to the conclusion that æsthetic standards are necessarily relative, but the whole issue is highly speculative.

TABLE OF HUMAN NEEDS AND CULTURAL RESPONSES

NEEDS	EXAMPLES OF CULTURAL RESPONSES
1. Primary Needs:	
(*a*) Food.	Nutritional system.
(*b*) Other basic physiological processes, such as breathing, rest, excretion.	Systems of ventilation, sleeping arrangements, sanitation.
(*c*) Defence against, and infliction of, bodily injury.	Shields, armour, fortifications, weapons.
(*d*) Protection against climate.	Houses, clothing.
(*e*) Sex.	The social expression and control of sex behaviour.
(*f*) Reproduction.	The family, systems of kinship, and cultural activities connected with pregnancy, childbirth and the care of the young.
(*g*) Health.	Hygiene and the treatment of sickness, almost exclusively magico-religious in primitive society.
2. Derived Needs:	
(*a*) Transmission of culture.	Education.
(*b*) Communication.	Language.
(*c*) Material satisfactions, largely conditioned by manipulative ability.	Economic system, including material culture.
(*d*) Organization of collective activities.	Leadership, centralized or diffused, in traditionally defined systems of co-operation.
(*e*) Social control.	Sanctions of law and custom.
3. Integrative Needs:	
(*a*) Confidence and feeling of collective unity.	Magico-religious system.
(*b*) Relaxation, play, æsthetic satisfaction.	Æsthetic, recreational and ceremonial activities.

What is, however, empirically observable about primitive art, particularly representative art, is its close relationship to practical and social pursuits, a relationship which is much closer than among ourselves. It is rare to find *objets d'art* produced merely for the purpose of contemplation, as we do when we hang pictures on the wall or erect statues in public places. Primitive art rather takes the form of embellishing objects which are actually used in practical and ritual pursuits, for example, the decoration of a

South Sea canoe or the carving on an Australian aborigine's shield.

We have shown that the needs of man are integrally related to certain types of cultural response. The types of relationship involved are summarized in the table given on p. 235.

In connection with this table, it must be emphasized that the presentation is necessarily incomplete and that the relationships indicated are not exclusive. In the next section we shall seek to clarify the character of these relationships, and to describe the way in which any given culture is organized for the satisfaction of human needs.

5. Needs and Institutions

In the foregoing analysis of the basic needs of man and the types of cultural responses which they produce, the reader may have noticed the emergence of certain general principles. In the first place, while we can describe and seek to classify the needs of man, they are closely related to each other in their satisfaction. Thus the infant's need for food, satisfied in the first instance by suckling, forms a part of its more general need for care and protection; the individual's need for sexual satisfaction and the community's need for reproduction are closely related, not merely biologically, but also culturally, since both find satisfaction through the institution of the family. This leads us to a second conclusion—that there is no point-to-point relationship between needs on the one hand and cultural responses on the other. A single economic system provides for the satisfaction of the needs for food and for material equipment; a unitary educational system provides for the training of the young and for the transmission of culture.

The relation of cultural responses to human needs takes on different forms from one society to another. The political leader may or may not be identical with the expert in economic affairs; in some societies both political and supernatural powers are vested in a "sacred king", in others the two functions are differentiated. Furthermore, we have not isolated except by implication any observable cultural phenomena, and the cultural concepts which we have formulated are to a large extent abstractions not directly applicable to observation in the field. When we live in a primitive community, we do not observe an economic system —we see people hunting, working in the fields, preparing and eating food, or making and exchanging artefacts. Our concept of an economic system is an abstraction from numerous temporally disconnected observations, based upon the postulate that man must eat and provide himself with various forms of material equipment. Again, our residence in a primitive community being usually limited to a year or two, we never observe the "educational system"—we witness but a very brief part of the process of growth and learning in the case of any one individual. But we do see from time to time a number of immature individuals at different ages being bathed, chided, initiated and generally brought up in the way they should go, and from these observations we are able to synthesize an educational system.

We must therefore at this stage attempt to isolate the units of cultural reality which may be observed in any society as distinct from the network of relations between needs and cultural responses which, though common to all cultures, are almost infinitely variable in their character from one to another. We must seek to define what Malinowski calls the *concrete isolates* of culture. As a preliminary to this we must ask the question: what are the *facts* of anthropological science?

The reader who thinks that the answer to this is obvious will probably be wrong. The superficial answer would be to mention such statements as "among the Kariera it is the custom for a man to marry the daughter of his mother's brother", or "Maori feather boxes are decorated with incised spiral designs", or "among the Nyakyusa all trees belong by tradition to the chief". But *these are not facts in social anthropology* any more than the affirmation that "if you pour hydrochloric acid on marble the mixture will fizz" is a statement of chemical fact. The latter is merely an isolated observation which only becomes significant when it is related to other observations and can be embodied in a chemical formula. It is thus integrated with a body of theoretical knowledge about different forms of matter and their chemical relations to each other.

Precisely the same is true, though it is less obvious, in the case of anthropological observations. As Malinowski says, "In real science the fact consists in the relatedness, provided that this is really determined, universal and scientifically definable".[1] Failure to recognize this has stultified anthropological field-work which has too often consisted merely of an agglomeration of haphazard

[1] Malinowski (10), p. 27.

observations, unrelated to each other or to the system of needs underlying every human culture. "To put it paradoxically, one could say that 'facts' do not exist in sociological any more than in physical reality; that is, they do not dwell in the spatial and temporal continuum open to the untutored eye. The principles of social organization, of legal constitution, of economics and religion have to be constructed by the observer out of a multitude of manifestations of varying significance and relevance. It is these invisible realities, only to be discovered by inductive computation, by selection and construction, which are scientifically important in the study of culture." [1] The facts of anthropological science, then, consist of cultural relations, that is, the relations of the elements or "traits" of culture to one another and to human needs.

The way in which cultural responses are related to human needs is founded upon two universal characteristics of human social behaviour: in the first place, human beings satisfy their needs collectively—they band together in groups and carry out activities determined by certain explicitly formulated purposes and traditionally defined rules. At specific places and times, and employing a standard material equipment, they indulge in activities which serve a definite function in the satisfaction of human needs. In the second place, these activities are not carried out haphazardly—the aggregation of human groups does not occur *ad hoc*, nor do their activities arise spontaneously. The whole process is governed by cultural traditions which create **institutions.** These are the concrete isolates of culture, the basic units of our subject-matter, which can be listed for any given culture. An institution may be defined as "a group of people united in a common task or tasks, bound to a determined portion of the environment, wielding together some technical apparatus, and obeying a body of rules".[2] The conception of institutions as the concrete isolates of culture is vital to anthropological science, because no single item of culture, such as an artefact, a religious belief or a form of ritual, has any anthropological significance until it is placed within the framework of an institution or of a series of institutions. Only in this way can we fully understand its relation to other elements of culture and to the system of human needs to which culture is a response.

[1] Malinowski (5), Vol. I, p. 317.
[2] Malinowski, Introduction to Hogbin (2), p. xxxiii.

6. *The Structure of Institutions*

All human institutions have a certain basic structure, more or less implied in the definition given above. Thus, every institution has a *charter*, a culturally formulated statement of its justification and social significance. Usually this is referred back into the past—the charter takes the form of mythological or legendary events by which the institution was originally set up. Apart from possible reticence, suspicion or secrecy on the part of the natives, the charter of an institution can always be elicited by direct questioning. Even where the objective of institutional activity is fairly obvious—as in the case of house-building or the provision of food—specific phases of it are always justified by relating them to features of the culture—to the doings of ancestors in ancient times, to the special powers or privileges of individuals alive today, or to specific moral values connected with obligations between kin. This is particularly important in the fields of religion and magic—thus, in many elaborate ceremonies of the Australian aborigines, every detail of the ritual is justified by some tale of mythological ancestors, who laid down once and for all the pattern of ceremonial which must be followed. Frequently, the charter is less specific—thus payment of tribute to chiefs may be justified, not by any legendary events, but by the generally accepted feeling that chiefs are entitled to certain privileges on the basis of their birth, their wealth, their administrative and protective functions, or their magico-religious powers. Whatever its form, the charter of an institution—the official cultural explanation of its existence and statement of its aims—must be distinguished from the *motives* of the individuals carrying out institutional activity, which are essentially personal and often egotistical.

Both charter and motives must be studied if an institution is to be understood, but they must not be confused with each other, and each must be distinguished from the *function* of the institution, a subject to which we shall return later.

The charter of an institution lays down at the same time a body of rules or *norms*, officially approved standards of conduct governing institutional activity. It is important to note that the actual behaviour of individuals does not always conform to this standard, but as an ideal it is an ever-present cultural reality.

Another feature of an institution which is embodied in its charter is the division and alignment of the individuals participating—the *personnel* of the institution. As we have seen in the preceding chapters, all cultures possess a social organization or social structure in which the reciprocal relations, rights and obligations of individuals and groups to each other are defined by tradition, for example, the standardized relations between men and women, between chiefs and commoners, between the old and the young, or between priests and laymen. The various types of social groupings which we have described are, in their dynamic aspects, standardized ways in which the institutional activities of different individuals are organized.

All institutional activities involve a material setting—they do not take place *in vacuo*, but in a defined place and with the aid of elements of material culture. The environment is modified in order to make possible or facilitate the institutional activities of the culture—huts, meeting-houses or temples are built; tools, implements and weapons are fashioned of wood, stone or metal; and even the spiritual values of man find material embodiment, whether in totemic emblems, in idols or in sacred books such as the Bible or the Koran. It should be noted that the existence of the *material apparatus* or *material substratum* of an institution itself exerts a profound influence on the very character of the institution. We have mentioned (p. 3) how, in prehistoric times, the invention of new technological processes and techniques made possible the development of new forms of social grouping and institutional activity. Again, the institutions connected with warfare provide a striking example of the way in which the character of human activities is modified by the material apparatus connected with them. The introduction of the stabbing assegai by Chaka contributed greatly to the expansion of the Zulu; the introduction of firearms in certain American and Pacific communities produced drastic, and at times lethal, effects upon the character of indigenous warfare, sometimes leading to the extermination of whole communities; and finally, the development of new and more devastating weapons of war in recent times has profoundly altered, not only the sociological character and implications of war, but also the relative power and status, as well as the policies, of the great nations.

The statement of the charter of an institution gives us some idea of the *activities* involved, but not a complete one. In the first place, the actual behaviour of individuals often falls short of the ideal embodied in the charter and norms, particularly when these involve irksome restrictions, burdensome obligations, or acts of self-denial and self-sacrifice. Secondly, the activities involved in an institution are never fully defined in its charter—there are usually important collateral or subsidiary activities carried on apart from the major purpose of the institution as defined in its charter. Thus, in the case of the Kula, the ceremonial exchange of valuables is supplemented by a certain amount of trade, carried out from purely economic motives and clearly distinguished from the social and ceremonial activities of the Kula proper.

The final task in the analysis of any institution is the statement of its *function*, that is, its place in the total culture and the part which it plays in the satisfaction of human needs. This again is something much more profound than the statement provided in the charter. No native can give a full and accurate account of the functions of an institution as can the sociologist. This is particularly true of magico-religious institutions. Consider, for example, the magical ceremonies connected with agriculture. The explicit purpose of these as embodied in their charter is to promote the growth of crops, to provide rain, to guard against the menace of hurricanes, pests, blights and so on. Our knowledge of natural and biological science tells us that they are ineffective for this purpose. But they nevertheless serve a function in emphasizing the importance of vital food-getting activities, in mobilizing collective economic activity, and in promoting collective optimism and confidence. An appreciation of the rôle of any given institution in satisfying human needs—its function— involves a study of all its aspects—economic, legal, educational, magico-religious and so on. But the study of an institution should include also its negative aspects—the way in which it frustrates or limits, as well as facilitates, the satisfaction of human needs. Thus, in the case of magico-religious institutions, we should have to note the way in which they impose irksome restrictions on human activity as well as the question how far they inhibit the active search for scientific or practically useful techniques for the solution of human problems (Chapter X, Section 10).

7. *The Analysis of an Institution*

We might illustrate the structural character of an institution by reference to one of the institutions of our own society, a Local Authority in Britain, such as a County or Town Council. Because ours is a literate society with elaborate political institutions, we should find the *charter* of the institution embodied in various Acts of Parliament. These have progressively defined and re-defined the powers and responsibilities of local authorities. We should find that the rules embodied in the charter are prescriptive, proscriptive and permissive. For example, the Council *must* provide education, fire services and police; it *must not* run public utilities such as transport, gas and electricity services at a loss—these services must be self-supporting; finally, the Council at its discretion may or may not organize a municipal orchestra, theatre or golf-course. In addition to legal enactments, we should also be able to observe a number of generally accepted rules governing the institution, some of them uncodified—rules governing the conduct of elections, procedure at Council meetings and the ceremonial of civic functions.

We should have to distinguish the social purpose embodied in the charter—in general terms, the provision of good local government—from the *motives* of the individuals involved. We should find, for example, that while some councillors are actuated primarily by a sense of public duty, others seek merely personal notoriety or even economic advantage. The motives of municipal civil servants, employees of the local authorities and of ratepayers (that is, of the *personnel* involved in the institution) would likewise be found to be coloured by personal interests—social, economic and political. We should have to study the legal and social relations of these groups to one another and to outside groups, for example, Church and Parliament.

Our examination of the charter reveals to us the outline of the *norms* governing the institution. But even among those citizens who are not familiar with the details of the charter we would find expressed, more or less clearly, certain standards of civic responsibility felt as binding upon the individuals involved, standards reflected in the statement so often made about any public inconvenience or nuisance that "the Council ought to do something about it".

We should also have to examine the *material apparatus* connected with the institution—schools and other public buildings, equipment connected with the provision of gas, electricity, public transport, protection against fire and so on. In our civilization this would be a highly technical problem, but we should have to emphasize firstly the relevance of the efficiency of the material apparatus to effective local government, and secondly, the way in which the existence of this apparatus partially determines the structure of an institution itself. Thus, the expansion in the functions of local authorities during the last hundred years has been largely due to the new and more complex technical equipment which they have to handle.

In describing the *activities* connected with the institution— elections, Council meetings, and the day-to-day procedure of public administration—we should have to remind ourselves of the distinction between charter and motives. Owing to human shortcomings, intellectual and emotional, we should find that what is actually done never conforms with the ideal standard implicit in the charter.

Finally, we should have to draw together the threads of our discussion by describing the *function* of the institution, that is, its relation to the satisfaction of the human needs of the community as a whole or of special sections of it. We should find that the Council provides partially for nutritional requirements, for example, by the provision of meals in schools, civic restaurants and food for the inmates of public institutions; in time of war its Civil Defence organization provides protection against injury; various public institutions provide shelter for the homeless; the Council performs important functions in relation to the needs for sex and reproduction in the registration of births and marriages, in the provision of maternity services, and in the regulation of sexual behaviour by various edicts imposing standards of decency in public places; the care and education of the young are provided for by infant welfare services, schools and colleges; a large range of material satisfactions provides for the comfort, health and recreation of the community; the local authority also has certain well-defined legal powers which control the activities of individuals in a socially approved way; and although the Council does not possess any specifically religious functions, its activities are related to the generally accepted religious code, for example, in the restriction of public recreation and entertainment on Sundays.

Finally, we should have to consider the activities of the local authority in relation to the geographical environment, including the demography and ecology of the community, and to the life-cycle of the various individuals composing it. We should thus discern how political attitudes are built up in the growing individual, how these affect the structure of governmental institutions, and how various motives determine the interaction of individuals, for example at elections.

From the above type of analysis we see that while a local authority is primarily a political and legal institution, it nevertheless serves very much wider functions in the satisfaction of human needs, and only by a description of all of its functions can its cultural significance be understood.

Before returning to the primitive field, we may clarify some of the concepts which we have employed, namely—traits or elements of culture, anthropological facts and institutions. A lamp-post in a city street is an element of culture. One can take a tape-measure and define exactly its shape and dimensions, one can describe the metallurgical and other technical processes by which it is made and erected.[1] But the lamp-post is not an anthropological fact—it is merely a mass of metal. Only when we say that it forms part of the lighting system of a town or city, and that this is the responsibility of the local authority (which implies the type of institutional analysis given above), have we defined an anthropological fact by placing the material object within the framework of an institution. By recording a number of such facts we discern the total cultural function of the institution along the lines described in this section.

8. Cultural Efflorescence and Degeneration

The question is often asked why, since all human cultures are founded upon a set of universal human needs, they should vary from each other. In certain instances differences in geographical environment provide a partial explanation, for example, if we compare the culture of the Eskimo with that of the Australian aborigines. But in many cases geographical environment seems to have little if anything to do with cultural variation. We find patrilineal and matrilineal peoples, segmented and stratified societies, totemic and non-totemic peoples living side by side in substantially similar geographical environments. Much less does geographical environment explain certain exceptional, striking and complex developments in particular cultures—for example, the development of matriliny and political organization among the Iroquois, the dramatic institution of the potlatch, or the ramifications of kinship organization in Australia. We can de-

---

[1] In most works on primitive technology, this is where the description ends, that is, before any anthropological statements have been made about the artefact concerned.

monstrate that these are related to certain integrative needs in the societies concerned, but we cannot say why these needs have led to the particular cultural responses which we observe.

To the theory of needs, then, we must add two ancillary hypotheses. The first of these is **cultural efflorescence**.[1] This is merely a hypothesis because, owing to the paucity of reliable historical data in primitive societies, we cannot describe the process itself [2] but only its end-products. We can discern in general terms the processes of change which have operated in primitive society— the influence of outstanding individuals, migrations, diffusion, and a process analogous to "drift" in language.[3] All of these may contribute to cultural efflorescence, but only under exceptional circumstances can we describe how they have actually operated in any given primitive culture. We therefore affirm that such striking and exceptional developments as those mentioned above have been due to a process of cultural efflorescence, although we are unable to describe this process in detail.

Perhaps we might gain some light on the fundamental characteristics of the process from comparative psychology and even from our everyday experience. An ape in a zoo tends to follow certain rhythmical and recurrent sequences of bodily behaviour, and we can discern an analogous process in the repetitive verbal and motor habits of young children. Perhaps a closer analogy with the cultural phenomena we are considering, though by no means a perfect one, is to be found in compulsion neuroses. Here we observe repetitions of certain behaviour patterns, which at first seem quite unrelated to any emotional drive of the individual.

---

[1] This concept was first introduced into theoretical anthropology by Firth (8, p. 598) under the name of *institutional efflorescence*. The term "cultural" is preferred here in order to emphasize that the process of efflorescence, although always manifested in institutions, may apply to aspects of culture or to patterns of behaviour which pervade many institutions. For example, where practices of sorcery are highly developed, they tend to effloresce in all the institutions of the culture concerned.

[2] Perhaps this is because no one has attempted to review bodies of ethnographic data in the light of the theory of needs and the hypothesis of cultural efflorescence. Furthermore, the field of culture contact seems to be one in which the process can actually be observed, for example, in the case of the similar types of "adjustment cults" (Firth, 14, p. 16) which have arisen in parts of the world as remote from each other as South-east Africa, Fiji and New Guinea.

[3] For example, in the case of Indo-European languages, Grimm's law demonstrated such correspondences as Greek "th", German "t" and English "d" in *thugatēr*, *tochter* and *daughter*. Here the process is known to have been due to historical connection, because of the common origin of the three languages. In regard to primitive culture, as distinct from language, it is only occasionally or in limited fields that such common origins can be demonstrated. But the operation of the process can probably be assumed—for example, in Australian kinship the drift seems to be from simple to complex types of organization, stimulated by diffusion.

Only when psychological analysis has traced them back to the initial situation in which they arose can their full significance be understood. In all these cases we observe that habits which are not demonstrably or obviously related to any fundamental need of the organism seem to acquire a momentum and even a compulsive power of their own, and we may perhaps assume a similar basic process in the cultural behaviour of human groups, though here the problem is enormously complicated by the cultural environment by which the organism is conditioned and the consequent interaction of the behaviour patterns of different individuals.[1]

To the hypothesis of cultural efflorescence we should add the complementary one of **cultural degeneration,** a concept which has frequently been employed in anthropology. Unfortunately, most studies of degeneration have concentrated on the generally futile task of trying to discern how it has actually operated in particular cases, rather than upon an analysis of the general biological, psychological and sociological processes involved. These are the same kind as those already mentioned. Just as the influence of exceptional individuals, migration, diffusion and drift can lead to the burgeoning of certain cultural features, so they can produce attenuation and even extinction of others.

The theory of needs, supplemented by the hypotheses of cultural efflorescence and degeneration, enables us to understand, albeit in very general terms, why certain cultures have developed exceptional features. But it is important to remember that they *are* exceptional and should never form the basis of a general theory of human culture. Trite as this statement seems, it is important because it is often overlooked in criticisms, explicit or implied, of the functional interpretation. Thus, writers of the Configurationist school have seized upon cultures in which one form or other of cultural efflorescence is very marked, have exaggerated certain features and reached the conclusion embodied in Dr. Ruth Benedict's dictum: "No common measure of cultural phenomena can be found." Again, the general theory of functionalism has been challenged by the production of atypical customs and institutions which appear inconsistent with it. But it is important to remember that the vast majority of primitive peoples

---

[1] The interaction of the individual human organism and the cultural environment in childhood and adult life will be discussed in Volume II in relation to the concept of "basic personality".

are polygynous, while polyandry is extremely rare; that the relatively unstable family organization of the Nuer is by no means typical of primitive society; that almost all stratified societies practise endogamy or similar marriage rules which prescribe marriages between members of the ruling classes, although the Natchez and one or two West African peoples for some reason or other have a system of exogamy connected with their class structure; and that in the vast majority of societies men are men and not the effeminate creatures described (or perhaps caricatured) among the Tchambuli. To deny the general theory of functionalism by citing abnormal and atypical cultural features is analogous to saying that because polydactyly and syndactyly [1] exist, it is incorrect to say that human beings have five digits on each hand.

Some psychologists have attempted to short-circuit the controversy about instinct by employing the term "prepotent reflex". The value of this concept for systematic psychology does not concern us here, but we badly need a somewhat similar concept in our comparative studies of primitive cultures. In these we should emphasize the existence of *prepotent cultural responses* to the basic and universal human needs—primary, derived and integrative—in contradistinction to exceptional cultural end-products of the processes of cultural efflorescence and degeneration.

9. *The Universal Aspects of Human Culture*

It will be apparent that any given institution may be considered from many aspects. It will be useful at this point to list the aspects of culture, all of which will be found in its most important institutions, though some of them may be absent from those which are less significant and more highly specialized.

The **universal aspects of culture** may be subdivided into special aspects and general aspects, according to how far they correspond with specific types of human activity and how far they are more general and pervade every field of human life. We have considered most of the aspects of culture as responses to human needs. We must further emphasize the fact that all human activity takes place within a specific geographical environment, which is always significant, and may be of vital importance in determining the character of cultural institutions, particularly those connected with demography and ecology, the way in which a human group

---

[1] These are abnormal anatomical conditions in which the individual is born with more or less than the normal number of digits.

is distributed over its territory and exploits its natural resources. We must also refer to the last of the general aspects of culture, namely, the life-cycle of the individual. Culture may be viewed psychologically as well as sociologically, and it is important to know, not only the pattern of cultural relationships existing at any one time, but also how this pattern affects, and is affected by, the individual, not only during the early period of his education, but also throughout his life from birth to death. The universal aspects of culture are listed in the following table:

THE UNIVERSAL ASPECTS OF HUMAN CULTURE

Special Aspects	General Aspects
1. Economic.	1. Geographical environment, demography, human ecology.
2. Political.	
3. Legal.	2. Material substratum.
4. Educational:	3. Knowledge and belief.
i. Knowledge and technique.	4. Normative system.
ii. Sentiments and morals.	5. Language.
5. Magico-religious.	6. Social organization.
6. Art, recreation and ceremonial.	7. Life-cycle of the individual.

In connection with this table, it must be emphasized that the distinction between special and general aspects is a relative one, and that the categories are not mutually exclusive. On the contrary, they overlap, and the phenomena belonging to them interlock in a complex manner. The list is essentially a mnemonic device designed to ensure that in considering any culture or institution, the student shall consider it in all its aspects, neglecting nothing which may be relevant to an understanding of the significance of an institution or of a culture considered as a whole. Failure to do this has in the past very often had an adverse effect on anthropological field-work, and has led to theoretical speculations which are futile because they fail to take into account the multiple aspects of human cultural activity.

The systematic study of any given institution in relation to human needs on the one hand and to the universal aspects of culture on the other leads us to an understanding of its structural characteristics, as listed in Section 6, and of the relation of these to the culture as a whole. Thus, when we consider the aspect of social organization, we define, not only the personnel of the institution, but also their relation to other institutional activities of the people; the social norms governing the institution are seen to be part of a very much wider normative system, and so on.

It may therefore be asked why we require two lists of phenomena to be considered—namely, the structural characteristics of institutions and the universal aspects of human culture. The answer is that, whereas the former applies to all institutions, the latter does not always do so; some aspects may be absent from certain institutions, though they must all be considered in any institutional analysis lest any important aspect should be forgotten. Moreover, the relation between the two lists varies from one institution to another—thus, the charter may be primarily related to the political system (as in a modern parliament) or may belong rather to the magico-religious aspect of culture, as in the case of a religious cult. The two lists are merely different ways of considering the same phenomenon—an institution— either in terms of its basic structure or in terms of its relation to the wider cultural framework of which it forms a part.

10. A Recreational Institution

It must be emphasized that the above type of analysis is not reproduced in the ordinary ethnographic account of an institution. This usually takes a more simple and narrative form. But if it is an adequate description, it will be possible to rearrange the material in a systematic form designed to show the basic structure of the institution and its relation to culture as a whole. To illustrate this, let us consider an abridged account of a recreational institution found in a primitive community—namely, a dart match in Tikopia.

The game of darts as played in Tikopia is a good example of an institution directed towards public recreation. The game consists of competitive throwing of the *Tika* or dart. This is really more like a small javelin. It consists of a reed shaft about four feet long, with a hardwood head at one end. Because of its lack of balance, the dart being exceptionally heavy at the front end, it is impossible to throw the *Tika* in the ordinary way. It is held at the back end, with the first finger placed against the butt. As there is considerable pressure on the finger at the moment of throwing, a protective ring of coco-nut fibre is placed between the finger and the butt.

Dart throwing is carried out on a pitch about 130 yards long, called the *Marae Tika*. The game is played between two teams of from twelve to twenty men—women attend the games, but do not play. Each team is captained by an expert, who is called "chief of the dart group". This man is always an excellent player, and is chosen by the chiefs and men of authority. His main function is to decide the order of throwing, so that his side has the best chance of scoring.

The teams are called "the bachelors" and "the married men". These terms are purely figurative—men play in the two teams irrespective of their marital state. In actual fact, the two teams are based upon the organization of the islanders into four clans. In general, the bachelors are drawn from Tafua clan. The married men come primarily from Kafika, but also from Fangarere and Taumako. The organization of the teams reflects the traditional opposition between the two Tikopia districts of Faea and Ravenga, and men from these districts sometimes belong to the team which is not associated with their own clan.

Because it can draw upon three clans, the team of married men seems to have the advantage so far as getting good players is concerned. But on the whole, the teams seem to be fairly well matched.

The scoring of the game is complicated. The general principle is that the longest throw wins, but if the other side can throw a dart so that its head comes level with any part of the leading dart, it is said to "eat" the first dart, the score of which is thus wiped out. A leading dart scores one, and each dart of the same side lying behind it also scores one, provided that it has not been "eaten" by the opponents. The rule is thus that only a dart unbeaten by the opposition counts. The procedure is that one side "goes in" and continues to score until its score is wiped out by the other side, which then goes in and continues to score until in its turn it is beaten. The method of scoring is slightly varied if one side succeeds in scoring ten without a check. After such a win, the winners go off to their orchards and gather coco-nuts, which they present to the losers. This principle of "winner pays" depends upon the feeling of shame which the losers feel after such a defeat. Their self-respect is restored by the gift—a typical Tikopia way of dealing with such situations.

The game of course has its own jargon—terms of praise and blame, terms for experts and terms for different kinds of throw.

A game of darts is an important episode in Tikopia life. The people, brightly decorated, assemble, and the match is a subject of gossip throughout the island for some time before and after it takes place. But the game has a more serious aspect. It is known as the "sport of the gods". There are special ceremonial matches from time to time. The gods are believed to be in attendance at such matches, and it is believed that the playing of the game promotes the growth of crops. At ceremonial matches, the chiefs of the island compete with one another through their young relatives—the chiefs themselves do not play.

An elaborate procedure is carried out before and during such matches. The ground is cleared and the pitch carefully smoothed over. The gods are invoked for success by the elders. On these occasions, special sacred darts, the property of the chiefs, are used. These darts have special individual names, and the night before the match their heads are smeared with coco-nut oil. During the night the darts are placed leaning against the wall, and if in the morning it is found that they have fallen down, the owners are pleased, for it is a sign that the gods have been playing with the darts during the night, and will be interested in the outcome of the match. In the morning the right arms of the players are smeared with coco-nut oil, and the elders again invoke the gods. This is a translation of one of their prayers:

> *"There! Turn to your foremost dart*
> *To a win for you to be gained this morning.*
> *Make it slide on your back for a win for you."*

There are two interesting points about this prayer. In the first place, it reflects the Polynesian belief that gods may be incarnate in birds and other creatures. The god to whom this prayer is addressed is incarnate in the lizard. The prayer envisages the lizard-god running along the pitch, carrying the dart on its back. Secondly, the phrasing of the prayer is of interest. The god is tactfully invoked to secure a win for himself. The interest of the human group is not mentioned.

After these prayers and ritual, the game is ceremonially opened by the pouring of a libation of *kava*. During the game the old chiefs sit with bowed heads murmuring invocations as the younger men throw the darts. If a chief is losing, he rebukes the gods, as in the following text:

> *"Look here! Your kava which is made here*
> *Why not turn to it!*
> *You don't look at the kava.*
> *But there you are facing the woods."*

This text reproves the god for not paying sufficient attention to the game, and invites him to show his appreciation of the *kava* libation which he has received. In addition to praying for success, the chiefs also seek to divert the darts of their opponents so that they fall harmlessly in the bush at the side of the pitch:

> "*Be glanced aside by you, Te Amafakaro!*
> *Block it for a win for yourself.*"

Again notice how the personal interest of the chief himself is tactfully omitted from the prayer.

The game is governed by many usages and rules of good manners. For example, a player must not show any satisfaction after an exceptionally successful throw. He must remain impassive, except when he is playing with a new dart. In this case, he may celebrate its success by crying out "iefu"—roughly equivalent to our "hurrah". On the other hand, the spectators may cheer, particularly if a long throw carries the dart beyond the end of the pitch.

There are legends of great players. These are often fantastic, as in the story of the man who, by tapping the ground with his finger, could direct the course of his dart in flight by a sort of remote control. The sacred darts mentioned above are used very sparingly, as it is believed that if they are thrown too often they will make the shoulders of the players ache.

If a man achieves an exceptional score, he presents food to the other men of his team. In the case of an exceptionally good player, this duty may be onerous. In fact, there is a record of one man whose play was so good that he was forced to economize by deliberately throwing short.

The importance and significance of the game are reflected in the dance songs which are composed about it. The dance song is a regular Tikopia way of expressing sentiment. Here is the song of a man who is not doing well, and is apprehensive of the criticism of the spectators:

> "*My dart has sped down from the throwing sands,*
> *It has been caught up by the experts,*
> *I shall be sorry and not shout.*

> "*Throbbing, throbbing is the heart.*
> *Eyes of the land*
> *Are all assembled at the pitch.*"

On the other hand, here is the song of a successful player:

> *"My dart is superior.*
> *It comes down, strikes the ground with its wooden head,*
> *Then it is lost to the eye (in its swift flight)*
> *in the middle of the pitch."*

It will be seen that the dart match, although only a game, is a significant element in Tikopia life. It is related to the needs of the people, particularly the need for social integration on occasions of community activity. It also provides recreation, relaxation, interest and an occasion for display and competition. It will be obvious that the Tikopia feel strongly about the game, and that the players are elated by success and cast down by defeat, which is a reflection, not only on the players, but also upon the chiefs and gods whom they represent.

Furthermore, the game is related to every other aspect of Tikopia culture. There are *economic* obligations concerned with the gifts to the defeated side and those given by a successful player to his own team. The *political* structure of the island is reflected in the direction of the game by the chiefs and elders and their selection of the captains of the teams. Because no very profound passions are concerned in the game, the *legal* aspect is less important; but it should be noted that incompetence is condemned, and that the rules of etiquette connected with the game are enforced by the chiefs. Thus, on one occasion, a player who appeared ostentatiously decorated was publicly rebuked by the chief, and as a result ceased to attend the matches. The *educational* aspect is to be found in the fact that children play and practise the game and are allowed to attend the important matches between adult teams. The *magico-religious* element in the game is most striking in the prayers and ritual connected with it and the belief that the playing of the game promotes the growth of crops. The game, too, has an *artistic* interest reflected in the decorations of the spectators, the careful smoothing over of the pitch before the game, and the workmanship of the *tika*. The *geography* and *demography* of the island, with its traditional opposition between the districts of Faea and Ravenga, is reflected in the organization of the teams. The *material substratum* is of course the tika itself and the throwing ring. Many elements of *knowledge* and *belief* enter into the dart match—the fine points of the game, the technique of throwing, and the beliefs connected with the participation of the gods. The rules of the game and regulations of good manners and ceremonial form part of the *normative system* of Tikopia culture, and are typical of the importance which Polynesian peoples attach to such matters. The *language* of the game includes a special jargon, terms of praise and blame, and names given to the sacred *tika* of chiefs. The grouping of people according to their functions in the game reflects the *social organization*, including kinship structure, local affiliation, and the social position of chiefs and elders. During the *life-cycle of the individual*, the part played varies: the children watch, the young men compete, and the older people encourage their side by cheering and by the invocation of the gods.

The reality of the game of darts in Tikopia is thus to be found in its relations to the culture as a whole, to the needs of the individuals composing it, and to its special and general aspects.

We have chosen the Tikopia dart match as an example of a primitive institution, because the description of it is comprehensive and at the same time capable of condensation. The full description of a primitive institution usually occupies many pages, sometimes a complete volume. The student is advised to apply the above criteria of analysis to institutional descriptions which he may encounter in further reading, since it will not only help in gaining a systematic understanding of the institution concerned, but will often reveal gaps in what appears to be a comprehensive description, particularly in the older field records.

The method of institutional analysis described in this chapter is not the only technique employed in social anthropology. Because of the characteristics of human culture which we have described, it is possible to study culture also from the point of view of one or more of the human needs which form its dynamic basis, or in terms of one or more of the universal aspects of culture. Such studies cut across the institutional type of analysis, since they involve a description of the satisfaction of needs through several institutions, or of more than one institution considered from a specific aspect. In the next chapter we shall exemplify these other two types of approach to cultural phenomena in relation to the satisfaction of the need for food and the economic aspect of human culture. But whatever type of analysis we adopt, we must never lose sight of the basic principles outlined in this chapter, namely, the dynamic basis of culture in human needs, the organization of human activities in the form of institutions, the universal aspects of human culture, and the interrelationships between needs, institutions and aspects. These interrelationships constitute the reality of culture scientifically understood, as distinct from a mere catalogue of beliefs, customs, artefacts and other items of ethnographic gossip.

11. Bibliographical Commentary

With regard to the relevance of the data of physical anthropology to the study of culture, cursorily treated in Section 1, reference should be made to Elliot Smith (1), though it must be stressed that Elliot Smith's subsequent theory of the derivation of all culture from Egypt is not accepted by the majority of modern anthropologists. For valuable discussions of the differences between man and the anthropoid apes and of the general lines of human evolution, see Stibbe (1) and Howells (1).

Malinowski's functional theory of culture, upon which the present chapter is four led, is stated in Malinowski (8 and 9) and most recently and comprehensively in Malinowski (10). This theory has been criticized by several writers, and the reader who is interested in theoretical issues may follow up the two more important lines of criticism which have appeared in recent anthropological literature. The first of these comes from the historical schools, and is exemplified by Lowie (2), Lesser (1) and Adam (1). A view in opposition to those of the writers mentioned is stated with reference to a specific ethnographic province in Piddington (5).

The other main line of criticism comes from what has been termed the "structural" school, the basic principles of which are stated in the writings of Radcliffe-Brown (especially 5 and 6). See also Gluckman (2).

The Tikopia dart match, briefly reviewed in Section 10, is more fully described in Firth (6).

CHAPTER VII

FOOD AND WEALTH

1. Nutrition and Culture

OF the fundamental needs which constitute the dynamic basis of human culture, the need for food may well be regarded as the most vital. In the current psychology of motivation, under the stimulus of the Freudian school, much attention has been paid to sex, and the repression of sex, as a determinant of human behaviour, and even of cultural institutions. It must be remembered that the Freudians use the term "sex" in a sense different from that of ordinary usage, and that the initial quasi-sexual experience (suckling) to which they attach so much importance is also an alimentary one. From it, in the life-history of the individual, become differentiated the more specifically "sexual" impulses on the one hand, and the urge of hunger on the other.

There are certain striking contrasts between the need for sex and the need for food. Firstly, an individual can live a lifetime without sex, but denial of food means certain death. Secondly, while an undernourished individual may suffer in health and efficiency, malnutrition produces neither the neuroses and maladjustments nor the cultural sublimations associated with sex repression. The explanation of this is probably to be found in the fact that while sex is a potentially disruptive force,[1] the need for food encourages, in fact necessitates, human co-operation.[2] Consequently, the human desire for food is not culturally disavowed as the sexual impulse tends to be, in our own society at least. The desire for food may be suppressed, but it is never repressed. People may be forced to go without food, for example, in a famine or religious fast, but they are not ashamed to admit that they are hungry. Such an attitude would, in fact, be absurd in such circumstances. In the former case, the community would

---

[1] Cf. what has been said concerning the prohibition of incest.

[2] There are certain exceptions to this statement—thus, the sexual relations between husband and wife are an integrating factor in family life, while competition over food may at times have disruptive effects in a community. But in general the contrast between the two impulses holds good.

take no steps to increase the food supply and so would starve to death; in the latter, the religious object of fasting would be defeated if it were believed that no self-denial was involved.

These facts have led to a neglect of the importance of hunger as a human drive. As Dewey says: "If a society existed in which the existence of impulse towards food were socially disavowed until it was compelled to live an illicit, covert life, alienists would have plenty of cases of mental and moral disturbance to relate in connection with hunger."[1]

Another reason for the failure to appreciate the importance of hunger is that in our own society (at least for those who contribute to its thought and literature) food is rarely a problem. In the case of the impulses connected with sex, psychological maladjustments arising from their frustration are common to all classes of the community, while it has been held that much creative art arises from sex repression or suppression. Certainly the theme of much drama and literature is sexual maladjustment of one kind or another. This has no correlate in the case of hunger. Consequently, food is not surrounded by a complex set of values—sociological, ethical, æsthetic and religious—comparable with that associated, directly or indirectly, with sex. To a community living well above a subsistence level, or at least to its more fortunate members, a regular supply of food is taken for granted.[2]

In this regard our own civilization differs in a marked way from most primitive societies, in which hunger frequently occurs and famine is a constant possibility. The emotional reponse to this is well expressed in the description of times of scarcity among the Eskimo (p. 45) and in the following extract from the Trobriand account of a famine which occurred about the end of the last century:

"Molubabeba in his childhood witnessed a famine. At that time the people first became ill with a skin disease. Some people died in the bush; some in the swamps; some in the *rayboag* (coastal ridge); some round the water-holes. They went to the

[1] Dewey, J., *Human Nature and Conduct*, p. 165.

[2] "We do not write poems, novels or plays about a poached egg. This is an interesting fact, because Arctic explorers have been known to dream of poached eggs. It seems that the class of people who write novels are more successful in budgeting their food than their erotic requirements, and that their books sell because the social regulation of the latter leaves a number of other people in the same predicament. If our social arrangements were better adapted to ensure happy sexual union, and if the sciences of human biology and psychology were sufficiently advanced to tell us how to make marriage a success or how to choose a satisfactory partner, the theme of Othello would give us no more excitement than a lament on an overdone poached egg" (Hogben, *Dangerous Thoughts*, pp. 215–16).

water-holes so as to moisten their hands, their feet, and then they died. All this was because of hunger. There was no food to be eaten." [1]

Even where the natural environment provides a fairly regular and adequate diet, the getting of food absorbs by far the greatest amount of the economic effort of the community. Its importance is reflected in the attention paid to food-getting activities and in numerous beliefs and practices connected with food. These are apparent in every phase of native life, particularly in a number of ceremonial usages. One of the most striking examples is the ritual of the sacred dairies among the Todas. There are many other less spectacular, though no less significant, illustrations of the importance attached to food. Success in the food quest is highly honoured, for example, in the respect paid to skilled hunters, gardeners and fishermen.

Probably the most significant usages in which the importance of food is emphasized are the magico-religious practices connected with food production. In contradistinction to that of animals, man's interest in food does not cease with the satisfaction of immediate hunger. He can, in fact must, plan for the future to some extent. And in doing this he can envisage failure or an inadequate return for his efforts. He gains a feeling of security, and to some extent avoids anxiety, by carrying out magico-religious rites to guard against failure, and these also emphasize the social importance of his food supply.

Among the magico-religious beliefs and practices connected with food are those of a negative character, commonly called food taboos. Of these the commonest are those usually (though not always) connected with totemism. Numerous other food taboos are observed by special individuals or classes of individuals, or at times of social crisis, the latter term having a very wide interpretation. Food taboos of this kind must be considered in relation to taboos on activities other than eating, which will be discussed later. In different communities, food taboos are found in connection with pregnancy, birth, childhood, adolescence, initiation, courtship and marriage, sickness, death and mourning; social undertakings, particularly those of a hazardous kind, such as hunting, deep-sea fishing and war; and the performance of magic or religious ritual. Taboos often restrict the consumption of certain foods to chiefs, priests and other men of rank.

[1] Malinowski (5), Vol. I, p. 163.

But food taboos are merely a part of the nutritional aspect of chieftainship in politically organized societies. Tribute is normally paid to the chief in the form of food. But as the chief obviously cannot consume all the food which he receives in this way, he redistributes it to the community either as largesse given at feasts, as payment for wives, or in other ways. This in turn increases his prestige. Generosity, in socially stratified societies, is often the high road to high rank.

In communities possessing legal institutions, deprivation of food is often a form of punishment; for example, a fine may be collected by a chief, or restitution for a wrong made, in the form of food. An extreme example is the Samoan punishment *o le sala*, in which live-stock, plantations and other property of an offender were completely destroyed by order of the village council.

One of the most important aspects of the cultural significance of food is to be found in the part which it plays in the life-cycle of the individual. Starting with suckling (normally carried out for much longer than among ourselves), the individual's social relations are largely concerned with food, first in the family circle and later in the wider community. The child learns the rules of ethics and good manners connected with the consumption of food, and the current food taboos of the people. At first entirely dependent upon kinsfolk for food, the child later learns the obligations which it owes to others, and the whole set of cultural values centring round food. This process, as it occurs among certain southern Bantu tribes, has been described by Dr. Audrey Richards, and the following is an abridged version of her analysis.

2. *The Genetic Study of Nutrition among the South-eastern Bantu*

Infancy.—The most striking feature of nutritional life in infancy among Bantu peoples, as in the majority of primitive communities, is the extremely long period of suckling, which is continued until the second or third year of the infant's life. The mother usually delays weaning until she is aware that she has conceived again. Sexual intercourse between husband and wife is taboo for the first two years after the birth of a child, so that the period of lactation is necessarily a long one.

In other respects, too, the life of Bantu infants differs from our own. Among ourselves a fixed routine of sleep, waking and periodic meals is imposed upon the infant, and the baby is accustomed to having its meals preceded by a regular sequence of events—lifting from the cot, changes of lighting, preparation of the bath and so on. It has been noted that among infants in our own society the presentation of one of these stimuli will quieten a child's cry of hunger. It will be seen that the mother's presence is but one element in a complex situation, from which it may perhaps be inferred that the emotional fixation upon her is less than in the case of the Bantu infant, for whom no training of habits in regard to feeding is organized. The mother will give the child the breast at any time; furthermore, the child is much more closely associated physically, both in sleeping and waking, with the mother's body; for example, it may be strapped to her back when she goes to work, and continue to doze in its sling of goat or antelope skin while she tills the field. One writer has suggested that the Bantu child is more like a marsupial cub than "the baby in our own civilization lying separated from its mother in a cot or perambulator". The Bantu mother thus becomes the centre of all the emotions associated with the gratification of the child's appetite—other stimuli are of little importance to it.

As the child learns to crawl and walk, it widens its environment and finds other sources of pleasures and excitement, but the original physiological relationships produced by suckling remain undisturbed, as does the close bodily association.

The biological basis of infant nutrition is expressed in several features of Bantu culture—in family usages and in magico-religious beliefs. In daily life the segregation of women and children is fairly complete, especially in polygamous households, where each wife has her separate hut. The husband rarely eats with his wife and children, taking his food either at the men's place in the centre of the kraal, or in a separate division of the hut. In daily life, too, the mother and her small child spend their day in the fields, while the father remains in the kraal or tends the cattle. At this stage the father pays little attention to his children —a marked contrast with certain Oceanic societies. This may be connected with the conception of ritual danger associated with birth, lactation and infancy. The father may not touch his child until a ceremony has been performed three months after birth, and he does not mourn for it if it dies before a ceremony has been carried out to mark its first crawling. Among the Basuto the mother and baby actually live for two months after birth in the home of the maternal grandmother.

Another taboo is that on sexual intercourse, which it is believed would harm the child. The significance of the father's paternity is, however, socially emphasized. He must provide special food for the mother during her confinement, and is responsible for sacrifices to the ancestors in connection with ceremonies marking the birth and growth of the child. As has been stated, the father has little to do with the child in these early years, and in case of divorce he cannot claim the offspring, even though they are his by right of *lobola* payment. Socially, as well as physiologically, it is the mother with whom the child is almost exclusively concerned during the first two or three years of its life.

Weaning.—As stated above, weaning takes place at a later date than in civilized society. The child is not weaned until it has developed emotionally a much more complex attitude towards the mother and has reached a physiologically independent stage. It has been suggested that this means that the emotional trauma associated by some psycho-analysts with weaning is less marked in the case of the Bantu child. So far as the evidence goes, it appears that weaning takes place in Bantu society at a time when the child is old enough to understand the meaning of punishment and rebuke. Drastic measures are sometimes taken to wean the child from the mother's breast, which is sometimes smeared with repulsive vegetable juices. Children are sometimes slapped for approaching the breast or rebuked in terms of annoyance. Weaning, then, does not take place gradually and without effort, but has actually to be enforced, and constitutes the first barrier placed between the child and its mother. The child's interest is centred almost exclusively around its mother's breast, which provides, not merely a physiological pleasure, but a feeling of comfort and dependence. The forcible severance of this relationship constitutes one of the child's earliest experiences of social prohibition or taboo.

In certain tribes there is yet another factor of separation from the mother in that temporary adoption at weaning sometimes occurs—the child may be taken to the house of its grandparents for a while. It should be noted that sexual intercourse between parents is resumed at about the same time as weaning takes place, and in a society where privacy in such matters is unknown and sex relations are observed and discussed among children of all ages, it may be assumed that this has some effect upon the child's emotional attitude towards the father. Suckling is not a purely physiological process, but also part of the legal code centring around kinship obligations. Suckling is a legal obligation of motherhood, and is expressed in the rule whereby if the infant is suckled by anyone except the mother, she must be paid for the service; or that the child may not be suckled by anyone except the mother or mother's sister. The service of suckling is regarded as one of the ways in which the mother's brother derives his rights over his nephews because they have derived nourishment from his sister's breasts.

Early childhood.—Weaning leads to a new phase in the life-cycle of the Bantu child, lasting from the age of about three years to about seven or eight. During early childhood children continue to live in close association with the mother; the mother's rôle as provider of food takes on a different character, and she fulfils her obligations in this respect by a series of complicated activities in the production and preparation of food-stuffs, and what may be called the child's nutritive horizon becomes widened by the realization that other members of the household play a part in the task of food production and preparation. The children at this stage feel little anxiety about their food or responsibility in regard to its production. They feed with their mothers, and as the women act as food distributors, the child is not likely to go short. They are also allowed to beg from their elders at meal-times, behaviour which would not be allowed in the case of older children. The child at this stage, too, becomes aware of the mother's rôle as a cook, competence in this activity being regarded as an essential part of the duties of a wife. The child also becomes aware that the mother is almost exclusively responsible for the provision of vegetable food, since she is the tiller of the soil. The little girl at this stage begins in a rudimentary way to share in her mother's tasks, and as the obligations regarding cooking become known to her, she comes to realize that her *lobola* price may depend upon her skill.

The growing realization of household co-operation in the production of food at this stage breaks into the child's consciousness, giving an early appreciation of the importance of social co-operation. The father, however, still plays but a small part in the child's life. He may provide special treats for the children, but normally eats in the men's place and does not appear in the family circle at meal-times. He does not appear as the chief provider of food, nor does he ask for the help of his son in food-producing activities.

The individual who is most significant for the child from the nutritional point of view is still his mother, and he becomes aware of the differentiation in his relationship to other women in the kraal. In polygynous kraals each household is a self-contained unit, and a mother may rebuke her children for straying into other huts at meal-times. The attitude of co-wives towards each other becomes reflected in the consciousness of the children. They are brought up together, but are separated at meal-times, and the jealousy which is apt to arise between co-wives is frequently reflected in hostility between their children. This becomes more significant at a later age, as children of different co-wives become aware that they are competitors in matters of privilege and succession. The child at this stage realizes the difference between his mother's sisters who may be substitute mothers and the co-wives or wives of his father's brothers, who are treated with less tenderness and affection, though the same kinship term (*manana*) is applied to all these women.

A further widening of the child's consciousness is produced by the inclusion of the rules of eating etiquette and good manners connected with food. Greed is rebuked, particularly if it is manifested in the house of a stranger. Children going to visit their friends are specifically cautioned against eating crumbs off the floor, not from any hygienic motive, but because it suggests that the child is not well fed at home.

The duty of sharing food is also taught. The basest deed conceivable is to fail to divide a tempting morsel with everybody present. This forms the initial situation for the rules of hospitality which play such an important part in later life. The importance of age and sex is also reflected in the distribution of food.

Later childhood.—The phase of early childhood is differentiated from that of later childhood, not by any physiological change, but by the fact that with the beginning of later childhood, the life and occupations of the boy become sharply differentiated from those of the girl.

The period between the eighth and tenth year and the attainment of puberty is marked by three important social changes: (1) the division of children according to sex and altered occupations; (2) the clear demarcation of age distinctions; and (3) the beginning of economic activities proper. The child begins to join other groups of his fellows on a basis of age and sex as distinct from the life in the household which he has previously led. He forms a new routine in regard to his daily meals, and becomes aware of the general sense of insecurity which Bantu peoples necessarily have in regard to their food supply. The boy at this stage is forbidden to eat any longer with his mother and sisters. He eats with youths of his own age; he associates less with his sisters, who are encumbered with the care of babies, while he sets out on adventurous expeditions such as tending goats on the hillside. He becomes more and more aware of the authority of his older brothers, father and paternal uncles; for example, his father may rebuke him for slinking back to the fireside where there is more security but less prestige. The age distinctions also become marked—between the boys who merely tend the goats and the youths who are promoted to the care of the cattle. A similar differentiation takes place in the case of the girl when she begins to sleep in the unmarried women's hut in the kraal.

In spite of the partial disassociation between mother and children, the former continues to act as the entrepreneur in matters of food which she cooks and sends either to the men's place or to the young boys. The children are still dependent upon her, though new ties of loyalty are being formed. Against the frequent statements of communism in matters of food in Bantu society, it must be stressed that the community is divided into well-marked units; food must be shared, but it must be divided only within the group and only in accordance with strict rules of precedence. This is particularly important to the growing child at this stage, when it becomes actively and painfully aware of the shortage of food and consequently of the need for observing the rules which regulate food distribution. There is much evidence that at this stage children are frequently hungry, and this is apparently not peculiar to Bantu society.

Adolescence.—While it is difficult to gather at what age older and younger children become differentiated from each other, the superiority of the cattle-herd over the goat-herd is undoubted. He must be treated with great respect by his juniors, and has complete licence to order them about or bully them. At meal-times it is the seniors' right to help themselves first from the dish which the mother sends.

After initiation, which takes place at varying ages, the young men appear to lead an easy life. They have certain duties in the care of cattle, but these are not arduous, and they are beginning to be concerned with begging *lobola* cattle from the members of their kinship group. It is at this point that the father becomes a definite social factor in the individual's life. It is he who enforces the separation of the boys from their mothers and corrects their manners. He controls their economic activities and is treated with respect. With this authority is associated the father's rôle in the provision of the food supply, the cattle herd and their products and, to some extent, the grain supply also. He is obliged to support his sons until the age of marriage and even after. The receipt of food marks the dependence of the child on his father to an extent which we find hard to realize. He simply cannot acquire food except from his parents' hands. Food is not a commodity which can be bought and sold, and the Bantu youth's dependence on his family is marked by the receipt, not of a money allowance, but of actual food. The father has another important rôle to fulfil at this time, namely, the provision of *lobola* cattle which the son could not accumulate for himself except by waiting for many years.

The father's authority is in fact expressed in his rôle of possessor, gatherer and controller of food, and this attitude towards authority is subsequently extended to the chief. The distribution of a slain beast among most Bantu peoples is carried out by the head of the family or the village headman—in a small kraal they may be the same person. The portions of the beast are distributed according to certain set rules. The ideal man in Bantu society is he who is never in want, and the enjoyment of plenty of food and its generous distribution to friends and dependents is recognized as an attribute of authority, whether of the father or of the chief.

Many observers have been so impressed by the offering of food to travellers that they have implied that Bantu hospitality is offered indiscriminately, but it appears that in fact the provision of food for strangers is strictly regulated according to kinship rules. Firstly, the duty of hospitality does not seem to be invariably carried out—as in the case of other irksome rules, there are frequent cases of evasion. Food may be cooked and hastily eaten when guests are believed to be imminent, and there are magical rites whereby guests and travellers on their way to the kraal may guard themselves against such a calamity. The good Ba-Ila wife is adjured at marriage to hide food for her husband so that he should not have to do without, and there is a case recorded in which a father beat his son for giving food to two men who were unrelated to him. It seems, then, that hospitality was an expression of kinship and other social obligations, though the complexities of these may well have given an impression of indiscriminate hospitality.

3. The Material Setting of Human Life and the Study of Primitive Economics

The quest for food forms but a part, albeit the most important part, of a very much wider cultural scheme by which human groups adapt themselves to their geographical environment and fashion objects of material culture. These two general aspects of human culture will be discussed in Volume II, but at this point we must again emphasize their importance. Even our superficial survey of the cultures of such peoples as the Eskimo, the Tungus and the Australian aborigines has revealed the intimate relationship between geographical environment and all the other aspects of culture—economic, political, magico-religious and so on. We have also referred to the significance of material culture in conditioning the character of human institutions (p. 240) and to the importance of artefacts *considered in their cultural context*. Too much emphasis cannot be placed upon the latter point, because it is one which has been consistently ignored in most descriptions of primitive technology.

Though it seems obvious today that no description of primitive culture can be adequate without a consideration of the material basis of human life, the scientific study of primitive economics is of comparatively recent growth. This aspect of primitive life was largely neglected in the earlier field records, for, to the untrained observer, it is an aspect of the native's life which appears to be hardly worthy of study. It lacks the glamour of ceremonial, the weirdness of magic and the piquancy of sexual customs. On the theoretical side the economic systems of primitive peoples have not always been treated realistically. In this field, "stages" of economic life were invented *ad hoc* without the slightest empirical enquiry as to whether any primitive economic institutions do actually correspond with the supposed sequence of stages. For Adam Smith, and other exponents of the "three-stage" theory, men were first hunters, then shepherds, and finally agriculturists; for Bruno Hildebrand, they passed through successive stages of exchange—barter, money and credit; and for Lewis Morgan, the history of man's economic development was divisible into two stages of "savagery" and three of "barbarism".

Again, the economics of primitive peoples were contrasted with those of civilized nations, and were held up as simple prototypes of modern forms of society, as exemplifying a mode of life from which our own economic organization has emerged. According to Karl Bücher, man's original state was characterized by the "individual search for food" without any social regulation; for Engels, on the other hand, it was one of "primitive communism", a view in direct opposition to Bücher's. None of these theories was based upon a thorough empirical study of the realities of primitive economic life. They selected only those aspects of it which, from a very superficial examination, seemed to fit in with the view which it was desired to establish. Only in recent years has any attempt been made to study the economic systems of primitive peoples in their own right, not as stages in a hypothetical evolutionary process, but as working mechanisms whereby man adjusts himself to his environment. By this method it has been found that economic facts have important relationships to religion, law, political organization and family life. The functional approach to the problem has thus revealed the social significance, as well as the great complexity, of primitive economic systems.

The existence of such systems is at first obscured by the absence, in primitive societies, of the elaborate institutions of our own society—banks, industries, complex systems of international trade, and in particular the existence of money (as a medium of exchange and measure of value) upon which all of these are founded. This accounts for many of the significant differences between primitive economic systems and our own. Many of the concepts of modern economics are not applicable without radical reformulation to primitive society, as will become apparent when we review the economic activities of primitive peoples in terms of the traditional concepts of production, exchange, distribution and ownership.

4. Production

The exploitation of the natural resources of the environment constitutes the productive system of any people, and the organization of this system in primitive society differs in several important respects from our own. The first point which must be mentioned is the character of work. As we have said, most economic effort in primitive society is devoted to the production of food. The activities involved in this have, quite apart from the stimulus of real or potential hunger, a spontaneous interest lacking in the ordinary work of an office or factory in contemporary civilization. This will become clear when we reflect that most of the food-getting activities of primitive peoples, such as fishing, hunting and gardening, are recreations among ourselves. It does not follow that primitive man takes an undiluted pleasure in such activities—much of the labour connected with them is heavy, monotonous or hazardous. But they do possess an inherent interest lacking in most of the economic labour in modern civilization, and much the same applies to primitive technology, in which the craftsman himself creates an artefact, rather than being merely a human cog in the machinery of production.

The spontaneous interest of work under primitive conditions is reinforced by a number of social values attached to it. Skill and industry are honoured and laziness condemned, a principle exemplified in the folk songs and proverbs of the Maori: From childhood onwards the virtues of industry are extolled, as in the term *ihu puku*, literally "dirty nose", applied as a compliment to an industrious man because it implies that he is continually occupied in cultivation with his face to the ground [1]; on the other hand, the twin vices of greed and laziness are condemned in the saying: "Deep throat, shallow muscles". Such social evaluations as these give pride in successful and energetic work, and stimulate potential laggards to play their part in productive effort.

Another feature of primitive production is the close relationship of art to work. One has only to walk through the galleries of an ethnological museum to appreciate the way in which almost all primitive artefacts are decorated or are constructed according to symmetrical and graceful designs. Nor is æsthetic enjoyment absent even from the quest for food. Thus the complex of social, material and æsthetic values connected with agriculture in the Trobriand Islands has been described as follows: "The Trobriander is above all a gardener, who digs with pleasure and collects with pride, to whom accumulated food gives the sense of safety and pleasure in achievement, to whom the rich foliage of yam-vines or taro leaves is a direct expression of beauty. . . . To the Trobriander all that is lovely to the eye and to the heart, or—as he would put it more correctly—to the stomach, which to him is the seat of the emotions as well as of understanding, lies in

[1] Cf. our own expression "nose to the grindstone".

things which promise him safety, prosperity, abundance and sensual pleasure." [1]

The interest of primitive work is increased, and its drudgery mitigated, by the fact that it is often co-operative. Major undertakings, such as house-building or the construction of large canoes, usually require the labour of more than one person. And even when the task concerned could be done individually, primitive peoples often prefer collective labour. Thus, in Hehe agriculture much of the cultivation is done individually or by small family groups. But at the time of the annual hoeing of the ground, it is customary for a man to announce that on a certain day his wife will brew beer. His relatives and neighbours attend, help with the hoeing, and are rewarded with beer in the middle of the day and in the evening. This is not to be regarded as payment, since casual visitors who have not helped with the hoeing may also take part in the beer drink. Under this system, each man helps others and is helped by them in turn. From the purely economic point of view, the system has no advantage, since each man could quite well hoe his own ground and the preparation of beer adds substantially to the work involved. But the system does possess psychological advantages. The task of hoeing might well appear endless if undertaken by each individual separately. Collective labour, and the collateral activity of beer-drinking, changes a dreary task into a social occasion. The same principle applies to collective labour in general in primitive society, and to the social activities of feasting, dancing and other forms of collective enjoyment which frequently accompany it or mark its conclusion.

In a similar way, magico-religious beliefs and practices reinforce the purely material motives in productive effort. These beliefs and practices not only give confidence in the face of possible failure, but also emphasize the importance of work and help to organize productive effort. The magician is often also an expert, and in this case beliefs in his magical powers reinforce his authority in the organization of work. Again, there is usually a magical or ritual cycle running parallel with the yearly cycle of productive activity, different phases of which are inaugurated by magico-religious ritual, thus ensuring that all members of the community undertake their productive tasks in good time. Finally, such ritual gives an added value to the bare struggle for existence, by bringing it into relation with supernatural forces and mythological tradition.

[1] Malinowski (5), Vol. I, p. 10.

In regard to the division of labour in primitive production, we have already mentioned that this is founded almost entirely on distinctions of sex. Apart from this, there is but little economic specialization. This is to some extent implied in the low level of technical achievement and lack of an economic surplus in primitive communities. Such communities are unable to provide support for a number of specialists or to allow for the leisure necessary for invention and the elaboration of the specialist skill of individuals freed from preoccupation with the food quest. Thus, in primitive society a man may be an expert craftsman, but he normally indulges also in the ordinary subsistence activities of his culture—hunting, cultivation and so on.

We must refer in conclusion to some forms of economic grouping which might be described as "trade guilds" or occupational groups. Thus, in Samoa carpenters were organized into a special group called *Sa Tangaloa*, that is, "the Family of Tangaloa", one of the greatest gods in the Samoan pantheon. They were entitled to material rewards and ritual privileges in connection with the building of houses and canoes and, in western Samoa at least, were organized into a well-defined trade guild. Again, among many African tribes the importance of iron is reflected in the occurrence of guilds of blacksmiths, having elaborate religious cults and initiation ceremonies connected with membership. Here, as in the Tobacco Society of the Crow, a particular type of economic organization becomes an important focus of community interest and the centre of magico-religious observances.

5. Exchange

Wherever a division of labour occurs, some mechanism of economic exchange is necessary. Since the division of labour in primitive society is founded primarily on sex, the basic form of exchange is between men and women, especially between husband and wife in the family. Such exchanges, which form part of the wider system of mutual obligations between the two, are usually informal in character and take place as part of ordinary day-to-day activities. But the more spectacular and public exchanges of wealth between individuals and groups are of a different kind, and are usually not founded primarily on economic necessity or convenience. For example, the exchange of *tonga* and *oloa* at a Samoan marriage is not dictated by economic necessity. Both consist of goods which the parties concerned in the transaction are quite capable of producing for themselves and the whole motivation of the elaborate system of exchange is social in character. Much the same applies to the transactions connected with cattle which are involved in *lobola*. These tend ultimately to cancel out, since a woman's *lobola* is normally used to procure a wife for her brother, and so on indefinitely. This does not mean that natives are indifferent to the material side of the transaction —on the contrary, they are keenly aware of it, as is clearly seen in the backbiting, quarrels and litigation which are apt to arise from *lobola* transactions. But as purely economic mechanisms, that is, mechanisms to provide people with goods which they could not otherwise obtain, the transactions involved in the payment of bride-price, and in primitive systems of exchange generally, are of minor importance.

The exchange of goods and services in primitive society cannot be understood in terms of such modern economic concepts as "barter", "purchase" or "wages". When a service is rendered or a material object handed over, there is usually no stipulation in regard to return. Furthermore, services are often rendered and goods handed over at collective gatherings; for example, in house-building, in agricultural work (as described for the Hehe in the preceding section), or at ceremonial distributions of food and gifts.

These two facts—the lack of a stipulated return and the collective character of many economic exchanges in primitive society— have been partly responsible for the mistaken assumption of a system of "primitive communism". No interpretation could be more misleading. Irksome services are not rendered, nor valuable gifts given, indiscriminately to everyone in the community or from a diffuse feeling of benevolence and lack of self-interest or sense of private property. They are regulated by tradition, and are in the vast majority of cases associated with an expectation of return, even though this may not be stipulated.

This basic characteristic of economic and social relationships in primitive society has been termed the **principle of reciprocity** which implies that the receipt of any service or material benefit imposes upon the recipient an obligation to return to his bene-factor at a later stage an equivalent service or material benefit. The nearest approach, in our society, to an example of this principle as it operates in primitive culture is the exchange of gifts between friends. If a man gives his friend a gift on his birthday or at Christmas, he will normally expect to receive a similar return gift in due course, and will be disappointed and probably annoyed if such a gift is not forthcoming. The last sentence indicates how the principle of reciprocity differs from the unspecified and uncritical generosity implied in "primitive communism". But our example also illustrates how the operation of the principle of reciprocity based upon social traditions differs from the impersonal and calculating transactions which form the core of modern economic systems and the basis of economic analyses.

In connection with most transactions based on the principle of reciprocity, the following common features should be noted:

1. There is, at the initial giving, no stipulated return, though such return is expected by the individual and sanctioned by social tradition.

2. The exact value of the return is usually not precisely specified, though it is normally expected to approximate to that of the original benefit.

3. The rendering of the return benefit may be delayed for a considerable period.

4. The exchange involved does not take place in a haphazard way between any two members of the community—it is based on such relationships as friendship and kinship existing between them, and is thought of primarily as a reflection of such relationships, rather than as a mechanism for economic gain.

5. The exchange frequently takes place in connection with specified occasions, for example, seasonal festivals and marriages.

Very broadly, the above principles are applicable to economic exchanges in primitive society, though some of them do not apply, and others require qualification, in connection with specific transactions. And in most cases other principles must also be added. Among these a common one is the existence of *closed circuits of exchange*, in which the nature of the return benefit, and occasionally its value also, is traditionally defined. Thus in the Kula, to be described presently, the two kinds of valuables involved can only be exchanged for each other, and not for other economic goods. In the case of bride-price, the nature of the payment, for example, cattle and hoes among Bantu peoples, is specified, and the amount is frequently a matter for bargaining and haggling, though the latter are absolutely unthinkable in connection with the Kula.

The fourth point mentioned above is of special importance in primitive society. In our own society there are certain kinship relationships which imply the giving of gifts, but these are for the most part restricted to the individual family, though they may include such close kin as uncles and aunts. In conformity with what we know of the extensive ramifications of kinship bonds in primitive society, the economic obligations of any individual are more far-reaching than anything which occurs in our own society. In addition to the bonds of kinship, other culturally defined relationships may be expressed in the giving of gifts or the rendering of services, for example, the relationship between bond-friends, or between a chief and his people. In all these cases the economic exchanges are essentially personal in character, and reflect the social relationships existing between the individuals and groups concerned. Finally, we must emphasize the importance of traditional occasions of exchange—births, initiations, marriages, deaths, feasts, religious ceremonies, and major economic enterprises such as house-building and collective agricultural labour.

Many economic exchanges are not private transactions between individuals, but are a matter of public interest and are sanctioned by tradition. This has an important bearing on productive effort. People are stimulated to work, not only by their own economic needs, but also by the knowledge that they will in the future have to honour traditional economic obligations, and that failure to do so will lead to opprobrium, ridicule, or even supernatural punishment.

The mutual character of economic obligations is seen most clearly in collective undertakings, for example house-building or communal labour in agriculture, such as we have described for the Hehe. Here the observation of a single undertaking might create the impression that individuals are prepared to work for one another out of the sheer goodness of their hearts, and without the anticipation of any reward commensurate with the effort which they expend. But when we consider a series of such undertakings, we find that each individual helps and is helped in turn; that he is prepared to put forth effort to assist a neighbour or kinsman largely because he knows that he will need similar help in the future; and that when laggards are consistently slack in rendering assistance, they become the object of public condemnation and in the last resort many find themselves unable to claim the services of others whom they have themselves failed to help. Similar principles are operative in the case of the exchange of gifts. While it cannot be asserted that such considerations as we have described are always present in the consciousness of individuals, they nevertheless constitute the dynamic core of primitive systems of exchange and mutual service based on the principle of reciprocity.

The simplest paradigm of the principle of reciprocity is the exchange of gifts or mutual services between two individuals, a relationship which may be graphically represented as follows, the arrows indicating the handing over of material goods or the rendering of some service:

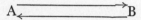

But it will be realized that most transactions in primitive society are far more complex than this would suggest. Thus, in a typical *lobola* transaction most of the cattle are provided by the father of the bridegroom but with the assistance of other kin; and though they are formally handed over to the father of the bride, some of them are distributed by him among her other kinsfolk. We might represent such a transaction as follows, the arrows pointing to the right indicating the transfer of cattle:

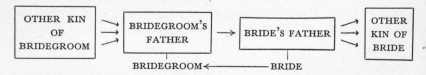

This illustrates the way in which the payment of *lobola* binds together, not only the two parties to the marriage and their respective families, but also their remoter kin. Much the same applies to other economic exchanges which, though founded on the principle of reciprocity, are much more complex than the simple exchange of gifts or services. Thus, in dealing with Hehe chieftainship, we had occasion to comment on the system of reciprocity existing between chief and people. The general outline of this system may be represented as follows:

Obedience, service in war, tribute, ivory
and other traditional gifts.

Leadership in war, organization of ivory
trade, public administration, religious services, and traditional disbursements, for
example, feeding warriors at war.

It follows from this that any particular transaction can only be
understood as part of a very much wider system. Let us consider,
for example, the way in which a man obtained a spear from a
blacksmith among the Hehe. The former, whom we may term the
"purchaser" in spite of the misleading implications of this term,
first supplied the smith with iron and charcoal in excess of that
required for his spear. While the smith was working upon the
spear, the purchaser either assisted him in the task or cultivated
his plantations for him, since Hehe blacksmiths, like most specialist craftsmen in primitive society, also engaged in the ordinary
food-getting activities of the people. The surplus iron and charcoal accumulated by the smith in a series of such transactions
was used to make spears and other artefacts which were sent to
the chief, who in due course would reciprocate with a gift of
cattle, this being one of the traditional forms of disbursement
mentioned above. The purchaser in his turn would, as a warrior,
take part in cattle raids, by which the herds of the chief were
partly supplied. The individual transaction between a purchaser
and a blacksmith can therefore be fully understood only by considering it within the very much wider system of reciprocity of
which the institution of chieftainship was the focal point.

The character of primitive systems of exchange is partly
conditioned by the absence of money as a medium of exchange
and measure of value. It is true that most primitive societies have
traditional objects of more or less standardized value which are
prominent in particular exchanges—for example, the valuables of
the Kula, cattle among most Bantu peoples, pigs and shell ornaments in Melanesia, and the blankets, whale-oil and coppers which
figured so prominently in the dramatic exchanges of the potlatch.
Such objects of ceremonial value do not normally constitute
ordinary media of exchange, which can be freely used as is money

in our own society. Even in those primitive societies in which some form of currency exists, the value of the objects concerned and the way in which they are employed in economic transactions vary from anything with which we are familiar. This may be illustrated by reference to certain phases of economic life in Rossel Island.

The natives of Rossel Island have two systems of currency, known respectively as *ndap* and *nko*. The former consists of single pieces of *Spondylus* shell, and the latter of strings of perforated discs of the shell of the Giant Clam. Only the first of these will be considered here. It is believed that most of the currency in Rossel Island was made by the gods at the beginning of time at spots which are now sacred centres in the various districts. The making and handling of currency is a matter of strict ceremonial observance, and is subject to numerous taboos. There are twenty-two values of *ndap*, each having a special native name, but it will be simpler if we refer to them as No. 1, No. 2, No. 3 and so on in ascending order of value. The value of the different *ndap* is not determined by scarcity, but by the traditional significance attached to them, as will be seen from the following rough estimate of the numbers of the higher-value *ndap* on the island:

No. 22	.	.	. 7
,, 21	.	.	. 10
,, 20	.	.	. 10
,, 19	.	.	. 10
,, 18	.	.	. 20
,, 17	.	.	. 7
,, 16	.	.	. 7
,, 15	.	.	. 10
,, 14	.	.	. 30
,, 13	.	.	. 30–40

Thus, while there is a general tendency for the more valuable coins to be more scarce, this tendency is not consistently operative. Among the lower values, No. 4 is the most plentiful item on the island, yet it is of higher value than Nos. 1–3, which are less common.

A complication in understanding the values of items of Rossel Island currency is that the higher values cannot be expressed as multiples of the lower, as they can in our own monetary system.

They can only be expressed in terms of interest on loans, and more-over the "interest" is not calculated as a percentage on the loan, but in terms of the time for which it is operative. The rule is that a man who borrows a *ndap* of a given value must return at a later date a *ndap* of higher value, the position of the latter in the value scale being determined by the time which elapses between the making of the loan and its repayment. Thus, a man who borrows a No. 1 and keeps it for only a week or two must return a No. 2, but the longer he keeps it the higher the value which must be given in return, so that if the loan extends over several years, one of the highest-valued *ndap* must be returned.

The system is complicated by several features. The return must be made in the form of the single appropriate value, and not by a number of *ndap* of lower value; it is, moreover, impossible to obtain "change," since the values are not multiples of each other; and as there is a shortage of currency on the island, this entails constant borrowing and lending. Moreover, the exact periods of time involved in the increments of value are not definitely fixed, and certain individuals take advantage of this. They accumulate capital which they keep out on loan, and manipulate their various monetary transactions to their own advantage. They perform magic to secure the acquiescence of their debtors and creditors in these negotiations.

The currency of Rossel Island is used in a variety of economic transactions which also possess a social significance. We may illustrate this by reference to the elaborate transactions involved in the purchase of a pig, diagrammatically represented in Fig. 16. This is a very much simplified version of the transaction, which involves *nko* as well as *ndap*. It must be regarded as schematic rather than descriptive.

When a man buys a pig, for example for a feast, the beast is ceremonially divided into ten portions, each of which is paid for by a particular item of currency. The highest value of *ndap* pays for the best portion; the next highest for the next portion; and so on, down to the worst portion, which is paid for by the lowest value of *ndap* involved in the transaction. All the currency in-volved is not provided by the buyer, though he must pay for the best portion and sometimes for other good-quality portions, as indicated by dotted lines. His relatives and other members of the community also contribute, each individual providing a special item of *ndap* which pays for a specified portion of the pig. These

other contributors are concerned mainly with the purchase of
the inferior portions, though they may contribute towards payment for the better portions also, as indicated again by dotted
lines.

The currency thus mobilized for the purchase of the pig is not
all taken by the seller, who claims the higher values only. The

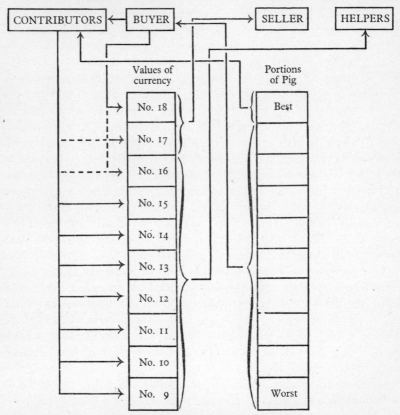

FIG. 16.—Buying a Pig in Rossel Island

remaining currency he redistributes, according to specified rules,
among his relatives and helpers who have assisted him in
feeding the pig.

The rules governing the distribution of the portions of pig are
likewise complex. Though the buyer has acted as entrepreneur
in the whole transaction, and though nominally he has bought at
least the best portion, he and his close relatives are forbidden by

tradition to eat any of it, in fact, they carry out a sort of mourning for the pig. The buyer hands over the best portion to one of the contributors and the remaining portions are divided among the others. An interesting rule governs this distribution. So far as the highest values at least are concerned, a man may not consume the actual portion for which he has paid.

The monetary system and principles of economic exchange in Rossel Island, like the corresponding mechanisms in other primitive societies, strike us at first as unnecessarily complicated, but this is so only until we realize that their implications extend far beyond the economic field. Though based upon the material needs of the community and the material satisfactions of individuals, their main function is in establishing and maintaining social relationships. Thus, the sale of a pig is not merely an economic transaction, but reflects the bonds of kinship and economic obligation existing between a number of individuals in the community. As with production, so with exchange, we find the economic systems of primitive peoples coloured at all points by non-economic values and motives, a principle which is well illustrated by the organization of the Kula.

6. The Kula

The Kula is an institution found amongst peoples who inhabit some of the islands to the east and north of the eastern end of New Guinea, for example, the Trobriand Islands, the Amphlett Islands, the Loughlan Islands and Dobu. These people are of diverse cultures, and though all co-operate in practising the Kula, some details of the institution differ among the various communities concerned. The details described here refer to the Kula as practised by the Trobriand Islanders.

The core of the Kula is the exchange of two kinds of articles, red shell necklaces and white shell arm-bands between individuals living in different communities. The articles (together called vaygu'a) are used, apart from the Kula, only on rare occasions for ornament, are easily manufactured in plentiful supply, and yet are to the native the most valued objects which he possesses. They are graded in value, and particularly valuable specimens have special names, their history is known to all, and there is fierce competition to obtain them. The communities form what might be called an "exchange ring", around which the two kinds of articles are constantly passing from person to person in opposite directions, the necklaces moving clockwise and the arm-bands anti-clockwise. An article of one type is exchanged only for an article of the other type: two articles of the same type are never exchanged. No specimen is ever held by any one individual for any length of time, for to hoard *vaygu'a* is contrary to the code of exchange. The transaction, the actual exchange, is performed according to strict rules and a definite code of etiquette. It must start with the presentation of an opening gift, a *vaga*, by one trading partner to another, and close by a return presentation of a counter gift or *yotile*, the value of which must be equal to or greater than the value of the opening gift. Several other types of gift may be given to smooth the deal, but are not obligatory. There is no haggling or bargaining, and the gifts are made ostentatiously and in public.

There are four types of Kula transaction: individual unco-ordinated exchange between men of the same Kula community, inland exchange between two contiguous communities, relatively unceremonious exchange overseas between communities near each other, and ceremonial overseas exchange. This last, with which we are mainly concerned, sometimes involves voyages of over a hundred miles, and differs from the others in the higher degree of organization which it entails; in that commodities such as pottery, food and wood utensils are also exchanged; in the pomp, ceremony and competition which mark its performance, and in the danger, hazards, magic and myth associated with it.

Before examining the many activities involved in a large-scale Kula expedition, we may consider the Kula community, that is, the group of persons who act as a unit in overseas expeditions and who exchange *vaygu'a* amongst themselves. Sometimes the group consists of the adult males of a single village, though usually it includes the men of several neighbouring villages, or of a district or federation of districts. A district is a political unit which has at its head a chief or sub-chief. It is the chiefs who initiate and lead the expeditions, who provide most of the finance, and who gain most wealth and prestige from them. A man must belong to a Kula community before he can participate in the Kula, and he may exchange *vaygu'a* only with certain members of the limited number of communities with which his own community traditionally deals. Each community must of course deal with at least two other communities. Moreover, there are definite rules regulating the entry of individuals into the group. Not everyone may belong to a group. A youth must be past adolescence, must know some Kula magic, and must possess some *vaygu'a*, and in a few communities must be of a certain rank. Magic and *vaygu'a* are inherited from a mother's brother, so that a man may only enter the group if his maternal kinsmen are already in it. The only exceptions to this rule are the sons of wealthy chiefs, who may be presented with magic and *vaygu'a* by their father. Women generally do not take part in Kula exchange; the sporadic exceptions to this show, as do the chiefs' sons, how the rules governing the Kula are modified by political rank, for occasionally a chief's wife may be permitted to exchange valuables with her husband. Though women and children do not participate in the exchanges, which constitute the core of the Kula, the institution impinges upon their lives. They take part in the celebrations associated with it and enjoy the benefits of exchange of goods, while women obey certain taboos in connection with it.

The initiation of a large overseas expedition, *uvalaku*, sets in motion a train of associated activities. New sea-going canoes have to be built and old ones overhauled. A chief or headman finances the building of a canoe; a canoe expert prepares and fits the materials, carves the prow-boards and performs the magic necessary to canoe-building; kinsmen and friends of the chief provide a constant labour force, while his subjects help at some stages when communal labour is required. The people are paid mostly in food, while the chief's maternal kinsmen secure a claim to form the crew of the boat. The technological process includes the felling and hollowing out of a tree, the preparation of planks, poles, an outrigger and a sail, the fitting of these items, and the lashing of them together to form the canoe. The building of a vessel capable of carrying a crew of at least six across a hundred miles or more of Pacific Ocean requires a body of detailed knowledge and a high degree of skill. Canoes are not navigable in all weathers, however, and the times of sailing are partly determined by weather and direction of wind. Punctuating the technological process, but never supplanting knowledge and skill, are magic rites to increase the efficiency of the canoe and to ward off dangers from it.

The new canoes having been ceremonially launched, all the canoes about to sail are displayed in a review, while the whole community, men, women and children, join in a feast and celebration. Shortly afterwards the crews collect certain goods from neighbouring districts who specialize in their production, and provision their vessels with gifts from friends and neighbours. All these must later be repaid. Finally, the fleet assembles and departs for distant shores.

Magic has been mentioned in connection with canoe-building. The Kula, an institution bound up with the most intense interests of the natives, has its own specific magic embodying a variety of rites and spells designed to ensure success for the individual by making him irresistible to his trading partners, by safeguarding him from dangers, and by preventing his companions from being too successful. The magic of the Kula is rooted in a body of myths believed by the natives to be accounts of events which once happened, for example, the legend of the Kudayuri canoe described in Chapter X.

It will be seen that the Kula is an institution which embraces many activities and commands much of the interest of the communities which practise it. In its major function it is both ceremonial and economic. Though the Kula exchanges themselves are not thought of as commercial in character, the overseas expeditions do provide opportunities for collateral trade which are of considerable economic importance. But these, like the Kula exchanges proper, cannot be understood apart from the context of social values—economic, political, ceremonial and magicoreligious—to which they are related.

7. Distribution and Ownership

The question of the claims exercised by individuals over the products of economic effort in primitive society has often led to considerable misunderstanding, epitomized in the hypothesis of "primitive communism". It is easy to see how this fallacy has arisen. The principle of purely individual and exclusive ownership unconditioned by the claims of others which constitutes our idea of private property [1] has a limited application in primitive society. Very broadly it applies only to personal possessions such as tools, utensils, clothing, ornaments and so on. As regards these, ownership is generally individual, though there may be a certain amount of borrowing and lending as there is in our own society.

---

[1] It is worth noting that even in our own society this conception of property does not correspond absolutely with the facts—thus, a man's exclusive enjoyment of his own income is limited by his obligation to support his family as well as by taxation, and he can only erect and use buildings on his own land subject to the regulations of a local authority.

Even in societies where women occupy a relatively subordinate position, their exclusive claims to their own belongings are usually recognized, and the same may even apply to children. Thus, Professor Lowie records that he once offered to purchase a blanket belonging to a small boy among the Paviosto. The parents referred the request to the lad and were prepared to abide by the price which he fixed.

The claims to minor possessions, then, are more or less exclusively individual and rest upon the principle of individual effort or upon utilization. Individuals own items of personal property, either because they have produced them or because they regularly use them. As regards food, the former principle is also operative, though here the question of ownership becomes more complex and the existence of individual claims to the food supply is apt to be obscured by the obligations of distribution, some of which we have mentioned in connection with nutrition among the southeastern Bantu. In the next chapter we shall find many examples of how individual productive effort establishes a claim to a portion of the food supply, and also of how this principle is modified by the traditional claims of other individuals.

When we come to more elaborate forms of property such as large canoes, which require collective labour in their construction and employment in productive activity, the superficial impression of collective ownership becomes even more misleading. Thus Rivers remarked that "one of the objects of Melanesian culture, which is usually, if not always, the subject of common ownership, is the canoe". Malinowski has demonstrated the superficiality of this statement with specific reference to fishing canoes in the Trobriand Islands. It is true that several individuals are involved in the scheme of "ownership" of the canoe, but the place of each in this scheme is clearly defined. The master of the canoe, who is also the captain of the crew and their official magician, finances the initial building of the craft, and with the assistance of other members of the crew is responsible for keeping it in good repair. In the actual employment of the canoe, each man has a defined place, such as "steersman", "keeper of the nets", or "watcher for fish". These positions, which are allocated on a basis of rank, age and personal ability, define, not only the tasks which each man carries out in fishing, but also his claims to a share of the catch.

Even a statement of these individual rights and obligations in the case of a single fishing crew does not exhaust the sociological study of canoe ownership, which is conditioned by external obligations. Thus, when a communal fishing expedition has been organized, every canoe is bound to attend. Furthermore, the catch is not consumed exclusively by the crew and their families. Part of it is exchanged with people of inland villages for vegetable food, a transaction based on the principle of reciprocity which is not merely economic but also social, in so far as it emphasizes the interdependence of the two types of community. But here, again, it must be emphasized that the transaction is not "collective". Each fisherman indulges in a series of exchanges with individuals from inland villages. These are based on the principle of reciprocity; for while they are conducted in a free-and-easy manner and are governed by rules of good manners, they involve definite self-interest, and there is much keen calculation of the advantages involved.

The relation of a group of men to a canoe in the Trobriand Islands is no more an example of "communistic ownership" than is a Joint Stock Company in our own society. This is broadly true of all other alleged examples of "collective ownership", though there are naturally extensive variations in the rules of property from one primitive society to another. The principles of distribution and the ownership of property must be defined for each primitive community in relation to different types of material objects. To this statement it must be added that in many primitive societies various forms of immaterial property exist, and these bear at least a superficial resemblance to our own laws of patent and copyright. Thus, among many Amerindian tribes the right to perform specific songs and dances may be "bought" by individuals and even inherited in the same way as material property. Sometimes, as we have seen among the Crow, such rights may be exercised by all members of a voluntary association, but each member must acquire them by the individual payments which constitute his membership fee. In a similar way magical spells and ritual privileges may be purchased in many primitive societies.

Closely related to the possession of such immaterial property, which confers prestige upon the owner, is the ownership of objects of ceremonial value, for example, the valuables employed in the Kula or the coppers and other forms of wealth used in the potlatch. Ownership of such objects is always circumscribed by traditional rules and above all by the obligation of generosity. Though wealth confers prestige in many primitive communities, it is the giving away of such wealth rather than its mere possession which is significant. Generosity is honoured in primitive communities, whether in an informal way as merely enhancing a man's reputation and popularity, or in the highly developed institutions of ceremonial exchange and distribution which we have mentioned. Finally, it must be mentioned that this principle is often restricted at the point where generosity becomes ostentation. In such cases the individual is forbidden to display generosity above his station, and social sanctions, ranging from ridicule to severe penalties imposed by outraged chiefs, are employed to restrict the extent to which a man may acquire prestige by the display of generosity.

Something must be said in conclusion about the economic evaluation of women in primitive society, concerning which it has often been said that they are regarded as property. This is one of those dangerous half-truths which lead to a complete misunderstanding of the position. It is true that women are the subject of many economic transactions; and that material goods are handed over in return for their economic, biological and personal services, as we have seen to be the case in the custom of *lobola*. The economic value of women is even more striking where, owing to the poverty of material culture and a simple ecology, there is little else in the nature of wealth. Thus in Australia women are concentrated in the hands of the old men, and in this regard they play much the same rôle in maintaining the position of a privileged class as does material wealth in other communities. But the economic evaluation of women does not mean that they are "mere chattels", as has been asserted in many of the less reliable ethnographic records. In all primitive societies women have, as we have seen, certain definite rights in the economic, social and even the magico-religious spheres. The fact that their services are often evaluated in economic terms implies, not degradation or anything approximating to it, but a material recognition of their value to the community, a value which is at the same time social and economic. Here, as in primitive economics generally, the two kinds of values—social and economic, spiritual and material— are inextricably intertwined in a way which makes it impossible to interpret primitive attitudes in terms of our own more rigidly defined categories.

While it is difficult to generalize about the ownership of property in primitive communities, it is clearly wrong to describe it as communistic. When a number of persons are involved, their specific claims are usually clearly defined, and are furthermore limited by a variety of social, political, ceremonial and magico-religious rights and obligations. The complex interlocking of such individual rights and obligations differs profoundly from anything which can be called "primitive communism". This will become apparent when we turn in the next chapter to the most significant form of ownership of all—namely, that which defines the rights of men to the land which they inhabit and to the food and other benefits which it provides.

8. Bibliographical Commentary

For a general survey of primitive types of economic activity, consult Herskovits (3), also Thurnwald, R. (1), and the chapters by Bunzel and by Lowie in Boas (3). For a comparative study of primitive types of ecology see Forde (1).

The best introduction to the study of nutrition in primitive culture is Richards (1). Valuable accounts of the place of food in social life are contained in Bell (1), Fortes, M. and S. L. (1), and Richards (4), as well as in more general works on primitive economic systems. Among these may be specially mentioned Firth (5, 10 and 13), Schapera and Goodwin in Schapera (1) and Stevenson (1). Particular phases of primitive economic life are discussed in Baumann (1), Benedict (1), Elkin (1), Fei (1), Field (1), Firth (2),[1] Forde (2), Garth (1), Hogbin (1, 6 and 8), Krige (1), Oberg (3), Stanner (1 and 2), and Thurnwald, R. (2).

For a fuller discussion of the types of economic activity briefly described in this chapter, consult, on nutrition among the southern Bantu, Richards (1); on Trobriand agriculture, Malinowski (5); on agricultural co-operation among the Hehe, Brown and Hutt (1); on the carpenters' guild of Samoa, Mead (1); on the currency system of Rossel Island, Armstrong (1); on the Kula, Malinowski (1), and on the ownership of Trobriand canoes, Malinowski (2).

[1] Reprinted and revised in Chapter IV of Firth (5).

CHAPTER VIII

LAND TENURE

1. Man and his Land

THE study of land tenure in any primitive community involves a statement of the relations of the human beings composing it to the land which they occupy, relations which are culturally defined in terms of several aspects of culture—economic, political, legal, magico-religious and so on. As we saw in the preceding chapter, our own legal conception of "ownership" is to a large extent inapplicable to primitive property, and this is particularly significant in the case of land.

The three aspects of culture which are of primary importance in the study of land tenure are geographical environment, economics and law. The first of these is significant in determining to some extent the character of ecological adjustment. Even if we did not know from observation, we could predict that land tenure would be different among the Eskimo, the Bantu, and again on the north-west coast of America, because of the very different geographical and climatic conditions under which the various communities live, the different natural resources available to them and the different systems of material culture by which they exploit their environment.

But although geographical environment is a limiting factor in the ecological adjustment of any people, it cannot be regarded as a simple determinant. Under similar geographical conditions, different peoples have developed widely varying economic systems, involving ways of organizing production and the traditional rules governing the exchange and distribution of food and wealth. All of these have an effect in determining the relationship of a human community to their land and its resources.

But a simple statement of ecological adjustment and of the principles of economic organization does not exhaust the field of land tenure. This involves rules and customary usages which often impose irksome obligations upon individuals or frustrate their desires by limiting their claims to the good things of life. As always, attempts are at times made to flout or evade such rules and obligations. There is consequently a need for a legal sanction for land tenure in order to enforce the cultural norms upon which it is founded.

Though we have mentioned the three aspects of culture which are of major importance in the study of land tenure, we must refer also to the relevance of other aspects in particular systems. Some political authority, centralized or diffused, is necessary to organize the relationship of a human community to its land. The rules of land tenure are largely, though not entirely, observed from habit, based upon the fact that they have been inculcated into the mind of every individual reared in the culture concerned as part of its educational system. As we shall see, land tenure is frequently supported by magico-religious sanctions. And in all human communities the recreational, æsthetic and ceremonial activities of the people serve to establish bonds between them and their common territory. These sentimental bonds are reinforced by day-to-day activities within the territory in which life is lived. Though it is difficult to define them with any precision, they are among the most important motives in the social life of human beings, who are often prepared to sacrifice comfort, convenience and even life itself for the land to which they are united by cultural bonds.

The study of primitive land tenure is thus one which requires an elaborate theoretical background, and a keen appreciation of the many factors involved in the definition of man's relationship to his land. The lack of these in the past has often led to misunderstandings which, in the relationships between Europeans and natives in regard to land, have produced far-reaching and tragic consequences.

Sometimes the maladjustments following the acquisition of native lands by Europeans have been due to ruthless expropriation. More frequently they have been due to failure to recognize the manifold aspects of primitive land tenure: the importance of food resources, and the effect upon these of European intrusion; the complex interlocking of individual economic and legal claims, such that no one individual can be said to "own" the land or to be legally entitled to "sell" it; the distinction between our legal conception of permanent ownership and native practices in regard to temporary use of land; and finally the complex sentimental values and magico-religious beliefs which establish a bond between man and his land that transcends a material interpretation in purely legal and economic terms. The importance of the theoretical study of land tenure in the practical problems of native welfare and administration will be discussed in Volume II. For the moment we are concerned with the mechanisms of land tenure as they operate under primitive conditions.

Among hunting and food-gathering peoples the principles of land tenure are most difficult to define. Such peoples usually have a segmented political organization, and live in small groups or bands which wander in search of food over a defined area of territory, a typical example being the Australian horde. Superficial observation at once suggests a system of primitive communism, but closer investigation reveals the existence of individual rights and obligations. It is true that all members of the horde may hunt game and gather vegetable foods over the whole of the horde territory. But the food thus acquired belongs in the first instance to the individual who obtains it. This individual ownership is conditioned by the claims of other individuals, and specifically by the mutual obligations between husband and wife and between fellow-members of the same camp. These obligations are expressed in some of the Karadjeri myths given in Chapter III, Section 10. But it must be remembered that the individuals concerned in the distribution of food are kinsfolk to each other and their mutual obligations derive from the individual bonds of kinship existing between them. There is a certain amount of casual hospitality and generosity, as in all societies, but the dynamic core of the system of economic distribution is to be found in the individual obligations arising from kinship, obligations which are sometimes very precisely defined. Thus, among certain tribes, a kangaroo is divided according to a traditional pattern, special portions of the carcase being allocated to specific kinsfolk.

The economic exploitation of land among the Australian aborigines, then, can only be understood in terms of their social organization. It has also a magico-religious sanction in terms of the myths of the dream times and the contemporary ceremonial, totemic and otherwise, which binds an individual to his horde territory. Though an aborigine enjoys a "walkabout", he always wishes to return to his horde territory to die, for it is to this land that he is bound by material, social and religious ties.[1]

[1] For a moving description of the strength of such motives, see the novel *Coonardoo*, by Katherine Susannah Pritchard.

Though our information for other hunting and food-gathering communities is less complete, we can discern in each of them examples of the individual character of rights to land and its resources. But this becomes more apparent when we come to pastoral and agricultural peoples, among whom it is usually necessary to define the allocation of good pastures and agricultural land. Here again we readily gain a superficial impression of collective ownership, but closer investigation reveals once more the essentially individual system of rights and obligations under-

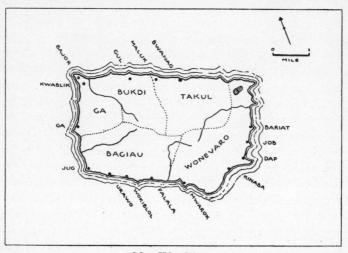

MAP IV.—Wogeo

lying such systems of land tenure. To provide examples of these, and to indicate how land tenure operates in primitive society, we shall, in the next two sections, give digests of two excellent ethnographic records of land tenure among the people of Wogeo and among the Nyakyusa respectively. It will be seen that they differ considerably from each other, as they do from other primitive systems of land tenure. But they both exemplify certain principles of explanation and interpretation which are applicable in primitive society generally.

2. Land Tenure in Wogeo

Wogeo is one of the Schouten Islands situated off the northern coast of New Guinea, not far from the mouth of the Sepik River. It is divided into five districts, each containing a number of villages situated on the coast (Map IV). Usually two patrilineal clans occupy a village, each clan having a headman and deputy-headman. A plan of the village of Dap is given in Fig. 17.

Except in a few places, the soil of Wogeo is everywhere rich.

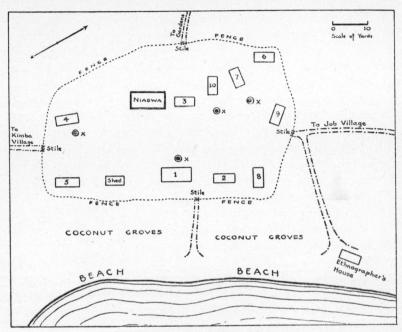

FIG. 17.—Dap Village, Wogeo

The names of only the principal householders are given below; where two men share a house the name of the one responsible for its erection is put first.

House 1. Clan A; Marigum, the *kokwal*
    „ 2. Clan A; Waru (Marigum's father's "classificatory" brother's son)
    „ 3. Clan A; Tafalti (Marigum's eldest son)
    „ 4. { Aligned with Clan A; Sakum
         { Clan A; Sawang (Marigum's brother's son)
    „ 5. Aligned with Clan A; Kalal
    „ 6. Clan A; Jaua (Marigum's sister's son)
    „ 7. Clan B; Bagasal, the *kokwal*
    „ 8. Clan B; Sabuk, a *ngaro*
    „ 9. { Clan B; Wiawia (Bagasal's brother)
         { Clan A; Wiap (Marigum's father's sister's son)
    „ 10. { Clan B; Sabwa (a distant relative of Bagasal)
          { Clan B; a widow and her family

The symbol × indicates the position of *nanarang* stones

For a consideration of the principles of land tenure, the land may be divided into three types: forest land, building sites in the villages, and land used for agricultural purposes.

Forest land.—The dense vegetation of the forest provides timber

for houses and for canoe-making. Wild pigs and smaller game are
hunted and certain fruits and berries collected. Particular shrubs
and creepers are necessary for magical purposes, and deposits of
ochre provide cosmetics and hair-dyes.

Within each district all persons have an equal right to the
products of the forest. But once a man has cut down a tree, it
belongs to him. Likewise, fruit and ochre when gathered are
individual possessions of the person who collects them. All
members of a communal hunt may claim a portion of the bag,
and a special joint of every pig snared is reserved for the man who
has provided the snares, even if he has taken no part in the hunt.

People seldom venture into the forest land of districts other
than their own, because the occasion for doing this rarely arises.
If they should do so, their action is likely to lead to suspicion that
they are there for some evil purpose, such as adultery or sorcery,
since it is assumed that they can have no legitimate business on
forest land other than their own.

The same principles apply to the sago swamps, which provide
thatch and farinaceous food, except that here the rights are
exercised by the village instead of the district. The question
whether a man might take produce from the sago swamps of
another village is regarded by the natives as foolish—why should
they go on a journey when they need only take a short walk?
Much the same applies to questions asked by the ethnographer
regarding the ownership of rock outcrops and patches of poor soil,
to which the natives replied: "Do you say that the ash which falls
from your cigarette is yours—that no one else may touch it?"

Building sites.—Each village is inhabited by two (or rarely
three) clans, at the head of each of which is a headman (*kokwal*)
who has a subordinate or deputy (*ngaro*). Ties of loyalty and day-
to-day co-operation are determined more by common residence
than by kinship, though for the most part these coincide, owing
to patrilineal descent and inheritance of agricultural land,
coupled with patrilocal marriage. But this is not universally
followed. A man with much land may hand over some of it to a
favourite daughter, in which case he insists that her husband
should come to the village to live. In this case the children are
associated with their mother's father's clan, with the same
privileges as if they were descendants in the patrilineal line. This
is not, however, the case when a man voluntarily comes to live in
his wife's village owing to friendship for her kinsmen, quarrels

with his own, or ill-health, which is always attributed to evil magic. In such cases the man receives no land of his own, and the children revert at maturity to membership of their father's clan.

The rule regarding building sites is that a man has a right to build a house in the village nearest to the agricultural land which he is entitled to cultivate. In the case of matrilocal marriage dictated by the woman's father's wishes, the husband acquires full rights in his wife's village. When matrilocal residence is due to free choice, it is a temporary arrangement, and his sons finally migrate back to their father's village.

The position of widows in this residential system varies according to circumstances. The widow of a headman is expected not to re-marry, and to remain in her deceased husband's village, where food is provided for her by her sons and her husband's brothers. Widows of ordinary men have a choice of residence. If they decide to return to their parents' village, they may take their young children with them, but these are expected to return at puberty to their father's village. This obligation, however, is sometimes neglected when the widow's brothers have surplus land which they are prepared to allocate to her children.

Each village contains a men's house (*niabwa*), a more impressive structure than ordinary dwellings, which serves as a club, meeting-house, a store for sacred objects and sleeping quarters for the unmarried men. All men in the village, and their close relatives from elsewhere, have an obligation to help in the construction of a *niabwa*. These are the only people who have a right to enter without invitation.

In the construction of dwelling-houses a man is helped by his fellow-clansmen, who are given a meal at the end of each day and a feast at the conclusion of the work. Fellow-clansmen assisting in this way have a right to demand a return in kind at a later date, and this is their principal motive in rendering assistance. The house is the husband's property—he may destroy it in anger if he wishes. But he must then provide another, for he has an obligation to provide shelter for his wife and family. In polygynous households each wife has her own portion of the dwelling beyond which she is not supposed to go. The husband visits each wife in turn. Only bond-friends and close kin may enter the house without permission.

Usually each clan occupies one end of the village, with the *niabwa* in the middle, but a choice of site is allowed, subject to the rule that the headman of the village may intervene if the proposed location is likely to cause inconvenience to others. A man usually chooses to build alongside his father's dwelling, or if the latter be dead, upon the identical site. One spot in the village, adjoining the *niabwa*, where materials employed in ceremonies are thrown after use, is avoided by both sexes. The beach adjoining the village is divided among the branches of the clans, but the boundaries are not precisely defined nor is any objection raised to trespass. A man normally draws up his canoe on the portion of beach associated with his branch of the clan, but in the season when gales are frequent, all canoes may be drawn up in the most sheltered section of the beach.

Agricultural land.—The whole of the coastal belt of the island, with the exception of village sites, marshes and waste land, is used for cultivation. No manures are employed, nor is rotation of crops practised. Plots must therefore be left to lie fallow for about ten years after cultivation. The soil is rich, and provides plentiful supplies of taro, bananas and other crops throughout the year. Coco-nuts are available perennially, and there is an annual harvest of Canarium almonds and other nuts. The importance attached to the produce of the land is exemplified in the custom of calling a good strain of taro after the man who developed it, and of naming trees after the man who looked after them during the earliest years of their growth.

The belt of coast flanking each village for about a third of a mile on each side is known by the name of the village—for example, "the ground of the Dap folk"—while the villagers distinguish sections of the land associated with the two component clans. These sections are subdivided into named allotments, boundaries being fixed by crests of hills, streams, pathways, boulders or trees. Great care is taken to train children in a knowledge of the names and approximate limits of these allotments, and most adults know the boundaries of all allotments in their district.

Some of the allotments are large (about twelve acres) and some much smaller, different rules of land tenure applying to the respective types. In the case of a large allotment, all members of the clan in whose territory it occurs, and their close blood relatives living elsewhere, have an equal right to cultivate a portion. After the fallow period the headman either clears a portion himself or permits another man to do so, others following on as new gardens are required. The clan does not collaborate in clearing the area, and neither the group as a whole nor any member of it has the power to determine the size or location of portions selected for cultivation. When a man has selected a site, no one may take it from him, and his crop is private property.

The large allotments are used exclusively for cultivation, but the smaller ones are valued also for their fruit and nut trees. The smaller allotments constitute the bulk of the agricultural land. Apart from occasional cases of joint cultivation by fathers and sons or by brothers, every adult male claims from ten to twenty allotments from which he takes the crops which he cultivates and also collects fruit and nuts. His right to such produce is individual and absolute, and he may dispose of it as he wishes, subject to certain customary obligations and privileges. Thus a man will not object if a kinsman takes coco-nuts from his trees, provided that a statement of the number taken is made afterwards, and of course he may claim a similar privilege in return. Protection against imposition or deliberate theft is provided by putting a taboo sign near the land and reciting spells, which are believed to bring illness to the culprit. Some fruits, such as pawpaws, are so common that it is not thought worth while to ask permission to take them.

Agriculture demands a certain amount of co-operation, but there is no organized gardening team. A man asks for the assistance of his neighbours, giving them a meal and returning the favour at a later date. Most of the land surrounding a village belongs to the villagers, though outsiders sometimes have rights to parts of it as a result of matrilocal marriages and other anomalies.

Disputes over boundaries are rare, since the limits of these are well known to the villagers, to whom appeal may be made. In one dispute over three self-sown almond trees, one of the claimants ringbarked the three trees to end the quarrel, since kinsmen should not squabble. The other, a bad-tempered man, retaliated by ringbarking three of the first man's trees. It was agreed that the first man had the better claim, but, though he won universal sympathy, no further action was taken. In another similar dispute the trees were also killed "so that the anger, by dying in the forest, might leave the village at peace". It is stated that if such a dispute should lead to an open breach, the headman would intervene, either by a formal decision as to ownership, or by ordering the trees to be destroyed.

Inheritance.—The right to practise agriculture and to collect

S.A. I—21

fruit and nuts normally passes from a father to his sons, to each of whom several plots are given during childhood, and more are subsequently allocated until the rights to all have been given up. The father is expected to be fair in this, though his two eldest sons usually receive more than the others. If a man dies while his sons are still young, his brother holds the land in trust for them.

After a man has declared which plots will be inherited by each of his heirs, his death is never followed by disputes between them. But the sudden death of a man who has not declared his wishes may be followed by serious quarrels. The eldest son in such cases is supposed to make a suitable distribution, but sometimes the younger sons are dissatisfied. In such cases the dispute is settled by elder relatives or by appeal to the headman.

This system means a disadvantage for persons descended from a long line of men, each of whom was the member of a large family. Men thus handicapped may appeal to relatives or to the headman to allow them the use of some of their land. In such cases the original owner receives a small portion of the harvest, not as rent, but in recognition of his kindness and the fact that "the man who cares for the trees is a stranger to the land". Rights of usufruct acquired in this way may be passed on to heirs, though it is said that the descendants of the original owner who permitted the planting of trees might cut them down without giving compensation. It is stated, however, that a man would need grave provocation to do this. A man who has the right to cultivate more land than he needs may, with the approval of his near kinsfolk, transfer some of it to some particularly unfortunate distant relative. Such voluntary transfer demands no return.

As there is no shortage of land in Wogeo, wars over land are unknown. Rivalry between districts is keen, and cases of theft and adultery have in the past led to fights; but these were never followed by territorial readjustments or changes in the normal sequence of inheritance.

Marriage and land.—The only persons, apart from legitimate heirs, to whom land may be handed over in perpetuity are daughters, who are sometimes given land as a dowry. Such women do not take the land for their private use, but entrust it to their husbands. In these circumstances the man uses the land in the normal way for the benefit of the whole family, but he has no personal claims. In the case of divorce, all land rights revert to the wife. A man using dowry land is expected to hand over some of the produce to his wife's father or brother. Such land is inherited by the woman's son, usually the eldest, but the obligation to hand over produce to her relatives is not passed on. There is a strong feeling that dowry land should ultimately revert to the patrilineal group to which it originally belonged, and marriages are often arranged so as to effect this. For example, a man who has inherited land from his mother may give it as a dowry to his daughter and marry her to his mother's brother's son's son. Sometimes the return may be delayed for a generation, and may be effected by a woman being given the land as dowry and marrying her father's father's mother's brother's son's son's son (Fig. 18).

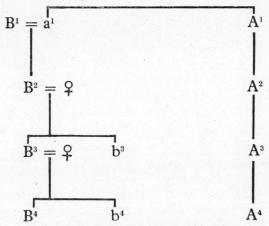

FIG. 18.—Reversion of Dowry Land in Wogeo

In the first instance, a woman a^1 of clan A marries B^1 of clan B and is given dowry land which passes to her son, B^2. This land may be made to revert to clan A as dowry land either by marrying b^3 to A^3 or by marrying b^4 to A^4.

A man who inherits from his mother also has rights, under patrilineal inheritance, to land in his father's village. The situation may sooner or later be resolved by two brothers separating, one cultivating the dowry land and the other taking up the patrilineal inheritance in another village.

Women and land.—Land is regarded primarily as the men's affair. This does not imply loss of status by women, since they have their own spheres of activity, such as cooking and care of the house, from which men are excluded. Men and women share equally in agricultural work, but control over land is exercised by the men, who make all decisions regarding its use and dis-

posal. Women, however, have definite claims in regard to land—
they must be given sufficient plots by their husbands to maintain
the family food supply. Widows returning to their own people are
likewise entitled to claim the use of land from their brothers, and
this may also occur in the case of divorce.

Inheritance by distant relatives.—If a man dies leaving no male
heir, his land goes to his daughter. In such cases, however, and
also when a man has no children at all, the difficulty is often forestalled by adoption, which is practised by the majority of childless couples. If this does not occur, cultivation rights of a childless
man pass to his nearest male kinsman, stress being laid on priority
of birth. Relationship in this case may include a female, though
the patrilineal principle takes priority. The system of inheritance
is identical with the rule of succession in the Royal Family in
England, except that in Wogeo women rarely actually hold the
property, whereas in the English monarchy they may succeed to
the title.

Though this is the officially correct legal rule, it is frequently
varied in practice, for there is a tendency for the property of a
man who dies without male heirs to be confiscated by the headman. This would never occur if there were a male heir. High-
handed action by the headman in such cases is condemned but
usually accepted in practice. There is some justification for it,
since a headman, having more wives and therefore a larger
family than a commoner, normally needs more land. Furthermore, his official position entails more calls on his generosity, and
his authority in the village is largely dependent upon his wealth.
In order to meet his obligations, the headman has the right to
demand help from his clansmen in agricultural work—they spend
an average of one day in eight in his service. At the time of village
feasts, the headman may prohibit the gathering of certain crops
to ensure an adequate supply for all guests—the only occasion
when any person is permitted to interfere with the harvest of
another.

Land tenure and religion.—Wogeo land tenure is influenced by
beliefs in certain spiritual beings called *nanarangs*. These are of
several types, but certain types only are connected with land
tenure.

In native thought Wogeo is the centre of the earth, and has
always existed. It is likewise the cradle of the human race. In
the beginning it was surrounded by empty sea and was populated

exclusively by *nanarangs*. Several of these sailed away in canoes, eventually changing themselves into new lands—the mainland of New Guinea and neighbouring islands—which represent parts of their bodies. The *nanarangs* left behind on Wogeo instituted all social customs and technical practices, which were subsequently taken over from them by human beings, whose origin is obscure. After the appearance of human beings on Wogeo, the *nanarangs* disappeared, but before they did so they created the inhabitants of all other places. When natives of Wogeo meet people from other areas, whose cosmogony is different, they dismiss their beliefs with contempt: "They are so stupid that they even deny the truth of what we tell them". The insular myths of Wogeo provide a charter for its occupation by its present inhabitants, much as in civilized countries national history is often used to provide a justification for traditional boundaries and national aspirations.

Other *nanarangs*, who were responsible for the details of Wogeo topography, probably provide a similar charter for the division of the island into districts. Each district has its own set, and its members refer to these as "our own *nanarangs*". These beings created the natural features of the several districts, and a moral tale is associated with such acts of creation. They also gave the knowledge of particular varieties of magic to the inhabitants of their own districts, who have the exclusive right to practise them.

Finally, another group of *nanarangs* left commemorative blocks of stone in each village (Fig. 17), and handed over the rights to building sites and agricultural land to the patrilineal ancestors of the present inhabitants. The large blocks of stone are associated with the land rights and rank of headmen and their deputies. They are surrounded by a pavement of smaller stones—the "*nanarang*-helpers"—which provide a vague sort of authority for the land rights of commoners.

"*Title Deeds*."—Though the natives of Wogeo are illiterate, the inhabitants of each village have material embodiments to their claims to particular allotments of garden land in the *niabwa* (men's house). When a *niabwa* is constructed, each rafter is lashed in place by one male villager, or occasionally two. This gives them a title to particular garden land, and the privilege of lashing a particular rafter is passed on from father to son. The legal association of lashing the rafter and cultivation rights is clearly recognized in native statements, for example, "I fasten this rafter; that is why I have gardens in those plots".

The sentimental value of land.—The culturally defined relationship of a Wogeo native to his land is supplemented by a sentimental attachment. Old people like to work in the gardens as long
as they can, even after they have ceased to be of practical assistance—it was said of an old woman: "She wishes to have earth
upon her hands until she dies". A dying man will sometimes ask
to be carried on a stretcher around his garden plots, so that he
may look for the last time upon the land he has tilled so often.
The fact that a man cultivates certain land is expressed by the
native term "he watches over it", the same phrase as is used in
connection with caring for children. A man will often "watch
over" his land in another village, even when this entails considerable inconvenience. This has a supernatural justification: "We
wish to use all the land, to till it everywhere. The *nanarangs* used
all their allotments and we follow them."

3. Nyakyusa Land Tenure

The Nyakyusa, a Bantu tribe of southern Tanganyika, are
divided into about a hundred small but traditionally independent
chiefdoms. The many streams running from the north into Lake
Nyasa and the crests of the ridges between them form natural
boundaries between the chiefdoms. On the lower ground to the
south, the land is more fertile than on the higher ground to the
north, parts of which are stony and mountainous, though there
are many old volcanic craters which are filled with rich soil and
which are greatly valued by the Nyakyusa.

Uses of Nyakyusa land.—The Nyakyusa use their land for building on, for agriculture, for pasture, for hunting and fishing; they
collect firewood, reeds, thatching-grass, mushrooms and other
wild vegetables there; they draw water from its streams and bathe
daily in them; on their land they grow bamboos, bananas,
syunguti trees and coffee; they keep bees; they dance, they fight,
they walk and lie down upon it; their land is both the receptacle
of refuse and the location of religious ritual, while their doctors
continually wander over its surface in search of magical medicines.

Not all these uses of land give rise to laws, moral rules or conventions, but only those uses which tend to lead men into conflict
with one another or into mutual embarrassment. The only
reasons for the existence of rules of land tenure are firstly to
prevent, as far as possible, such conflicts and embarrassments
from arising, and secondly, to facilitate their resolution when

aroused. If, then, there is no danger of conflict or embarrassment, neither is there a need for any rule at all.

Scarcity of land is a matter of quality rather than quantity, though in the future the Nyakyusa may be afflicted by land shortage as a result of the development of export crops. At the moment it is the *best* land which is scarce, not land as such.

The Nyakyusa practise intensive cultivation with rotation of crops. The success of this method is due partly to the variety of their crops and partly to their extensive knowledge of the uses and potentialities of different varieties of soil, both for agriculture and pasturage. Thus, although the cattle are herded during the daytime by small boys, a man always goes out with them in the morning to show them where the cattle may best be pastured.

Though the value of land is primarily determined by utilitarian considerations, sentiment also plays a part. Other things being equal, a man prefers to make his gardens where he or his father and brothers have done so before, and to build his house on a site which has family associations. Religious beliefs also play a part. One man who did not move to his father's site on the latter's death subsequently suffered a failure of his millet crop. This was attributed by a diviner to the anger of the father's spirit because no one had "swept his grave". The man did not actually move, for he preferred his own site, but he performed a ritual sacrifice to propitiate his father's spirit. In such cases a man will often move to his dead father's site for fear of further misfortune.

Land tenure and social organization.—The system of land tenure of the Nyakyusa is intimately bound up with their local and political organization. They are predominantly patrilineal. Inheritance is in the male line, but goes to brothers before sons. Inherited wealth is thus in the hands of the older men, though these have obligations towards their sons, both real and classificatory. For example, a man must provide *lobola* cattle both for his own sons and for the sons of any man from whom he has inherited. In return the son must hoe his father's fields and maintain a respectful bearing towards him. In cultivation, hoeing is done by men, and planting, weeding and reaping by women. Polygyny is the rule rather than the exception among middle-aged men, each wife having her own garden plot. Polygyny is an economic advantage—the more wives and children a man has, the more wealth can he produce.

Boys leave their father's village at the age of about eleven, and build together a new village nearby on ground allocated to them by the parent village. It is not regarded as decent for a boy to sleep at home as he approaches puberty. Between the age of about eleven and marriage (which takes place in the late twenties) the youth lives with his bachelor friends in the new village. At marriage he brings his wife to live with him. As the members of a village grow older, younger boys begin to be refused admittance, and are forced to start a new settlement of their own. Each village is thus in origin an age-group, but its population

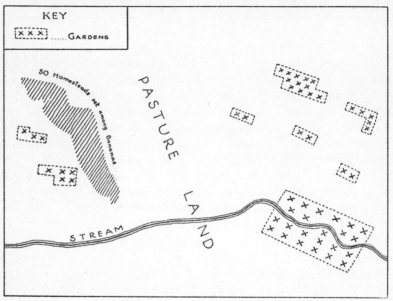

FIG. 19.—A typical village of the Nyakyusa

may be augmented by men (and their families) who are not exact contemporaries, by the sons of dead villagers, and by strangers, who are never refused admittance on the ground of age. Villages on an average number from forty to fifty households. The plan of a typical village is given in Fig. 19.

Every generation each chiefdom is divided into halves. This is based on the Nyakyusa practice of chiefs having two "great wives". When a chief begins to grow old, the sons of his respective great wives are ceremonially "brought out" and recognized as chiefs, though they do not assume full powers until their father's death. Traditionally they assumed authority over the "young" villages in their half of the chiefdom as soon as they were "brought out". Sometimes, however, two such chiefs would fight, and one would become subordinate to the other, most of the subordinate chief's subjects going over to the more powerful and wealthy chief who could afford to give more feasts to his warriors. A subordinate chief might thus end his days in authority over one village only, composed of the remnants of the original four to eight. In such cases only one son would succeed.

Each village has a headman,[1] selected for his wealth and ability by the older headmen of the chiefdom. In the boys' villages they are selected by the headmen on their side of the chiefdom, and if they prove satisfactory, their appointment is confirmed at the "coming out". If not, another candidate is selected. From this stage onwards they hold office for life.

At the "coming out" the young headmen are ritually treated with medicines to give them the power of witchcraft which they are expected to use in the interests of morality, while the young chiefs are treated with medicines to make them fierce and impressive themselves, and to ensure the fertility of their land and the prosperity of the people under them.

It should be noted that the above system has been changed under European influence. The Administration does not recognize the authority of an heir until after his father's death, and only one chief is officially recognized, his co-heir being subordinate to him. In Christian villages elders and deacons take the place of headmen.

Land rights within the "homestead".—The land in and near the homestead, which may consist of the houses of several wives, may be classified as:

1. The house site itself.
2. The adjoining portion of the open space.
3. Adjoining banana groves.
4. Garden plots allocated to wives by husbands.
5. *Busongo* plots and banana trees (optional).

A plan of the first three of these is shown in Fig. 20 and the division of a typical bean garden in Fig. 21.

The garden plots are hoed by groups of male villagers, and each wife plants, weeds and reaps her own plots, allocated to her by

---

[1] This more common word has been substituted for the term "Great Commoner" used by Wilson.

her husband. Rights to garden produce vary according to the nature of the crop. Millet and rice belong exclusively to the husband. In the case of other crops, the woman is the effective owner, subject to specific obligations. She must feed her children and her husband from time to time. She must also prepare meals for his guests and provide him with cooked food to present as gifts. She normally does these things willingly in order to retain his affection and in return for his obligations towards her —he builds her house, hoes her garden, and provides her with a

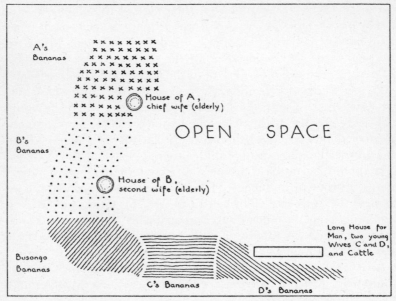

FIG. 20.—The homestead of a rich man among the Nyakyusa

share of the household milk. But if this system of co-operation breaks down, there are sanctions which operate. A quarrel may develop and he may strike her, or she may refuse conjugal rights. In such cases the injured party may appeal to neighbours for support. The neighbours censure one or the other, or try to make it up between them. If this fails, one party may claim compensation in court. Or it may happen that, without any quarrel or formal appeal to neighbours, one party becomes aware that his or her conduct is provoking mockery or criticism, and mends his or her ways. Or if one or other falls ill, he or she may attribute this misfortune to spiritual retribution in the form of witchcraft.

Subject to the obligations mentioned above, a woman may use her own crops to entertain friends, and to make gifts to her relations, without consulting her husband. Co-wives may entertain one another, but there are no obligations between them. If a woman's crop fails, her co-wives may refuse to assist her, though they usually do so out of charity, pity for her children, or in deference to the husband's wishes.

Each wife weeds and sweeps the portion of the open space adjoining her house, though her husband may assist her. Pride is

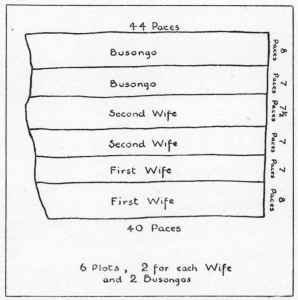

FIG. 21.—A typical bean garden among the Nyakyusa

an important motive in this activity. She must keep her banana trees free of weeds, and the bunches of fruit are her own property —not even her husband may cut them without consulting her.

The husband in a polygynous homestead must make a fair division of land and banana trees between his wives. He always has a favourite wife, but he must not show favouritism towards her. If he does, the injured wife or wives may spread whispering complaints among the people, and this may bring witches to kill him or the favoured wife. Or the offended wife may sulk and refuse to plant. Or she may appeal to her own family, who will accept her back if they are convinced that she has been ill-treated.

The disposal of surplus crops differs according to whether a husband has reserved *busongo* plots and banana trees for himself. If he has, all his wives co-operate in planting, weeding and reaping such plots, but the crops are entirely his own. Conversely, each woman has an absolute right to dispose of all the surplus of her own plots—her husband cannot touch them at all. But if the husband has reserved no *busongo* plots for himself, the surplus of each wife's plot is owned jointly with him. Neither can dispose of it in large quantities without consulting the other; neither can be denied the right to dispose of it for any urgent need. The same principles apply to the disposal of surplus crops for cash.

The most important reason for the *busongo* system is the lack of affection and generosity of women towards their married step-children.[1] If the married children of a dead wife come to visit their father, they frequently receive scanty entertainment and go away empty-handed. To guard against this, some men reserve *busongo* plots from the crops of which they can draw without argument. In addition, *busongo* plots are useful to meet the demands of the chief and to secure the household against a shortage of food.

The obligations of sons in regard to hoeing vary from one household to another. Sometimes sons hoe the plots of their own mothers only, sometimes father and sons work as a team hoeing the plots of each wife in turn. Provision of meals follows the same pattern as the hoeing. The custom of hoeing may be determined by lack of friendliness between the women, by the slackness of the husband, or by inadequate provision of food by co-wives. Under the system of separate hoeing, a woman who has no sons may be forced to call in people from outside the homestead, rewarding them for their services by the provision of food.

When a man dies, his widows pass to his heir, with the exception of the heir's own mother, who may be given to a half-brother. Or the heir may build for her at a little distance and look after her. In such cases she is treated, in matters of land tenure, as a wife. A man often supports an old woman—mother, mother-in-law or elder sister—whose husband is still alive, but is unable to hoe for her, and who has no unmarried sons. He may either hoe for her on her husband's land or assign her a plot or two of his own.

---

[1] It should be noted that *unmarried* motherless children, who from the age of six or so are economically useful, do not present the same problem as married ones. They are allotted to one of the other wives, and this is facilitated by the practice of a man marrying two sisters.

The gardens of a household are not only worked by its members. Both husband and wife invite neighbours to help them with their respective tasks, rewarding them with food and, in the case of men, with beer.

When a man inherits his dead father's wealth, he assumes the position of father towards his younger unmarried brothers—he is responsible for their marriages, and they hoe for him just as do unmarried sons. Young married men are expected occasionally to help their wives' fathers, particularly if they are behindhand with *lobola* payments. When the work is finished, they are entertained as sumptuously as neighbours. The son of a poor man will often attach himself to the household of a rich kinsman—for example, a brother of his father or mother—and hoe regularly for him. The kinsman thus acquires an obligation to help with his *lobola*.

The above account of the land rights of the household must be supplemented by reference to the rights of the village and of the chief, for Nyakyusa land tenure consists of an interlocking of these rights. The rights and obligations of land tenure are essentially personal in character, for among small and isolated communities such as those of the Nyakyusa there are few or no impersonal relationships.

As stated above, the boys of each village set up a new village on land assigned to them by the parent village, the allocation being made by the headman in consultation with other villagers. At first building sites only are allocated, but as the youths grow up and marry, these are supplemented by garden land. The boundaries of the village are confirmed at its "coming out", which coincides with that of its future chief.

Individual land rights in relation to the village and the chief.—Individual land rights in relation to those of the village are best seen in cases in which a man moves from one village to another. Such moves are fairly frequent, owing to the magico-religious beliefs of the Nyakyusa. Sickness or other misfortunes in a household are frequently attributed to the witchcraft of neighbours. This witchcraft cannot operate at a distance. Traditionally, the victim might have the witch identified and expelled from the chiefdom. Nowadays, his only course of action is to move, either to another village within the chiefdom, or to another chiefdom. It is estimated that 80 per cent. of pagan Nyakyusa have at some time moved away from the villages in which they first cultivated gardens. The man who moves may stay away only a few weeks, a matter of months or years, or permanently. Usually his neighbours go after him, perhaps several times, and try to persuade him to return—this is an expression of friendship designed to allay his suspicions and to clear them of the slur of witchcraft. A man can always return to his original village even if he has not been invited, unless he himself has been expelled for witchcraft or some other offence. The majority of people who move do eventually return, particularly if they suffer ill-health or misfortune in their new village, or are slighted by the villagers.

A stranger moving to a new village is normally granted land by the headman of the village, not by the chief, who is informed but seldom interferes. It may be said that "the chief gave him the land", but this is merely a figure of speech, a polite recognition of the chief's overlordship. In practice the headman grants land on , his behalf, but also acting for the villagers. It is incorrect for the chief to grant land directly, except in very unusual circumstances. Thus, only a member of the chief's own family or a very important stranger may approach the chief directly, and the chief may then exercise his right of overlordship. In other cases he is restrained from making improper grants of land, not only by public opinion, but also by fear lest the headmen and villagers may bewitch him. All this illustrates the danger of relying too much on verbal statements of custom in regard to land tenure.

Strangers are normally welcomed because men are scarcer than land and a new member helps to bring prestige and prosperity to a village. The precision with which a new-comer's land is demarcated depends upon the value and scarcity of the land concerned.

The position is different in the case of a man returning to his original village. He has a claim to enter again into possession of his old building site and gardens, but this claim is not absolute— it depends on his relationship to the villagers and to the chief. Thus, if he has been expelled for witchcraft, he has no claim. If he returns before his house has fallen into disrepair, or a new house has been built on the site, the person to whom the site has been temporarily allocated will be evicted. Such persons should be told, when the site is allocated to them, that their tenure is conditional upon the original owner remaining away. But sometimes this is not done—the villagers may be indifferent to his return or he may have been away so long, and may have refused so many invitations to return, that they have come to regard his absence as permanent. If the new-comer has thus been given the site unconditionally, and if he has built his own house upon it, the villagers cannot evict him. The original owner may appeal to the chief as overlord, and the latter may or may not evict the new-comer. In the latter case the original owner will have to build elsewhere, and in any case he may prefer to do this rather than to dispute the matter. The same principles apply to garden land with the following *de facto* reservations: (i) a man will only seek the eviction of the new-comer in the case of scarce or valuable land; (ii) it is easier to get back old gardens than old building sites, since it involves less hardship for the evicted man; (iii) a man may claim the garden sites of his father, even if he has never hoed them himself. But the last type of claim is more difficult to establish— it may be refused or the land may be divided between the claimant and the present possessors.

Three features of the customs governing the return of people to their own chiefdoms are: (i) that the chief may take the initiative in inviting a man to return, (ii) that he may widen the invitation to include all villages of his chiefdom, and (iii) that a man may live in one village and cultivate gardens in another. Thus, one man so invited by the chief refused to return to live in the village where he had suffered misfortune. He continued to cultivate his gardens there, but took up residence in a neighbouring village.

When a man moves from his village, his land rights pass temporarily to the headman and his fellow-villagers. But an exceptionally valuable plot of land may be claimed immediately on his departure by his nearest kinsman—it is not clear whether the latter can subsequently be evicted as described above. A man who moves may reap his standing crops when they ripen, but his building site and bananas revert to the village immediately. Neighbours care for the banana trees and eat the fruit until the site is reallocated—the man may ask for bananas from them if there are none at his new home, but he receives them as a favour and not as a right—his request may be refused if he is unpopular and the villagers do not wish him to return.

When a man dies, his heir takes his wives, his cattle and his movable property and, if he comes to live in the dead man's village, his land also. But if he remains in his own village, he has no rights over the dead man's land.

Pasture-land.—In the case of pasture-land adjoining a village, all villagers have a right to graze their cattle on it. The headman, in consultation with his neighbours, may also grant grazing rights to outsiders. Members of the village taking up new garden land must be careful not to encroach unduly on the village pastures.

Ownership of indigenous trees.—Indigenous trees, other than bananas, are of two kinds—bamboos, and fruit trees known as *syunguti*. There are also trees, of which coffee is the principal one, introduced by Europeans. Ownership of indigenous trees is complicated by the fact that different groups of Nyakyusa have two different systems of rights.

Under the one system, ownership resembles that connected with exceptionally valuable garden plots. When a man moves, rights to the use of his trees do not revert to the villagers, but are taken up by his nearest kinsman in the chiefdom concerned. If the man's building site is given over to a new-comer, this man has no right to use the trees unless given permission by the kinsman. In the case of *syunguti* trees the kinsman often does not bother to exercise his rights, and in this case they are treated in the same way as banana trees. Bamboos are men's property and only a man can claim them, but *syunguti* trees may be claimed by a kins-woman. If a man moves without leaving kinsfolk near at hand, the chief, as supreme overlord, has a right to the trees, and if they are near to the chief's home the right is exercised. If a new-comer moves to the site, he goes and asks the chief for some trees and the chief usually divides the *syunguti* trees between himself and the new resident. But bamboos, the more valuable of the two types, he usually keeps for himself. If the trees are at some distance from the chief's residence, he normally does not claim the *syunguti* trees, but only the bamboos, leaving the former to be used by the villagers meantime and subsequently handed over to a new-comer. Even bamboos may sometimes be ceded by a "good chief" in this way.

Under the other system *syunguti* trees are treated like bananas. When a man moves they revert, not to a kinsman, but to the village, subject to the rule that the chief may claim them if he so desires. Bamboos, however, pass to the nearest kinsman. It is uncertain whether here also the chief has an option.

Trees introduced by Europeans.—It has been ruled by the Federation of Chiefs that coffee trees, and other introduced trees, are the property of the planter, even if he has moved to another chiefdom.

But this has required modification in the case of coffee, since these trees require constant care if they are to remain free from pests and bear fruit. So the man who tends the trees has an admitted claim to the crop unless he is paid by the planter for his labour. However, the planter, on surrendering the trees to him, may compel him to pay something for their initial value. Sometimes the Agricultural Department takes over the trees and cares for them by paid labour. Profits from subsequent sales go to the native treasury.

Chiefs and commoners.—The interlocking rights and obligations of chiefs and commoners in regard to land form part of a wider system of reciprocity. When a new-comer arrives in a village, the chief is not only nominally a party to the granting of land to him, but also in most cases extends a ceremonial welcome to someone who comes from outside his chiefdom by sending him a present of cooked food. He has gained a new subject and his power and prestige are thereby increased. The chief has certain traditionally defined rights. Commoners must provide cooked food for ceremonies in the chief's own immediate family, such as the marriage of his daughter. The right is not so much legal as reciprocal and conventional—the chief is expected in return to kill one or two beasts, and if he is mean in this regard, commoners will be reluctant to bring food in future. The commoners are constrained to carry out their obligations by the public opinion of their fellow-villagers. Failure to meet their obligations towards the chief occasions adverse comment in the village. The chief has a traditional right to demand food, particularly milk and bananas, from his subjects.[1] This right is not nowadays recognized by the Administration, on the ground that the chief receives a salary of about 10s. per month, though this is not commensurate with the rights which he originally exercised. These rights, however, are still very largely observed in practice.

The chief had a traditional right to evict any subject if he desired the man's site for his own use, but he was obliged to provide alternative accommodation. This right is now abrogated, but a chief may still take any unoccupied site for himself or for a kinsman. It is only if he gives the site to an ordinary commoner than his action will be criticized. Land allotted by the chief is associated with a greater security of tenure, for even if the tenant moves away, the land may not be reallocated by the headman without his permission or that of the chief.

---

[1] Cf. what has been said above about *busongo* bananas.

4. The Scientific Study of Land Tenure

From our review of two primitive systems of land tenure we may now abstract certain general principles of interpretation. The first of these is that legally enforced rules of land tenure emerge and become significant only when there is competition for land and its resources. The function of such rules is to regulate the differential claims of individuals who are, actually or potentially, in competition with each other. Where land is valueless or its resources abundant, there is no need for the legal definition of conflicting claims to the land itself. But the distribution of resources won from it is nevertheless the subject of customary rules, as in the case of forest land in Wogeo. Similarly, even waste land, streams and geographical features which are not economically significant may nevertheless be important in the total scheme of land tenure because of their sentimental or magico-religious associations.

The second principle which emerges is the importance of the preliminary definition of land tenure in terms of verbally formulated claims to specific areas of territory. This is particularly important in field-work. It is the point at which modern ethnographers begin and where the older ones left off. One can obtain from informants verbal statements such as "this land is my brother's", "this plot belongs to my extended family", "this field belongs to my wife's clan", or "all land belongs to the chief". All such formulations are partial statements of the truth, each by itself is misleading. Thus we have seen how among the Nyakyusa the titular ownership of land by the chief is an important factor, particularly in regard to trees and traditional claims to tribute; but we have also seen to what extent this titular ownership is modified by the claims of other individuals in the community.

This brings us to our third principle of interpretation, namely, the economic rights and obligations in regard to the use of land and its resources. In our own society a man may own a piece of land and leave it unused. In primitive society the ownership of land is always conditioned by actual use, and some claims are exercised by virtue of productive effort expended upon it. This is often done collectively, and the claims to the products of economic effort are exercised by several individuals, and are defined by the kinship relationships existing between them, and by their sex, rank and age.

The fourth and most important principle in the study of land tenure is the integration of verbally defined rights and economic claims with the whole cultural framework, so far as this is concerned with the regulation of the relationship between man and his land. As we have seen, the verbal statements of legal rights by themselves may be mutually contradictory and misleading. Likewise, a mere inventory of natural resources and a bald statement of how these are divided among members of the community refers only to the material aspect of land tenure, and gives no idea of the basic cultural doctrines which govern its operation. The principles of kinship and family organization, the traditional recognition of the prerogatives of rank, and magico-religious beliefs defining man's relation to his land must be recognized as the dynamic forces giving validity to legal claims and customary principles of economic exchange and distribution. It must be emphasized that the nature and method of operation of such cultural doctrines vary from one system of land tenure to another. Thus, the permanent occupation of land by specific groups in Wogeo is sanctioned partly by mythology and its visible embodiment in the *nanarang* stones. Such a doctrine does not operate, and indeed could not operate, in the more mobile community of the Nyakyusa. But even here it should be noted that it is an activity within the magico-religious sphere—namely, witchcraft—which determines the mobility itself. The relevance of this to the system of land tenure will be seen if we consider what might be expected to happen if the belief in witchcraft should decay. Under these circumstances we would expect less migration and the principle of more or less permanent residence would increase in importance compared with the distributive powers of the headmen, which would necessarily be exercised to a lesser extent.

The scientific approach to the problems of primitive land tenure outlined in this section is more than a heuristic device for the theorist and a useful recipe for the practical man who desires to achieve an enlightened understanding of native land tenure as a means to progressive native development. It gives us an appreciation of what land means to the native in terms, not only of law and economics, but also of the subtle and intangible values resting upon the experiences of everyday life, on sentimental attachment and on magico-religious belief. For the native, his land is not merely that which provides his livelihood and the environment in which he is born, grows up, loves, hates and dies. It is culturally evaluated in terms of mythology and tribal history, it is the place where generations of men and women have preceded him and where others will follow him after his own individual death, a conception summarized in the Maori proverb: "Man perishes, but the land remains".

5. The Fiction of Primitive Communism

In dealing with various phases of primitive economic life, we have on several occasions pointed out the misleading implications of the term "primitive communism". These implications have led to more muddle-headed thinking in relation to land tenure than in any other field.

Most primitive communities—even those with a relatively complex political and economic organization—have at some time or other been described as "communistic"; the existence of individual ownership has been denied; or it has been said that land is owned "communally" or, what amounts to the same thing, "by the tribe" or "by the clan". Such statements contribute nothing to ethnographic knowledge—on the contrary, they tend to prevent the detailed study of recondite problems of primitive economics and law which modern field-work has shown to be necessary. They obscure the complicated network of definitely *individual* rights and obligations which arise from membership of family, household, clan and tribe, and from participation in the activities of social institutions, particularly those connected with the production, exchange and consumption of food and material wealth.

The complex ramifications of such systems of rights and obligations give the superficial observer some ground for speaking of natives as living "communistically". This affirmation crops up over and over again in quasi-anthropological works. It sounds impressive, even though it is in fact a confession of ignorance. Furthermore, it accords well with certain European values, oddly enough of a contrasting kind. From the point of view of European economic interests, the statement that the native has a communistic attitude towards land interprets his motives and aspirations in a way quite alien to European thought. It puts the occupation of native lands by Europeans in a category different from downright trespass, which it would be if land were owned "individually". At the other extreme, kindly and well-meaning people are all too ready to contrast "primitive communism" with the manifestations of greed and acquisitiveness found in civilized society, and even to find in it a paradigm of the Christian life.

The dogma of primitive communism, however, is not merely a popular fallacy. It was accepted by many of the earlier ethnographers and theoretical anthropologists. Thus Rivers speaks of "the great extent to which communistic sentiments concerning property dominate the people of Melanesia". Of Bantu communities, very different from those of Melanesia, we find such statements as that all such things as "food, beer, private earnings, blacksmithing, and matrimony" are more or less tribalized, or that the distribution of food is the highest expression of "communism".

A special formulation of the doctrine of primitive communism is found in the developments arising from the work of Lewis Morgan, which was taken over by Engels as an appendage to the Marxist theory of social history.[1] It is theoretically more refined than the other interpretations, and refers primitive communism back to a primordial, nascent state of human society which, together with "primitive promiscuity", gave way, as a result of development of technology and the socio-economic organization of production, to the forms of society which we know, neatly arranged into "stages" of savagery, barbarism and civilization. The lower stages are said to reveal "survivals" of primitive communism and sexual promiscuity. Like all existing theories of social evolution, apart from those which are backed by solid archæological evidence, this view rests on a selection of some facts to the neglect of others in order to support a preconceived theory. Whenever individuals in primitive society share their property or their womenfolk, this is a "survival" of primitive communism and promiscuity. When they display qualities of greed, acquisitiveness and jealousy, this is due to later developments in socio-economic history. But it would be equally plausible to formulate a theory of "primitive individualism" and regard all individualistic behaviour of natives as a survival of this, the "communistic" features being dismissed as the result of a growing control by society over the behaviour of individuals. In fact, if the researches of Zuckerman on primate behaviour be regarded as relevant, the latter theory would seem to offer a more plausible picture of the transition from anthropoid to human existence. But both interpretations are worthless. They contribute nothing

[1] Engels, *The Origin of the Family, Private Property and State.*

to the empirical study of contemporary primitive societies or of the impact of European civilization upon such societies in the culture contact situation.

The protagonists of the theory of primitive communism are not, however, concerned with such scientific pursuits. The theory, like primitive myths and the Aryan dogma of the Nazi regime, serves the function of justifying a particular set of social values and specific lines of conduct in social life. This is why Morgan has been hailed in the U.S.S.R. as an anthropological hero—incidentally doing his memory a disservice by stressing his valueless evolutionary theories to the neglect of the pioneering work which he did in the empirical study of kinship and social organization.[1] And it may be remarked that the whole paraphernalia of propaganda and pseudo-science involved in this seems quite unnecessary. Arguments about remote evolutionary origins among small, isolated societies at a low level of technological development have no bearing on the social, economic and political problems of masses of human beings in the complex, largely industrialized world of today. Whether Neanderthal Man did or did not become annoyed when his neighbour appropriated his hand axe or his wife seems to have no possible bearing on whether the U.S.S.R. is an instalment on the Millennium or a Hell of totalitarian despotism.

The term "communism" refers primarily to developments in modern civilized society. It is variously used to refer to an abstract social philosophy or to conditions actually realized in the U.S.S.R. And it carries different implications for different individuals. The emphasis may be on:

(a) Equality in social status.
(b) The organization of production by social planning in contradistinction to individual enterprise.
(c) The ownership of the means of production by the community.
(d) Equality, or relative equality, in the standards of living of different individuals.
(e) The obligation to work, and the conception of productive effort as constituting the only valid claim to a share of the common income.
(f) The way in which political authority is organized and exercised.

[1] Cf. Lowie (2), pp. 54 and 66; Firth (10) p. 362.

Theoretically one or more of these might exist independently in a given society, or they might all co-exist.

The above implications refer to the socio-economic organization of a society. But the use of the term "communism" is apt to let in, by the back door, a number of assumptions concerning individual psychology. Granted that individuals living in primitive societies do in fact upon occasion forgo material advantages, the motives lying behind such conduct demand investigation and precise description. We have seen that among them there loom large the anticipation of reciprocal advantages in the future; fear of unpleasant consequences from supernatural causes; desire for social prestige and conversely the fear of public disapproval, contempt or ridicule, which lead to the honouring of social obligations, particularly those of kinship. Only in the case of near kin, bond-friends, and others towards whom the individual has a sentimental attachment, is the fulfilment of such obligations backed by genuine altruism. Yet the use of the term "communism" is apt to imply, albeit vaguely, quite different motives—the operation of a mystical "group sentiment", an indifference to material rewards or advantages, or a diffuse benevolence towards humanity at large.

From the above we see that no two individuals mean precisely the same thing when they speak of "communism". Furthermore, those who use the term are generally thinking in emotional terms when they do so. So that when different people speak of "primitive communism" they mean different things about primitive society, and what they do mean often carries a heavy "emotional freight", implying that primitive economic organization is either a Good Thing or a Bad Thing. As we shall see in Appendix C, there are an almost infinite number of interpretations which may be put upon the term. The only thing which they have in common is that they obscure the complex nature of socio-economic relations in primitive society.

6. Bibliographical Commentary

The best study of land tenure from the point of view of theory and method is contained in Malinowski (5), Vol. I, Chapters XI and XII, but the theoretical arguments involved may be found somewhat difficult to follow. The reading of this work is therefore better deferred until the student has studied several other modern ethnographic accounts of land tenure, such as those contained in

Brown and Hutt (1), Fei (1), Firth (8), Forde (2), Mair (1, 2 and 3), Nadel (6) and Richards (4). The chapters on land tenure in Herskovits (3) should also be consulted.

The material on land tenure in Wogeo and among the Nyakyusa presented in this chapter has been abstracted from the accounts given in Hogbin (9) and Wilson (2), to which reference should be made for further details.

CHAPTER IX

PRIMITIVE LAW

1. Law and Custom in Primitive Societies

THE study of primitive law, in its widest sense, is perhaps the most general and difficult task of the social anthropologist. Legal institutions take on a fundamentally different form in primitive communities as opposed to modern civilizations; and law cannot be considered apart from the whole normative system—the body of moral codes, æsthetic standards, rules of good behaviour and the like—of which institutionalized methods of legal procedure are but a part, albeit an extremely important part.

This is perhaps the most important fact to be borne in mind in considering primitive law. It was for a long time obscured because ethnographic observations in the field were confined almost entirely to accounts of crime and punishment, and to the procedure adopted in the settlement of disputes. The approach was that of the lawyer rather than that of the scientist. The former, who earns his livelihood in righting the wrongs committed by others, is only interested in the comparatively few instances of breach, as against the overwhelming majority of cases of observance. Like his counterpart in the medical profession, he is only interested when things go wrong, for this is his function in society. But the anthropologist who sets out to study law in its entirety is not merely interested in the comparatively few instances in which the law is broken; he must also consider the vast majority of cases in which it is kept. He must study all the **forces of social conformity,** including those positive inducements which ensure that, generally speaking, honesty is the best policy. But he must not ignore the fact that cases of breach do occur, and that, in such instances, legal mechanisms are brought into play. Law cannot be considered apart from other forces of social conformity, but its existence as a specific element in culture must also be recognized.

An approach such as this immediately brings before us an initial difficulty—the problem of definition. In our own society law is highly institutionalized. It has its own special personnel—

judges, advocates and police; legal business is transacted in special places, is subject to highly codified rules, and is correlated with a specialized terminology. But in many primitive societies there is nothing corresponding to this elaborate body of legal institutions, with their complex and highly differentiated organization. For this reason no purely formal definition of law, as operative in our own society, is applicable to primitive communities. The definition of primitive law is to be found ultimately in an empirical description of the way in which primitive communities cope with situations comparable to those which arise in our own courts of law, a subject to which we shall return at the end of this chapter.

The scientific study of primitive law and custom—the normative systems of primitive peoples—is fraught with many difficulties, which have in the past produced many misleading interpretations. The first impression was that epitomized in the word "savage". Early travellers were shocked, horrified or disgusted by the ways in which primitive types of behaviour differ from our own. Thus arose the figment of primitive conditions marked by anarchy and internecine hostility, by constant war of all against each other, by dominance of the instinct of self-preservation, "an insatiable appetite for power leading each individual to pursue his own aggrandizement at the cost of any loss or suffering to the rest".

At the other extreme there was the diametrically opposite view of the "Golden Age", of primitive man as an essentially kind, unselfish and law-abiding being. This view was strengthened when early field-workers studied more closely, though by no means thoroughly, the social life of primitive communities. Their observations revealed, instead of anarchy and chaos, a well-ordered social system in which tradition, taboo and the "cake of custom" laid down certain rules which members of the community invariably obeyed, *or said they did*. Hence arose the artificial conception of the savage "automatically" obeying the traditional rules of his society, either from his own goodness of heart, or because of some almost mystical quality of primitive social behaviour such as "group consciousness" or "communistic organization".

The following quotations exemplify various interpretations of why primitive peoples conform to custom:

"Envy, malice and all uncharitableness usually have for the

object of their expression some artificial aim, from the pursuit of which Primitive Man is exempt." . . . "So long as he is free from the disturbing influence of civilization, the nomad is by nature a happy and well-behaved child, full of generous impulses and free from vice." [1]

"The savage . . . is hemmed in on every side by the customs of his people. He is bound in the chains of immemorial tradition, not merely in his social relations, but in his religion, his medicine, in his industry, his art: in short, every aspect of his life. . . . These features are accepted by him as a matter of course. He never seeks to break forth." [2]

"Among such people as the Melanesians, there is a group sentiment which makes unnecessary any definite social machinery for the exercise of authority in just the same manner as it makes possible the harmonious working of communal ownership and ensures the peaceful character of a communistic system of sexual relations." [3]

"Regulations bearing upon the conduct of life, which Western culture might be deemed to come within the province of government, were controlled automatically by established customs. Custom indicates appropriate procedure under the various circumstances which face the individual or the community. Children, by observing their elders or by parental instruction, are taught the correct procedure, and no other mode of action occurs to them in life. . . . Customs act automatically, and there is no need for Government control. . . . What constituted right and wrong conduct had been defined by custom. Custom was obeyed without thought of opposition, and there was little need of courts of law with police to hale malefactors to justice. Prohibitions by tapus were observed out of fear and ingrained obedience." [4]

Both of the contrasting views—of primitive anarchy on the one hand and of "automatic conformity" on the other—have been shown by modern field-work to be exaggerations. Primitive societies are governed by laws and moral rules, but these are by no means obeyed invariably, and certainly not automatically. The study of primitive law and custom has thus two aspects: the

---

[1] Elliot Smith, *Human History*, pp. 189 and 199. Note that these assessments are associated with Elliot Smith's discredited theory of the origin of all but the most rudimentary cultural elements in ancient Egypt.
[2] Hartland, S., *Primitive Law*, p. 138.
[3] Rivers (2), p. 169.
[4] "Te Rangi Hiroa" (P. H. Buck), *Ethnology of Tongareva*, pp. 52–3.

forces which induce people to conform in the vast majority of cases, and the procedure adopted in cases of evasions and breaches of normative standards.

2. *The Variety of Primitive Legal Systems*

The manner of dealing with legal problems varies greatly from one primitive community to another. The most important variation is between stratified and segmented societies. In the former the study of law is simplified by the fact that they usually have a system of legal institutions which bears at least some resemblance to our own. In the latter there is an almost complete lack of such institutions. Yet they do not live in a state of anarchy, and we are driven to enquire how social conformity is ensured in communities which lack legal institutions.

In segmented societies we find a number of autonomous political units based on kinship and locality, local clans being the commonest types. Such units are a law unto themselves in the sense that they are not subordinate to any higher political authority or legal agency—they resemble in this respect the sovereign states of the modern world. Injuries inflicted on a clansman by members of another clan are resented by all the members of the victim's clan, who usually seek compensation or inflict some form of retribution. The latter procedure is known as **clan vengeance**, and its actual operation varies from one community to another. In some it may develop into a *blood feud* or vendetta, in others the incident is closed after vengeance has been exacted by the injured clan.

A much-discussed feature of clan vengeance in primitive society is the fact that injury inflicted by way of retaliation may be visited, not upon the offender, but upon some other member or members of his clan. This doctrine is known as **collective responsibility** and, though commonest in the case of the clan, sometimes applies to other social groups also. Thus, voluntary associations often protect the rights of their members on lines comparable with clan vengeance, and here too the principle of collective responsibility may apply, all members of a society being jointly responsible for the misdeeds of one of its members. Again, in some communities punishments may be inflicted, not only upon the offender, but also upon members of his family.

It follows that in communities where the doctrine of collective responsibility applies, there is a lack of emphasis upon criminal intent, that is, the legal principle of *mens rea*. Thus, in a fight which forms part of a clan feud, any clansman, and not merely the original offender, may be killed or injured, even though he cannot be regarded as morally responsible for the original wrong.[1] In a striking incident recorded from the Hupa, a child was accidentally burned to death by a fire which a woman had started to heat washing water. Although the woman was in no way responsible, the life of her son was sought in recompense.

The principle of retaliation, usually carried out by the clan or other kinship group, may co-exist with systematic legal procedure and the existence of legal authorities. Sometimes these authorities do not exact punishment themselves, but merely allow the kinsmen of the injured party to do so.

Where systems of collective retaliation exist, typically in the form of clan vengeance, it is customary for the group of the wrongdoer to stand by him, to protect him, and to resist attempts by the group of the victim to exact vengeance. Such behaviour is determined by the solidarity of the clan, rather than by abstract moral principle, as is clearly seen when a series of acts of retaliation develop into a blood feud. On the other hand, the tendency for the clan to protect its members varies in its operation from one society to another and within any given society according to the circumstances of the case. Thus among the Chukchi members of a kinship group may actually kill an offender in order to avoid becoming embroiled in a vendetta, but this is unusual. More commonly the principle of "my clansman right or wrong" determines behaviour, except where the wrongdoer has frequently offended before or has otherwise made himself unpopular. In such cases, as we shall see, his clansmen will often let vengeance take its course.

We have so far spoken only of injuries inflicted by a member of one clan upon a member of another. As regards injuries inflicted upon a fellow-clansman, the procedure again varies, but most commonly no action is taken. Because of the feeling of clan solidarity, members of a clan are unwilling to punish a wrongdoer who is a fellow-clansman, and other clans are not interested in the

---

[1] That this is not really so alien to our own ways of thinking becomes clear when we reflect that in modern warfare an individual may suffer for acts which were carried out by his national government, and of which he himself may have disapproved or been ignorant. The main difference between primitive and civilized society in this respect is the size of the groups within which collective responsibility operates, these being very much smaller in primitive society.

matter. Even such dire offences as incest and parricide may go
unpunished, in the sense that no steps are taken to inflict punishment or to exact compensation. But this does not mean that there
are no deterrents against them. On the contrary, they are regarded with the utmost horror. They bring abject shame upon
the offender, and are often believed to lead to drastic punishments of a supernatural order. Consequently, in spite of the
general lack of formal "punishment" as we understand the term,
wrongful acts against fellow-clansmen are far less common than
against outsiders.

In considering conformity to, and breach of, law and custom in
primitive society, it is useful to distinguish between those wrongs
which may or may not provoke retaliation by an injured party,
and those which provoke a public reaction by society at large.
These are roughly equivalent to "torts" and "crimes" respectively
in our own legal system. But the offences which belong to the two
categories are different in primitive society. Thus wrongful acts
which provoke a general public reaction are usually confined to
such offences as sacrilege, witchcraft, incest, treason and what
can only be defined as "being a bad lot".[1] On the other hand,
certain offences, which in our own society are regarded as crimes,
are in many primitive communities treated more as "civil"
wrongs against a victim or his kinsmen, for example, theft and
murder.

We must, however, avoid carrying over our own legal concepts
into the field of primitive law and custom, where there is little or
no codified law, and where reactions to breach of custom are
conditioned to a very large extent by the social context in which a
wrong is committed, and by the personal character, status and
personality of the wrongdoer, rather than by rigidly defined laws.
The way to understand primitive legal systems is to define what
actually happens, for this is often very different from what the
natives say *should* happen.

3. The Sanctions of Social Conformity

As we have said, to understand why people conform, it is
necessary to study law as a part of a wider system of principles,

---

[1] As regards the latter, we always find that consistent breaches of tribal custom lead
to some form of public reaction. This may consist merely of an extreme degree of un-
popularity with the consequent social and material disadvantages to be mentioned
presently, or may take the form of violent injury or even death inflicted upon the
habitual offender.

moral rules, traditional lore and customary procedure, involving both positive and negative **sanctions.** The working of institutions provides rewards for conformity which are quite as important as penalties for breach. We must therefore consider creditable acts and their rewards (positive sanctions) as well as derelictions from duty and their punishments (negative sanctions). Since obedience to custom is not "slavish" or determined by "automatic conformity", the real problem lies in defining all the forces which induce people to behave traditionally.

Among the **positive sanctions** which are operative, perhaps the most important is the pressure of public opinion, which is particularly strong in small and isolated primitive societies, where everybody knows most of everybody else's business and privacy is practically non-existent. Under these circumstances, people are far more keen to win the approval of society at large than in the more impersonal atmosphere of modern urban civilization.[1] The acquisition of a good reputation has both social and material advantages—it provides satisfaction for personal vanity and enhances self-respect, it is often culturally recognized in terms of political and social status, and usually brings economic advantages. Sometimes there exists a belief that ancestors and other spiritual beings are pleased by good conduct. Occasionally there is a belief in rewards after death, but these are never so significant as they are, for example, in the Christian religion, and their truly indigenous character is sometimes doubtful. In primitive society generally the effects of wrongful acts upon an offender during his lifetime are far more significant than anything which may happen to him after death.

Among the **negative sanctions** which make for conformity. we must again mention public opinion, this time in its negative effects. Just as people are eager to win a good reputation, so they are anxious to avoid a bad one. The fear of public condemnation or ridicule is extraordinarily powerful in primitive society, and here again the effects are not only social but also material. The principle of reciprocity ensures that a man who consistently fails to honour his obligations will find himself not only condemned or ostracized, but also at a disadvantage in material matters. He cannot expect material benefits from those whom he has treated badly, neither can he expect them to uphold

---

[1] Note in this connection how the force of public opinion varies, under modern conditions, between urban and rural communities.

his rights or to support him in quarrels. One of the most effective
social sanctions of all is the condoning of reprisals by injured
parties—what might be termed the "serve him right" sanction.
The force of the negative sanctions provided by public opinion
is most clearly seen in those primitive communities where a man
who has violated some important custom actually goes into
voluntary exile or commits suicide because he cannot bear the
shame of public humiliation.

Among the most important forces of conformity in primitive
society are the negative sanctions based upon magico-religious
beliefs. Though we know such beliefs to be unfounded, they are
nevertheless firmly held by the natives, for reasons which we shall
discern in the next chapter. Magico-religious sanctions are
broadly of three kinds, and their occurrence and operation vary
from one society to another: firstly, there are beliefs in the effects
of breach of taboo; secondly, there are beliefs in drastic consequences arising from the anger of ancestors or other supernatural
beings; and finally, there are beliefs in the power of sorcery which
restrain individuals from doing injury to others through fear of
magical retaliation.

Such sanctions as we have described support tribal custom
wherever conformity with custom is irksome, difficult or contrary
to the individual desires of human beings. They reinforce the
manifold obligations connected with kinship. Together with the
other motives in economic activities described in Chapter VII,
they ensure the honouring of co-operative obligations in economic
affairs. They serve to make binding the legal rules of land tenure
reviewed in the last chapter. They ensure respect for individual
life, property and reputation. And they control the sexual behaviour of individuals, particularly through the sanctions for the
prohibition of incest and the rules of exogamy.

Our discussion of sanctions leads us to consider them in a much
wider sense than is implied in the term "punishments", even if we
add to this the category of "rewards". This becomes clear when
we consider the sanctions of conformity in primitive society in the
light of two popular and humanitarian interpretations of the
function of punishment in our own society, namely, the *reforma-
tory* and the *deterrent* theories. According to the former, the function of punishment is to reform the criminal. This view is clearly
inapplicable to capital punishment, and is inconsistent with the
fact that the less appears to be the likelihood of reforming a

criminal, as in the case of habitual offenders, the more severe is the punishment in primitive and civilized societies alike. According to the deterrent theory, wrongdoers are punished in order to deter others from following their example. While this is probably a valid ethical basis for punishment in our own society, it is inapplicable to instances where the principle of collective responsibility is operative.

A third view might be called the *expiatory* or *kathartic* theory. According to this view, the commission of a wrongful act shocks the moral sentiments of society, and creates, in the words of Professor Radcliffe-Brown, a condition of *social dysphoria*. There is therefore a need for some action which will restore the *euphoria* of society, and this most commonly takes the form of some punishment inflicted on the criminal. But it may take other forms, for example, the payment of compensation or some other action designed to expiate the offence and mitigate the damage done to the feelings of an injured group.[1]

An important fact stressed by the expiatory theory is the mutual relationship between moral sentiments on the one hand and overt acts of punishment on the other. Offences are punished because they are wrong, but they are also wrong because they are punished. The public action, even if limited to a verbal or symbolic expression of disapproval, which follows upon a wrongful act serves to establish moral sentiments in the young and to keep them alive in those of riper years. It is upon the existence of such sentiments that much, if not most, social conformity rests. It is only occasionally that individuals are seriously tempted to flout the most fundamental rules of society, and it is in these instances only that the deterrent function of punishment becomes operative.

In connection with the relation of moral sentiments to social conformity it is important to recognize that this is expressed in linguistic terms. In all societies we find emotionally significant terms of praise and blame, proverbs, maxims or other verbal expressions in which the conduct of individuals is evaluated by public opinion in terms of currently accepted standards of right and wrong. These are learned as part of language in early childhood, and come to possess a binding force on the conduct of individuals through psychological mechanisms which will be discussed in Volume II.

We have outlined some of the ways in which social conformity

[1] For an exposition of this view, see Radcliffe-Brown (7).

is ensured in primitive society. But we must again emphasize the differences between various communities in this respect. Just as each primitive society has a different set of rules from any other, so it has also different mechanisms by which these rules are made valid. Primitive law can only be understood by a study of the legal systems of various primitive societies. In the two following sections we shall review two such systems in relation to particular types of wrongful acts, selecting in the first instance a segmented society—that of Wogeo—because it is in such societies that the specifically primitive characteristics of law and custom are most apparent, and the consideration of legal problems presents the greatest theoretical and practical difficulties.

4. Law and Custom in Wogeo

The way in which the people of Wogeo deal with certain offences provides a useful insight into the working of law in a community which does not possess legal institutions. The two offences to be considered are adultery and theft. These are particularly suitable for our purpose, because in our own legal system the former falls within the province of civil law and the latter within that of criminal law. Yet in Wogeo, as we shall see, the sanctions connected with them operate in very much the same way in the two cases.

Adultery.—Adultery is fairly common in Wogeo, but is described as wrong by all natives. Some informants will even deny that it ever occurs in their district. The reason for adultery is, of course, primarily the desire of the persons concerned for sexual variety. But there are other factors involved:

(a) Adultery in certain circumstances does not lead to serious consequences, and it is often possible to carry on an intrigue without discovery.

(b) The Wogeo attitude towards pre-marital intercourse lacks any strong feeling, and it is generally ignored provided that the couple are not found out. In this case the situation is embarrassing for them, but no more. This must tend to produce the impression that in sexual matters a good deal is permitted provided that it does not become generally known.

(c) At initiation, boys are solemnly warned against adultery and told of the punishments meted out to adulterers in the past. At the same time the instructors seek to glorify their clan by telling how *their* ancestors were always successful in the most flagrant adulteries. This must foster the view that the condemnation of adultery is a purely official and conventional attitude, which need not have implications in actual practice, provided that the adultery is successfully concealed.

(*d*) Adultery with a woman of another clan is probably to some extent a reflection of clan rivalry, a permissible means of scoring off one's neighbours.

(*e*) Although young men are constantly told of the punishments which follow adultery—sorcery, public abuse and physical violence—they observe that many men continue to offend without producing any unpleasant consequences.

(*f*) Finally, adultery is attractive because it is forbidden and slightly dangerous. When a basis of confidence is established, informants will boast of their conquests and the devious means by which they carried them out.

The practice of adultery is, then, founded upon strong passions of lust and vanity. On the other hand, it almost always produces a violent emotional reaction on the part of the wronged husband. This is likely to cause disruption in the community. So clearly adultery in Wogeo presents a legal problem.

How is this problem solved? The reaction of the community varies according to whether the adultery has taken place with a woman of another district, with a woman of another village of the same district, with the wife of a fellow-clansman,[1] or of a headman. It also varies according to the personalities and social relations of the individuals directly or indirectly concerned.

Adultery with a woman of another district.—In view of the rivalry between districts, this is very lightly regarded, and is only condemned because it may lead to trouble. Usually it is the result of an amorous expedition of men from one district to another. The men take advantage of the fact that at certain tasks, such as weeding large gardens, the women are alone. When the men of the offended district hear the news, they send a challenge to the offenders. In the old days a fight took place with spears, but was usually not a serious matter, and ceased as soon as blood had been drawn. Since the prohibition of fighting by Government, the challenge is to a football match. From twenty to forty men take

[1] Adultery with the wife of a fellow-villager who is not a clansman appears to be regarded in much the same light as adultery within the clan.

the field and the game usually develops into a brawl. Friendly relations between the districts are afterwards restored, food is sometimes exchanged, and things return to normal until the next amorous expedition.

When inter-district adultery is an individual matter, the wronged husband and his relatives wait for one of the ceremonial fights which precede large distributions of food and other ceremonies (Plate VI). They take this opportunity of manhandling the adulterer.

Adultery between different villages of the same district.—The wronged husband feels violent anger because his rights have been interfered with and his pride hurt. His anger is directed primarily against the adulterer. The woman usually escapes with a beating unless she has been frequently unfaithful, in which case she may be divorced. The clan of the husband also feels affronted and assists him in securing redress. They do this partly because of the strength of the clan tie and partly because each member may some day require similar assistance.

On discovering the offence, the husband may beat the slit-gong in his village and publicly abuse the adulterer. He may repeat this performance at the latter's village. He may also perform black magic against the man who has wronged him. Apart from this, his redress consists of receiving a present from the adulterer or of inflicting violence on him at the next ceremonial fight.

The adulterer is embarrassed and ashamed, especially if he is insulted in public, when he must listen in silence. He feels a fool for having been found out. He also knows that he will probably be roughly handled in a few months' time, but he does not view this so seriously as he does public humiliation.

The adulterer's fellow-clansmen are angry with him, since he has brought shame upon them. Also they may have to subscribe to the present which he gives to the wronged husband. Their clan loyalty forces them to help him in this way unless he is an habitual offender. They would not, however, help him if he took any action in reprisal for the insults heaped upon him, for they know that he is in the wrong. But their resentment at these insults probably adds zest to the subsequent ceremonial fight.

People who are not linked by bonds of clan membership, or otherwise, with the parties concerned describe the adultery as wrong, though they do not feel strongly. Their main reaction is that the adulterer was a fool to let himself be found out.

PLATE VI

A CEREMONIAL FIGHT IN WOGEO

Observe the man in the centre with a decorated conical mask ; he is there to keep
the peace.   On this occasion he was unsuccessful.   Note also the man on the left
preparing to throw a stone.

While this is the general pattern of reaction, there are variations which depend on special factors in the situation. For example, an adulterer's clansmen will normally support him in the football match which sometimes follows an act of adultery. One adulterer who was challenged to such a match was confident that some of his clansmen, who had just returned from work on a plantation, would support him. But when the day arrived they went over to the other side, with the exception of two men. Their reason for deserting their clansman was that they had heard that he had been carrying on with their sweethearts while they were away.

Again, if a man is a notorious adulterer, his reputation suffers, even so far as his own clan is concerned, and public disapproval is much greater than in ordinary cases. It is said that in the old days such a man would have been killed. On the other hand, in one case of adultery the husband had a reputation for being both jealous and cruel to his wife, and her action was regarded by some as a justifiable return for the treatment which she had received.

Adultery within the clan.—This is a much more serious matter. It is generally condemned in the strongest terms. Many natives insist that it never occurs, though in fact it does, albeit less frequently than other forms of adultery.

The reason for this strong condemnation is that the adulterer "breaks the clan". In native thought all the members of a clan are brothers and owe loyalty to one another. Adultery with the wife of one of them is inconsistent with this sentiment. Moreover, it is said that an adulterer always feels ashamed in the presence of the husband he has wronged, an impossible situation when the two are near neighbours. Finally, the wives of clansmen are addressed as "mother", and men are expected to behave towards them in somewhat the same way as they do towards their own mothers. This sentiment again is utterly inconsistent with any sexual relations between them.

When adultery does take place, however, the injured husband is expected to refrain from any kind of vengeance, for this again would "break the clan". He is expected to pretend that he knows nothing unless the couple are caught by him *in flagrante delicto*, in which case it is understood that he cannot restrain his anger. But even in other cases he is frequently unable to control himself. He may relieve his feelings by trying to burn down his house or cause it to collapse by chopping down a corner post. He is usually restrained by fellow-villagers. On one occasion, the husband

beat the slit-gong and indulged in a public harangue, but re-
frained from mentioning any names. He merely talked in general
terms of the unfaithfulness of wives and the untrustworthiness of
brothers.

If a case of adultery within the clan thus becomes a public
scandal, the adulterer usually hands over a present to the husband,
and an influential man may arrange a public reconciliation in
which the two men take a meal together in the presence of the
villagers. But even these measures are often inadequate to restore
harmony between the two, and the adulterer frequently leaves
the village for a while. He may even feel constrained to go away
from the island and work on a plantation for a year or two.
Whether he does this or not depends largely upon the reaction of
the husband. If he remains hostile, the adulterer cannot very well
remain in close association with him. If he is thus forced to go
away for a long time, public antagonism is apt to shift and be
directed against the husband, who by his obstinacy has further
"broken the clan". Later, however, it is recalled that a husband's
anger cannot be expected to die in a few minutes, and public
condemnation is once more directed against the adulterer.

Adultery within the clan is strongly condemned, even outside
the village in which it occurs. But no general punitive action is
taken by outsiders, and would be bitterly resented by the clan if
it were.

Adultery with wives of headmen.—This is regarded as particularly
reprehensible, and young men are warned about the serious
consequences which may follow this form of adultery. The adulterer may lose his life, and a man was actually killed for this
offence as recently as 1929. Even the adulterer's own clan will
not attempt to protect him in such circumstances, though they
would not join in inflicting the punishment. Even if the adulterer
escapes death by violence, it is believed that sooner or later the
offended headman will use black magic against him, causing
disease or death. All headmen are regarded as competent
sorcerers, and such employment of magic by the headman is
regarded as entirely justified. The natives are genuinely afraid
of it.

In one case of adultery with the wife of a headman, the offending couple ran away into the bush. Some of the older men were
with difficulty restrained from murdering the guilty man. A
message was sent around the island asking all villages to refuse

them shelter, and in fact they were ordered to leave one village in which they had sought refuge with the relatives of the woman. After a while the woman returned to her husband, who treated her with indifference and contempt. The adulterer then persuaded her to run away again, and they lived in the bush for awhile. Later they built a hut and made a garden near a village where they had relatives. They were fed by the villagers until crops in their garden had ripened, but they took no part in village life, and no one helped them in their garden. In spite of public indignation and the fact that the headman said that he would charge the young couple with adultery when next the District Officer visited the island, their determination won a certain amount of sympathy among the younger generation. But if any evil should overtake them, it will inevitably be attributed to the black magic of the offended husband.

The headman as adulterer.—There are recorded cases in which the headman was the adulterer. If the injured man is of lower rank, he has no redress. But if the headman takes advantage of his position too often, he loses the respect of his clansmen, and runs the risk of seducing the wife of a man with sufficient force of character to organize a punitive expedition.

Finally, there were in the past cases of adultery by a headman with the wife of another headman. Such offences led to murder, raiding and warfare. This sometimes developed into a vendetta. The clan of the adulterous headman would support him, since no clan likes to lose its headman, and its prestige as a group is bound up with his.

Theft.—Theft is also condemned as wrong, but nevertheless occurs. The man who is robbed is annoyed, and his clansmen help him to gain redress. Strong public indignation is felt only when the theft has been committed within the village. As with adultery, there are different kinds of theft, and the reaction of the community is again variable.

Theft of garden produce. — Petty thieving of garden produce within the village is rare, since it implies admission that the thief is lazy and improvident. It is a disgrace to be without food, and no one who had food would be forced to steal. When such thefts occur, the man who is robbed may publicly abuse the thief, and the villagers express contempt. Only those who are indifferent to their reputation would commit such an offence, though there is one shameless family which lives entirely on charity and theft.

Their fellow-villagers give them food, partly because of the primitive sense of obligation in such matters, and partly because they know that they will be robbed if they do not. Such habitual thieves are not usually abused. What would be the use, since they are utterly without shame?

A second type of theft of garden produce occurs when the young men of one village raid the gardens of another and distribute the food among their relatives. The latter regard the episode as a good joke, reflecting credit on the pluck and virility of the boys, though when the compliment is returned they are apt to be annoyed. But no open dispute results, since "boys will be boys".

Pig-stealing between districts.—The Wogeo natives are attached to their pigs, not only for economic reasons, but also as pets. Pig-stealing is regarded as wrong, but no very great indignation is expressed. The pigs, which are earmarked, often wander away from the village and may be killed by a man from another district. If the owners can discover the thief, they demand the exact equivalent in return. Such demands may lead to arguments and brawls, since the thieves will plead innocence unless irrefutable proof is produced. If they cannot deny the offence, they will protest that the pig had damaged their taro, or that the theft was a just reprisal for an earlier theft committed against themselves by the complainants.

In the case of an open quarrel, the accused man's clan and village will support him, since they too feel insulted. They are not much concerned with the question of guilt or innocence, though the latter increases their indignation.

Often, however, it is difficult to prove the theft, or even to detect the thief. No one in the latter's village will give him away, and in any case there is always the possibility that the pig may have died naturally or been bitten by a snake and afterwards devoured by dogs.

Pig-stealing within the district.—Thefts of pigs between different villages of the same district usually occur when the animal has done damage to gardens. A man is justified in killing a pig in such circumstances, but should notify the owner. In fact, he often remains silent. Nevertheless, the theft is quite likely to become known. There is much coming and going between villages, and the news is often conveyed by one of the married women in the thief's village who happens to be related to the injured parties.

If the owners get to know of the theft, they can demand an equivalent return. If this is not forthcoming, they may carry out magic to cause the thief's pigs to wander into other districts and be killed.

An accusation of theft is often met, as before, by pleas of innocence or extenuating circumstances. But the theft is not always denied. In fact, a headman may even offer a larger pig as compensation, thus enhancing his reputation for generosity. The complainant may refuse this, in order to show that he, too, can be liberal.

It is worth noting that when a dispute arises over the theft of a pig, the sympathy of persons not directly concerned is determined by their relationship to the contending parties rather than by sense of justice.

Pig-stealing within the village.—The natives do not say that theft of pigs within the village never takes place, as they do with adultery. But some of them are reluctant to admit that it ever takes place in *their* village. The reason for condemnation is that the rights of relatives and fellow-villagers should be respected. It is also pointed out that the theft affects, not merely the owner, but also other villagers who would later have received a share of the pig when it was killed.

But if a theft occurs, the owner is expected to ignore it so as to preserve the harmony of the village, which would otherwise be upset. Though it causes disapproval at the time, the offence is not held against the guilty man for any length of time, and his reputation does not suffer greatly. The whole tendency seems to be to hush the matter up and forget about it.

Theft of pigs within the clan is extremely rare. Quite apart from moral considerations and fear of public disapproval, it is not of any great advantage to the thief. When a pig is killed all clansmen normally receive a share. So as the thief can only consume a portion of the pig himself, he is merely illegally taking in the present what he would in any case legitimately receive in the future.

Theoretical conclusions.—The above description illustrates several theoretical points in connection with primitive law and custom:

(a) Although Wogeo has no legal institutions, there are social mechanisms which serve the same function as legal institutions in civilized society. They curb the selfish passions of lust, vanity and greed by threatening offenders with consequences which are emotionally unpleasant—the violent infliction of physical pain or death, a social situation so intolerable that the offender is forced to seek relief in voluntary exile, and the fear of disease or death resulting from the sorcery of the offended party.

(*b*) But the dire consequences involved, including real and imaginary dangers, are backed by other sanctions. In fact, where no great disruption is involved, these are the only sanctions which operate. In minor cases, or where the parties are not relatives or neighbours, the only public reaction is to regard the offender as being a fool to let himself be found out. The sanctions which operate in such cases include the fear of ridicule or contempt, embarrassment, the feeling of guilt at having done something which is regarded as wrong or of having "broken the clan", and the alienation of fellow-clansmen so that they do not provide support when needed.

(*c*) The sanctions mentioned above are negative ones. But custom is also supported by *positive* sanctions, or inducements to good behaviour. There is the desire for the favourable reputation which results from good conduct, or perhaps more correctly from a minimum of bad conduct. This is connected with the wish to stand well with (and therefore be able to rely on) fellow-clansmen. And, finally, there is for the individual the pleasure derived from a feeling of moral righteousness. Thus, one informant stated that if he refused temptation "his inside felt good" because he knew he was a worthy man.

(*d*) What is known as "superstition" supports tribal morality, by inducing fear of retaliation by magic, which is believed to be a real threat and is regarded as justifiable retribution. The special reputation which headmen have as sorcerers reinforces their authority and leads their rights to be respected, rights with which their clan feels itself to be associated.

(*e*) In spite of the fact that certain acts are generally regarded as wrong and their very occurrence denied by certain informants, they do nevertheless occur. There exist cases of evasion and even open defiance of custom. Furthermore, although everybody says that certain acts are wrong in the abstract, they do not, in actual practice, evince signs of moral indignation unless the crime is a serious one or they are themselves involved. They may even feel a certain satisfaction if they have a grudge against the offended party. *These considerations stress the importance of distinguishing between what natives say they do or feel, and what their actions and feelings are in reality.*

(f) Individuals vary greatly in their reactions to temptation and to the dictates of custom. Some are completely shameless, and where the offences are minor ones, nothing much can be done about them. But where more serious offences are habitually committed, or in the case of a single crime of a particularly heinous character, the offenders may be killed (this does not apply since the Administration intervened) unless they prefer voluntary exile. Habitual criminals receive no support from their fellow-clansmen, who have so often been put in a difficult position by them.

(g) Primitive peoples do not "conform automatically" to the dictates of custom. They are, in fact, tempted from time to time, and a man's behaviour on such occasions is determined by a balance of motives which are conditioned by his individual temperament and the particular circumstances of the case.

(h) The operation of legal and other sanctions is modified in each particular case by factors peculiar to it. These include ties of blood and neighbourhood; the rank of culprit and victim; whether there was provocation; whether really uncontrollable passions were involved; whether the culprit was a first offender; whether there were extenuating circumstances; and the age, prestige and personality of the parties directly and indirectly involved. It may be noted that, although some of these circumstances are allowed to modify the rigid application of our own legal code, primitive law is much more flexible in this regard. It might be argued that it is more efficient in terms of wider social considerations. Thus, it seems unjust that a commoner should have no redress against an adulterous headman. But this is a recognition of respect for his authority, and indirectly for the clan which he represents.

(i) The study of primitive law includes the examination of reasons why the law is obeyed in the vast majority of cases, and not merely the occasional instances of breach. For example, even in Wogeo, not *all* of the people are committing adultery *all* of the time. Married life goes on, not unhappily, for husband and wife are bound together by close ties of affection, day to day co-operation, and common interests such as children and gardening. While mistrust is easily aroused, few husbands are suspicious all the time. Those who are become objects of ridicule. Some men reassure themselves by the belief that though the wives of other men may be unfaithful, their own wives would be incapable of such conduct. Others face the fact that their wives are probably much the same as other women, but since nothing can be done about it, unless they have direct proof, they consider complacency preferable to endless suspicion.

5. *Legal Institutions of the Southern Bantu*

In contradistinction to the Melanesian community previously studied, the Bantu stribes of South Africa possess definite legal institutions. The working of these institutions as they operated in pre-European times reveals (*a*) the ways in which they differ from our own; (*b*) the existence of "primitive" conceptions of law comparable with those of Melanesia, and (*c*) variations from one Bantu tribe to another.

The nature of Bantu law.—Bantu law is not codified, either in writing or in any well-defined body of legal maxims or principles. Apart from proverbs and similar sayings, the legal rules are inherent in the social system, a system of rights and obligations generally recognized as binding. The Bantu speak of the bulk of their laws as having always existed, or having been created by God or by the ancestor spirits.

Children are taught by their parents the difference between right and wrong, and at initiation more formal instruction is given. The function of the latter is not so much to impart new information as to impress upon the novice the importance of social codes which he already knows. In later life any man may attend the hearing of law-suits, so that the law, being generally known, requires no codification. Diligent observance of the law leads to social esteem and material rewards from tribal authority. Failure to comply means shame or ridicule; the offender may be denied services akin to those which he has failed to render; or sickness and misfortune may result from the anger of ancestor spirits or from other supernatural causes. When these sanctions fail the material power of the tribal courts comes into play. They may force a man to carry out obligations which he has neglected, or to make restitution, or to suffer punishment for an offence he has committed.

The work of the courts consists mainly of enforcing laws upon the validity of which there is general agreement. Occasionally, differences of opinion arise and are discussed among the old men; or they may be referred to a neighbouring chief with a view to ascertaining whether there is any precedent in the matter. The legal system of the Bantu thus consists of a body of "case law", which is capable of slight modification from one case to another but not of drastic change. In addition, the chief has the power to make new decrees, but these must be made with the approval of the tribe in council.

Civil and criminal law.—The legal code of the Bantu may be roughly divided into two sections, corresponding to our distinction between civil and criminal law. But the categories differ greatly from those of European systems of law. The principal crimes are offences against the tribal authorities, homicide, violent assault, sorcery, incest and other "unnatural acts". In addition, certain civil injuries are also treated as crimes, the offender being forced, not only to make restitution, but also to suffer punishment. Similarly, certain crimes, particularly against bodily security, may also give rise to civil remedies. In European law the two aspects of such offences are the subjects of separate proceedings, but in Bantu law they are tried as a single action, and it is only in the verdict of the court that the two aspects find expression. But the distinction is also clear in the way in which the matter is brought to court. The victim of a civil wrong may take no action, or may reach a private settlement with the offender, or may sue him in court. But unless the victim takes the initiative in this way, no action can be taken by the courts. A criminal offence, however, cannot be compounded and must be reported to the chief or other tribal authority, who will then summon the offender to court. If the punishment is a fine, it is paid to the court, although, as stated above, the victim may also be awarded some compensation.

The principal remedies for a civil wrong are restitution and compensation. The former aims at cancelling the wrongful act when this is possible—a trespasser may be removed, borrowed or stolen property restored, or an unfulfilled contract carried out. Compensation is paid usually in livestock, when the wrong cannot be undone, for example, in cases of seduction, damage to property or defamation. In many tribes the amount of such compensation is traditionally standardized for certain kinds of wrong.

Occasionally, the victim may "take the law into his own hands", but the tendency of Bantu law is to limit this kind of "self-help". It is condoned only in exceptional circumstances, such as the killing or assaulting of an adulterer, homicide, or thief caught red-handed.

The most common form of punishment is a fine, also generally paid in livestock. The amount varies with the seriousness of the offence, the position of the offender, his previous record and his ability to pay. It ranges from the fine of a single beast to confiscation of the offender's entire property. Among certain tribes corporal punishment is frequently imposed as an alternative. In one tribe the *lex talionis* applies—for example, in cases of assault, particularly between women, the victim is allowed to inflict an injury similar to that which she has received. In most tribes certain offences may be punished by bodily mutilation, for example, the removal of ears or hands. Serious crimes are commonly punished by death or banishment, both generally accompanied by confiscation of property.

Contracts.—Apart from various aspects of the marriage contract, the commonest forms of contractual obligation relate to alienation of property by gift, barter or sale; permissive use of property, and service. All important contracts must be concluded before witnesses, the property concerned being produced, or the service specified, at the time. Breach of contract entitles the victim to compensation, or to an order by the court that the contract shall be carried out. Women and children are normally incapable of entering into contracts without the consent of their guardian, who may nullify any independent contract they may make, but may be held liable for breach of a contract which he has approved. In the case of certain types of contract, for example, sale or barter, if a man is unable to pay, his near relatives, such as his father or brothers, may be called upon to do so. A dead man's heirs are expected to settle his outstanding debts before taking over his estate.

A common form of contract, known as *ukusisa*, is for one man to place some of his cattle in the care of another. The latter may use the milk of these cattle, but may not sell or slaughter them. He must tend them as he does his own, is answerable to the owner for their welfare, and must report any loss or death, in the latter case producing the skins. If the cattle thrive under his care, the owner may reward him from time to time by the gift of a heifer, but there is no legal obligation in regard to remuneration unless it has been specified in the contract.

In the case of children temporarily entrusted to the care of persons other than their lawful guardians, a fee, usually one beast, may be claimed when the children are returned. In a similar category are the fees payable to professional magicians. For the "doctoring" of huts, fields or cattle, the fee is payable on the completion of the rite, but in the case of illness the fee is payable only if the treatment has been successful. Payment is rarely refused in the case of successful "doctoring" of a patient, for the magician might use his art to undo the effects of his treatment or even bewitch the defaulting clients. But if the fee is not paid within a reasonable time, the magician can recover it in court.

Marriage is one of the most important legal contracts in Bantu law. Marriages are normally arranged between the parents of the two people concerned, and some tribes practise infant betrothal. But in any case the parties cannot be married until they have passed through the initiation ceremonies. The prohibited degrees of relationship differ from one tribe to another, and the following variations are found:

(a) No marriage restrictions outside the immediate family circle.

(b) Marriage permitted with mother's brother's daughter, but forbidden with all other blood relatives, however remote.

(c) All blood relatives forbidden as mates, and clan exogamy also practised.

Breach of these regulations is regarded as incest and is punished as such. In addition, the marriage itself is nullified.

The essentials of a legal marriage are the formalities of betrothal, the payment of *lobola*, and the handing over of the bride by her relatives to those of the husband. Unless these conditions exist, any co-habitation between a man and a woman is regarded as concubinage, and no legal obligations exist on either side. The man is not bound to support the woman, nor she to remain with him, and no legal action can be taken if one abandons the other. Children of such a union belong legally to the mother, though the father may, under certain circumstances, claim them by a special payment of cattle. Normally, it is only by payment of *lobola* that a man acquires any right to the children he begets by a woman.

Though the payment of *lobola* is essential to a legal marriage, the contract is effective from the time of betrothal. For example, if the girl becomes pregnant by another man, her intended husband can claim damages from her lover. Should she or her family refuse without just cause to let the marriage take place, they are liable for return of all payments and gifts made to them by the young man and his relatives. But if the man should unjustifiably break the engagement, he forfeits all such payments and gifts, and among some tribes is also liable for damages.

Though such contractual obligations exist from the time of betrothal, the marriage itself is not complete until the woman has been formally handed over to her husband and the marriage has been consummated. In some tribes the husband goes to live with his wife's relatives for awhile, returning with her to his own people after the birth of a child. In other cases marriage is patri-local from the outset. The wedding festivities may take place either before or after the handing over of the *lobola* cattle. The number of cattle handed over is usually agreed after negotiations between the parties. Even when in theory the cattle should be handed over before the woman goes to live with her husband, this is often not observed in practice. Failure to complete payment within a reasonable time renders the bridegroom's relatives liable to an action in court.

The *lobola* for a man's first wife must be provided by his father or guardian, assisted by contributions from other relatives. The girl's father receives them, and first satisfies certain traditional claims by specified relatives, for example, the mother's brother. He then allocates them to the household from which the girl came, and they are subsequently used to *lobola* a wife for her brother. For marriages subsequent to the first, a man must provide his own *lobola*.

Though polygyny exists, it is not practised to any marked extent except by chiefs and other prominent or wealthy men. The first wife married is normally the "great wife", but there are exceptions to this.

A husband may repudiate his wife for sorcery, barrenness, repeated adultery, desertion, refusal of conjugal rights or failure to perform domestic duties. A woman may leave her husband for desertion, cruelty or flagrant ill-usage, or non-support. A divorced woman normally returns to her parents' home, where she reverts to the status of an unmarried daughter and may be married again. If the husband is regarded as being in the right, the *lobola* cattle are returned to him, unless there are children, in which case none, or only some, of the cattle are returned. But if the husband is in the wrong, he has no claim to the cattle. In either case the children always belong to him.

Other civil wrongs.—Apart from breaches of contract, the main civil wrongs are: (*a*) seduction, adultery and similar offences against family rights; (*b*) theft, trespass and other offences against property, and (*c*) defamation and other wrongs against reputation.

Wrongs connected with illicit sexual relations are regarded as wrongs against the father, husband or guardian, not against the woman herself. Seduction is a wrong against the father or guardian, because the woman's marriage value has been reduced. In adultery it is the husband who is wronged. Abduction is likewise an offence against the male individual concerned. With a few insignificant exceptions, only men can sue in such cases, and it is to them that any damages are paid.

The law in regard to seduction varies from one tribe to another. In some there is no liability unless the girl conceives, in others seduction is in any case a wrong, though a more serious one if the girl becomes pregnant. In some tribes an action may be brought in respect of every seduction of a girl, in others the initial seduction only can be the subject of an action. The amount of damages is often standardized, though at a different rate in various tribes, the rate varying from one to five head of cattle. In most tribes the seducer has the right to marry the girl, subject to the consent of both families, and in such cases the damages are counted as part of the *lobola* payment. In one group of tribes the seducer is not liable if the girl's parents refuse his offer of marriage.

The adultery of a married woman does not entitle her husband to a divorce unless the offence is frequently repeated. But he can claim damages from the adulterer, the extent of these sometimes varying according to whether the woman becomes pregnant or not. A husband catching an adulterer *in flagrante delicto* has the traditional right to thrash or even to kill him. Adultery with the wife of a chief is a crime subject to capital punishment, or mutilation and confiscation of property. A woman has no right of action in respect of her husband's adultery.

In one group of tribes abduction of an unmarried woman is one of the recognized preliminaries to marriage, and no damages can be claimed over and above the marriage payments. But if for any reason the marriage does not take place, damages can be claimed, especially if the girl has been seduced. Other tribes do not regard abduction as a preliminary to marriage, and treat it in the same way as seduction. The abduction of a married woman is regarded as an aggravated form of adultery, and therefore liable to greater damages. In one group of tribes the husband is actually allowed to take for himself all the cattle of the transgressor.

Wrongs against property. — Encroachment on the gardens of another is not usually an actionable wrong. The trespasser is merely asked to move away or is forcibly ejected, if necessary with the support of an order or messengers from the tribal court. But if cattle enter gardens and cause damage, the owner of the gardens is entitled to compensation. Sometimes the extent of damage is agreed between the parties concerned, but if this cannot be done, an assessment is made by a court messenger. In one group of tribes there does not seem to have been any provision for compensation in cases of damage to gardens by cattle, but the right of self-redress existed in that the women whose gardens were damaged had the right to drive the cattle back into the gardens of their owners.

Other kinds of damage to property entitle the owner to compensation, which in the case of arson and other forms of malicious damage may greatly exceed the actual damage done.

Theft is a civil wrong which may be compounded by payment of property of greater value than that stolen. Often this takes the form of twofold restitution. If the case comes to court, the culprit may also have to pay a fine to the chief or other tribal authority. Theft of cattle is regarded as particularly reprehensible, and among some tribes a man caught red-handed stealing cattle might be killed or have his hands cut off.

Defamation.—The law in regard to defamation varies from one group of tribes to another. In one group the only actionable kind of defamation is an accusation of witchcraft. Elsewhere such statements as that a person has committed a crime or that a girl is unchaste are also actionable, unless made in good faith to a person in authority. Finally, in other tribes defamation is not an actionable wrong unless the allegation has exposed the victim to some danger, for example, a trial in court.

Penal Offences.—Variation is again found in the treatment of crimes against the person. In one tribe the legal theory is that injury to a member of the tribe is an injury to the chief as representative of the tribe. No damages can be claimed by the victim or his relatives for such an injury to the "chief's man". A fine is levied and paid to the chief, who may give some of it to the person injured, but this is a gift and not a legal privilege. A homicide caught in the act may be killed immediately, but all other killings must be reported to the chief, who may confiscate varying amounts of the culprit's property. Any person taking the law into his own hands, except under the circumstances mentioned above, is himself punished for the same offence.

In other tribes murder and culpable homicide are punished by death or banishment. Furthermore, the culprit's property and family may be confiscated by the chief, but here again no compensation is paid to the relatives of the deceased. In other tribes the homicide is killed and his relatives must in addition give to the family of the victim enough cattle to *lobola* a woman—to replace the deceased if she was a woman, or to raise seed to him if he was a man. No tribes permit the vendetta system of self-help. It may be added that in all cases in which the homicide is not actually killed he must undergo a purification ceremony to free him from the pollution of having shed blood. Accidental homicide, too, is differently treated from one tribe to another. In most the homicide must pay something either to the chief or to the relatives of the victim, in the latter case often a woman. One group of tribes impose no penalty if the killing has been accidental, but punish negligence with a fine.

There are various kinds of justifiable homicide, for example, the killing of adulterers or murderers caught in the act, or nocturnal wizards found in a homestead, or a thief found with stolen cattle or in the cattle enclosure. In most tribes it is not only justifiable but customary to kill twins, or children born feet first, or cutting their upper teeth first, or presenting some other abnormality. Such children are evil omens and must be put out of the way lest they should bring disaster to the family. All other forms of infanticide, and also abortion, are treated as penal offences if they come to the notice of the chief, but frequently they are kept secret, especially in the case of unmarried girls who become pregnant.

Assaults in which blood is shed, or serious injury inflicted, must also come before the chief. The punishment is payment of a fine to the chief or compensation to the victim, or both. Rape is treated along the same lines as assault. Vulgar or obscene abuse against an older or senior person is also an offence, since it is apt to lead to fighting. The penalties are various—thrashing, fining or payment of compensation to the person abused.

Crimes against tribal authorities.—Disobedience to an order given by the chief or other tribal authority is an offence punishable usually by a fine—this applies also to such acts as misbehaviour in court, impudence, or refusal to give evidence. In cases of flagrant or repeated insubordination, the offender may be punished by sudden seizure of some or all of his stock. Actual rebellion or conspiracy against the chief is one of the greatest crimes in Bantu society, punishable by death and confiscation of property.

Sorcery and other unnatural offences.—Sorcery is dreaded by the Bantu and is drastically punished. The offence cannot be tried in the ordinary way by the courts, since the sorcerer is often un-conscious of the evil he is doing. So various forms of divination are employed—legitimate magicians use their art to detect him or he is compelled to undergo an ordeal. If guilt is established, the sorcerer is brought before the chief and punished by banishment or death, accompanied by confiscation of property.

Incest and sexual perversions are likewise looked upon as ill-omened actions, and culprits are killed, often violently. Among tribes practising clan exogamy, however, sex relations or marriage between members of the same clan are not necessarily regarded as incest if the relationship between them is sufficiently remote. In such cases the two branches of the clan to which the parties belong may separate, thus establishing two clans in place of one and legalizing the marriage and all subsequent marriages between the two groups.

Procedure.—Chiefs and other tribal authorities are assisted by a panel of assessors or "remembrancers" who advise on points of law and assist in arriving at a verdict. They must attend and participate in all cases coming to court. Some of them are senior patrilineal relatives of the chief or headman, others are elderly commoners noted for their legal sagacity. Among them is always the chief's *induna* who, in addition to other political and adminis-trative functions as the chief's right-hand man, receives all complaints and arranges trials. He must also see that fines are paid and detail messengers for any work connected with the administration of justice. Sometimes the messengers are permanent officials, but usually any man may be called upon to summon litigants and witnesses or to enforce the payment of fines. Every adult man has the right to be present at the trial of any case and to take part in the discussion.

Apart from ordinary courts, other bodies help in the settlement of disputes. Thus, nearly all cases affecting family relations, such as disputes between husband and wife, are discussed in a family council, composed of all the near male relatives of the parties concerned. When women are directly involved, mothers and wives are included in the council. The settlement reached by such a council may involve payment of damages, but the council cannot enforce payment or inflict any penalty on an offender without his consent. If agreement cannot be reached in the family council, the case goes to the local court. There are also regimental courts which deal with offences in connection with the initiation schools or regimental duties, and these courts have power to punish offenders by thrashing or fining. One group of tribes has special women's courts, presided over by a woman of high rank. These courts can take disciplinary action where women quarrel over a man or break any of the sexual taboos.

Cases are usually tried first in the court of the authority under whom the defendant is residing. But if the court is not competent to give a final verdict on the case, it is merely discussed and passed on to a higher court. The lowest courts, with very limited jurisdiction, are those of the headmen. Next come those of the sub-chiefs, and above these is the chief's court, the supreme tribal authority. The chief can try cases on appeal from a lower court and also those which are beyond the latter's competence. Such cases include all penal offences, except refusal to obey orders and contempt of court. The headman's court can deal with all forms of civil injury, but in important or difficult cases the headman is bound, after discussion, to forward the case to a superior court. Cases involving important persons are usually treated in the same way, partly out of courtesy and partly from the common-sense realization that an appeal is sure to be made.

Trials.—Procedure varies with the status of the court—the smaller the court, the simpler the procedure—though the pattern is the same throughout the judicial system. An injured party who wishes to take action reports the matter to the defendant's head-man, who fixes a day for the hearing of the case. There are no fixed sessions.

On the appointed day, all parties concerned assemble. Any male member of the tribe may be present, even a stranger. But women may not be present unless they are actually involved in the case. Each party in the case is responsible for the appearance of his own witnesses, who must attend and may, if necessary, be summoned by messengers. Failure to appear is contempt of court.

The judge outlines the case and the plaintiff is asked to state his grievance. This he usually does at great length and he is seldom called to order for straying from the point. The defendant similarly states his case. Both may be asked questions by any person present. Witnesses are called and similarly questioned. The case is then usually thrown open for public discussion. The assessors speak one by one, in ascending order of seniority, pointing out what appear to them to be the rights and wrongs of the case according to the evidence, and also stating the law on the subject, referring if possible to precedents. The judge finally sums up the evidence and opinions advanced, and gives his verdict. In theory he should base it, not on his own opinion, but on what he thinks is that of the majority. Where he disagrees, he may try to win the others round to his way of thinking, but he cannot go against the united opinion of the assessors.

Direct, circumstantial and hearsay evidence are all admitted, though not much importance is attached to the latter in the absence of more direct proof. The court also relies on evidence as to the character of the defendant, particularly as to whether he has offended in other similar cases. No oath is taken, nor is there any form of ordeal or divination, except in cases of witchcraft. Perjury is difficult, owing to the close questioning, and if detected is punished.

Cases on appeal to a higher court are heard all over again from the start, and the verdict may be confirmed, modified or reversed. An unsuccessful appellant must not only abide by the original verdict, but may in addition have to pay a fine for having taken the matter so far without good cause. The chief's verdict is final, but a man who thinks that he has been unjustly treated by the chief may take the matter up with one of the latter's senior rela-tives, or with his *induna*, who may induce the chief to diminish the penalty or remit it altogether. If he refuses to do this, the man's only alternative is to leave the tribe and settle somewhere else.

Sentences of corporal or capital punishment are carried out immediately after being pronounced, but in one group of tribes a man sentenced to thrashing may run away and find asylum in the homestead of the chief's wife, mother, or other prominent relative, after which he cannot be thrashed. Damages and fines are paid on a fixed day. Fines are paid to the headman or to the *induna* of a chief. Usually a beast is killed and eaten by the men present, the remainder going to the headman or chief as his own property. Unreasonable delay in paying fines or damages is penalized by augmenting them.

Factors affecting liability.—Every adult person is presumed to know the law and to have intended the results that follow an act he has committed. Motive is not generally taken into consideration, but allowance is made for provocation. Malicious prosecution may entitle the victim to damages for defamation. Negligence usually involves liability for resulting damage, but purely accidental wrongs are almost invariably excused or far less heavily penalized. Less liability is attached to unsuccessful attempts to do wrong than to those which have succeeded; in fact, the former are seldom brought to trial. Bantu law in the main takes cognizance only of wrongs actually perpetrated.

The character and attitude of the wrongdoer play an important part in determining the attitude towards him. If he readily admits his offence, he may be lightly dealt with or even excused altogether. If he is insolent or obstreperous, even in the face of overwhelming evidence, he will be penalized more heavily than usual, as are habitual offenders.

The relative status of the parties is also an important factor. In general, offences against a person senior in age or status to the offender are regarded as more reprehensible than they would have been if the relative positions had been reversed, and are more severely punished by the courts, particularly if the offence is against the chief. Conversely, it is difficult, sometimes impossible, to obtain justice when the chief or one of his senior relatives is the offender. Offences against kinsmen or members of the same local group are often treated more lightly by the victim than where the offender is an outsider. There is a greater readiness to accept nominal damages or even to overlook the offence altogether. So, too, offending foreigners are on the whole more harshly treated than members of the tribe.

There is no time limit within which an action must be brought—"a wrong does not decay". A case cannot be tried in the absence of one of the parties, unless he is dead, in which case, for example, action may be taken against his heirs for recovery of debt. The sooner a case is dealt with the better; but if a defendant hides or runs away, the complainant can still bring an action even years afterwards. But the complaint must be lodged immediately after the offence, or it is likely to be regarded with suspicion.

The principle of collective responsibility plays an important part in Bantu law. Every man is held responsible for the delicts of his wife and unmarried children, and must pay their debts and any fines or damages which they may incur. Moreover, if a man himself is unable to pay a fine or damages, his near relatives are expected, and can sometimes be forced, to come to his rescue. This does not normally apply to cases where corporal or capital punishment is involved, but in some tribes, if a man is sentenced for sorcery or treason, not only he but also his whole family may be punished. Collective responsibility is further seen in the "spoor law" of certain tribes, whereby if the tracks of missing cattle are traced to a certain kraal, the onus of proving that they are not there lies upon the members of the kraal. If they fail to do so, they are held collectively liable for the missing animals.

Conclusion.—The above is a brief summary of Bantu law in South Africa as it existed in pre-European times.[1] Bantu law reveals interesting contrasts with the legal systems of segmented primitive communities on the one hand, and with that of our own society on the other. The following points should be noted:

1. Laws are not formally codified as among ourselves, yet are more systematized than in Melanesia.
2. The distinction between "civil" and "criminal" law (or, in Radcliffe-Brown's terminology, between private and public delicts) is more evident than in Melanesia, yet not so clearly drawn as among ourselves. Differences in the classification of theft and sexual offences should be noted.
3. The occurrence of specific legal institutions (tribal courts) means that the operation of legal sanctions becomes more regular and more consistent than, for example, in Wogeo,

---

[1] It should be noted that, though the present tense has been used throughout, many of the practices mentioned have been abandoned under European influence.

and less dependent upon the context of particular social situations and the motives and personalities of individuals. Yet in this respect Bantu law seems to be more flexible than our own.

4. The ability of men of rank and influence to "get away with" violations of the social code is less marked than in Melanesia, though more so than among ourselves.

5. The examples of the doctrine of collective responsibility contrast with our own conception of individual responsibility, as does the tendency under certain circumstances to neglect the question of criminal intent or *mens rea*.

6. The *lex talionis*, a prominent feature of legal systems in which clan vengeance plays an important part, appears only sporadically, but is in marked contrast to the absence of this principle in our own legal system.

7. The settlement of disputes, for example regarding family matters, by negotiation is more marked than in our own legal system, though here it seems to be playing an increasingly important part.

6. *The Definition of Primitive Law*

There has been considerable controversy regarding the definition of primitive law and particularly as to whether, or in what sense, "law" can be said to exist in primitive societies which have no legal institutions. If we accept Roscoe Pound's definition of law as "social control through the systematic application of the force of politically organized society", we are forced to deny that the term "law" can be applied, for example, in the segmented societies of Melanesia. Many anthropologists adopt this view, for example, Professor Radcliffe-Brown, who states that " some simple societies have no law, although they have customs which are supported by sanctions".

An objection to this formulation is that it may obscure the significance of certain specific types of normative rules—those protecting human life and property, the prohibition of incest, the condemnation of adultery and other sexual offences, and rules designed to inhibit greed, vanity and inordinate ambition. Generally speaking, such rules are found in all societies, and are enforced by sanctions of a broadly similar character: the fear of death, mutilation or physical pain, whether inflicted by society or through the operation of supernatural agencies; loss of material advantages; expulsion from the community; or a degree of social opprobrium so intolerable that the wrongdoer is driven to suicide or voluntary exile.

The same criticism applies to the formulation of Hobhouse in regard to tribes at a low level of culture: "Such societies, of course, have their customs, which are doubtless felt as binding by their members, but if we mean by law a body of rules enforced by an authority independent of personal ties of kinship and friendship, such an institution is not compatible with their social organization." [1] More recently the late Godfrey Wilson expressed a similar view when he defined legal action, as distinct from other types of sanction, as follows: "Legal action . . . may be defined as any customary action on the part of some member, or members, of a social group, one or more of whom are not themselves directly and personally concerned in the issue, to prevent breaches in the pattern of social conformity, to ensure the recurrence of human actions in the customary form which obtains in that particular social group." [2]

The formulations of Hobhouse and Wilson do not postulate legal institutions as necessary to the existence of law, as does Roscoe Pound's definition. But the conception of law as involving essentially an appeal to some independent and disinterested party again tends to obscure the fundamental similarity in the consequences of violently anti-social conduct in all human societies.

An entirely different approach to the problem of definition lays emphasis upon the way in which sanctions operate in deterring wrongdoers, rather than upon the social mechanisms—for example, clan vengeance, chiefs' courts or beliefs in supernatural punishments—through which they operate. Thus Malinowski states that "the fundamental function of law is to curb certain natural propensities, to hem in and control human instincts and to impose a non-spontaneous, compulsory behaviour".[3] This view has been elaborated by the present writer in such a way as to stress, firstly, the fact that legal sanctions only operate when violent human emotions tend to burst through the limits of customary behaviour; and secondly, the integral relation and similarity between psychological motives leading to legal offences and those upon which the effectiveness of legal sanctions is based.

---

[1] Hobhouse, *Morals in Evolution*, 1915, p. 73.
[2] Wilson (1), p. 25.   [3] Malinowski (2), p. 64.

We have seen that law, and particularly primitive law, cannot be considered apart from the totality of customary rules governing human behaviour. But the phrase "cannot be considered apart from" is not synonymous with "is". Law is not merely part of a vague continuum of custom. Compare the statement: "It is the custom to eat a meal at midday" with "It is the custom to kill a man convicted of witchcraft". Entirely different human motives are involved in maintaining the effectiveness of the two customs. The former is observed largely as a matter of convenience and because no one particularly wants to deviate from it. In the second case violent anti-social passions are involved and the most stringent penalty is imposed by society. This gives us a clue to a possible distinction between law and custom. It might be held that law only enters where selfish anti-social and disruptive tendencies are likely to violate customary usage. Drastic measures are taken to prevent this and to express horror at its occurrence.

In no human community, then, do we find an undifferentiated continuum of custom which we can vaguely label "law"—on the contrary, there is always a co-ordinated system of specific rules which define correct behaviour in social situations, and which are supported by various types of sanction. The latter term, as we have seen, must be used in a very wide sense to include, not only the repressive forces which prevent breaches of custom, but also the positive inducements towards social conformity. Defined in this way, sanctions are essentially *mechanisms of validation*, or forms of human behaviour which make custom effective. And the differences between various social rules within the normative system are most plainly demonstrated by a description of the sanctions by which they are enforced. By considering rules in their integral relationship to the sanctions which support them, it is possible to differentiate between various aspects of custom, and in particular between legal and non-legal rules of behaviour.

In speaking of primitive communities, then, what do we mean by the specifically legal aspect of their institutions? The first step in answering this question is to ask what we really mean by "law" in the context of European civilization. If we were to ask whether, in our own society, we should define law in terms of murder, theft, bigamy and libel, or in terms of such offences as selling groceries after hours or parking cars in the wrong places, the answer would be fairly obvious; and it is upon the first group of functions, upon the most vitally significant aspects of law in our own society, that we must concentrate if we are to obtain a conception of law which we can extend to primitive communities.

The interesting thing is that we find parallels with the above offences in all treatments of primitive law, with the addition of one important offence which is specific to primitive communities, namely, witchcraft. Offences such as theft, adultery, incest and murder occur with monotonous regularity in discussions of primitive law, and it is in this fact that the definition of law is to be found. All communities have rules which direct human behaviour and curb human impulses, and for the most part these are obeyed fairly generally, because it is usually easier and more profitable to conform. But certain rules have as their function the repression of human passions such as greed, fear, hate, jealousy, vanity and sexual desire; and the nature of these impulses is such that they are apt to sweep everything before them, to blot out from the individual consciousness all future considerations or moral restraints in the passion of their immediate appeal, and to render quite useless the usual forces of social restraint. Such cases society meets by an appeal to, or harnessing of, those very forces which tend towards disruption. Physical violence, the confiscation of material goods, exile, abject humiliation or death are the sanctions which society employs to frustrate the more passionately disruptive forces within it.

We might then define the functional significance of law as being to control the most violent, passionate and disruptive propensities of the individual by the frustration, actual or potential, of the same or similar propensities in the interests of social order. This definition applies primarily to what we usually call criminal law, but it is also applicable to civil law, because the latter depends, in the last analysis, upon a trial of physical force between the individual on the one hand and the officers of the law, or the supporters of the aggrieved party, on the other.

We must not forget that legal mechanisms, as defined above, may have secondary functions. They may be extended to the correction of minor offences, to the settlement of trifling disputes, and to the regulation of administrative procedure. We are justified in relegating these to a position of secondary importance since they might be regulated in other ways. But the primary function of law as we have defined it is something vital to the existence of every human society.

We have reviewed several approaches to the problem of the

definition of primitive law, not because any satisfactory conclusion can be reached on this subject, but because the discussion brings to light the complex theoretical problems connected with the study of primitive law and custom. None of the above definitions is really adequate, since each seeks to define primitive law by stressing one aspect of the legal system of our own society. Thus our own suggested definition would bring within the scope of law the drastic supernatural punishments which reinforce many customs in primitive society. To describe the beliefs in such punishments as a form of legal sanction is hardly in accord with ordinary usage. Yet our definition is significant as emphasizing that, for example, the fear of death operates in very much the same way as a deterrent whether the agency of execution is a living hangman or an outraged ancestor. The other definitions which we have discussed lay emphasis on other aspects of the problem, in particular the importance of differences in the social agencies through which sanctions operate, specifically in a comparison between those communities which possess legal institutions and those which do not. Thus, while each definition is in itself open to objection, each is nevertheless valuable in emphasizing certain features which must be studied in considering the legal and normative systems of primitive communities.

7. Bibliographical Commentary

Many of the nineteenth-century discussions of primitive law centred around the light which, it was thought, the study of this subject could cast on the early origins of our own legal institutions. For a discussion of the more important of these, see Lowie (2), Chapter V.

For discussions of the theoretical problems of primitive law see Radcliffe-Brown (7), Wilson (1) and Malinowski (2) and Introduction to Hogbin (2).

The material presented above from Wogeo and from the Bantu peoples of South Africa has been abstracted from Hogbin (7) and Schapera (1). Other valuable discussions of primitive law and political organization are contained in Brown and Hutt (1), in the various essays contained in Fortes and Evans-Pritchard (1), and in Hogbin (2), Kaberry (2), Malinowski (2), Meek (1), Schapera (3), and Wilson (1).

CHAPTER X

RELIGION AND MAGIC

1. Some Early Theories of Primitive Religion

By contrast with the more mundane phases of native culture, such as economics, education and family life, the religion and magic of primitive peoples loom large in the older field records and in the history of anthropological theory. Spectacular ceremonies, queer rites and weird beliefs immediately attracted attention, were meticulously described and produced a spate of theoretical interpretations. Magico-religious beliefs and practices were explained as the results of intellectual speculation or of the specifically "primitive" condition of "pre-logical mentality". But little attempt was made to relate these beliefs and practices to everyday life, to individual hopes and fears, or to the collective pursuits and organization of human communities. Religion and magic can only be understood in terms of what they do, the needs which they satisfy, and the influence which they have on human behaviour.

To study primitive religion and magic scientifically, it is essential to lay aside our own beliefs and categories. Christian faith and atheism are alike irrelevant to the sociological interpretation of magico-religious beliefs, whether primitive or civilized. We must simply accept the fact that such beliefs exist, that they are instilled and reinforced by powerful cultural forces which make them valid for the people who hold them, and that they exert a significant influence on individual and social behaviour.

This approach to magico-religious institutions is a comparatively new development. The earliest discussions of primitive cults treated them as prototypes of more advanced religions, and the chief object in studying them was to gain an understanding of the *origin* of human religion and of the psychological processes whereby man first arrived at a belief in the supernatural.

Animism.—The first of these attempts to explain the origin of religion was the animistic theory propounded by E. B. Tylor, and subsequently adopted by Herbert Spencer. According to this view, the idea of the soul was the essential fact in the genesis of religion, which was held to have been due to a process of reasoning carried out by primitive man.

The steps in the intellectual process whereby man arrived at a belief in the soul were, according to the animistic theory, as follows: the idea of the soul was derived originally from the experiences of dreams when, apparently, a part of the sleeper leaves his body and wanders abroad as a separate entity, from which was inferred an essential dualism in the nature of man. Fainting and other similar conditions provided further examples of a temporary separation between the body and the soul, while at death a further separation took place, this time of a permanent character. The soul, which left the body permanently at death, was held still to influence the lives of the survivors for good or ill, and this led to prayers and sacrifices designed to secure blessings and avert evil. The first religion was thus the cult of ancestors, which subsequently gave rise to other forms.

Among the most important of these later religious forms was the worship of nature, based upon the belief in the supernatural qualities of animals, plants and material objects. This cult Tylor and Spencer derived from the worship of ancestors, though in different ways.

According to Tylor, the extension of religious interest from the souls of ancestors to the phenomena of nature was due to the peculiar mentality of the primitive, who, like the very young child, did not distinguish between the animate and the inanimate, and thus came to endow the phenomena of nature with a spiritual quality analogous to his own.

The manner in which Herbert Spencer derives the worship of nature from that of ancestors is rather different. For him, the transition was due to linguistic errors: men are frequently known by the names of animals, plants or other natural objects, and Spencer suggested that, after such a man had been dead for some time, his descendants would mistake his name for a descriptive title—if he had been called "Tiger", his descendants would, in time, come to believe that he really was a tiger, and since the ghost is often believed to revisit its old home, the divinity of the ancestor would eventually come to be regarded as incarnate in the animal. He offers similar explanations of other aspects of nature worship.[1]

---

[1] *Principles of Sociology*, Vol. I, Chaps. XXII–XXIV.

Naturism.—As we have seen, the animistic theory gives primacy to the worship of the soul, and derives the worship of nature from it. But another school of thought, associated particularly with the name of Max Müller, reverses the order, and derives the belief in supernatural beings from the sensations aroused in man by the overwhelming and at times cataclysmic manifestations of nature. These, far from being "natural", were calculated to make the human mind aware of "the overwhelming pressure of the infinite". Such sensations were the germ of religious experience, which grew into religion proper through a disease of language. Müller holds that man first called the striking phenomena of nature by terms which denoted their activities—"a thunderbolt was called *something* that tears up the soil or that spreads fire; the wind *something* that sighs and whistles",[1] and so on. This description of the phenomena of nature in terms of human or quasi-human activities led to an interpretation of them in anthropomorphic terms, and divine personalities were invented to account for the activities of natural phenomena. The origin of religion thus lay in a disease of thought and of language—since the words used to describe the awe-inspiring phenomena of nature were terms denoting human activities, these terms were taken to imply the existence of personal agencies operative in the natural phenomena themselves.

The theory of Frazer.—The theories so far mentioned derive religion essentially from the supposed primordial speculations of man concerning phenomena with which he came in contact, whether spiritual or material, religious beliefs arising from the impressions, intellectual or emotional, produced by a contemplation of these phenomena. They assumed a certain abstract philosophical curiosity concerning the phenomena of human life and of nature, which drove man to a series of inferences, the end-product of which was religion. It was Sir James Frazer who first introduced the pragmatic element into the study of primitive religion by attributing its growth to an active desire for effective control of the phenomena of nature, rather than to passive impressions derived from the contemplation of them. The sources of primitive religion he finds in the failure of magic to effect the desired results. Magic he believes to be a mistaken application of principles of association which, properly employed, lead to science:

[1] Quoted by Durkheim (1), p. 77.

"The fatal flaw of magic lies, not in its general assumption of a sequence of events determined by law, but in its total misconception of the particular laws which govern that sequence. . . . The principles of association are excellent in themselves, and indeed absolutely essential to the working of the human mind. Legitimately applied, they yield science; illegitimately they yield magic, the bastard sister of science." [1]

Magic, then, seeks directly to influence the natural sequence of cause and effect, and shares with science the fundamental belief that this sequence is absolute and invariable. But religion rests upon a different assumption, namely, the belief in the existence of "powers superior to man which are believed to direct and control the course of nature and of human life." [2] This stage of belief, which is a step beyond that of faith in magic, is reached when man realizes the futility of his magical practices, and instead offers supplications to powers higher than himself, who can, he believes, alter the normal sequence of cause and effect at his behest. This theory goes far beyond those which we have mentioned previously, in stressing the part played by human needs in the genesis of religion, as well as philosophical speculation. Such speculation is held to be carried out under the stimulus of man's desire to control life and nature in accordance with his own wishes, a desire whose first manifestation is found in magic. But like the other theories, that of Frazer is orientated from a specific methodological point of view, based upon a desire to discover the origin of religion in the history of mankind, rather than to understand the reality of existing religions, and the part which they play in living human cultures.

This specific orientation of early theories of religion was due to the hypothesis of evolution, which had, at the time when they were conceived, revolutionized biological science; and it seems not unnatural that the first attempts at a scientific study of religion should have regarded present-day phenomena mainly as a means of understanding the past. The most striking example of this tendency is, as one would expect, the sociological system of Herbert Spencer, who sought, in every phase of social life, a progression from simple to more complex forms comparable with that which is observable in biological evolution.

Based upon this common *motif*, each theory developed along particular lines, understandable in terms of the context in which

---

[1] Frazer (3), pp. 49–50.   [2] *Ibid.*

it was conceived. It seems natural that Tylor, reviewing for the first time the range of primitive religious beliefs, should be struck by the active part which ghosts and spirits of the dead play in many primitive communities, as opposed to their nebulous character and the apathy towards the concerns of the living which they exhibit in a civilized European community. In view of this, it is not surprising that he should find the origin of religion in the cult of ancestors. Again Max Müller, studying the history of religion as a philologist, quite naturally found its beginnings in linguistic usage. Finally, Sir James Frazer, bringing to the study of primitive society a wealth of classical scholarship, emphasizes just those facts which were important in the religion of ancient Greece, namely, on the one hand the active influence of the gods on human affairs, and on the other that intellectual curiosity which led to the birth of philosophy. His theory may perhaps be regarded as a synthesis of these two conceptions.

The theory of Durkheim.—The work of Émile Durkheim, the French sociologist, for the first time shifted the emphasis in the study of primitive religion from the past to the present. He criticizes in detail the earlier theories,[1] the main point of his argument being that they all regard religion as a survival of some elementary intellectual blunder, some primordial process of muddled thinking. Any such theory, he holds, fails to explain why religion, founded upon a great illusion, should have survived so long, and should play the part which it does in human communities. If, on the other hand, we regard religion as corresponding to *some* reality, as meeting some actual human requirement, this problem does not arise. The reality upon which religion is founded is, for Durkheim, essentially social, and is based upon the solidarity and spiritual communion which the individual feels with the fellow-members of his social group, and he proceeds to elaborate this theory in relation to Australian totemism.

The defect of Durkheim's view is that he regards social solidarity, which is nowhere adequately defined, as an end in itself, and does not attempt to relate it to other aspects of native life, nor to individual urges considered apart from "collective representations" superimposed upon the individual by society. Undoubtedly a sense of solidarity or community feeling exists in all social co-operation, but such co-operation depends upon individual needs attaining their ends through social institutions. Religion has an

[1] Durkheim (1), Book I, Chapters II and III.

effect in expressing and maintaining social cohesion of a non-religious character. Concretely, for example, Australian totemic increase ceremonies do undoubtedly serve the function which Durkheim attributed to them, namely, that of increasing the sense of the individual's participation in the life of his social group. But they do far more than this; in the first place, they possess a marked economic function [1]; they imply organized co-operation in productive activities, and they are very definitely related to the practical pursuits of a hunting and collecting people; their control by the old men emphasizes the political organization of the community, and their associated mythology is closely related to family life through the totemic theory of reproduction. The social solidarity which they express can therefore only be understood by considering it in concrete terms, that is, in relation to the extraneous institutional activities to which they are so closely related.

2. Religion and Magic

As with the definition of religion, so with the differentiation of magic from religion, several divergent views have been advanced. That of Frazer has been mentioned above. For Durkheim, religion is essentially social, while magic is individual and even anti-social: "There is no Church of magic. Between the magician and the individuals who consult him, as between these individuals themselves, there are no lasting bonds which make them members of the same moral community, comparable to that formed by the believers in the same god or the observers of the same cult. The magician has a *clientèle* and not a Church." [2] It should be noted that this distinction would not be applicable, for example, to Trobriand garden magic or to the magical practices connected with the Kula. In both of these magical systems, rites which are concerned with the common aspirations of the whole community are inextricably interwoven with those designed to promote the interests of individuals.

A different distinction between religion and magic is drawn by Malinowski: "Compare [he says] a rite carried out to prevent death in childbed with another typical custom, a ceremony in celebration of a birth. The first rite is carried out as a means to an

---

[1] Cf. Malinowski, "The Economic Aspect of the Intichiuma Ceremonies," in *Festskrift tillegnad Edvard Westermarck, i anledning av Hans Femtioarsdag.*

[2] Durkheim (1), Book I, Chapter I, Section IV.

end, it has a definite practical purpose which is known to all who
practise it and can be easily elicited from any native informant.
The post-natal ceremony, say a presentation of a new-born or a
feast of rejoicing in the event, has no purpose; it is not a means to
an end, but is an end in itself. It expresses the feelings of the
mother, the father, the relatives, the whole community, but there
is no future event which this ceremony foreshadows, which it is
meant to bring about or to prevent. This difference will serve us
as a *prima facie* distinction between magic and religion. While in
the magical act the aim is always clear, straightforward and
definite, in the religious ceremony there is no purpose directed
towards a subsequent event." [1]

The objection to this as a basis of classification is that it leaves
many of the phenomena unclassified. Most religious systems include ceremonies with a definite and clearly formulated objective,
such as the provision of rain, the aversion of public calamities, or
success in war. On the other hand, many acts usually classified as
magical lack entirely a "clear, straightforward and definite" aim,
as in the many minor observances which have only a very vague
objective of avoiding "bad luck", which is probably not by any
means always envisaged during their performance. Again, many
religious ceremonies have an objective which, though not as
specific as it might be, is none the less present, such as pleasing a
deity, or removing sin from a congregation. Further, even such
predominantly self-contained ceremonies as Malinowski cites
have a general, if not a specific, objective. For example, initiation
ceremonies are aimed at "making the boy into a man". This fact
comes out very clearly in the beliefs concerning the results of
non-performance, for in many religious ceremonies there exists
a specific fear of evil consequences if the ritual is omitted or
negligently carried out. Thus, though we may agree with Malinowski's formulation as representing a general tendency, we must
not lose sight of the fact that religious ceremonies cannot be
considered apart from subsequent events supposed to follow from
their performance on the one hand or from failure to carry them
out on the other.

Probably no attempt to differentiate between religion and
magic in primitive communities can be satisfactory. It is a waste of
time to attempt to lay down dogmatically what *is* religion and
what *is* magic, as though there were some pre-ordained distinc-

[1] Malinowski (12), p. 38

tion between them. Any distinction drawn must rest upon the procedure of abstracting from religion and magic *as conceived by ourselves* two contrasting elements which are then applied to the quite different categories of primitive magico-religious systems. For us, religion, for example Christianity or the paganism of Greece and Rome, includes :

(a) A belief in one or more spiritual beings;

(b) Collective activity (the "church" of Durkheim);

(c) Gatherings which have no special object except worship and communion, for example ordinary church services; and

(d) The pursuit of ends approved by society.

On the other hand, our idea of magic is of something which:

(a) Produces results directly, that is, without the intervention of spiritual beings;

(b) Is essentially individual and often secret;

(c) Has a definite objective in view; and

(d) Is often malicious and therefore socially condemned.

Taking *any one* selected criterion, we can define a given primitive rite as "religious" or "magical"; but the classification will often change if we select a different criterion, and will in any case probably prove inapplicable to primitive magico-religious systems, as distinct from particular rites. In terms of the above criteria, most of the phenomena with which we are dealing are "religious" in some respects and "magical" in others. For example, Australian totemic increase ceremonies involve spiritual beings, but not in the ordinarily "religious" sense; they are collective in character, sometimes secret and sometimes not; they have a definite end in view, namely, the increase of the species; and they are socially approved. So they are "religious" according to some definitions and "magical" according to others.

It is therefore better in general to speak of "magico-religious" phenomena, institutions, beliefs and practices without trying to fit them into any hard-and-fast division between "religion" and "magic". For descriptive purposes we may use the term "religious" to refer to the ways in which belief in the supernatural is established and reinforced and collective sentiments are expressed, reserving "magical" for the cases where such beliefs are used to produce practical results. Avoiding pedantry, we may roughly label any phenomenon we are considering either "religion" or "magic" according to which of the above functions seem to predominate.

Not only are the words "religion" and "magic" used in ambiguous and varying senses by different writers, but so also are other terms connected with man's relation to the supernatural. Thus, the terms *witchcraft* and *sorcery* are often used synonymously, the former being commonly applied to beliefs in Africa and the latter to those of Oceania. The commonest distinction drawn between them is based upon the possibility of the practices described actually occurring. Thus, when an informant can describe and actually demonstrate a technique of black magic, for example, breathing on a bundle of herbs and reciting a spell, the practice is usually described as sorcery; it is demonstrably possible for a person to do the things described, even though the alleged results do not follow from them. On the other hand, when it is believed that an injurious substance may emanate from the body of an evilly disposed person and enter the body of his victim, or in the case of the common Australian and Melanesian belief that a man may extract some vital part of his victim's body and seal up the wound so as to leave no trace, it is manifestly impossible for the events described to take place and the procedure is referred to as witchcraft.

Another possible distinction is on the basis of the reaction of society. Some writers use the terms "black magic" and "white magic" for practices which are condemned or approved respectively by the community in which they occur. A similar distinction is sometimes drawn between witchcraft and sorcery. The activities described as witchcraft are socially condemned, and the convicted witch [1] is often killed or otherwise severely punished. Sorcery, however, though it may be resented by the injured person and his kinsfolk and may lead to retaliation, is not subject to social condemnation to the same extent. In many Oceanic communities sorcery, as such, is not the subject of any moral judgment. In dealing with such communities, Dr. Hogbin has aptly compared sorcery with a weapon such as a dagger. It is neither moral nor immoral in itself. If it is used to punish a thief or adulterer, then its use is justifiable. If it is employed for anti-social purposes and without provocation, then its employment is wrong, not because there is anything inherently evil in sorcery, but because the ends for which it is employed are unjustified.

---

[1] The term "witch" is generally employed in ethnographic writings to include both males and females, though the term "warlock" should more properly be applied to the former.

In conclusion, we may refer to some beliefs connected with witchcraft which are never associated with the activities commonly called sorcery. In many cases it is believed that a person may be a witch without being aware of the fact, and can inflict harm without intending to do so. It is held that such persons simply cannot avoid having a malevolent influence, which they exercise through the possession of the "evil eye" or some similar characteristic.

Similar ambiguities exist in the case of terms used for magical practitioners of various kinds. The term *magician* is employed both for those who practise black magic and for those who carry out magical rites approved by society, and it must be emphasized that the same person is often a practitioner in both fields. The term *medicine-man* is similarly used, though by derivation it should apply to an individual who employs magical substances or "medicines" to secure good or evil results, as is common among many African and Amerindian tribes. But it must be emphasized that elsewhere, for example in Melanesia and Australia, magical substances are often absent from magical practices or play a minor part in them. In these instances it is the rite or the spell, rather than the employment of herbs or other substances, in which magical potency is believed to reside.

In anthropology the term *witch doctor* is usually applied to individuals who possess the power of detecting witchcraft and identifying witches by magical practices, but in popular writings it is often used in a sense more or less equivalent to "medicineman", that is, as applying to someone who effects cures by the employment of magical substances or supernatural techniques. The term *shaman* is mainly used with reference to the Siberian tribes among which it originated and also Amerindian peoples. Shamans are broadly distinguished from priests, in that their activities are related to private or individual magic, such as diagnosing and curing illness, exorcizing evil spirits and providing charms to ensure success or good luck. The term *priest*, on the other hand, is usually restricted to functionaries who carry out public ceremonies on behalf of the community at large. But in many cultures, for example among the Eskimo, we find the two functions combined in the same individual.

It is impossible to be more definite on the use of all these terms. As with the terms "religion" and "magic", so with the names applied to various functionaries connected with these activities, we are unable to reach any satisfactory set of definitions. And as we saw in the case of law, attempts to define European terms in their application to primitive categories can never lead to any definite conclusion. Discussions on definition are useful as emphasizing first one and then another of the manifold facets of the phenomena we are considering, and as indicating in a very general way the sense in which various terms are employed. But we cannot reach anything approaching scientific definitions of general applicability, because the categories of primitive cultures vary greatly from our own and also from one another. The only way of achieving precision is to define the sense in which a series of terms is employed *with specific reference to each magico-religious system in turn*. This is done, for example, by Professor Evans-Pritchard in his study of witchcraft and its associated beliefs and practices among the Azande. He gives a list of native terms, an approximate English equivalent and a brief definition of the term *as it is employed by the natives*. In this way he ensures that the reader knows exactly what he means by such terms as "witch", "magician" and "witch doctor" in speaking of the Azande, though the meaning of such terms necessarily changes as soon as they are applied to any other culture.

3. The Cultural Function of Religion and Magic

Our emphasis upon the diversity of magico-religious beliefs, practices and functionaries must not blind us to the universality of beliefs connected with the supernatural and the common functions which they subserve in all human communities. Though various primitive peoples have different conceptions of the operation of supernatural forces, of the extent to which these act directly or through the agency of spiritual beings, of the moral justification or culpability of magical practices and of the specific powers of particular individuals, they all possess a *magico-religious system*. Very broadly, the function of this is to provide psychological safeguards against failure, methods of controlling the incalculable, expressions of collective optimism, explanations of failure and disaster, and ways of securing and enforcing socially orientated co-operation. This is not, of course, done consciously. We do not know how primitive peoples first arrived at beliefs and practices connected with the supernatural. All that we can observe is that they all have such beliefs and practices which are passed on from generation to generation as part of the cultural tradition, and that the existence and vitality of such beliefs and practices depend upon certain universal characteristics of human life.

All peoples possess a body of technical knowledge and equipment which enables them to satisfy their individual and social needs. But this is never entirely adequate. The need for food is menaced by shortages, droughts, hurricanes, pests and other dangers ; sickness is always possible and death inevitable; some pursuits, such as navigation and warfare, are specially hazardous; individuals suffer misfortune, and communities are sometimes visited with public calamities. On the other hand, there are windfalls and unexpected successes. All of these are, for the native, determined by factors not controllable by his scientific and technical equipment.

There exist, therefore, beliefs and practices which supplement the gaps in practical knowledge, give confidence against possible failure and stimulate hope of success. Magico-religious beliefs and practices provide (a) an explanation of incalculable and uncontrollable events in human life, and (b) a putative way of controlling them and steps which can be taken to express the hopes of the human beings concerned and to establish their faith that these hopes will be realized. This is vividly reflected in the way in which spells, rites and prayers envisage, anticipate and dramatize the result desired. Consider, for example, the following condensed extract from a spell of Trobriand garden magic:

"The belly of my garden grows to the size of a bush-hen's nest,
The belly of my garden grows like an ant-hill;
The belly of my garden rises and is bowed down,
The belly of my garden rises like the iron-wood palm,
The belly of my garden lies down,
The belly of my garden swells,
The belly of my garden swells as with a child."

To appreciate the meaning of such a spell, it is necessary to appreciate the position of the Trobriand gardener. Agriculture is the main pursuit of his life; a good harvest means a condition of *malia* or plenty, a bad one may mean *molu*, shortage, or even starvation; not only hunger, but self-respect, expressed in the obligations to present food to kinsfolk, are involved in the success of gardening. The Trobriander has a body of practical agricultural knowledge which he applies in gardening. But the outcome of his efforts is determined partly by factors which he cannot control by the employment of his practical knowledge and technique. Hence the significance of the above dramatic representation which envisages the desired result in a series of striking and often hyperbolic metaphors.

Not only the language but also the ritual of magic and religion provide a symbolic expression of the result desired. Sir James Frazer drew a distinction between two varieties of what he called *sympathetic magic*, namely, *homœopathic* and *contagious* magic. Sympathetic magic is founded, on Frazer's theory outlined above, on a mistaken application of the principles of association which may take two forms, based respectively upon similarity and contiguity. Thus, there are two widespread types of sorcery which exemplify the two kinds of magic. In one, an effigy of the victim is made in wax or some other substance, and is burned, pierced or otherwise injured in the belief that this will produce a similar effect on the victim. In the other type, something which has been in close contact with the victim—an item of clothing, nail parings, hair clippings or excreta—becomes the object of destructive magic. In both cases the emotional basis is similar, and hatred is expressed by destructive action against some material object which represents symbolically the hated person. The bodily expressions involved in magic are thus not unlike such actions as the clenching of the fists in anger, or the action of the lips, as though expelling some unpleasant substance from the mouth, in expressions of disgust. They are culturally standardized ways of expressing certain emotions for which they provide at least a partial satisfaction.

The universal tendency to express human hopes and desires in magico-religious speech or ritual does not mean that the native neglects practical measures to achieve his ends. He does not believe that he can produce fertility by spells and rites alone. He adopts all the practical measures provided by his culture, and in addition carries out magico-religious practices. Far from distracting from practical effort, these actually stimulate it by inhibiting apathy and despair and by providing a public stimulus towards constructive collective effort. We must distinguish between the illusory and the real effects of magico-religious practices. The results thought by the natives to follow are illusory, but the stimulating, vitalizing and organizing effects are real. In addition, as we shall see, a number of subsidiary functions are served: authority of parents and chiefs is reinforced, wrong-doers are deterred, and traditional standards generally are maintained. In addition, religious beliefs produce personal as well as social integration.

Before concluding our discussion of the cultural function of religion and magic, we must refer to an analytical discussion in which the explanation of magico-religious phenomena in terms of human anxiety is criticized with special reference to ritual. Professor Radcliffe-Brown writes: "I think that for certain rites it would be easy to maintain with equal plausibility an exactly contrary theory, namely, that if it were not for the existence of the rite and the beliefs associated with it, the individual would feel no anxiety, and that the psychological effect of the rite is to create in him a sense of insecurity or danger." [1] Professor Radcliffe-Brown goes on to emphasize the rôle of ritual in expressing social values. For him, such practices as the taboos observed by a father in connection with his wife's pregnancy are to be explained in terms of the obligatory social sentiments connected with the family, rather than as a psychological safeguard against the dangers awaiting the mother and newly born infant.

In view of what we have said concerning the unitary nature of magico-religious beliefs and practices, there does not appear to be any contradiction between the two theories. All magico-religious systems, and most magico-religious acts, have two aspects, which might be called respectively *consecratory* and *prophylactic* the latter term being employed in a psychological sense. These, of course, correspond with "religion" and "magic" in Malinowski's sense. But in the actual study of magico-religious phenomena they are inextricably interwoven, and can only be isolated by a process of abstraction. Thus, the taboos connected with childbirth serve both to express its social importance and to allay anxiety concerning the risks inevitably connected with the event. Similarly, the spell of Trobriand garden magic cited above stimulates confidence in a good crop, and also emphasizes the social importance of agriculture, which is one of the most important institutional activities of the Trobriand Islanders.

4. The Charter of Mythology

Among the beliefs connected with the magico-religious systems of primitive peoples, some of the most important are to be

[1] Radcliffe-Brown (8), p. 39.

found in the field of mythology. Almost all primitive peoples have some systematic account of how the world, and the various social institutions which make up their culture, came into being. Such beliefs interlock with others referring to the contemporary operation of supernatural forces, so that the two sets of belief form an integrated whole, myth and miracle being complementary to each other. But the effects of mythology extend beyond the purely magico-religious field. Mythology provides a charter for existing social institutions in a way which may be illustrated by reference to one of the many Trobriand myths connected with the Kula, namely, the myth of the Kudayuri flying canoe.

The story relates to the village of Kudayuri, on the island of Kitava. This island is fringed by a coral ridge surrounding a central declivity; large canoes are therefore dug out and lashed on the beach, as it would be difficult to carry them over the coral ridge if they were constructed in the villages.

At one time in the distant past the people of Kitava decided to go on a Kula expedition. All the villages set about constructing their canoes on the beaches except the village of Kudayuri, whose headman, a man called Mokatuboda, ordered the villagers, in spite of their protests, to prepare their canoe in the village. The myth goes on to describe the various technological activities of canoe building, as carried out in the village of Kudayuri under the direction of Mokatuboda and on the beach by members of other villages. When all was ready, Mokatuboda ordered his crew to man the canoe (which still lay in the village) and to hoist the sail. He recited magical spells and struck the canoe with a charmed adze, and the canoe flew into the air. A rock stood before it, but the flying canoe pierced through it. Mokatuboda looked out and saw the canoes of the other villages sailing upon the sea below. There are many incidents connected with this magical canoe, tales of how on the Kula expedition it always sailed last of all the fleet, but because of its superior speed arrived first at its destination.

The myth goes on to tell how Mokatuboda made evil garden magic to bring rain to his own garden but not to those of others, so that their crops were burned in the sun. The people decided to kill Mokatuboda so that they could perform magic for all the gardens. But they did not know that Mokatuboda had kept back some of the most powerful of his magic both for gardening and in connection with the flying canoe. They killed him, but when next year his younger brother attempted to carry out magic to make the canoe fly, this proved ineffective—when the crucial and dramatic moment came the canoe would not rise into the air, because some of the most vital parts of the magic had been kept back.

The three sisters of Mokatuboda, who had learned his flying magic, were angry at his murder and decided to leave Kitava. They flew about among neighbouring islands in a flying canoe, piercing certain rocks and sailing round promontories. One of them became a stone which can still be seen in the sea. The other two sailed on. One of them ate men, and she cast her eyes on the island of Dobu, hence the Dobuans are cannibals to this day. The other who was not a man-eater turned her face to Boyowa, hence the natives of this island do not eat human flesh. These two women were also changed into rocks visible in the sea, but spiritually they became flying witches.

This legend appears at first to consist largely of pointless incidents, and, indeed, it is a characteristic of primitive mythology that the behaviour of the characters often appears to be unmotivated. On the other hand, the myth possesses a very real significance in terms of the Kula and its associated magic. The first point to note is the emphasis on the efficiency of magic—it was because Mokatuboda possessed such extraordinary magic that he was able to cause his canoe to fly. Much of his magical knowledge died with him, but he did leave *some* of his magic, and this gives validity to beliefs in the magic actually performed today to impart speed to canoes. The myth, moreover, in the complete version, embodies a fairly complete description of a Kula expedition, even embracing details of technology involved in the preliminary preparation of a sea-going canoe.

The myth thus provides a charter for the institution of the Kula as it exists today, and in particular for the authority of the headman of a village as master of the canoe and organizer of the activities connected with it. It also gives an account of the origin of the flying witches, who are believed, among other malevolent activities, to menace the safety of men at sea. Finally, the myth explains certain contemporary features both of geographical environment and social custom. Certain rocks visible in the sea are connected with the doings of the sisters of Mokatuboda, as is the difference in the attitude towards the eating of human flesh in Dobu and in Boyowa respectively. The miraculous events narrated in the myth, with the sanction they provide for magical belief and social practice, thus become, as it were, embedded in reality. Visible features of the landscape provide tangible evidence of the truth and social relevance of the myth.

Many primitive myths are specifically concerned with accounting for and validating features of the social organization of the people concerned, for example, the Tikopia myth of the origin of totemism, which runs as follows: in the distant past a god called Tikarau came to Tikopia from distant lands. A feast was prepared to welcome him and a huge, pile of food laid out. By a ruse Tikarau disposed temporarily of his hosts, and while they were away seized all the food which had been laid out. Carrying this burden, he fled to the hills with the ancestor deities of the Tikopia in close pursuit. He tripped and fell at a certain spot, where a deep groove in the hillside today bears witness to the truth of the story. The ancestors of the Tikopia came up and, before Tikarau reached a cliff and launched himself into space, were able to seize four items of food. One seized a coco-nut, another a taro, another a breadfruit and others a yam. Thus, though Tikarau succeeded in stealing most of the feast, the ancestors of the Tikopia were able to preserve the principal food-stuffs and transmit them to posterity. The ancestral deity of Tafua clan saved the coco-nut, that of Taumako the taro and so on, so that the ancestor of each clan saved the particular food-stuff which is associated with it as a totem and which is believed to be under its special jurisdiction by virtue of the particular associations established in the myth.

A recognition of the function of myth in establishing a social order, linked with the natural order and going back to the beginning of time, helps to explain a feature of certain primitive theologies which is perplexing to us. The supreme deities of many primitive peoples are believed to play little part in contemporary affairs. Thus, in parts of Polynesia some of the greatest gods who played a leading part in the cosmogony were not actively worshipped and were believed to be remote from the affairs of men. The gods actually worshipped and believed to be powerful in affecting human destiny were lesser deities. Again, in Ashanti, the creator god 'Nyame was believed to be remote from everyday affairs, which were the province of the ancestral deities which ranked below him in the pantheon. The occurrence of such "lazy gods" can be understood if we appreciate the fact that the honour accorded to them and the tales of their miraculous deeds serve to establish social codes which are thus made binding and intelligible by virtue of their association with the very origin of the world.

In a rather special category of mythology we find widespread varieties of myths of the origin of death. These envisage a time in the distant past when man was immortal. They tell a story in which, usually through some lapse of attention or moral fault on the part of one of the characters, death was introduced. One type of such myths is that of the two messengers, as in the Zulu story of how the great creator spirit Unkulunkulu sent the chameleon with a message to mankind saying, "Let not men die". But the chameleon loitered on the way, and in the meantime Unkulunkulu changed his mind and sent the lizard after the chameleon with the message: "Let men die". Because of the chameleon's tardiness the lizard passed him on the way, and arrived first with his message of death, so that when the chameleon arrived, men said: "We have heard the words of the lizard—we cannot hear your words. Through the words of the lizard, men will die." The implication is, of course, that if the chameleon had arrived first, men would have remained immortal.

Another type of myth of the origin of death compares the mortality of man with the apparent revivification of reptiles and crabs which cast their outer covering from time to time. One such story from the Banks Islands tells of a time when human beings never died; when they became old they cast their skins, as snakes do, and so became young again. One day an old woman went to a stream to cast her skin, and when she threw it into the water it floated downstream, but caught on a stick. The woman, who was now young and attractive again, went home, but when she arrived her child did not recognize her. The child cried so much that the woman went back to the stream, fished out her old skin and put it on again. So that nowadays people become old and die, and do not cast their skins and renew their youth as reptiles appear to do.

These and several other types of myths of the origin of death [1] serve to make this phenomenon intelligible in moral or social terms, so that the individual and social tragedy of death appears less repellent than it would otherwise be.

[1] See Frazer (2), Vol. I, pp. 59–86.

Finally, we must refer to the importance of mythology in validating ceremonial, many examples of which we saw in our review of Karadjeri increase and initiation ceremonies. In other primitive communities also we find ceremonial accounted for and justified by myth in general terms if not specifically. In fact, the actual character of the relation between mythology and ceremonial is very flexible. Thus, among various tribes of the Gulf of Papua we find almost identical ceremonies validated by entirely different myths; in dealing with the Poro, we mentioned that there are several legendary accounts of its origin; and in any given mythological account of the origin of a social custom or ceremony there are usually gaps, confusions and even contradictions. The significance of mythology is not in the precision of its content, but in its symbolic expression of social values relating present-day practice and belief to events in the distant past, in such a way that the full significance of neither can be understood without reference to the other. Present-day custom, and its binding emotional force, can only be understood in terms of its mythological charter; while on the other hand, as Malinowski says, "living, recurrent, regenerated myth is a constant by-product of living faith which is in need of miracles; of sociological status which demands precedent and example; of moral rule which requires sanction".[1]

5. The Social and Individual Significance of Magico-religious Belief

This brings us to a consideration of religious beliefs which refer to the present-day operation of supernatural forces, distinct from, though related to, mythological beliefs referring to the distant past. This subject has not received the attention which it deserves in recent studies of primitive religion. In the reaction against the facile intellectualistic interpretations typified by the theories of Tylor and Frazer, modern anthropologists have tended to concentrate on ritual activities and the social functions of magico-religious institutions, to the exclusion of their dogmatic aspect. The study of the latter, as Professor Firth has pointed out, is less straightforward, and is made difficult by the absence in most primitive religions of anything approximating to a creed.[2] Their body of dogma must be inferred from observations of human behaviour and verbal statements, which are often confusing and contradictory.

[1] Malinowski (5), Vol. I, p. 464.   [2] Firth (14), p. 3.

These characteristics emerge from the fact that, in any given culture, religious beliefs may be divided into three kinds. There is a solid core of *nuclear* beliefs, never challenged by true believers; there is a set of *ancillary* beliefs or personal elaborations on the central themes of religious dogma; and finally there are *peripheral* beliefs which are even more flexible as a result of difficulty of formulation or lack of certainty or conviction.

All of these types of belief serve, in Firth's words, to "place the facts of emotion within an intellectual system". But the social, as distinct from the individual, significance of belief varies from one category to another. Nuclear beliefs are binding upon the whole society, and embody interpretations of nature and statements of social values to which all right-thinking individuals subscribe. They thus bind together the community by imposing upon its members a common set of intellectual interpretations and social values. The more flexible and fluctuating beliefs in the second two categories provide more scope for individual adjustment and expression for particular temperamental types. Thus, while in one sense religious belief is an integrating force in society, the expression of particular deviations from the normal in the more variable types of belief may lead to a splitting of society and, at more advanced stages of cultural development, to the conflicts of religions and sects which contrast so markedly with the relative homogeneity of religious belief in primitive society.

Among the most widespread types of religious belief found in primitive society are those relating to the survival of the soul after death. Some form or other of the *belief in immortality* is found in all primitive societies, though its character and social significance vary from one people to another. Sometimes it is only the souls of people of rank which are believed to be immortal; sometimes the belief is not in perpetual existence after death, but in survival for a period only; often the conception of survival takes the form of a belief in reincarnation.

A common characteristic of beliefs in immortality is their vagueness. While the belief in *some* form of survival is held by everybody, there are apt to be considerable differences of opinion among informants as to the actual conditions of the life after death. In fact, it would probably be true to say that native peoples are more interested in the social implications of death than in the fate of the individual soul.

Beliefs in immortality, together with mortuary ritual and

mourning, are to be conceived as a human protest against the social loss and disruption caused by a death as well as a negation of individual annihilation; in fact, the former aspect tends to receive more emphasis than the latter. This is particularly true in societies which practise some form or other of ancestor worship, or who look to the souls of the dead for help in day-to-day affairs and succour in time of crisis. Here the continued social effectiveness of the dead contrasts in a marked way with corresponding beliefs in modern civilization, where the dead are not believed to be able significantly to influence the fortunes of the living.

Before leaving the subject of magico-religious belief, we must refer to certain communities in which beliefs in supernatural power are generalized in a native term which has no English equivalent. Such a concept is that of **mana** found in the religious systems of Polynesia. *Mana* refers to supernatural power or extraordinary efficacy derived from the gods and affecting the lives and fortunes of human beings in different ways. A tool or weapon is effective because it possesses *mana*; temples, chiefs and sacred objects derive their sanctity from the *mana* which is associated with them and which makes dangerous any approach to them except in a ritually correct way; chiefs owe their authority, and craftsmen their success, to the *mana* which they possess. Clearly such a term as *mana*, which has been variously rendered as meaning strength, prestige, efficacy, skill or sanctity, cannot be simply translated by any of these terms, particularly as it is used in different senses in various contexts. But it is nevertheless profoundly significant in religious belief as representing an embodiment of supernatural power, respected in custom and sanctioned in mythology.

Much the same applies to similar concepts among other primitive communities. Thus the term *mana* also occurs in Melanesia, but with slightly different implications owing to the lesser elaboration of religious belief in this area, while in several Melanesian communities no such concept exists. Among many Amerindian tribes comparable beliefs are found, for example, the beliefs in *orenda*, the basis of magical power among the Iroquois, in *wakonda* or *wakang* among the Omaha, and in *manito* among Algonquian tribes. As in the case of *mana*, these terms cannot be simply translated into English—thus *manito* has been variously translated as spirit, god, devil, demon, guardian spirit and fetish. Thus it clearly differs from *mana* in its personal or anthropomorphic implications, but no simple comparisons can be instituted. Each of these embodiments of beliefs in the power of supernatural agencies can only be understood in terms of the specific magico-religious system and cultural context in which it occurs.

While we have recognized the importance of the dogmatic aspect of magico-religious systems, we must not forget its expression in human conduct, whether in the stylized procedure of ritual or in its more general ethical effects on human behaviour. These two aspects of primitive religion and magic will occupy our attention in the two succeeding sections.

6. Magico-religious Ritual

The standardized types of behaviour which we call magico-religious ritual may be of two kinds—bodily or verbal. Bodily ritual consists of stylized behaviour which reflects in a symbolic or dramatic way the result desired or the social attitudes expressed. We have already referred to the former in connection with magical ritual. In the case of forms of ritual which are religious, in Malinowski's sense, we find various types of social relationships expressed in an appropriate way. Thus, initiation ceremonies express dramatically the removal of the novice from society, his admission to a new place in the social structure, and his final return to the community as an adult.

The symbolic significance of ritual is perhaps best revealed in mortuary ceremonial, and particularly in the widespread occurrence of weeping, self-mutilation and other violent expressions of grief on the part of the mourners. Probably this does not bear any direct relationship to the grief actually experienced. In the case of near kin, it does as a rule involve genuine emotion, but in other cases it appears to be mainly a ceremonial affair. Weeping has been interpreted as a physiological reaction to a situation in which emotional readjustment is necessary. It does not occur only in connection with death, but also on such occasions as initiations, marriages and the return of members to the community after an absence.

The practices connected with the disposal of the dead vary greatly from one community to another. As to the psychology of mortuary ritual, it frequently appears to involve an ambivalent attitude—on the one hand an attitude of fear and horror towards the corpse, coupled with a desire to dispose of it as completely as possible; and on the other hand the desire to preserve and retain a close association with the body which has been an object of affection during life. Cremation and mummification respectively might be regarded as expressing the two opposite extremes of this ambivalent attitude. A compromise is sometimes reached by disposing of the corpse (for example, by burial) for a time, and thereafter recovering some special part of it, frequently the skull. This may be kept or even worn as a treasured relic.

Magico-religious ritual must always be considered in relation to the dogmatic beliefs with which it is correlated. This is particularly important when it brings human beings into relationship with gods, ancestor spirits or other supernatural beings. This relationship is frequently interpreted in terms of current social usage by a process which might be termed *socio-religious parallelism*. Thus offerings, sacrifices and libations express in economic terms the relation of human beings to supernatural beings who are pleased by the same things as are ordinary living men; ancestor worship reflects the social structure, in that each clan or family group appeals to its own ancestors; gods and spirits are subject to the same motives as human beings, and can be influenced in a similar way by requests, adulation and economic advantages.

Verbal ritual consists of chants, spells, prayers and other sacred formulæ. These reflect *the compulsive power of the word* in reinforcing belief, in achieving results and in inducing emotional attitudes. This is probably founded on early experiences of childhood, when individuals *can in fact* achieve results by uttering appropriate words, that is, by determining the conduct of adults. Human beings can be influenced by words, and so in native belief can supernatural beings and agencies. It should be noted how repetition, the use of secret or archaic words and formulæ and the reflection of the desired result in spell and prayer tend to reinforce the belief in the compulsive power of language. This is a very general feature of human psychology reflected in a wide range of phenomena from primitive magical spells to the elaborate techniques of modern advertising and propaganda.

We have so far dealt with forms of ritual which prescribe certain types of bodily or verbal behaviour at specific times and in order to achieve certain results or to express social attitudes. Contrasting with these are practices which we might describe as negative ritual, namely, rules which forbid certain types of speech or behaviour. Such rules are commonly referred to as taboos.

The term **taboo** is derived from the Oceanic word *tápu* or *tábu*, and refers to certain specific types of prohibition, violation of which is believed automatically and by supernatural means to produce undesirable consequences. It is important to emphasize the automatic operation of taboos, which are distinct from beliefs in supernatural punishments arising from the anger of ancestors or other supernatural beings. In the words of the Ganda, "It is the sin itself which kills". The nearest parallel among ourselves is to be found in certain beliefs of superstitious people, for example, that to walk under a ladder will bring "bad luck". But primitive beliefs in the operation of taboo are far more significant socially; they are held by all members of the community; the consequences of breach are more drastic and are usually more clearly defined than in the term "bad luck"; such consequences include illness or death for the offender or members of his family, failure in economic or social undertakings and other types of misfortune. As in the case of positive ritual, the proscriptions of taboo often bear a symbolic relationship to the results believed to follow from breach.

The specific types of behaviour forbidden by taboo among various primitive peoples cover practically every act of which a human being is capable. Food taboos, of which those connected with totemism are the commonest though by no means the only examples, may forbid the consumption of specific foods either temporarily or permanently. Such taboos often reflect the social structure, as when specific foods are reserved for men of rank, or are taboo to women or to the young. Another widespread group of taboos refer to sexual intercourse, as in those connected with the prohibition of incest and the Bantu custom of forbidding sexual intercourse between husband and wife while the latter is suckling an infant. Taboos on sexual intercourse are often imposed upon men in connection with dangerous or important social undertakings such as hunting, warfare, economic enterprises and the performance of magico-religious ceremonies.

Some taboos serve to protect the privileges of sacred persons or the sanctity of temples or other sacred places, any unauthorized approach to such persons or places being followed by dire consequences for the offender.

The term "taboo" cannot be simply translated by any English equivalent, since ideas of uncleanness, danger, sacredness and prohibition may all enter into situations to which the term is applied. Moreover, though natives are usually quite clear on the nature of the evil consequences which are believed to follow from breach of taboo, they are generally vague as to how taboo operates. They are not interested in metaphysical interpretations; the really significant thing to them is that certain acts are followed by unpleasant consequences. The acts forbidden are often of an anti-social character, for example, adultery, theft, incest and homicide. Beliefs in taboo thus serve a useful function in tending to discourage such conduct, and in this respect they serve the same function as beliefs in supernatural punishment through the intervention of sentient supernatural agencies, to which we shall refer in the next section.

7. *The Ethical Implications of Religion and Magic*

We have already encountered many examples of how magico-religious beliefs and practices provide sanctions for tribal custom in primitive society. Before going on to examine in detail the operation of a specific magico-religious system, we must refer in general terms to certain respects in which the influence of such a system in primitive communities differs from that which exists in our own society.

In the first place we have seen that primitive religious systems lack any explicit statement of dogma embodied in a creed. They likewise lack any comprehensive statements of moral injunctions, comparable, for example, with the Ten Commandments. There are certain cases of moral exhortations with a religious background, as in the *fono* [1] of Tonga and Tikopia, which consists of a set of moral precepts uttered by a chief to an assembly of the people. But more commonly the influence of magico-religious systems on human conduct in social affairs is not explicitly formulated, though its operation can be clearly discerned.

The general lack of abstract moral formulations in primitive religious systems is connected with the fact that the relations between supernatural beings and those who worship them are essentially personal. Wrongful acts may lead to supernatural punishment, because they rouse the personal anger of spiritual beings rather than because they are offences against a general moral order, as in more developed religious systems. But the effects on social order are very much the same, since the types of

---

[1] The meaning of the term *fono* in the areas mentioned should not be confused with the employment of the same word in Samoa to refer to political and ceremonial assemblies of chiefs and other men of rank.

anti-social acts which anger the spirits tend to be of the same kind as the "sins" of more advanced religions—adultery, murder, theft, greed, sacrilege and so on. The relationships between human beings and their deities, however, are based essentially on the principle of reciprocity—the former should render homage and follow lines of conduct pleasing to the latter, who in turn bestow blessings on the righteous and visit punishment upon offenders. If they fail to do this, active resentment may be aroused in the worshippers, an attitude quite different from passive acceptance of the Divine Will. We have seen how in the Tikopia dart match a man does not hesitate to rebuke a god who has failed to respond to the *kava* libation. An extreme but very illuminating example of this attitude comes from the Society Islands, where ancestral deities were sometimes discarded if they failed to discharge their obligations. It sometimes happened that when members of a family had suffered much from illness, and had appealed to their ancestral god in vain, they would decide to cast him off and seek protection from another deity. When this happened, the priest or head of the family would go to the ancestral temple and address the god as follows:

"There is casting off, I am casting thee off! Do not come in to possess me again; let me not be a seat for thee again! Let me not know thee again; do thou not know me again. Go and seek some other medium for thyself in another home. Let it not be me, not at all! I am wearied of thee—I am terrified of thee! I am expelling thee. Return not again to me. Behold the family, they are stricken with sickness; thou art taking them, thou art a terrible man-devouring god!"

Though such action as this is exceptional, it does illustrate a fundamental difference between such a religion as Christianity and primitive magico-religious systems. The former stresses the duty of men to do the Will of God, which should not be questioned; the latter lay more emphasis on the means by which the gods may be induced to do the will of the community.

Many magico-religious beliefs and practices support social codes indirectly. For example, seasonal agricultural rites tend to emphasize the essential economic activities of the seasonal round, to concentrate attention on the due performance of necessary work and to stimulate laggards to keep up with the rest of the community. Ancestor worship supports parental authority, since a father will one day be an ancestor of his lineage and must accordingly be treated with respect. Finally, beliefs in sorcery tend to protect individual rights and privileges, since a man will hesitate to do injury to another if he believes him to be armed with a weapon of supernatural retaliation—in particular this belief, as we have seen, often supports the political authority of chiefs and headmen.

It may be said, then, that all magico-religious systems provide sanctions for socially approved conduct, though the way in which they do so varies from one community to another. In order to gain an understanding of one such system, and of the integral relation between magico-religious belief and social behaviour, we shall in the next section refer briefly to Professor Evans-Pritchard's comprehensive description of witchcraft and related phenomena among the Azande.

8. Witchcraft among the Azande

The Azande are an African people whose territory lies partly in the Sudan, partly in the Belgian Congo and partly in French Equatorial Africa. They are politically organized in several autonomous kingdoms, each subdivided into provinces and districts, and ruled by kinsmen of a royal clan. The traditional form of settlement is the single homestead occupied by a polygamous family. The relative isolation of each homestead may be partly explained by the belief that witchcraft cannot operate at a distance.

A witch, to the Azande, is a person who harms other people by virtue of witchcraft, or *mangu*, a small ball of some hard substance located inside the belly and inherited patrilineally. It acts mysteriously; its "soul" leaves the body of the witch and so operates on the souls of inanimate objects or of organs of its victim as to cause misfortune or even death. It is the major cause of all misfortune and failure in Zandeland. If a man's crops fail, if he falls ill, if his house collapses and injures someone, he knows that witchcraft is at work. This theory does not exclude appreciation of natural causation. The Zande know, for example, that termites eat foundations of houses, causing them to collapse, but that does not explain why someone should be injured by a collapsing house. A boy who knocked his foot on a stump, receiving a cut which festered, explained the matter thus: It was not witchcraft which put the stump there, or which caused the cut—that was to be expected. It is not necessarily witchcraft which makes a person stub his toes, for people are often careless. But, he claimed, knocking a foot on a tree-stump does not usually result in a festering sore, whereas in his particular case it had, therefore it was due to witchcraft. Witchcraft explains why a person is brought into relation with a set of circumstances in such a way that he sustains injury.

Not every misfortune is allowed (by society as opposed to the individual sufferer) to be explained in this way. When a techno-logical, moral, legal or customary rule has been broken, any resulting misfortune is due, not to witchcraft, but to inefficiency or immorality. It is not witchcraft which makes a man commit adultery, be found out and punished, but his own evil nature. Thus the Zande belief in witchcraft is compatible with personal responsibility. Any culture necessarily postulates, not only that its standards of action ensure life, but also that obedience to them guarantees a successful life. In spite of obedience, however, failure and misfortune constantly occur. By accounting for this unpleasant truth, belief in witchcraft validates the normal Zande standards and by providing a protective course against witchcraft, to be described below, Zande culture ensures individual adjust-ment to misfortune with the minimum disturbance to society. The belief is also compatible with personal interpretation of events. The husbandman whose crops fail blames witchcraft, more fortunate neighbours his incompetence or immorality. The correct interpretation can be established by consulting an oracle.

A witch attacks only persons whom he or she dislikes, so if a man wants to know who is bewitching him, he puts before the oracle the names of his enemies, who he knows wish him harm. Witchcraft is a function of misfortune and bad personal relations. The range and character of a person's social relationships deter-mine who are his enemies, and hence whom he accuses of witch-craft. Thus, a male commoner never accuses an aristocrat, or a prince's deputy, rarely a woman or a child, but usually a male neighbour of equal status. Most adults have been accused of witchcraft, but no stigma attaches to this. Nevertheless, the Azande dislike being accused, and fear of it is a sanction for sociable behaviour.

Action against witchcraft is socially controlled. If, for example, a man falls ill, he summons witnesses and consults the oracle, which exposes the witch responsible. The witch's name is sent to the governor of the victim's province, who consults his own oracle. If the governor's oracle does not confirm the accusation, the victim must hold another seance—his oracle has been faulty. If the governor's oracle does confirm the victim's, then the accusation becomes a legal verdict. The governor sends the verdict to the witch, who must ritually withdraw his witchcraft and apologize for the trouble he is causing. The victim is informed, and the incident closes. The victim either gets better, proving the judgment of the oracle, or he does not, proving that other witches are also at work. In the latter case he consults the oracle again, and the procedure is re-enacted with reference to another witch. Eventually he recovers—or dies. The procedure at death is described later.

Oracles are the Azande's main weapon against witchcraft. They expose witches and divine the future presence of witchcraft. There are several kinds of oracles, differing in degree of fallibility, but all serve the same functions; only the poison oracle need be described. It consists of a poison administered to a chicken and questioned according to a stereotyped formula: its effect on the chicken is unpredictable. Any adult male may consult the oracle, on purchasing a dose of poison and obeying some preliminary taboos, but two persons must be present at a seance, one to administer poison and one to question it, while for important seances witnesses must also be present. Women and children cannot consult the oracle, but may obtain verdicts through a husband or father. The questions take the following form: "If X is a witch, poison oracle kill the fowl; if X is innocent, poison oracle spare the fowl." The chicken either dies or lives, thus answering yes or no.

The Azande do not manipulate the oracle so as to provide the answers they want. That would merely be to cheat themselves when it is vital for them to obtain accurate information on witches and witchcraft. Faith in its efficacy is sustained, because the information it provides cannot be empirically verified and because its advice is accepted and acted upon. Azande do not, for example, ask it if a certain plot of land will grow good crops, for they know which plots grow good crops. They ask the oracle whether, if crops are planted in a certain plot, they will fail through witchcraft. If the oracle replies in the affirmative, then they do not plant crops in that plot (unless a later consultation advises that the danger is over); hence they remain ignorant of what would have happened had they disregarded its advice. If the oracle replies "No", and the plot is cultivated and yet the crops fail, several beliefs may be invoked to safeguard faith in the oracle. There may have been no danger at the time the oracle was consulted, or a moral rule may have been broken since. Finally, witchcraft itself is able to damage the oracle, so that it answers incorrectly. Witchcraft and oracles are complementary, belief in one reinforces faith in the other.

Faith is also sustained by the oracle's connection with the rulers. The oracles of the kings and princes are ultimately infallible. To question their verdicts is to question political authority itself, a crime punishable at law. The oracle thus buttresses and is buttressed by political authority. It also enhances the authority of the head of the household, since its members can obtain advice only through him. Oracle verdicts have a compulsive force apart from the exposure of witches. A man may try to evade an obligation by saying (without consulting it) that his oracle warned him against it, but if he procrastinates too long, persons interested in the fulfilment of the obligation will consult their own oracle, a favourable verdict from which can be used in a law-court to compel the man to carry out his duties. Oracle verdicts are also used in court in cases of adultery.

Another weapon against witchcraft is the witch doctor, who by the aid of medicines which he swallows can divine witchcraft and by magical surgery and medicine can cure the illnesses which it causes. Only men are doctors, and become so by paying an established practitioner to teach them the secret skills of the craft, swearing a vow of secrecy, and undergoing a painful initiation. A doctor's seance is a communal entertainment, directed by up to a dozen doctors, and paid for by a wealthy man to whose prestige it redounds. In the course of the seance, drumming, music, dancing and gashing of the body may induce in the doctors a state of dissociation. In this condition they hint that members of the audience are witches, and proceed to banish witchcraft from the community. Doctors are not, however, as effective as oracles. Their hints have no legal standing, and they have neither authority nor high prestige. One of their favourite devices in curing illness is to conceal a small splinter of bone in the mouth, suck the afflicted part of the patient's body, and claim to have extracted the splinter, which is believed to cause pain. The Azande know that with some doctors this is merely a trick, and are sceptical of the powers of these particular doctors, but firmly believe that other, better, doctors can cure in this manner. Trickery can only be recognized as such, but scepticism in regard to particular doctors is an essential element in faith in witch doctoring.

The magic of witch doctors is only a part of the battery of rites and medicines available to the Azande. Zande magic differs from Melanesian magic in that there are few communal rites, in the privacy of its use, and in that medicines and not spells are its effective agent. Nevertheless, it is used for the same object—to ensure success where success is endangered by factors beyond control by the Azande. In agriculture, in love, in war, the Azande seek success through magic. Since witchcraft is the main cause of failure, most magic is bound up with protection against, or destruction of, witchcraft. Witchcraft, oracles and magic are interdependent components of a coherent and logically consistent system of behaviour and beliefs. Witchcraft endangers success, oracles disclose its presence, magic counteracts it.

There is an important distinction between two types of Zande magic, namely, good and evil magic (sorcery). The distinction is that sorcery flouts moral and legal rules, whereas good magic does not, and is often a sanction for obedience to them. Both may be used to destroy persons, but whereas to use magic to kill a law-abiding citizen is sorcery, a criminal offence, to use magic to punish a thief is approved; while to use vengeance magic to kill a witch who has killed one's kinsman is obligatory. What sanctions have the Azande to ensure that no one will use good but harmful magic for illegal purposes? The sanction is a belief that good destructive magic is by its very nature morally discriminating, will only attack criminals, and if wrongly used will kill the user himself. Good magic is only employed against unknown persons; if, for example, a thief is known, he is tried in court. Sorcery is directed at specific persons, with intent to kill, hence is evil, and a sorcerer would be killed on sight. There are very few sorcerers.

There is a wide range of plants providing the Azande with medicines. The plants themselves have no magic virtue; the extracts and concoctions from them acquire magic power because the Azande make them according to formulas which give them magical power. Magic is man-made. Anyone can acquire the knowledge of how to make medicines either by way of gifts from kinsmen or by buying it, but naturally the types of activity which a person engages in most, and his wealth, determine the types and amount of magic he will use. A prince will use much magic to attract followers, a husbandman to grow crops, a youth to gain success in amorous adventures. Spells and rites are often perfunctorily performed, consisting often simply of an order to "the soul" of the medicine to achieve the result desired. There are few myths accounting for Zande magic, but current "success stories" affirming its power are common everyday talk. If pressed to account for the origin of many medicines, the Azande attribute it vaguely to Mbori, the Supreme Being.

This brief account of some Azande supernatural beliefs and practices may give rise to two misconceptions. The first, that the Azande are preoccupied with the supernatural. This is not so. The greater part of their time is devoted to mundane affairs. Small failures and misfortunes do not occasion an oracle consultation, and, as they point out, it is not worth while finding out who bewitched you once your temporary misfortune has passed. The second, that all Azande would think alike in any one situation into which the supernatural enters. This also is not the case. Some men have more faith than others in particular medicines and witch doctors, and we have seen how their beliefs in witchcraft allow scope for individual interpretation of events. In any situation each person selects and uses the concepts and techniques most useful to himself.

There is one situation in which certain beliefs and actions are obligatory, and in which the interrelations between witchcraft, oracles and magic are most clearly seen. It is axiomatic that the death of a kinsman is always due to witchcraft, or occasionally to sorcery. When a man dies, his kinsmen ask the oracle to select two persons to avenge him, one to observe stringent sex and food taboos, and one to provide vengeance magic to kill the unknown witch. The accurate, honourable and unfailing vengeance magic is set in motion. Sooner or later someone else in the neighbourhood dies. The oracle is asked whether this person was the guilty one. Sooner or later the oracle will give an affirmative reply to some recently dead neighbour's name. This answer must be corroborated by a governor's oracle, and this invariably occurs sooner or later. The kinsmen cease mourning and rejoice. The magic has done its work, and the final justice of the universe has been triumphantly vindicated.

9. The Validation of Magico-religious Beliefs

Our review of the interrelationships of belief, ritual and ethics in primitive society generally, and with more detailed reference to a particular magico-religious system, reveals how far the modern anthropologist's approach to primitive beliefs differs from that which inspired the earlier theories mentioned at the beginning of this chapter. Considered as scientific interpretations or even as metaphysical speculations, the beliefs of primitive man do not command our respect. This is why they have so often been interpreted as the result of faulty logic, or even, as by Lévy Bruhl, as due to a "pre-logical mentality" which is incapable of the ordinary processes of reasoning known to civilized man. Some support appears to be given to this view by the tenacity with which primitive peoples cling to their "superstitions" in the face of what appear to us to be convincing demonstrations of their falsity.

A study of the social implications of magico-religious beliefs, however, shifts the emphasis away from the purely intellectual assessment of their logical bases. We find that such beliefs are not maintained merely by illogicality, ignorance of cause and effect, or blind faith in tradition, but by *positive* factors which validate them, that is, make them convincing, effective and acceptable to the human beings who hold them. Among these factors of validation are the following:

(*a*) The cultural limitations of knowledge in backward communities make plausible the magico-religious theories of success and failure. For example, the absence of scientific knowledge about disease does not mean that it is left unexplained; it is interpreted in terms of the anger of ancestors, breach of taboo, witchcraft, or the machinations of sorcerers.

(*b*) Early training in magico-religious beliefs leads them to be accepted as part of the whole cultural heritage. In particular we find that myths, legends, tales of the achievements of culture heroes and of famous magicians living and dead, reinforce belief in individuals with special powers and in supernatural agencies generally. What has once by general assent been effective is still effective; the forces which once produced disaster or outstanding success can still produce them.

(*c*) Magic is sometimes supported by trickery, for example, in the production of blood by Eskimo magicians at the annual expulsion of Sedna, or the extraction of foreign substances from the body of a sick man by Australian medicine men.

(*d*) The conditions under which activities are carried out are often such that beliefs are reinforced. For example, Australian totemic ceremonies are performed at places where the species is usually plentiful and at the time of the year when it normally becomes abundant, so that increase of the species *does in fact* generally follow the performance of rites, though not for the reasons given by the natives.

(*e*) Positive cases receive more attention than negative, successes more emphasis than failures, just as they do, for example, in popular anecdotes about the prophetic significance of dreams among ourselves.

(*f*) Many magical practices are secret, and it is therefore impossible to say whether they have been carried out in any given instance. What actually occur are cases of illness or other misfortunes, and these are *explained retrospectively* by postulating sorcery. This can never be proved or disproved, and an important ethnographic problem is whether many practices of black magic are ever in fact carried out. Often, as we have seen, they are obviously figments of the imagination, and from their very nature can never have occurred.

(*g*) The reputation and status of performers, who are often also expert in practical affairs, the taboos which they observe, the special and often esoteric language which they employ, and their use of substances of magical potency, may all serve to reinforce beliefs in their supernatural powers. In many cases their behaviour is abnormal and therefore impressive as suggesting that powers and forces beyond the ordinary experience of mankind are at work. In many of the phenomena of inspiration, possession and divination, the special qualities of neurotic or eccentric individuals are employed, these qualities being interpreted as manifestations of supernatural agencies.

(*h*) Explanations of failure form a most important part of the ideology of the supernatural among primitive peoples. As we have said above, positive cases receive more attention than negative. But when magico-religious techniques demonstrably fail to achieve their objective, this is never taken to indicate their futility. On the contrary, a variety of explanations are produced. Either the rites have not been properly carried out, or taboos have been neglected, or counter-magic has been performed, or "divine option" has been exercised. An example of the last of these is found among those peoples who believe that illness is caused by the anger of ancestral spirits. When this occurs, the ancestors may forgive after supplication or may remain adamant, the former explaining recovery and the latter a fatal termination of the illness. Whatever the result, ancestral power is not questioned. Much the same applies to beliefs in counter-magic, since no one can be really sure whether it has or has not in fact been carried out. The outcome is determined by a battle of forces on the supernatural plane, one or other being successful. The result, whatever it is, still supports belief in the power of supernatural agencies.

(i) Some beliefs connected with sorcery postulate "delayed action". It is held that the victim will *sooner or later* become ill or die, a statement which cannot be challenged.

We have mentioned some of the mechanisms by which magico-religious beliefs are validated. Their incidence and importance naturally vary greatly from one primitive community to another. But in every magico-religious system the context of belief ensures that it shall be acceptable and satisfying to the human beings concerned. In view of what has been said, we are no longer surprised at the tenacity of magico-religious beliefs, or at the way in which the native clings to his "superstitions" in the face of preaching by missionaries, solemn demonstration and argument by Government officials and ridicule by other Europeans.

10. Religion and Human Welfare

Throughout our discussion of magico-religious beliefs and practices, we have emphasized their culturally useful functions. But it is also necessary to question how far beliefs in supernatural causation prevent natives from experimenting with new practical measures. For example, Professor Firth has suggested that the Tikopia might have experimented with irrigation as a safeguard against drought if they did not believe that rain is controlled by special deities.[1] In the wider field of human experience the rôle of beliefs in supernatural forces in inhibiting material progress has been stressed by many philosophers and publicists. It is not necessary to go to primitive society for illustrations. Consider, for example, the following inscription from the churchyard at Silkstone, Yorkshire, commemorating the death in a mine disaster of twenty-six children, aged between seven and fifteen:

[1] Firth (10), pp. 89-91.

"This monument was erected to perpetuate the remembrance of an awful Visitation of the Almighty which took place in this Parish on the fourth day of July, 1838. On that eventful day the Lord sent forth his thunder, lightning, hail and rain, carrying devastation before them and by a sudden eruption of water into the Coalpits of R. C. Clarke, Esq., twenty-six human beings whose names are recorded here were suddenly summoned to appear before their Maker.

"Reader remember! Every neglected call of God will appear against thee at the Day of Judgment.

"Let this solemn warning then sink deep into thy heart, and so prepare thee that the Lord when he cometh may find thee watching."

It is impossible to say how far beliefs such as those reflected in the above text delayed the introduction of safety precautions in mines. It is, however, certain that they played an important part in maintaining social codes and in reconciling human beings to disaster. As in primitive magico-religious systems, human misfortune was exploited in the interests of social morality and human contentment. The general question whether the social advantages of such systems are offset by their disadvantages is one which cannot perhaps be answered entirely in terms of an empirical examination of their contributions to human happiness or misery. Many would hold that the question involves metaphysical premises which lie beyond the province of science.

11. Bibliographical Commentary

The theories of Tylor, Frazer and Durkheim have been selected for special treatment, and references have been provided in the text. The theory of "pre-logical mentality" is stated in Lévy Bruhl (1 and 2), and though this view is not acceptable nowadays, it is of interest from the point of view of the history of theories of primitive religion and magic. Other landmarks in this field are Lang, *Magic and Religion* and *The Making of Religion*; Robertson Smith, *The Early Religion of the Semites*; Marett, *The Threshold of Religion*, and Lowie, *Primitive Religion*. Of the many works by Sir James Frazer, *The Devil's Advocate* is undoubtedly the best by modern standards and provides many illustrations of the rôle of "superstition" in supporting cultural standards.

As regards more modern theories of primitive religion and

magic, that of Malinowski is expounded in Malinowski (12), critical comments on which are presented in Radcliffe-Brown (8). For an attempt to reconcile the two points of view, see Homans (1). For an elaboration of the theoretical point of view adopted in the present chapter, together with a description of the place of magico-religious beliefs and practices in various Polynesian cultures, see Piddington (4). The material contained in Section 8 of the present chapter is taken from an outstanding contribution to the ethnography of magico-religious institutions, namely, Evans-Pritchard (2). A valuable comparative study of magic in the Trobriand Islands and among the Azande is contained in Evans-Pritchard (8). On the psychological significance of religious belief see Firth (14) and for a comparative study of taboo consult Webster (1).

Descriptions of magico-religious beliefs and practices in relation to social life are contained in all good ethnographic records. Among those in which they receive special attention may be cited Firth (11), Fortune (1 and 2), Hogbin (2 and 3), Kuper (1), Nadel (1), and Strehlow (1).

CHAPTER XI

THE NATIVE AND OURSELVES

1. The Savage in Fancy Dress

WE have now completed our survey of some of the more important cultural activities of primitive peoples. The understanding which we have gained enables us to dispose of certain popular misconceptions. We have seen many times how untrained ethnographers and theorists who had never seen a native have completely misinterpreted the facts of primitive life and have, as it were, arrayed the savage in fancy dress, making him appear as a weird and exotic being quite distinct from ourselves and characterized by motives and ways of thought quite incommensurable with our own. A scientific study of primitive culture, on the other hand, enables us to see him as a human being like ourselves, whose apparently irrational, conventional or brutal behaviour can be understood in terms of the cultural context in which he lives, from which he derives his knowledge of the world and his system of values, and on which he depends for everything which makes life worth living for him.

Thus we have disposed of the "noble savage", that amiable imbecile who meanders through the ethnological writings of Elliot Smith. We have seen that primitive man is upon occasion aggressive, greedy and even disloyal to the cultural standards by which he lives. We have seen that his economic life is dominated, not by a "communistic group sentiment", but by a complex of motives in which self-interest, personal sentiment, respect for tradition and fear of supernatural sanctions are inextricably interwoven.

This implies that primitive man is also capable of altruism, of self-sacrifice in the interest of those he loves, and of adherence to the normative standards of his culture. We have thus also disposed of the "savage savage", described by one New Guinea missionary as "guided in his conduct by nothing but his instincts and propensities, and governed by his unchecked passions . . . lawless, inhuman and savage". This conception of primitive man is much more prevalent than the other, and many "barbarous" customs such as cannibalism and infanticide have been cited in support of it. Though most of these customs are of minor sociological importance, we may refer briefly to some of them.

2. Barbarous Customs

The incidence and importance of cannibalism have been greatly exaggerated in popular thought. Though it occurs sporadically throughout the world, the majority of primitive peoples are not cannibals, and most of the remainder eat human flesh only occasionally. The motive is only very rarely a crude appetite for human flesh as a delicacy. Sometimes it is a matter of necessity as among the Eskimo, where, as we have seen, some individuals were occasionally eaten in order that the remainder of the community might survive. Elsewhere, slain enemies are the most common victims, and such customs can frequently be interpreted as a dramatic expression of revenge, or in terms of the magico-religious belief that by the eating of a dead warrior his physical prowess and courage may be acquired by the consumer. This was the case among many Amerindian tribes, who scorned to eat human flesh other than that of valiant warriors. In other communities, again, cannibalism is connected with the institution of human sacrifice and is imposed as an obligation by magico-religious belief. An entirely different type of cannibalism is found among peoples who eat the flesh of their dead kinsfolk as part of mourning ritual which affirms the continued association between the living and the dead. Finally, in primitive societies in which slavery exists, we sometimes find that slaves are eaten, as among certain tribes of the north-west coast of America. It is impossible to assess the frequency of such practices, but it may be inferred that they were to some extent limited by practical if not by humanitarian considerations. You cannot have your slave and eat him.

The sporadic custom of infanticide is another feature of certain primitive cultures which has often shocked the European. Sometimes, like cannibalism, it is a necessity imposed by inadequacy of the food supply, the alternative to it being famine. The Tikopia, for example, are keenly conscious of the need to maintain a balance between population and food resources, and one of the means which they adopt to achieve this is infanticide. In some communities female infants are killed more frequently than males because of their lesser economic value or social prestige. In other communities male infants may be killed for political reasons, for example, the offspring of the inferior wives of chiefs whose survival might lead to conflicts over succession. Sometimes the death of one or other parent, particularly of the mother in childbirth, or the birth of illegitimate children, are reasons for infanticide. We can see how such practices are related to the importance of the family as the basic unit of kinship structure—in some communities this is expressed in the feeling that a child who lacks one or other parent should not be allowed to survive. In an entirely different category belong the Bantu practices connected with the killing of twins and abnormal children, the magico-religious basis of which we already know.

The occasional occurrence of infanticide does not indicate that primitive peoples are incapable of parental affection. On the contrary, most married people want to have children, and soon become fond of them when they are allowed to live. In individual cases motives of shame or laziness may lead to infanticide as they do occasionally among ourselves. But in the vast majority of cases the custom is related to such specific economic, political and magico-religious considerations as we have mentioned. In conclusion, it should be pointed out that the high rate of infant mortality in most primitive societies means that infanticide appears as less of an interference with the normal course of nature than in more advanced societies where it is expected that the vast majority of infants will survive.

Again, head-hunting, practised by several peoples of Malaysia and Melanesia, has, like the Amerindian practice of scalping, excited the horror of Europeans. But we invariably find that such customs are rooted in a social system in which the taking of a human head is a necessary step in attaining adult status, in proving manhood, or in attaining prestige within the community. We may condemn such systems of moral values as undesirable. We cannot blame individuals or communities for living by the normative standards of the culture into which they happen to be born.

Oddly enough, the practices connected with primitive warfare have often been cited in indictments of the savage. Wherever European administration has penetrated, attempts have been made to eradicate primitive forms of armed conflict; and a pursuit which among ourselves has been regarded for centuries as an honourable profession and a legitimate testing ground for human courage has been condemned and visited with drastic punishments.

A scientific and comparative study of warfare does not merely consist of assessing whether the refined forms of torture which the Society Islanders and the Natchez inflicted on their enemies were more horrible than the effects of an atomic bomb. The socio-logical task is to discern the entirely different characteristics of warfare among various human communities. Thus, in Australia the commonest causes of wars between hordes are to be found in the abduction of women and in beliefs in sorcery which, after an inquest to determine guilt, may lead to an avenging expedition. Wars for booty or territorial conquest are unknown in Australia, the former because of the poverty of material culture, and the latter because of the close association, both economic and magico-religious, of every aborigine with his own horde territory.

Warfare in Australia, based as it is on magico-religious beliefs and socio-sexual jealousy, and lacking altogether any traditions of martial prowess as an end in itself, differs profoundly from the cattle-raiding practised as a lucrative pursuit and honourable adventure by many African pastoralists. In a different category again must be placed wars for the conquest of agricultural lands as found among many Polynesian communities. Here, too, motives of economic gain and prestige were closely interwoven. But a comparative study of Polynesian communities sheds much light on the alleged inevitability of war and its supposed basis in human aggressiveness or a mystical entity called "the tribal spirit".[1] In the major island groups of Polynesia, with their elaborate political organizations and dynasties of ruling chiefs, warfare was common. But in the smaller islands there was con-siderable variability. In Manihiki and Rakahanga there were occasional family quarrels, but nothing which could properly be called warfare. In Mangaia there were constant and bitter wars over land. The natives of the former islands had a special official, the *tuha whenua* or land distributor, whose function was to forestall quarrels over land. In Mangaia the ownership of land was re-solved upon the battlefield. In Tikopia, again, a well-organized system of land tenure, based largely upon the authority of the chiefs, and thus integrated with a closely knit social and political structure, as well as the practices of birth control and infanticide, have prevented regular conflict.

[1] Cf. my controversy with Sir Arthur Keith on this point, *Man*, Vol. XL, Nos. 57, 76 and 122.

Our treatment of these various customs indicates that such terms as "infanticide" or "warfare" do not correspond to anthropological entities, much less are they manifestations of specific types of character or of "human nature". They are merely useful labels for certain broadly and superficially similar types of human behaviour. In various communities we find different institutional settings and different constellations of human beliefs and motives in the context of which such practices as warfare and infanticide must be considered. Whatever our ultimate moral judgment may be, such an approach makes the customs we have mentioned at least comprehensible in terms of the motives of human beings reared in a cultural environment entirely different from our own.

3. Savage Superstition

Our discussion of religion and magic has emancipated us from the popular belief that the native is irrational, that he is in all matters a slave to his superstitions, and that he feels himself beset on every side by terrifying supernatural forces. As regards the last of these fallacies, the true position has been admirably stated by Dr. Hogbin with reference to certain magico-religious beliefs in Ontong Java: "It has often been said that natives live in a constant state of dread of supernatural forces, which prevents them from committing the actions we have called sins. As a matter of fact, no natives do live in such a state of terror. The Ontong Javanese think no more of the kipua (ancestor spirits) than we do of divine punishment or of criminal procedure. At times they are afraid, just as Europeans sometimes fear the arm of the law or the Last Judgment, but such moments are comparatively rare."[1]

To this statement it should perhaps be added that in view of the inadequacy of technical, medical and scientific knowledge in primitive society, the field of magico-religious belief is in general wider than among ourselves. Since more events are incalculable and uncontrollable, the incidence of magico-religious practices is greater. In our own history, it has been the growth of scientific knowledge and techniques which has accounted largely for the attenuation of magical practices. Faced with, say, a diphtheria epidemic, we now have our children immunized instead of burning some unfortunate old hag at the stake as did our ancestors not so many centuries ago. But our ancestors were not obsessed by the fear of witchcraft, any more than are primitive peoples. One

[1] Hogbin (2), p. 162.

might as well say that modern parents live in a constant state of dread that their children will contract some disease with which medical science will be unable to cope.

4. Race and Culture

In our first chapter we distinguished between race, which is a subject of study in physical anthropology, and culture, which is our own subject-matter. These two concepts are often confused. For example, we are apt to meet such statements as: "The Polynesians were a warlike race". As we have seen in Section 2, whether any particular group of human beings of Polynesian race were warlike or not depended upon their culture; for example, whether they lived in the Society Islands or in Tikopia. Therefore, though the study of race is not within our province, we must say a word or two about what we mean by the term, and more important still what we do *not* mean by it.

It is obvious that the physical differences which are called "racial" exist, and are transmitted by heredity.[1] To realize this one has only to compare the ape-like lips of the European with the corresponding features of the African negro; and to note that the descendants of negroes in the New World continue (apart from racial mixture) to exhibit the same characteristics as their ancestors, while the lips of generations of Europeans born in Africa continue to resemble those of the chimpanzee. Thus, when groups of human beings possessing certain physical characteristics interbreed, these characteristics tend to be transmitted from one generation to the next, and groups of people sharing such characteristics may be loosely referred to as a race. But owing to centuries of migration and interbreeding throughout the world, there is practically no such thing as a pure race. For example, the writer of this book and most of its readers belong to a mongrel stock, contrasting with the relatively pure racial stock of the Australian aborigines who have been isolated for many centuries from extensive contacts with other peoples.

But apart from purely scientific studies in comparative somatology and human genetics, which are concerned with such problems, theories of race play a far more significant part in human relationships through the tendency to assume that *mental* differ-

---

[1] It should be noted that certain researches, such as those recorded in Shapiro (1), seem to indicate that the genetic characteristics of race are by no means so stable as was previously supposed.

ences, whether in temperament or intelligence, are associated with the physical traits which we call racial. There is no evidence for this assumption, which it is at present impossible either to prove or to disprove. It is possible, for example, that the average Australian aborigine may be slightly more intelligent than the average European or Chinese. But it is impossible to say whether this is so or not. As we shall see in dealing with mental tests in Volume II, the necessary instruments and techniques of measurement simply do not exist. In the words of an eminent biologist: "I do not hesitate to say that all existing and genuine scientific knowledge about the way in which the physical characteristics of human communities are related to their cultural capabilities can be written out on the back of a postage stamp."[1]

Why, then, do we find the beliefs in racial differences in mentality to which we have referred? They have been aptly described by Professor Ashley-Montagu as "man's most dangerous myth". This is not merely a striking metaphor. It is a profound sociological truth. As with the myths of primitive peoples reviewed in this book, the importance of beliefs in racial differences in mental capacity lies, not in their correspondence with established fact, which is negligible. It lies in the way in which they act as a charter for human conduct, or perhaps it would be better to say inhuman conduct. They support policies of racial segregation and discrimination, and they serve as a charter for the economic exploitation of one race by another.

5. The "Practical Man"

The doctrine of racial inequality finds expression, not only in the legal codes of South Africa and certain southern states of the U.S.A. In a more or less explicit form it is an essential part of the creed of the self-styled "practical man", whom one may meet in any far-flung outpost of Empire where Europeans are in contact with native peoples. He is usually a trader or employer of native labour.[2] He has perhaps never spent more than a few hours at a time in a native village, but he readily asserts that his years of residence in the country give him a better knowledge of the

[1] Hogben, "Race and Prejudice," in *Dangerous Thoughts*, p. 47. This essay should be read by all those who still have a lingering suspicion that there might be some evidence for popular theories about racial differences in mentality.
[2] I wish explicitly to exclude from the following strictures those few individual employers and traders who through inherent intellectual honesty or human sympathy are able to think beyond the mythology of their class, as I also exclude the vast majority of administrators and missionaries.

natives than can be acquired by the professional anthropologist, whom he dismisses as a "theorist". An analogy with this view would be the statement that an attendant who has spent twenty years of his life scrubbing out the wards of a hospital knows more of the treatment of disease than a newly qualified medical practitioner.

This type of practical man has a profound contempt for the mentality of the native, often expressed in the assertion that the native is a child and must be treated as such. This view is none the less wrong because it is sometimes not unkindly expressed. It is one of those popular fallacies which are produced by complete misunderstanding of the native point of view. The native sometimes *appears* to behave as a child because he is unfamiliar with our cultural material, with our feelings and standards of conduct, as we are with his. After all, most European adults handling chopsticks look very much like children handling a knife and fork, and for the same reason—they have not the necessary culturally acquired skill. But a Chinese would hardly be justified in saying that the manual dexterity of a European is like that of a child. And what can be said of manual dexterity is even more true of behaviour patterns such as manners, sentiments and the nuances of emotional response peculiar to each culture.

The native is a highly specialized adult with his own cultural equipment, which incidentally makes *us* look very foolish to *him* at times. If he appears gauche, obstinate, stupid or capricious, it is not for the same reason as with a child. A child has only a very imperfect understanding of any cultural values and ways of behaving. The native has a cultural equipment of his own, and when his behaviour seems to be queer, foolish and naïve, the European observer is more likely to be right if he attributes this to his own ignorance than if he assumes that "the native is like a child".

Another favourite assertion of the practical man is that the native is lazy. We know enough of the motives in productive effort to realize that, within the context of primitive economic institutions, this is not true. But these institutions differ markedly from our own, particularly in their seasonal rhythm. They call for periods of intensive effort, alternating with periods of leisure, festivities and ceremonial. This contrasts with our own conception of a regular daily routine of work throughout the year. There is, moreover, little stress upon promptness and a regular time-table of work. Whether a party of hunters in Australia sets out at dawn or two hours later does not matter very much. There is no need for the alarm-clock mentality which characterizes our own conception of work. Moreover, the tasks which the native carries out for his European employer are usually dull and menial ones, with poor pay and very little prospect of promotion. One is not surprised that, for example in New Guinea before the war, native indentured labourers were not enthusiastic about cutting grass on coco-nut plantations with a piece of hoop-iron for the princely reward of 10s. per month.

The most important consideration, however, is qualitative and not quantitative. The work which the native does for the European has none of the stimulating and exciting cultural context of productive effort under primitive conditions, and fails to provide the incentives to effort with which we are familiar. The native, then, is only lazy with reference to superimposed goals, motives and traditional standards of economic behaviour which are peculiar to European civilization.

Having affirmed that the native is superstitious, irrational, lazy and of childish mentality, the "practical man" will often go on to explain that he nevertheless possesses extraordinary and mysterious psychic powers such as a gift for telepathy or capacity to predict events. Now modern experimental psychology has amply demonstrated, in the case of some European subjects at least, the existence of extra-sensory perception, even though both descriptively and theoretically this is a relatively new field in which few very definite conclusions have been reached. Granted the existence of what psychologists call the "ψ" factor in human personality, it is possible that there are racial variations in this respect. But, as with other mental traits, there is no scientific evidence on this point. In the present state of our knowledge, all we can do is to exercise extreme caution in accepting the anecdotes which are told of the alleged psychic powers of natives, since the events described in them are in many cases at least capable of much more simple explanations. The writer was once sitting at dusk with a group of white people on a verandah in north-western Australia. Two or three native servants were sitting nearby, and during a pause in the conversation one native woman remarked with reference to one of the white women present: "I think Missis go inside soon". This astounded the white woman, who said afterwards that this was exactly the thought which was passing through her mind at the time. It is all too easy to attribute such incidents to supernormal psychic powers. Actually, as subsequent enquiries

revealed, the native girl had simply noticed that the white woman
had started to swat mosquitoes which were beginning to appear,
and, knowing the reaction of Europeans to these insects, had
accurately inferred her thoughts and predicted her behaviour.

When the practical man quotes such incidents in support of the
theory of native psychic powers, the interesting thing is not that
he is or may be mistaken, but that his interpretation is related to
his contempt for the other mental capabilities of native peoples.
It is precisely because he underestimates their capacity for
ordinary commonsense observation and their shrewd knowledge
of the ways of white people that he feels called upon to assume
mysterious psychic powers to account for manifestations of ordinary human intelligence.

6. The Place of Social Anthropology in Modern Culture

Like other sciences, perhaps more than other sciences, social
anthropology has a part to play in the rational adjustment of
present-day humanity to the chaotic world in which it finds itself.
It has obvious practical implications in the field of culture contact
and in the solution of the problems raised by the impact of modern
civilization upon primitive peoples, problems with which we shall
deal in Volume II. But these more obvious practical applications
of our science do not exhaust its contribution to human welfare.
Even a limited survey of primitive society serves indirectly to
widen our conception of our place in the universe in which we
live. The following statement expresses this point of view:

"Though it may be given to us for a moment to enter into the
soul of a savage and through his eyes to look at the outer world
and feel ourselves what it must feel to *him* to be himself—yet our
final goal is to enrich and deepen our own world's vision, to understand our own nature and to make it finer, intellectually and
artistically. In grasping the essential outlook of others, with the
reverence and real understanding due even to savages, we cannot
help widening our own. We cannot possibly reach the final
Socratic wisdom of knowing ourselves if we never leave the
narrow confinement of the customs, beliefs and prejudices into
which every man is born. Nothing can teach us a better lesson in
this matter of ultimate importance than the habit of mind which
allows us to treat the beliefs and values of another man from his
point of view. Nor has civilized humanity ever needed such
tolerance more than now, when prejudice, ill-will and vindictive-

ness are dividing each European nation from another, when all the ideals, cherished and proclaimed as the highest achievements of civilization, science and religion, have been thrown to the winds. The Science of Man, in its most refined and deepest version, should lead us to such knowledge and to tolerance and generosity, based on the understanding of other men's point of view." [1]

It follows from this that the scientific study of primitive cultures helps us in the understanding of our own. We can see ourselves as products of the values, material equipment, sentiments and systems of knowledge which constitute the culture in which we live and which has moulded our personalities, feelings and opinions as culture does and has done for every individual human being who has ever lived. We can view our most firmly held beliefs and our most cherished traditions objectively, as merely one form of cultural adjustment. But this does not imply, in the face of the overwhelming problems with which we are faced, an attitude of intellectual nihilism or moral apathy. On the contrary, the postulate of human needs enables us to consider our own institutions, customs and values in terms of an ultimate normative conception of how far they contribute to human happiness or misery. In this intellectual adventure, with its enormous potentialities for human welfare, we are faced with complex problems. Our solutions for them must almost always be tentative, and will, because of the limitations of knowledge, often be wrong. Our goals are distant and but dimly envisaged, our methods are at present crude and inadequate, our task seems overwhelming in its magnitude. But— and here we pass from demonstrable scientific principles to an assertion of personal conviction—the task envisaged is worth while.

END OF VOLUME I

[1] Malinowski (1), pp. 517-18.

AN ETHNOGRAPHIC DIRECTORY

THE following list indicates approximately the location of various peoples mentioned in this work, or which the student may encounter in further reading. The list is intended primarily for reference, and no attempt should be made to memorize it in its entirety. The index should also be consulted.

It must be emphasized that the peoples mentioned constitute only a minute proportion of the primitive cultures of the world, and that the definition of habitat in terms of modern political boundaries is only approximate (cf. pp. 31–2). In the case of Bantu peoples, the tribal prefix (p. 34) has usually been omitted.

In certain cases reference has been made to points of special interest in connection with the cultures concerned, and some limited suggestions for further reading have been included. In the case of peoples mentioned in the general surveys contained in Forde (1) and Murdock (1), references to these works are given. The digest contained in them should be sufficient for introductory reading, while they provide ample bibliographies for the student who wishes to refer to original sources.

Aborigines: This term refers to the native inhabitants of any area in pre-European times and their descendants. But it is rarely used except in reference to the Australian aborigines (*q.v.*). Note that : he adjectival form, "aboriginal", should not be used as a noun.

Ainu: A primitive non-Mongolian people of northern Japan. Murdock (1).

Aleut: A branch of the Eskimo inhabiting the Aleutian Islands.

Algonkin: A term originally applied to a small tribe of Algonquian-speaking Indians inhabiting territory east of Ottawa. More generally used to refer to the Algonquian Family of languages, a linguistic stock of North America covering extensive territory from Newfoundland in the east to the Rocky Mountains in the west, and from Pamlico Sound in the south-east to the Churchill River in the north-west.

Andaman Islanders: A hunting and food-gathering people of the Andaman Islands, Bay of Bengal. Radcliffe-Brown (1).

Ankole: A native kingdom of western Uganda. The Banyankole are remarkable for the system of economic and social symbiosis of the politically dominant pastoral Bahima and the socially inferior agricultural Bairu. Oberg (1–3).

Aranda (or *Arunta*): An Australian tribe inhabiting territory around Alice Springs, Central Australia. Murdock (1).

Arapesh: A mountain-dwelling people of northern New Guinea.

Arunta: See Aranda.

Ashanti: A native kingdom of the Gold Coast. The story of the Golden Stool of Ashanti illustrates very well the effects of misunderstanding native custom. Smith, E. W. (1).

Atsugewi: An Amerindian tribe of north-eastern California.

Australian aborigines: Hunters and food-gatherers of Australia. They should not be referred to as "blackfellows", though this is a common Australian usage, or as "Bushmen" (*q.v.*). In Australia the term "bushman" (usually with the adjective "good") is used to refer to a *white* man who is expert in bush craft, and can fend for himself when far from civilization. See also *Aborigines*. Elkin (3).

Azande: A group of kingdoms of Central Africa around the junction of the frontiers of French Equatorial Africa, the Belgian Congo and the Anglo-Egyptian Sudan. Notable for Evans-Pritchard's very detailed analysis of beliefs connected with witchcraft, and their social significance. Evans-Pritchard (2).

Aztecs: A people of the valley of Mexico. Murdock (1).

Bahima, Bairu, Banyankole: See *Ankole*.

Baiga: A primitive tribe of the Central Provinces of India. Elwin (1).

Bedouin (or *Badawin*): Primarily camel-keeping peoples of Arabia, though their culture has exerted an important influence on neighbouring desert regions of North Africa. The true Bedouins subsist mainly upon the milk of herds of camels, though among marginal groups inhabiting slightly more fertile territory other kinds of livestock are kept, and in certain areas some agriculture is practised. Economically the camel is the most important domesticated animal of this region, though horses are more highly prized for social reasons. Warfare, either to secure camels or as a means of obtaining prestige or avenging wrongs, is very common among the Bedouin, who are organized into patrilineal kinship groups under the leadership of a chief or *sheikh*. Forde (1) and Musil (1).

Bellacoola: A people of the north-west coast of America (*q.v.*) between Queen Charlotte and Vancouver Islands.

Bemba: A Bantu tribe of north-eastern Rhodesia. A matrilineal, matrilocal, agricultural people among whom work carried out by the bridegroom for the parents of the bride takes the place of the more common Bantu *lobola*. Richards (4).

Benin: A native city of southern Nigeria, famous for its very beautiful native work in bronze.

Blackfoot: An American Indian people of the Bison area, inhabiting territory on both sides of the Canadian-U.S.A. border, now Alberta and Montana. Forde (1).

Boro: A people of South America inhabiting territory around the junction of the frontiers of Brazil, Peru and Colombia. Forde (1).

Bushmen: A hunting and food-gathering people of the Kalahari Desert, South Africa. Forde (1).

Cayuga: One of the tribal groups composing the League of the Iroquois (*q.v.*).

Chaga: A Bantu tribe of northern Tanganyika. Raum (2).

Chenchus: A primitive people of southern Hyderabad, India. Fürer-Haimendorf (1).

Cherokee: A powerful Amerindian tribe of northern Georgia and the Carolinas.

Cheyenne: Traditionally the Cheyenne were an agricultural tribe of Minnesota, but they were driven westwards by the Sioux and southwards as far as Colorado by other hostile tribes. During this process they "lost the corn" and became bison hunters like other Plains Indians.

Chinook: A small tribe of South-west Washington who spoke one of the Chinookan family of languages, and also gave their name to the "Chinook Jargon" (*q.v.*).

Chinook Jargon: A trade language spoken in the Columbia River region of North America and along the Pacific Coast from California to Alaska. It existed in pre-Columbian times as an intertribal *lingua franca*, but was later supplemented by words from English, French and possibly Russian.

Chins: A primitive people of Burma. Stevenson (1).

Chippewa: One of the largest tribes of North America, occupying territory around the shores of Lakes Huron and Superior. Estimates of their numbers at different periods range from 15,000 to 30,000.

Chiricahua: A mountain tribe of South-east Arizona.

Chocktaw: An agricultural people of central Mississippi.

Chuckchi: Reindeer herders and seal hunters of the extreme north-east of Siberia. Forde (1).

Cochin: A native state of the Malabar coast, southern India. Forde (1).

Cook Islands: A group of islands of south central Polynesia.

Cree: An Algonquian tribe of Manitoba and Saskatchewan.

Creeks: A group of tribes of Alabama and Georgia, so called from the numerous streams in their country.

Crow: A western Plains Indian tribe of Wyoming and Montana. Murdock (1).

Dahomey: A once powerful negro kingdom forming part of what is now the French West African colony of the same name. Murdock (1).

Dakota (or *Sioux*): The largest group of the Siouan family occupying an extensive area of north central U.S.A., particularly the two states of the same name and Minnesota.

Dieri: An Australian tribe to the east of Lake Eyre, south central Australia.

Digger Indians: A term originally applied to the Nuanuints, a small tribe of South-west Utah, who were the only Pauite tribe to practise agriculture. The term is also applied to a number of western food-gatherers who relied largely on roots for food.

Dinka: A nilotic people of the Anglo-Egyptian Sudan. Seligman, C. G. and B. Z. (1).

Dobu: A Melanesian island south of the Trobriands. Fortune (1).

Dyak: A term somewhat loosely applied to a wide variety of non-Mohammedan peoples of Borneo. Cole (1).

Eskimo (or *Esquimaux*): Aboriginal inhabitants of northern Canada and islands to the north, also extending westwards over the Aleutian Islands to the north-east coast of Asia. Forde (1); Murdock (1).

Ewe: A linguistic group of the central West African coast.

Flathead: A term applied to various Amerindian tribes who practised artificial deformation of the heads of infants.

Fox: An Algonquian tribe of Wisconsin.

Fulani: Cattle-keeping people of the northern territories of West Africa.

Galla (or *Gallas*): A group of predominantly pastoral tribes of Abyssinia and northern Kenya.

Ganda: A Bantu people of Uganda. Mair (3); Murdock (1).

Gikuyu: See Kikuyu.

Guadalcanal: A Melanesian island of the Solomon Group.

Haida: One of the peoples of the north-west coast (*q.v.*) of America. Murdock (1).

Hausa: A large group of Mohammedan people of northern Nigeria.

Hawaiian Islands: Northernmost of the large island groups of Polynesia.

Hehe: A Bantu tribe of Iringa Province, Tanganyika. The Hehe are notable as the subject of an experiment in applied anthropology. Brown and Hutt (1).

Herero: A Bantu people of South-west Africa.

Hidatsa: A Siouan tribe of North Dakota.

Hopi: An agricultural people of northern Arizona. Murdock (1).

Hottentots: Nomadic herders of South-west Africa, distinct from the Bushmen of the Kalahari Desert and the neighbouring Bantu peoples. Murdock (1).

Hupa: An Amerindian tribe of the Trinity River, California.

Huron: A people inhabiting the strip of land between Lakes Huron and Ontario.

Ibo: A large linguistic group of south-eastern Nigeria. Meek (1).

Igorot: A term loosely applied to various pagan peoples of north-western Luzon. Cole (1).

Ila: A Bantu people of Northern Rhodesia. Smith and Dale (1).

Incas: A Peruvian people having a highly developed culture. Murdock (1).

Iroquois: The League of the Iroquois was a confederation of American Indian tribes of northern New York. They were remarkable for their complex political system and highly developed matrilineal organization. Murdock (1).

Jaga: A warlike tribe of Angola.

Kababish: A pastoral people of the Anglo-Egyptian Sudan whose ecology combines elements from the cattle-keeping tribes to the east and the camel-keeping peoples to the west.

Kaffir (or *Kafir*)*:* A popular name for the Bantu peoples of South-east Africa. Not used as a term in social anthropology.

Kano: A city of northern Nigeria, centre of the Hausa craft of leather-work.

Kaihsienkung: A Chinese village about eighty miles west of Shanghai. Fei (1).

Karadjeri: An Australian tribe inhabiting the coastal region and hinterland, La Grange Bay, north-western Australia.

Kariera: An Australian tribe inhabiting territory south of the De Grey River, Western Australia.

Kayan: An agricultural river-dwelling people of Borneo. Cole (1).

Kazaks: A pastoral people of Central Asia, between the Caspian Sea and Chinese Turkestan. Murdock (1); Forde (1).

Kede (or *Kyedye*)*:* A sub-group of the Nupe living in settlements on the banks of the Niger and Kaduna Rivers. Their livelihood depends mainly on fishing and the river transport traffic, of which they have a virtual monopoly. Nadel (3).

Khoisan Peoples: A term used in physical anthropology to denote the Bushmen and Hottentots.

Kikuyu (or *Gikuyu*)*:* A Bantu tribe of Kenya, north-east of Nairobi and east of Mount Kenya.

Kimberley Tribes: A number of Australian tribes inhabiting the Kimberley division of Western Australia. Kaberry (1).

Koryak: A people of eastern Asia to the north of Kamchatka. Their ecology depends largely on fishing and reindeer-herding. Forde (1).

Kwakiutl: One of the peoples of the north-west coast (*q.v.*) of America. Forde (1).

League of the Iroquois: See Iroquois.

Lepchas: A people of Sikkim, east of Nepal, northern India. Gorer (1).

Lovedu: A Bantu people of the north-eastern Transvaal.

Malaita: A Melanesian Island of the Solomon Group.

Manam: An island off the northern coast of New Guinea. Wedgwood (2-4).

Mangaia: A Polynesian Island of the Cook Group.

Manihiki and Rakahanga: Two small islands of Central Polynesia, approximately half-way between the Marquesas and Samoa.

Manua: An island of American Samoa. Mead (1).

Manya-Krobo: One of the peoples inhabiting the Shai Plain of the Gold Coast, between the River Volta and the Accra Plain.

Maori: The aboriginal Polynesian inhabitants of New Zealand. Firth (1).

Marquesas: A large island group of north-eastern Polynesia.

Masai: A tribe of northern Tanganyika and southern Kenya. An essentially pastoral people who despise agriculture. Forde (1).

Melanesia: An area of the Pacific. It includes New Guinea and the arc of islands to the north-east of Australia, extending southwards as far as New Caledonia and eastwards to Fiji.

Mende (or *Mendi*): A tribe of Sierra Leone. Their political system includes an interesting method of elective succession of chieftainship. Hofstra (1); Little (1 and 2).

Micmac: An Algonquian tribe of Nova Scotia and Prince Edward Island.

Micronesia: An area of the Pacific covering the small scattered islands to the north of Melanesia (*q.v.*).

Miwok: A tribe of central California.

Mohawk: One of the tribal groups composing the League of the Iroquois (*q.v.*).

Mundugumor: A New Guinea tribe of the Sepik River.

Munshi: A people of central Nigeria.

Murngin: An Australian tribe of north-eastern Arnhem Land, Northern Territory of Australia. Warner (1).

Nagas: A group of agricultural tribes of the Naga Hills of Assam.

Natchez: An agricultural tribe of the lower Mississippi, remarkable for their complex system of descent and rank. Swanton (1).

Navajo (or *Navaho*): A tribe of North-east Arizona, famous for the high development of the art of weaving.

Nez Percé: A group of tribes of western Idaho, North-east Oregon and South-east Washington. Their name was derived from their real or supposed practice of piercing the nose for the insertion of a piece of dentalium.

Ngonde: A district of Nyasaland, to the west of the northern end of Lake Nyasa. Wilson (3).

Ngoni: A Bantu people of Northern Rhodesia and Portuguese East Africa. Read (1 and 2).

Ngwato: The largest of the Bantu tribes of Bechuanaland.

Nootka: One of the peoples of the north-west coast (*q.v.*) of America. Forde (1).

North-west Coast: A culture area of the Pacific coast of Canada and adjacent islands. A distinctive cultural feature of this area was the potlatch.

Nuba: A group of tribes inhabiting the Nuba Mountains of Kordofan. They are primarily agriculturists, the keeping of livestock and hunting being of minor significance. Social organization varies greatly from one tribe to another. In some, chieftainship is highly developed, in others political authority is rudimentary. Nadel (5).

Nuer: A people of the southern Sudan. Evans-Pritchard (3).

Nupe: A large tribe around and to the west of Bida in Nigeria. Subsistence is mainly by cultivation of different varieties of grain and other crops, though some cattle and other livestock are kept. Culturally they are a heterogeneous people having a complex political organization at the head of which is a monarch, called the Etsu Nupe. The official religion is Mohammedanism interwoven with a variety of pagan cults. Nadel (4).

Nyakyusa: A Bantu tribe of southern Tanganyika. Wilson (1 and 2).

Ojibway: The common name for the Chippewa (*q.v.*).

Omaha: A Siouan tribe of eastern Nebraska.

Oneida: One of the tribal groups composing the League of the Iroquois (*q.v.*).

Onondaga: One of the tribal groups composing the League of the Iroquois (*q.v.*).

Ontong Java: An atoll to the north-east of the Solomon Islands. A Polynesian "outlier". Hogbin (2).

Ovimbundu: A Bantu people of Portuguese West Africa.

Paiute: A term somewhat loosely applied to an extensive group of western Amerindian tribes inhabiting parts of Utah and Nevada and eastern California. Forde (1).

Pavmotu, Tuamotu or Low Archipelago: Numerous small Polynesian Islands to the east of the Society Islands.

Paviosto: The northern Paiute, a food-gathering people of north-eastern California, Nevada and southern Oregon.

Pawnee: A tribe of south-eastern Nebraska.

Plains Indian Culture Area: A culture area of the Great Plains of central North America, bounded on the north by the Saskatchewan River, on the west by the Rocky Mountains, and on the east by a line joining east central Missouri with west central Manitoba. Its southern limits followed the southern borders of Utah and Colorado, with a roughly triangular extension southward into central Texas.

Polynesia: An area of the Pacific, roughly east of longitude 180° and also including New Zealand.

Pondo: A Bantu people of eastern Cape Province, South Africa. Hunter (2).

Pueblos: A term applied to a group of tribes of the south-western U.S.A. (South Colorado, Utah, New Mexico and Arizona) who lived in permanent stone or adobe houses built into compact villages, often in recesses in the walls of cliffs or canyons.

Pygmy: A term used in physical anthropology to refer to various peoples of unusually short stature found in various parts of the world.

Rakahanga: See Manihiki.

Reddis: A primitive people of eastern Hyderabad, India. Fürer-Haimendorf (1).

Rossel Island: A small Melanesian Island to the east of New Guinea. The unique system of currency in Rossel Island is of special interest. Armstrong (1).

Samoa (see also *Manua*)*:* Large island group of central Polynesia. Murdock (1).

Samoyeds: A hunting and deer-herding people of north central Asia, employing reindeer as draught animals. Forde (1).

Semang: A hunting and food-gathering people of the Malay Peninsula. Murdock (1); Forde (1).

Seneca: One of the tribal groups composing the League of the Iroquois (*q.v.*).

Senussi: A Mohammedan sect of Lybia.

Shawnee: An ill-defined tribal group of the eastern U.S.A., particularly Tennessee.

Shilluk: A Nilotic people of the Anglo-Egyptian Sudan. Seligman, C. G. and B. Z. (1).

Siouan Family: An extensive linguistic group of North America, extending from the junction of the Mississippi and Arkansas Rivers north-west as far as southern Saskatchewan. The largest and best-known tribal group of this area were the Sioux or Dakota (*q.v.*).

Sioux: See *Dakota.*

Society Islands: Large island group of east central Polynesia. Forde (1); Piddington (4).

Swahili: A mixed Bantu-Arabic *lingua franca* spoken on the east central coast of Africa. Not a tribal designation.

Swazi: A Bantu tribe of Swaziland Protectorate. Kuper (1).

Tahiti: Largest of the Society Islands.

Tallensi: A people of the northern territories of the Gold Coast. Subsistence is based on animal husbandry and agriculture. The social organization of the Tallensi is marked by emphasis on kinship and locality, there being no centralized tribal authority. Fortes (1–3).

Tchambuli: A small tribe of north central New Guinea.

Tebu (or *Tibbu*)*:* A camel-keeping people of the Tibetsi plateau, eastern Sahara.

Thonga: See Tonga.

Tikopia: Small island, a western "outlier" of Polynesia, south-east of the Santa Cruz Islands. Firth (8).

Tlingit: A people of the north-west coast (*q.v.*) of America.

Todas: A people of the Nilgiri Hills, Malabar Peninsula, southern India. Murdock (1).

Tonga, Thonga or *Bathonga:* A Bantu people of the northern and eastern Transvaal. Not to be confused with the Pacific island or island group (see next entry). Junod (1).

Tonga: A large island group of western Polynesia. Not to be confused with the Bantu Tonga (see previous entry).

Tongareva: Small Polynesian island to the north of Manihiki and Rakahanga.

Trobriand Islands: A Melanesian archipelago to the north of the eastern end of New Guinea. Malinowski (1).

Tswana: A group of Bantu tribes of the western Transvaal and eastern Bechuanaland.

Tuamotu: See Paumotu.

Tuareg: A camel-keeping people of the western Sahara.

Tungus: The *Northern Tungus* are reindeer-keeping peoples of Trans-Baikalia, eastern Siberia. The *Southern Tungus* of Manchuria and Outer Mongolia, on the other hand, are primarily agriculturists who also keep livestock (Forde (1).

Tuscarora: A group of tribes of North Carolina, the last nation to join the League of the Iroquois (*q.v.*).

Umor: A village of the Yakö tribe.

Veddas: A primitive hunting and food-gathering people of the forests of Ceylon. Seligman, *The Veddas* (1911).

Winnebago: A Siouan tribe of Wisconsin.

Witotos: A primitive people of the Amazon jungle, Brazil. Murdock (1).

Wogeo: One of the Schouten Islands off the northern coast of New Guinea, not far from the mouth of the Sepik River. The culture is Melanesian and the systems of law and land tenure are of special interest. Hogbin (7–10).

Xosa (or *Xhosa*): A Bantu people of eastern Cape Province around East London.

Yakö: A tribe of Ogoja Province, southern Nigeria. Forde (2–4).

Yakuts: A pastoral people of eastern Asia, whose territory lies between the Tungus and the Yukaghir. Forde (1).

Yokuts: An Indian tribe of central California.

Yoruba: A large group of tribes of south-western Nigeria. Forde (1).

Yukaghir: A reindeer-herding people of the Kolyma River, eastern Siberia. Forde (1).

Yurok: A tribe of north-western California.

Zande: Singular and adjectival form of Azande.

Zulu: A once powerful Bantu tribe of northern Natal, South Africa. The Zulu nation rose to power under Chaka (or Shaka) in pre-European times. Gluckman (1).

Zuñi: A Pueblo tribe of western New Mexico.

KINSHIP EXERCISE

READERS who wish to check their knowledge of some of the terms and principles connected with kinship organization outlined in Chapter IV may do so by attempting the following exercise and then comparing their answers with those given in Appendix D.

Part I: Terminology

1. What technical terms are used to denote the following?—
    i. Cousins who are related through parents of identical sex, i.e. the children of two brothers or of two sisters.
    ii. The system of kinship terminology whereby different kinds of relatives are grouped together under the same term.
    iii. The system whereby a man goes at marriage to live with the family of his bride.
    iv. The rule that a man must marry a woman of his own social group.
    v. The custom whereby, if a married man dies, his younger brother may, or must, marry his widow.
    vi. Both brothers and sisters.
    vii. A kinship term which refers to one type of genealogical relationship only.
    viii. The system whereby a woman may have more than one husband.
    ix. The rule that a man may not marry a woman of his own social group.
    x. The type of kinship which reckons consanguineous relationship through both males and females.
2. If, in studying primitive cultures, you were to find the following types of social groups, by what technical terms would you describe them?
    i. A group of adjoining huts inhabited by:
        (a) An old woman and her husband.
        (b) Her three daughters, two of whom are widows.
        (c) The husband of the third daughter.
        (d) The female children of the three daughters, but not the married son of one of them. This man lives in a different village.

ii. A group of individuals who, though they cannot all trace genealogical relationship to each other, nevertheless claim common descent in the male line from a mythical ancestor who was half man and half pigeon. Members of this group refuse to kill or eat pigeons, and the same taboos in regard to other natural species are observed by other similar groups in the same tribe.

iii. The tribe is divided into two groups which do not inter-marry. Membership of each group is inherited from the in-dividual's mother. One group is associated with the eagle and the other with the crow, and members of each group refrain from killing the bird with which their group is associated.

Part II: Construction of Genealogy

From the following data, construct the genealogy of GEORGE, who is EGO. (Note that order of birth of children is indicated by the order in which they are mentioned, unless otherwise stated.)

GEORGE is the son of DENNIS and Mary. DENNIS has two elder siblings, Freda and DUDLEY. Freda is married to ALBERT and they have a daughter Dorothy. DUDLEY is married to Roma and they have a son, DOUGLAS.

The father of DENNIS is dead. His name was WILLIAM, and he had an elder brother JAMES, who is also dead. JAMES had two sons, KEN and DAVID.

GEORGE has an elder sister Constance, who is married to NOR-MAN. NORMAN and Constance have two children, ARTHUR and Vera. Vera is married to RICHARD and has a son, HUGH.

EGO's mother, Mary, is the daughter of HAROLD, who is dead. The name of HAROLD's wife, who is also dead, is not known, but she had a brother, still living, whose name is KEITH.

Mary has two younger siblings, BERNARD and Bernice. BERN-ARD is married to Margaret, and they have two children, FRED and Audrey. Bernice is married to PATRICK, and they also have two children, Rose and Muriel.

GEORGE is married to Mabel, who is the daughter of JACK and Barbara. Mabel had an elder brother HOWARD, who is dead. Barbara has a younger brother ANDREW, who is married to a woman whose name is not known. JACK has an elder sister Violet, who is married to JOSEPH and has a son DANIEL. Violet and JACK are the children of DONALD and Jean. Jean has a younger brother JOHN.

GEORGE and Mabel have an infant son, ERNEST.

Having constructed a genealogy showing the above relationships, you should imagine that, in spite of the English names, the genealogy refers to primitive kinship, and attempt the following questions.

3. Which of the following pairs of individuals are *patrilineal kin* to each other?

WILLIAM and ARTHUR   RICHARD and Constance
GEORGE and DAVID   WILLIAM and Dorothy
HAROLD and FRED   Freda and Roma
ALBERT and DENNIS   Mary and Audrey
KEN and Freda   Audrey and Rose

4. Which of the following pairs of individuals are *matrilineal kin* to each other?

GEORGE and BERNARD   WILLIAM and Mabel
DOUGLAS and ALBERT   KEITH and Audrey
FRED and GEORGE   Mabel and Violet
KEN and BERNARD   Mary and Muriel
PATRICK and DUDLEY   Constance and Dorothy

5. Which of the following pairs of individuals would you normally expect to find living in the same village in a community practising *matrilocal marriage*?

DENNIS and PATRICK   BERNARD and Dorothy
JACK and ERNEST   DENNIS and Rose
RICHARD and Mary   GEORGE and ERNEST

6. Which of the following individuals are consanguineous, and which affinal, kin of DENNIS? In regard to consanguineous kin, you should reckon relationships through either males or females, or both:

DUDLEY   KEN
Mary   HUGH
ALBERT   ERNEST
RICHARD   Constance
FRED   Bernice

7. Under *patrilineal inheritance*, who would be the person last named in the genealogy who would ultimately inherit the wealth of (a) DENNIS and (b) HAROLD?

8. Under *matrilineal succession*, who is the person last named in the genealogy who would succeed to the rank and title of (a) KEITH and (b) JOHN?

9. Which of the following pairs of individuals are cross-cousins to each other?

GEORGE and DOUGLAS   FRED and Constance
ARTHUR and ERNEST   Rose and Audrey
DANIEL and Mabel   Dorothy and Constance

PRIMITIVE COMMUNISM—AN EXPERIMENT IN SEMANTICS

In Section 5 of Chapter VIII we set forth the reasons why the term "primitive communism" should not be used in anthropology. Some students find difficulty in following these arguments in the abstract. They ask why, since primitive economic systems bear some resemblance to their conception of a communistic society, they should refrain from applying the term "primitive communism" to them. A direct answer to this question in concrete terms helps students to appreciate the significance of the general arguments mentioned above. The following experiment was therefore carried out with two first-year classes in Social Anthropology in the University of Edinburgh during the sessions 1946–7 and 1947–8.

Members of the 1946–7 class were asked, after they had attended a series of lectures on primitive economics and land tenure, (a) to write out a brief definition of what they understood by the term "communism", and (b) to write down the word which they regarded as the antithesis of communism. In order to secure maximum freedom in the expression of opinion, students were told that they need not give their names in handing in their answers.

The heterogeneity of the definitions of "communism" may be judged from the range of terms given as its antithesis: individualism, capitalism, feudalism, autocracy, conservatism, laissez-faire, oligarchy, anarchy, fascism, caste, dictatorship, monarchy, despotism, plutocracy, autarchy, private enterprise, monopoly.

From the definitions of communism given by students, representative passages were abstracted so as to provide a series of twenty-seven statements all purporting to refer to a condition of "communism". These statements were subsequently submitted to both classes in the form of a questionnaire, the answers to which were again anonymous.

Questionnaire

Below are a number of statements, each preceded by a dotted line. On the dotted line to the left of each statement write a capital "T", "F" or "I" according to the following code:

(a) If the statement is true of the primitive societies which you know, write "T".

(b) If the statement is false in the same application write "F".

(c) If the statement is inapplicable write "I". By "inapplicable" in this context is meant either (a) true of some primitive societies but not of others, (b) true, in general, but only subject to important reservations; (c) meaningless when applied to primitive societies.

1. ..... The benefits of the land and the resulting economic wealth are for the use of the community without differentiation according to birth.

2. ..... The entire material resources of the community are owned jointly by all its members.

3. ..... Every member of the community has an equal share in the profits of the "national exchequer".

4. ..... All people of a "state" are brought to a common level in order to further the ends, usually material, of that state.

5. ..... Government is by rulers elected by the people.

6. ..... No part of the community has any economic or social advantage over another.

7. ..... The State controls all sources of production.

8. ..... No individual possesses other than small personal belongings. Buildings and other important things are allotted by the State.

9. ..... Food is given according to work done. Every able-bodied person, therefore, must work.

10. ..... Everyone works for the good of the State. The produce, etc., which is got from their labour is pooled and distributed among all. No one gets the produce of his own labour, but gets a share of all produce.

11. ..... Each individual has equal rights. Each individual works for the general good according to his or her ability.

12. ..... No one is in want.

13. ..... No one definitely owns any land or property for himself.

14. ..... The means of production, exchange and distribution are held in common.

15. ..... Men and women give to society according to their capacity and take from its products according to their needs.

16. ..... Individuals live in self-supporting groups.

17. ..... Individuals work towards equality both financially and socially.

18. ..... People all have the same privileges and status.

19. ..... People are intimately bound to help one another in any type of work.

20. ..... There is a belief in the universal brotherhood of man.

21. ..... Power is in the hands of the lower classes.

22. ..... There are no class distinctions.

23. ..... The interests of the individual are subjugated to those of the community as a whole.

24. ..... All property belongs to the group as a whole.

25. ..... There is no private ownership—an individual works, not for himself nor his kin, but for society.

26. ..... Economic life is centred around the community's needs, to which all contribute without expecting rewards.

27. ..... Inheritance of property does not exist.

From the answers returned to this questionnaire by the two classes, one hundred papers were selected at random, and the answers tabulated as follows:

TABLE A

Percentages of students regarding each statement as true, false or inapplicable

No. of Statement	Answers of Students			No. of Statement	Answers of Students		
	Percentage "T"	Percentage "F"	Percentage "I"		Percentage "T"	Percentage "F"	Percentage "I"
1	12	70	18	15	28	43	29
2	14	69	17	16	55	13	32
3	5	68	27	17	4	69	27
4	9	61	30	18	1	90	9
5	5	37	58	19	45	21	34
6	11	72	17	20	14	45	41
7	12	52	36	21	0	73	27
8	9	68	23	22	3	82	15
9	38	24	38	23	41	25	34
10	9	59	32	24	13	58	29
11	11	61	28	25	5	80	15
12	42	34	24	26	15	61	24
13	16	62	22	27	1	89	10
14	35	42	23				

TABLE B

Percentages of students regarding different numbers of statements as true

Total Number of Statements Regarded as True	Percentage of Students	Total Number of Statements Regarded as True	Percentage of Students
17	1	8	3
16	0	7	9
15	0	6	8
14	1	5	5
13	1	4	7
12	1	3	10
11	3	2	16
10	6	1	9
9	5	0	15

The results of this experiment reveal, not only the wide divergence of opinion among the students in regard to what is meant by "communism", but also disagreement as to whether characteristics which various students themselves regard as "communistic" can be attributed to primitive societies. The general tendency is to regard the statements as false.

The conclusions of the experiment, however, are not so much concerned with the truth or falsity of the statements as applied to primitive communities, as with the confusions and misunderstandings which arise in connection with the use of the term "primitive communism", which has widely differing meanings for different individuals.

In conclusion, it must be emphasized that it is also dangerous simply to *deny* that primitive society is communistic. To do so might imply that it is characterized by individualism, capitalism, feudalism, autocracy or any of the other features which various students regard as the antithesis of "communism". It would convey different meanings to different individuals. In fact, no such blanket terms are adequate to cover the complex realities of primitive economic organization. They are only used by those who, by implication, agree with Humpty Dumpty: "When I use a word it means exactly what I intend it to mean, no more and no less."

APPENDIX D

ANSWERS TO KINSHIP EXERCISE

Part I: Terminology

Question 1

i. Parallel cousins.
ii. Classificatory system.
iii. Matrilocal marriage.
iv. Endogamy.
v. Junior levirate.

vi. Sibling.
vii. Descriptive.
viii. Polyandry.
ix. Exogamy.
x. Bilateral.

Question 2

i. Matrilocal extended family.
ii. Patrilineal totemic clan.
iii. Matrilineal totemic moieties.

Part II: Construction of Genealogy

Question 3

GEORGE and DAVID
HAROLD and FRED

KEN and Freda
Mary and Audrey

Question 4

GEORGE and BERNARD

Mary and Muriel

Question 5

DENNIS and PATRICK
JACK and ERNEST
RICHARD and Mary

DENNIS and Rose
GEORGE and ERNEST

Question 6

DUDLEY—Consanguineous
Mary—Affinal
ALBERT—Affinal
RICHARD—Affinal
FRED—Affinal

KEN—Consanguineous
HUGH—Consanguineous
ERNEST—Consanguineous
Constance—Consanguineous
Bernice—Affinal

Question 7

(a) DENNIS—ERNEST

(b) HAROLD—FRED

Question 8
  (*a*) KEITH—HUGH   (*b*) JOHN—DANIEL

Question 9
  ARTHUR and ERNEST   Rose and Audrey
  DANIEL and Mabel   Dorothy and Constance
  FRED and Constance

BIBLIOGRAPHY [1]

Note

The system of references used in this work is not a common one and should perhaps be explained. Works are usually cited by the name of the author, followed by a number in parentheses, the latter corresponding to the numbers in parentheses in the Bibliography. Thus, Ashley-Montagu (1) is his work *Coming into Being among the Australian Aborigines* and Ashley-Montagu (2) is the book *Man's Most Dangerous Myth*. Where only a single work by a given author is cited, it may seem superfluous to add (1), but this is done so that this Bibliography may be used together with that which will appear in Volume II, where further works by such an author may be cited. This will ensure a uniform system of references throughout the two volumes. Works are generally cited in chronological order of publication, but this is sometimes varied in order to bring several of an author's works on a single subject or area together for ease of reference. It would in any case have been impossible to carry over a strict chronological order of citation into Volume II.

Adam, L.	(1)	"Functionalism and Neo-Functionalism," *Oceania*, Vol. XVII, p. 1 (1946).
Armstrong, W. E.	(1)	*Rossel Island* (1928).
Ashley-Montagu, M. F.	(1)	*Coming into Being among the Australian Aborigines* (1937).
——	(2)	*Man's Most Dangerous Myth: The Fallacy of Race* (1942).
Barnett, H. G.	(1)	"The Nature of the Potlatch," *A.A.*, Vol. XL, pp. 349–58 (1938).
Baumann, H.	(1)	"The Division of Work according to Sex in African Hoe Culture," *Africa*, Vol. I, p. 289 (1928).

[1] In connection with the citation of articles from anthropological journals, the following conventions should be noted:

Journal						Cited as
Africa	.	.	.	.	.	*Africa*
African Studies (previously *Bantu Studies*)	.	.	.	.	*African Studies*
The American Anthropologist	.	.	.	.	.	*A.A.*
The Journal of the Royal Anthropological Institute	.	.	.	.	*J.R.A.I.*
Man, A Monthly Record of Anthropological Science	.	.	.	*Man*
Oceania	.	.	.	.	.	.	*Oceania*

Beemer, H.   *See also* Kuper, H.
——   (1) "The Development of the Military Organ-
          ization in Swaziland," *Africa*, Vol. X,
          pp. 55 and 176 (1937).
Bell, F. L. S.   (1) "The Place of Food in the Social Life of
          Central Polynesia," *Oceania*, Vol. II,
          No. 2, pp. 117–35 (1931).
——   (2) "Sokapana: A Melanesian Secret
          Society," *J.R.A.I.*, Vol. LXV, pp. 311–
          42 (1935).
Benedict, R.   (1) "Marital Property Rights in Bilateral
          Society," *A.A.*, Vol. XXXVIII, pp. 368–
          73 (1936).
Bidney, D.   (1) "On the Concept of Culture and Some
          Cultural Fallacies," *A.A.*, Vol. XLVI,
          p. 30 (1944).
Blackwood, B.   (1) *Both Sides of Buka Passage* (1935).
Boas, F.   (1) "The Central Eskimo," in the *Sixth
          Annual Report of the Bureau of American
          Ethnology* (1888).
——   (2) "The Eskimo of Baffin Land and
          Hudson Bay," *Bulletin of the American
          Museum of Natural History*, Vol. XV
          (1907).
—— (Ed.)   (3) *General Anthropology* (1938).
Brown, E. F.   (1) "Hehe Grandmothers," *J.R.A.I.*, Vol.
          LXV, pp. 83–96 (1935).
Brown, G. G.   (1) "Bride-Wealth among the Hehe," *Africa*,
          Vol. V, p. 145 (1932).
Brown, G. G., and   (1) "Social Organisation and Social Struc-
Barnett, J. H.   ture," *A.A.*, Vol. XLIV, p. 31 (1942).
Brown, G. G., and   (1) *Anthropology in Action* (1935).
Hutt, A. McD. B.
Chadwick, N. K.   (1) "Shamanism among the Tartars of
          Central Asia," *J.R.A.I.*, Vol. LXVI,
          pp. 75–112 (1936).
Childe, V. G.   (1) *Man Makes Himself* (1936).
——   (2) *What Happened in History* (1942).
——   (3) *Progress and Archæology* (1944).
Clarke, E.   (1) "The Sociological Significance of An-
          cestor-Worship in Ashanti," *Africa*, Vol.
          III, p. 431 (1930).
Cole, F. C.   (1) *The Peoples of Malaysia* (1945).
Davis, K.   (1) "Intermarriage in Caste Societies," *A.A.*,
          Vol. XLIII, p. 376 (1941).

Deacon, A. B. (ed. Wedgwood, C. H.).	(1) *Malekula* (1934).
Driberg, J. H.	(1) "The Status of Women among the Nilotics and Nilo-Hamitics, "*Africa*, Vol. V, p. 404 (1932).
Durkheim, É., tr. by Swain, J. W.	(1) *The Elementary Forms of the Religious Life* (1915).
Eiselen, W.	(1) "Preferential Marriage," *Africa*, Vol. I, p. 413 (1928).
Elkin, A. P.	(1) "The Kopara," *Oceania*, Vol. II, No. 2, pp. 191–8 (1931).
——	(2) *Studies in Australian Totemism*, The Oceania Monographs, No. 2.
——	(3) *The Australian Aborigines* (1938).
Elliot Smith, G.	(1) *The Evolution of Man* (1927).
Elwin, V.	(1) *The Baiga* (1939).
Embree, J. F.	(1) *A Japanese Village* (1946).
Evans-Pritchard, E. E.	(1) "Zande Blood Brotherhood," *Africa*, Vol. VI, p. 369 (1933).
——	(2) *Witchcraft, Oracles and Magic among the Azande* (1937).
——	(3) *The Nuer* (1940).
——	(4) *The Nuer of the Southern Sudan*, in Fortes and Evans-Pritchard (1).
——	(5) *Some Aspects of Marriage and the Family Among the Nuer*, The Rhodes-Livingstone Papers, No. 11 (1945).
——	(6) "Bridewealth among the Nuer," *African Studies*, Vol. VI, No. 4, pp. 181–8 (1947).
——	(7) "Nuer Bridewealth," *Africa*, Vol. XVI, p. 247 (1947).
——	(8) "The Morphology and Function of Magic," *A.A.*, Vol. XXXI, pp. 619–641 (1929).
Fei, Hsiao-Tung	(1) *Peasant Life in China* (1939).
Field, M. J.	(1) "The Agricultural System on the Manya Krobo of the Gold Coast," *Africa*, Vol. XIV, p. 54 (1943–4).
Firth, R.	(1) *Human Types* (1938).
——	(2) "Economic Psychology of the Maori," *J.R.A.I.*, Vol. LV (1925).
——	(3) "Proverbs in Native Life, with Special Reference to those of the Maori," *Folk-Lore*, Vol. XXXVII, Nos. 2 and 3, pp. 134–270 (1926).

Firth, R.	(4)	"Maori Hill-Forts," *Antiquity*, Vol. I, No. 1 (1927).
——	(5)	*Primitive Economics of the New Zealand Maori* (1929).
——	(6)	"A Dart Match in Tikopia," *Oceania*, Vol. I, No. 1, pp. 64–96 (1930).
——	(7)	"Totemism in Polynesia," *Oceania*, Vol. I, pp. 291 and 377 (1930).
——	(8)	*We, the Tikopia* (1936).
——	(9)	"Bond-Friendship in Tikopia," *Custom is King*, Essays in Honour of R.R. Marett (ed. Buxton, L. H. D.) (1936).
——	(10)	*Primitive Polynesian Economy* (1939).
——	(11)	*The Work of the Gods in Tikopia*, 2 vols. (1940).
——	(12)	"The Sociological Study of Native Diet," *Africa*, Vol. VII, p. 401 (1934).
——	(13)	*Malay Fishermen: Their Peasant Economy* (1946).
——	(14)	"Religious Belief and Personal Adjustment," *Henry Myers Lecture* (1948).
Forde, C. D.	(1)	*Habitat, Economy and Society* (1934).
——	(2)	"Land and Labour in a Cross River Village, Southern Nigeria," *Geographical Journal*, Vol. LC, pp. 24–51 (1937).
——	(3)	"Fission and Accretion in the Patrilineal Clans of a Semi-Bantu Community in Southern Nigeria, *J.R.A.I.*, Vol. LXVIII, pp. 311–38 (1938).
——	(4)	"Kinship in Umor-Double Unilateral Organization in a Semi-Bantu Society," *A.A.*, Vol. XLI, pp. 523–53 (1939).
Fortes, M.	(1)	"Social and Psychological Aspects of Education in Taleland," Supplement to *Africa*, Vol. XI (1938).
——	(2)	"The Political System of the Tallensi of the Northern Territories of the Gold Coast," in Fortes and Evans-Pritchard (1).
——	(3)	*The Dynamics of Clanship among the Tallensi* (1945).
Fortes, M. and S. L.	(1)	"Food in the Domestic Economy in Taleland," *Africa*, Vol. IX, pp. 237–76 (1936).
Fortes, M., and Evans-Pritchard, E. E. (ed.).	(1)	*African Political Systems* (1940).

Fortune, R. F.   (1) "Manus Religion," *Oceania*, Vol. II, No.
                            1, pp. 74–108 (1931).
——   (2) *Sorcerers of Dobu* (1932).
Frazer, J. G.   (1) *Totemism and Exogamy*, 4 vols. (1910).
——   (2) *The Belief in Immortality and the Worship of
                            the Dead* (1913).
——   (3) *The Golden Bough: A Study of Magic and
                            Religion*, Abridged Edition (1925).
——   (4) *The Devil's Advocate: A Plea for Superstition*
                            (1927).
Fürer-Haimendorf, C.   (1) *The Chenchus* (1943).
——   (2) *The Reddis of the Bison Hills* (1943).
Garth, T. R. (Jr.).   (1) "Emphasis on Industriousness among the
                            Atsugewi," *A.A.*, Vol. XLVII, p. 554
                            (1945).
Gifford, E. W.   (1) *Tongan Society* (1929).
Gluckman, M.   (1) "The Kingdom of the Zulu of South
                            Africa," in Fortes and Evans-Pritchard (1).
——   (2) "Malinowski's Contribution to Social
                            Anthropology," *African Studies*, Vol. VI,
                            No. 1, pp. 41–6 (1947).
Goldenweiser, A. A.   (1) *Early Civilization* (1921).
——   (2) *History, Psychology and Culture* (1932).
Gorer, G.   (1) *Himalayan Village.*
Hambly, W. D.   (1) *Source Book for African Anthropology*, Field
                            Museum of Natural History, Anthropo-
                            logical Series, Vol. XXVI (1937).
Hart, C. W. M.   (1) "A Reconsideration of the Natchez Social
                            Structure," *A.A.*, Vol. XLV, p. 374
                            (1943).
Herskovits, M. J.   (1) "The Culture Areas of Africa," *Africa*,
                            Vol. III, p. 59 (1930).
——   (2) "A Note on Woman Marriage in Da-
                            homey," *Africa*, Vol. X, p. 335 (1937).
——   (3) *The Economic Life of Primitive Peoples* (1940).
Hill, W. W.   (1) "The Status of the Hermaphrodite and
                            Transvestite in Navaho Culture," *A.A.*,
                            Vol. XXXVII, p. 273 (1935).
Hodge, F. W. (ed.).   (1) *Handbook of American Indians North of
                            Mexico*, Bureau of American Ethnology,
                            Bulletin 30 (1907).
Hoernlé, A. W.   (1) "An Outline of the Native Conception of
                            Education in Africa," *Africa*, Vol. IV,
                            p. 145 (1931).
——   (2) "Social Organization," in Schapera (1)

Hofstra, S.   (1) "Personality and Differentiation in the Political Life of the Mendi," *Africa*, Vol. X, p. 436 (1937).

Hogbin, H. I.   (1) "Polynesian Ceremonial Gift Exchanges," *Oceania*, Vol. III, No. 1, pp. 13–39 (1932).

——   (2) *Law and Order in Polynesia* (1934).

——   (3) "Mana," *Oceania*, Vol. VI, No. 3, pp. 241–74 (1936).

——   (4) "Social Advancement in Guadalcanal, Solomon Islands," *Oceania*, Vol. VIII, No. 3, pp. 289–305 (1938).

——   (5) *Experiments in Civilization* (1939).

——   (6) "Trading Expeditions in Northern New Guinea," *Oceania*, Vol. V, No. 4, pp. 375–407 (1935).

——   (7) "Social Reaction to Crime: Law and Morals in the Schouten Islands, New Guinea," *J.R.A.I.*, Vol. LXVIII, pp. 223–62 (1938).

——   (8) "Tillage and Collection: A New Guinea Economy," *Oceania*, Vol. IX, pp. 127 and 286 (1938–9).

——   (9) "Native Land Tenure in New Guinea," *Oceania*, Vol. 113–65 (1939).

——   (10) "The Father chooses his Heir: a Family Dispute over Succession in Wogeo, New Guinea," *Oceania*, Vol. XI, No. 1, pp. 1–39 (1940).

Homans, G. C.   (1) "Anxiety and Ritual: The Theories of Malinowski and Radcliffe-Brown," *A.A.*, Vol. XLIII, p. 164 (1941).

Howells, W.   (1) *Mankind So Far* (1944).

Hsu, F. L. K.   (1) "The Problem of Incest Tabu in a North China Village," *A.A.*, Vol. XLII, pp. 122–35 (1940).

——   (2) "The Differential Functions of Relationship Terms," *A.A.*, Vol. XLIV, p. 248 (1942).

——   (3) "Observations on Cross-Cousin Marriage in China," *A.A.*, Vol. XLVII, p. 83 (1945).

Hu, H. C.   (1) "On the Chinese Conception of 'Face'," *A.A.*, Vol. XLVI, p. 45 (1944).

Humphrey, N. D.   (1) "A Characterization of Certain Plains Associations," *A.A.*, Vol. XLIII, p. 428 (1928).

Hunter, M.   (1) "The Effects of Contact with Europeans
                              on the Status of the Pondo Women,"
                              Africa, Vol. VI, p. 259 (1933).

——   (2) *Reaction to Conquest, Effects of Contact with
                              Europeans on the Pondo of South Africa* (1936).

Hutton, J. H.   (1) *Caste in India* (1946).

Junod, H. A.   (1) *The Life of a South African Tribe* (1912).

Kaberry, P. M.   (1) *Aboriginal Woman, Sacred and Profane*
                              (1939).

——   (2) "Law and Political Organization in the
                              Abelam Tribe, New Guinea," *Oceania*,
                              Vol. XII, pp. 79, 209 and 331 (1941–2).

Keesing, F. M.   (1) *Modern Samoa* (1934).

——   (2) *The South Seas in the Modern World* (1942).

——   (3) *Native Peoples of the Pacific World* (1947).

Kenyatta, J.   (1) *Facing Mount Kenya* (1938).

Kirchhoff, P.   (1) "Kinship Organization: A Study of
                              Terminology," *Africa*, Vol. V, p. 184
                              (1932).

Krige, J. D.   (1) "The Significance of Cattle Exchange in
                              Lovedu Social Structure," *Africa*, Vol.
                              XII, p. 393 (1939).

Kroeber, A. L.   (1) *Handbook of the Indians of California*,
                              Bureau of American Ethnology, Bulletin
                              78 (1925).

Kuper, H. (*née* Beemer).   *See also* Beemer, H.

——   (1) "A Ritual of Kingship among the
                              Swazi," *Africa*, Vol. XIV, p. 230 (1943–4).

Lesser, A.   (1) "Functionalism in Social Anthropology,"
                              A.A., Vol. XXXVII, p. 386 (1935).

Lévy-Bruhl, L., tr. by   (1) *Primitive Mentality* (1923).
Clare, L. A.

——   (2) *How Natives Think* (1936).

Li An-Che   (1) "Zuñi. Some Observations and Queries,"
                              A.A., Vol. XXXIX, p. 62-76 (1937).

Little, K. L.   (1) "The Poro Society as an Arbiter of Cul-
                              ture," *African Studies*, Vol. VII, No. 1,
                              pp. 1–15 (1948).

——   (2) "The Changing Position of Women in the
                              Sierra Leone Protectorate," *Africa*, Vol.
                              XVIII, pp. 1–17 (1948).

Lowie, R. H.   (1) *Primitive Society* (1921).

——   (2) *The History of Ethnological Theory* (1937).

Macleod, W. C.   (1) "Natchez Political Evolution," *A.A.*,
                              Vol. XXVI, pp. 201-29 (1924).

Mair, L. P.

(1) "Native Land Tenure in East Africa," *Africa*, Vol. IV, p. 314 (1931).

—— (2) "Baganda Land Tenure," *Africa*, Vol. VI, p. 187 (1933).

—— (3) *An African People in the Twentieth Century* (1934).

—— (4) *Native Policies in Africa* (1936).

Malinowski, B.

(1) *Argonauts of the Western Pacific* (1922).

—— (2) *Crime and Custom in Savage Society* (1926).

—— (3) *Sex and Repression in Savage Society* (1927).

—— (4) *The Sexual Life of Savages in North-western Melanesia* (1929).

—— (5) *Coral Gardens and their Magic*, 2 vols. (1935).

—— (6) "Parenthood, the Basis of Social Structure," in *The New Generation*, Ed. Calverton and Schmalhausen, (1930).

—— (7) Articles on "Kinship" and "Marriage," in the *Encyclopædia Britannica*, 14th Edition (1929).

—— (8) Article on "Culture," in the *Encyclopædia of the Social Sciences*, Ed. Seligman, E. R. A., and Johnson, A. (1931).

—— (9) Article on "Social Anthropology," in the *Encyclopædia Britannica*, 14th Edition (1929).

—— (10) *A Scientific Theory of Culture* (1944).

—— (ed. Kaberry, P. M.) (11) *The Dynamics of Culture Change* (1945).

—— (12) "Magic, Science and Religion," in *Science, Religion and Reality* (ed. Needham) (1926).

—— (13) *Myth in Primitive Psychology* (1926).

Mead, M.

(1) *Social Organization in Manua*, Bernice P. Bishop Museum, Bulletin 76 (1930).

—— (2) *Coming of Age in Samoa* (1928).

—— (3) *Growing Up in New Guinea* (1931).

Meek, C. K.

(1) *Law and Authority in a Nigerian Tribe* (1937).

Morant, G. M.

(1) "Racial Theories and International Relations," *J.R.A.I.*, Vol. LXIX, pp. 151–62 (1939).

Murdock, G. P.

(1) *Our Primitive Contemporaries* (1936).

Musil, A.

(1) *The Manners and Customs of the Rwala Bedouins* (1928).

430   BIBLIOGRAPHY

Nadel, S. F.   (1) "Witchcraft and Anti-Witchcraft in Nupe
                                  Society," *Africa*, Vol. VIII, p. 423
                                  (1935).
——   (2) "Nupe State and Community," *Africa*,
                                  Vol. VIII, p. 257 (1935).
——   (3) "The Kede: A Riverain State in Northern
                                  Nigeria," in Fortes and Evans-Pritchard
                                  (1).
——   (4) *A Black Byzantium* (1942).
——   (5) *The Nuba* (1947).
——   (6) "Land Tenure on the Eritrean Plateau,"
                                  Africa, Vol. XVI, pp. 1 and 99 (1947).
——   (7) "The Interview Technique in Social
                                  Anthropology," in *The Study of Society*,
                                  Ed. Bartlett and others (1939).
Nelson, E. W.   (1) *The Eskimo around Bering Strait*, in the
                                  Eighteenth Annual Report of the Bureau
                                  of American Ethnology (1896–7).
Oberg, K.   (1) "Kinship Organization of the Banyan-
                                  kole," *Africa*, Vol. XI, p. 129 (1938).
——   (2) "The Kingdom of Ankole in Uganda,"
                                  in Fortes and Evans-Pritchard (1).
——   (3) "A Comparison of Three Systems of
                                  Primitive Economic Organization," *A.A.*,
                                  Vol. XLV, p. 572 (1943).
Peristiany, J. G.   (1) *The Social Institutions of the Kipsigis*
                                  (1939).
Piddington, R.   (1) "The Totemic System of the Karadjeri
                                  Tribe," *Oceania*, Vol. II, pp. 373–400
                                  (1932).
——   (2) "Karadjeri Initiation," *Oceania*, Vol. III,
                                  pp. 46–87 (1932).
——   (3) *The Psychology of Laughter* (1933).
——   (4) Part II of Williamson (1).
——   (5) Preface and Part II of Williamson (2).
Powdermaker, H.   (1) *Life in Lesu* (1933).
Radcliffe-Brown, A. R.   (1) *The Andaman Islanders* (1933).
——   (2) "The Social Organization of Australian
                                  Tribes," *The Oceania Monographs*, No. 1
                                  (1931).
——   (3) "The Study of Kinship Systems,"
                                  J.R.A.I., Vol. LXXI, Parts I and II,
                                  pp. 1–17 (1941).
——   (4) "On Joking Relationships," *Africa*, Vol.
                                  XIII, p. 195 (1940).

Radcliffe-Brown, A. R. (5) "On the Concept of Function in Social Science," *A.A.*, Vol. XXXVII, p. 394 (1935).

——— (6) "On Social Structure," *J.R.A.I.*, Vol. 70, Part I, pp. 1–12 (1940).

——— (7) Article on "Primitive Law" in the *Encyclopædia of the Social Sciences*, ed. Seligman and Johnson (1933).

——— (8) *Taboo* (1939).

Raum, O. F. (1) "Some Aspects of Indigenous Education among the Chaga," *J.R.A.I.*, Vol. LXVIII, pp. 209–22 (1938).

——— (2) *Chaga Childhood* (1940).

Read, M. (1) "Tradition and Prestige among the Ngoni," *Africa*, Vol. IX, p. 453 (1936).

——— (2) "The Moral Code of the Ngoni and their former Military State," *Africa*, Vol. XI, p. 1 (1938).

Richards, A. I. (1) *Hunger and Work in a Savage Tribe* (1932).

——— (2) *Bemba Marriage and Present Economic Conditions*, The Rhodes-Livingstone Papers, No. 4 (1940).

——— (3) "The Political System of the Bemba Tribe—North-Eastern Rhodesia," in Fortes and Evans-Pritchard (1).

——— (4) *Land, Labour and Diet in Northern Rhodesia* (1939).

——— (5) "The Development of Field Work Methods in Social Anthropology," in *The Study of Society*, ed. Bartlett and others (1939).

Rivers, W. H. R. (1) *The Todas* (1906).

——— (2) *Social Organization* (1924).

Roscoe, J. (1) *The Baganda* (1911).

Schapera, I. (ed.) (1) *The Bantu-Speaking Tribes of South Africa* (1937).

——— (2) "The Political Organization of the Ngwato of Bechuanaland Protectorate," in Fortes and Evans-Pritchard (1).

——— (3) *Handbook of Tswana Law and Custom* (1938).

Seligman, C. G., and B. Z. (1) *Pagan Tribes of the Nilotic Sudan* (1932).

Shapiro, H. L. (1) *Migration and Environment* (1939).

Siegel, B. J. (1) "Some Methodological Considerations for a Comparative Study of Slavery," *A.A.*, Vol. XLVII, p. 357 (1945).

Smith, E. W.   (1) *The Golden Stool* (1926).
Smith, E. W., and   (1) *The Ila-speaking Peoples of Northern Rhodesia*
  Dale, A. M.   (1920).
Spencer, B., and   (1) *The Arunta*, 2 vols. (1927).
  Gillen, F. J.
Stanner, W. E. H.   (1) "The Daly River Tribes," *Oceania*,
                                   Vol. III, p. 377, and Vol. IV, p. 10
                                   (1933-4).
——   (2) "Ceremonial Economics of the Mulluk
                                   and Madngella Tribes of the Daly River,
                                   North Australia," *Oceania*, Vol. IV, pp.
                                   156 and 458 (1934).
Stevenson, H. N. C.   (1) *Economics of the Central Chin Tribes* (1943).
Steward, J. H.   (1) *Handbook of South American Indians, The
                                   Marginal Tribes*, Bureau of American
                                   Ethnology, Bulletin 143, Vol. I (1946).
——   (2) *Handbook of South American Indians, The
                                   Andean Civilizations*, Bureau of American
                                   Ethnology, Bulletin 143, Vol. II (1946).
Stibbe, E. P.   (1) *An Introduction to Physical Anthropology*
                                   (1930).
Strehlow, T. G. H.   (1) *Aranda Traditions* (1947).
Swanton, J. R.   (1) *Indian Tribes of the Lower Mississippi Valley
                                   and Adjacent Coast of the Gulf of Mexico*,
                                   Bureau of American Ethnology, Bulletin
                                   43 (1911).
Thurnwald, H.   (1) "Woman's Status in Buin Society,"
                                   Oceania, Vol. V, No. 2, pp. 142-70
                                   (1934).
Thurnwald, R.   (1) *Economics in Primitive Communities* (1932).
——   (2) "Pigs and Currency in Buin," *Oceania*,
                                   Vol. V, No. 2, pp. 119-41 (1934).
Torday, E.   (1) "The Principles of Bantu Marriage,"
                                   Africa, Vol. II, p. 255 (1929).
Wagner, G.   (1) "The Political Organization of the Bantu
                                   of Kavirondo," in Fortes and Evans-
                                   Pritchard (1).
Warner, W. L.   (1) *A Black Civilization* (1937).
Webster, H.   (1) *Taboo: A Sociological Study* (1924).
Wedgwood, C. H.   (1) "The Nature and Functions of Secret
                                   Societies," *Oceania*, Vol. I, No. 2, pp.
                                   129-45 (1930).
——   (2) "Girls' Puberty Rites in Manam Island,
                                   New Guinea," *Oceania*, Vol. IV, No. 2,
                                   pp. 132-55 (1933).

Wedgwood, C. H.   (3) "Sickness and its Treatment in Manam
                               Island, New Guinea," *Oceania*, Vol. V,
                               pp. 64 and 280 (1934–5).

——   (4) "Women in Manam," *Oceania*, Vol.
                               VIII, p. 170 (1937).

——   *See also* Deacon, A. B.

Williams, F. E.   (1) *Bull-Roarers in the Papuan Gulf* (1936).

Williamson, R. W.,   (1) *Religion and Social Organization in Central
   (ed. Piddington).   Polynesia* (1937).

——   (2) *Essays in Polynesian Ethnology* (1939).

Wilson, G.   (1) "Introduction to Nyakyusa Law," *Africa*,
                               Vol. X, p. 16 (1937).

——   (2) "The Land Rights of Individuals among
                               the Nyakyusa," *The Rhodes-Livingstone
                               Papers*, No. 1 (1938).

——   (3) *The Constitution of Ngonde,* The Rhodes-
                               Livingstone Papers, No. 3 (1939).

Wissler, C.   (1) *Man and Culture* (1923).

——   (2) *The American Indian* (1938).

——   (3) *Indians of the United States: Four Centuries
                               of their History and Culture* (1940).

Young, T. Cullen.   (1) *Contemporary Ancestors*.

——   (2) *African Ways and Wisdom* (1937).

Zuckerman, S.   (1) *The Social Life of Monkeys and Apes* (1932).

INDEX

NOTE: *On tribal designations the Ethnographic Directory should also be consulted*

Aborigines: 404; *see also* Australian aborigines
Acorn area: 43
Activities: institutional, 240–1
Adam, L.: 255
Adelphic polyandry: 112 *n.*
Adhesion: 22
Adjustment cults: 245 *n.*
Administrators: 12; value of social anthropology to, 10
Adolescence: 9; Bantu, 264–5; *see also* Education, Initiation
Adoption: 111, 226
Adultery: Bantu, 343–4; Iroquois, 56; Wogeo, 328–33; *see also* Marriage, Wife-lending
Advertising: 378
Æsthetic standards: 234
Affinal kinship: 111
Africa: agriculture in, 39–40; blacksmiths in, 270; cultures of, 33–40; pastoral peoples of, 37–9; pastoralists, and warfare, 396; references on, 58
Age: classes, 176 *n.*; grades, 176; groupings, 175–6; sets, 176 *n.*; *see also* Gerontocracy, Life cycle
Agnatic kin: 145
Agricultural peoples: and land tenure, 290
Agricultural rites: 381
Agriculture: African, 39–40; Amerindian, 43; Baiga, 65; Chin, 67–9; Iroquois, 55; Kazak, 64; Trobriand, 367–8; Wogeo, 294–5
Ambilateral kinship: 117, 151
Ambivalent attitudes: 138
American Indians: 40–59
Amerind, Amerindian, Amerindic: 40
Amerindian tribes: and cannibalism, 393
Amulets: Eskimo, 52
Ancestors and ancestor worship: 37, 144, 146, 147 *n.*, 164, 192, 200, 326, 357, 388, 397
Andaman Islanders: ix, 71, 105
Animism: 356–7
Ankole: 40; political organization, 200; *see also* Banyankole
Anthropoid apes: 219–20, 227
Anthropological sciences: 1–3
Anthropometry: 1

Aranda: 75, 79 *n.*, 106, 119, 203
Archæology: *see* Prehistoric archæology
Arctic hysteria: 51
Area of wild seeds: 43–4; political organization, 199
Arioi: 207, 211–13
Armstrong, W. E.: 286
Art: 19, 235; of Bushmen, 36
Artefacts: 4
Arunta: *see* Aranda
Ashanti: 151 *n.*; creator god, 372
Ashley-Montagu, M. F.: 29, 163; on race, 399
Asia: primitive cultures of, 60–9; reference on, 105
Assam: 66–7
Association areas: 220
Associations: 206–15; references on, 218
Australian aborigines: 6, 74–5, 244, 266, 405; division of labour, 169; kinship, 124; land tenure, 289; marriage, 142–3; medicine men, 389; paternity, 154; political organization, 199; polygyny, 112; references on, 106; sorcery, 364; status among, 189; totemic ceremonies, 389; tribal variations, 32; tribe, 164; warfare, 396; wife-lending, 114–15; women, 170, 285
Avoidance: 124, 136–8
Azande: 405; magic, 392; witchcraft, 382–7
Aztecs: 41

Ba-Ila: 265
Baboons: 227–8
Baganda: blood brotherhood, 214; totemism, 202, 205; *see also* Ganda
Bahima: 40
Baiga: 65
Bairu: 40
Banks Islands: origin of death, 373; secret societies, 207–8
Bantu: 6, 170, 275, 287; alleged communism of, 315; area, 35; bride-price, 139; languages, 33–4; legal institutions, 338–51; nutrition, 259–66; political organization, 190; preferential marriage, 142
Banyankole: 189; *see also* Ankole
Basic personality: 246 *n.*

434